Reading Herodotus

Reading Herodotus

A Guided Tour through the Wild Boars,
Dancing Suitors, and Crazy Tyrants
of *The History*

Debra Hamel

The Johns Hopkins University Press
Baltimore

© 2012 The Johns Hopkins University Press
All rights reserved. Published 2012
Printed in the United States of America on acid-free paper
9 8 7 6 5 4 3 2 1

The Johns Hopkins University Press
2715 North Charles Street
Baltimore, Maryland 21218-4363
www.press.jhu.edu

Library of Congress Cataloging-in-Publication Data

Hamel, Debra.
Reading Herodotus : a guided tour through the wild boars, dancing
suitors, and crazy tyrants of The History / Debra Hamel.
    pages. cm.
    Includes bibliographical references and index.
    ISBN 978-1-4214-0655-8 (hardback : alkaline paper) —
ISBN 978-1-4214-0656-5 (paperback : alkaline paper) —
ISBN 978-1-4214-0715-9 (electronic) (print) — ISBN 1-4214-0655-1
(hardback : alkaline paper) — ISBN 1-4214-0656-X (paperback :
alkaline paper) — ISBN 1-4214-0715-9 (electronic) (print)
    1. Herodotus. History. I. Title.
    D58.H473H36 2012
    938'.03—dc23   2012000578

A catalog record for this book is available from the British Library.

Cartography by Bill Nelson.

Special discounts are available for bulk purchases of this book. For
more information, please contact Special Sales at 410-516-6936 or
specialsales@press.jhu.edu.

The Johns Hopkins University Press uses environmentally friendly
book materials, including recycled text paper that is composed of at
least 30 percent post-consumer waste, whenever possible.

For my sweet Melissa

Τὴν δ' ἐκ μελίσσης· τήν τις εὐτυχεῖ λαβών·
—Semonides of Amorgos

Contents

Acknowledgments

I am grateful to a number of friends who read all or part of this book in manuscript form and otherwise provided encouragement and support. My thanks to Kyle Behen, Victor Bers, and in particular Clare Dudman, who not only offered her editorial assistance and unstinting enthusiasm for the project but also contributed a photograph to these pages. Thanks also to my husband, David Seidemann, for his contribution to a footnote on the subject of urine therapy; to Bill Nelson once again for his beautiful maps; to Matthew McAdam of the Johns Hopkins University Press for his early support of the manuscript and his work in getting it to print; to Martin Schneider for his careful editing; and to the publisher's anonymous readers for their thoughtful responses to the text. I am grateful also to Elizabeth Jane Shepherd and Jan Theo Bakker, who went out of their way to help me connect with the Ostia Museum in Italy: the casual kindness of far-flung strangers is one of the blessings of our connected world.

This book is dedicated to my younger daughter, Melissa (whose name means "honeybee" in ancient Greek). What Semonides of Amorgos writes of the bee woman in my dedication applies equally well to her and her sister Rebecca: whoever has them in their life is fortunate indeed.

Timeline

This timeline is adapted largely from the Dated Outline of Text that appears in Robert B. Strassler's *The Landmark Herodotus*. I have followed his practice of appending question marks to doubtful dates. In some cases dates appear below with a slash: Solon's archonship is dated to 594/3, for example. This is because the Athenian year ran from our midsummer to midsummer. All dates listed are B.C.

c. 1200	Greece–Asia Minor	Trojan War
716?	Lydia	Gyges kills Candaules
664–610	Egypt	Reign of Psammetichus
632	Athens	Conspiracy of Cylon
c. 630	Libya	Founding of Cyrene
625–585	Corinth	Tyranny of Periander
617–560	Media	Reign of Alyattes
594/3	Athens	Solon's archonship
589–570	Egypt	Reign of Apries
585	Lydia-Media	Total solar eclipse. End of war between Lydia and Media
584–550	Media	Reign of Astyages
c. 575	Persia	Birth of Cyrus
570–526	Egypt	Reign of Amasis
561–556	Athens	Pisistratus in power in Athens (first time)
560–546	Lydia	Reign of Croesus
559	Persia	Cyrus becomes king of the Persian city of Ansan
555?–?	Athens	Pisistratus in power in Athens (second time)
c. 555	Chersonese	Miltiades the Elder becomes tyrant in the Chersonese
550	Media-Persia	Cyrus defeats Astyages

550–?	Lydia	Croesus plans to challenge Persia
548–547	Sparta-Lydia	Spartans ally with Croesus
547?	Lydia-Persia	Croesus crosses the Halys River and attacks Persian territory
547–546?	Lydia-Persia	Persian invasion of Lydia and the fall of Sardis
546	Asia Minor	Ionians begin fortifying their cities
546–528	Athens	Pisistratus in power in Athens (third time)
c. 545	Lydia-Persia	Lydian revolt defeated
545?	Asia Minor–Persia	Persians subdue cities in Asia Minor
539	Babylon-Persia	Cyrus attacks Babylon
c. 532–517/6?	Samos	Tyranny of Polycrates
530	Massagetae-Persia	Cyrus killed in battle against Massagetae
530–522	Persia	Reign of Cambyses
526–525	Egypt	Reign of Psammenitus
525	Egypt	Cambyses conquers Egypt
525	Sparta-Samos	Spartan campaign against Samos
524?	Egypt-Persia	Cambyses' expeditions to Ammonia and Ethiopia
522 (Mar. to Sept.)	Persia	Reign of the False Smerdis
522–521	Babylon-Persia	Babylonian revolt
521–486	Persia	Reign of Darius
519?	Chersonese	Death of Miltiades the Elder
516	Chersonese	Miltiades the Younger becomes tyrant in the Chersonese
516?	Persia	Death of Oroetes
515?	Samos-Persia	Persian expedition to Samos
514	Athens	Harmodius and Aristogiton assassinate Hipparchus
513	Scythia-Persia	Darius' Scythian expedition
513	Libya-Persia	Persian expedition to Libya
512–511	Thrace-Persia	Megabazus' operations in Thrace and the Hellespont
c. 511	Sparta-Athens	Alcmaeonids bribe oracle. First Spartan expedition to expel Pisistratids
510	Sparta-Athens	Second Spartan expedition to expel Pisistratids. Cleomenes besieges Acropolis. Pisistratids leave Athens
510	Macedon-Persia	Persian embassy to Macedon

508/7	Sparta-Athens	Rivalry of Cleisthenes and Isagoras. First Spartan attempt to install Isagoras in Athens
506	Sparta-Athens	Second Spartan attempt to install Isagoras in Athens
504	Sparta-Athens	Cleomenes tries to install Hippias as tyrant in Athens
499	Naxos-Persia	Persian expedition to Naxos
499	Sparta–Athens–Asia Minor	Beginning of Ionian Revolt. Aristagoras visits Sparta and Athens
498	Athens–Asia Minor	Ionians and Athenians burn Sardis
498–454	Macedon	Reign of Alexander I of Macedon
494	Asia Minor	The Battle of Lade and the fall of Miletus
493	Chersonese	Miltiades the Younger flees the Chersonese
492	Thrace-Persia	Mardonius' expedition to Greece
491	Greece-Sparta-Persia	Darius sends heralds to Greece. Deposition of Demaratus
491?	Sparta	Cleomenes' madness and suicide
490	Athens-Persia	Battle of Marathon
490 or 489	Athens-Paros	Miltiades' expedition to Paros
487	Egypt-Persia	Egypt revolts from Persia
486	Persia	Death of Darius. Succession of Xerxes
485	Egypt-Persia	Egyptian revolt suppressed
c. 484–c. 424	Ionia-Greece	Herodotus
484–481	Persia	Preparations for Persian invasion of Greece
483	Athens	Athenians build navy
481 (Aug. or Sept.)	Athens	"Wooden Wall" oracle
481 (Sept. or Oct.)	Greece-Persia	Xerxes in Sardis, sends heralds to Greece
481 (Oct. or Nov.)	Greece	First congress of the Hellenic League
480–479	Greece-Persia	Second Persian War
480 (April)	Persia	Persians march from Sardis to Abydus
480 (spring)	Greece	Second congress of the Hellenic League
480 (May)	Persia	Xerxes crosses the Hellespont
480 (May)	Greece	Greek expedition to Tempe
480 (Aug.)	Greece-Persia	Battles of Thermopylae and Artemisium
480 (Sept.)	Greece-Persia	Battle of Salamis

479 (June)	Greece-Persia	Second Persian occupation of Attica
479 (Aug.)	Greece-Persia	Battles of Plataea and Mycale
431–404	Greece	Peloponnesian War
430	Sparta-Athens	Athenians execute Peloponnesian envoys*

*Latest event recorded by Herodotus

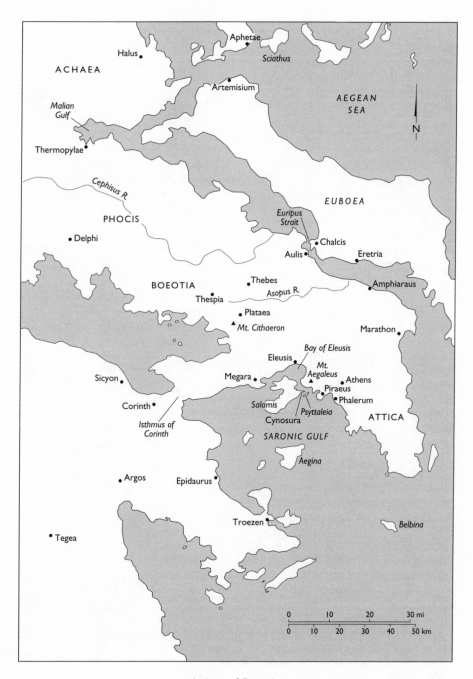

Attica and Boeotia

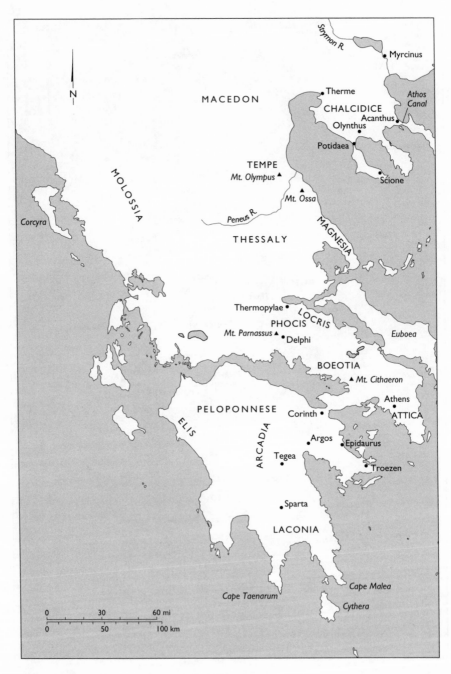

Greece

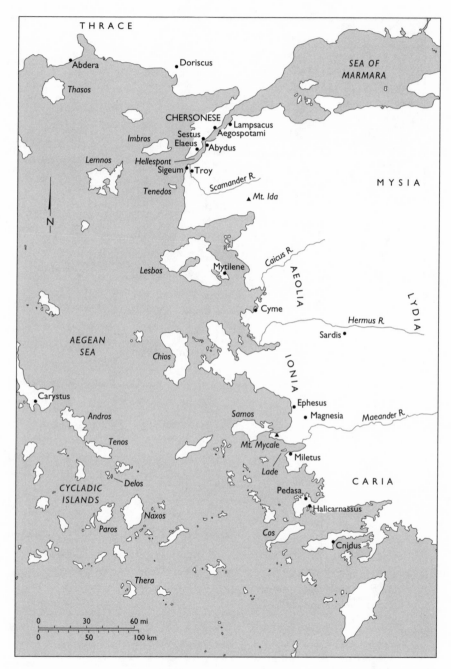

Asia Minor and the Aegean

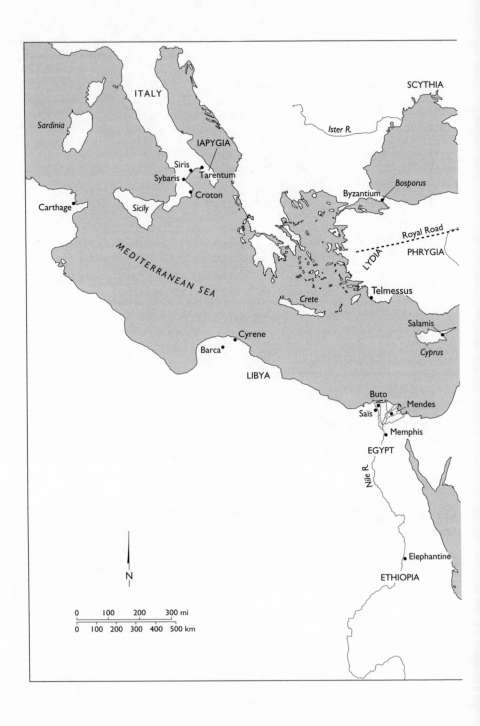

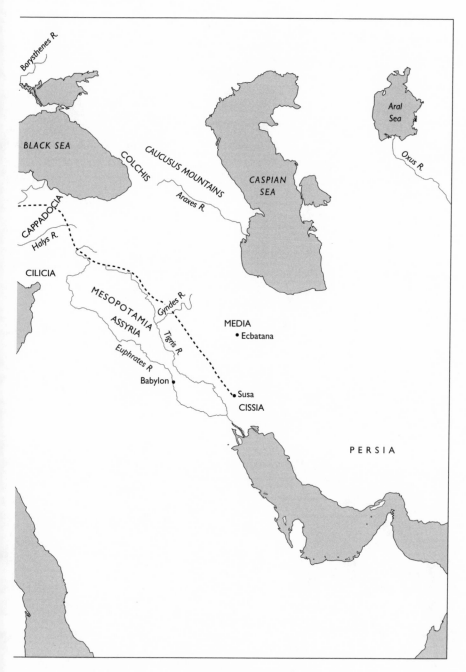

Asia and the Mediterranean

Reading Herodotus

Introduction

These are the researches of Herodotus of Halicarnassus, which he pub-
lishes, in the hope of thereby preserving from decay the remembrance of
what men have done, and of preventing the great and wonderful actions
of the Greeks and the Barbarians from losing their due meed of glory; and
withal to put on record what were their grounds of feud. (proem)

CHAPTER TIMELINE

c. 1200	Trojan War
c. 484–c. 424	Herodotus
490	First Persian War
480–479	Second Persian War
460–c. 400	Thucydides
431–404	Peloponnesian War

IT ALL STARTED WITH A WOMAN, that great clash of arms and cultures that
culminated in the battles of Marathon and Thermopylae and Salamis some
two and a half millennia ago. The Persians say the Phoenicians started it
by kidnapping Io, the daughter of the king of Argos in the Greek Peloponnese. And things escalated from there. The Greeks kidnapped Europa from
the Phoenicians, and Jason carried off Medea from Colchis, and finally Paris
stole Helen from her husband and brought her to Troy. And even that wouldn't
have been such a big deal if the Greeks hadn't overreacted: Helen's abduction
launched a thousand ships, as the saying goes, and Troy burned. The East's enmity toward the West was born in the ashes of Priam's toppled palace.

Herodotus summarizes all this backstory in the first five sections of the first
book of his *History of the Persian Wars* (1.1–5). He goes on to discuss his own
theory of the origins of the rift between East and West, an account which, like
that of the Persians, begins with a wronged woman. But we'll get to that in
chapter one.

Herodotus composed his *History* in the fifth century B.C., some decades after the Second Persian War had ended but while the embers of that conflagration were still smoldering and its veterans were still available for questioning. Born in Halicarnassus, a Greek city on the west coast of Asia Minor (modern Turkey), Herodotus traveled around the ancient world, from Egypt to Athens to Mesopotamia, sightseeing and talking to people and digesting their stories. The result of his inquiries is a seminal work of western literature, invaluable to historians and classicists for its preservation of an enormous amount of information about not only the Persian Wars but also the art and archaeology, mythology and mores of classical and preclassical Mediterranean and Mesopotamian societies.

Herodotus has often been faulted for being insufficiently critical of his sources, for including fantastic stories in his work that couldn't possibly be true. And his *History* is certainly not the scientific gem that his slightly younger contemporary Thucydides produced when chronicling the next great war, between Athens and Sparta, which brought the fifth century to its close. If Herodotus is the Father of History, then Thucydides is the father of modern, critical history (though this view of Thucydides has become controversial). But it must be remembered that Herodotus invented the genre. (The word he uses in introducing his work, translated as "researches" in the epigraph above, is *historie*, the source of our word "history.") The prose masterpiece he composed—a mix of geography and ethnography, political and social history, mythology and propaganda; part *Frommer's Travel Guide*, part *Ripley's Believe It or Not!*—can't be faulted because Herodotus fails to adhere to historical standards that didn't exist yet when he was writing.

Besides, Herodotus' *History* is a fun read—one doesn't often hear that said of Thucydides—filled with sex and violent death and divine prophecies. It's also a very long book, weighing in at five or six or seven hundred pages depending on the translation you grab. A modern editor, were the manuscript to cross his transom today, would advise pruning.

In the introduction to his novel *The Princess Bride*, William Goldman describes the (entirely fictional) genesis of his story. With great difficulty he'd managed to get his hands on a copy of a book his father had read to him as a child, S. Morgenstern's classic *The Princess Bride*, which in his memory was filled with fencing and fighting and monsters and poison and snakes and spiders and true love. He gives the book to his son to read but the boy, inexplicably, maddeningly, finds the story boring. Finally Goldman picks up the book himself. He's never read it, only heard it read, and he soon realizes what the problem is: his father's reading had been selective. He'd left out the boring bits. Goldman forsakes his other responsibilities to work on an abridgment of the book and the result—the *Princess Bride* that you can find in bookstores and that Rob Reiner later turned into a movie—is the "good parts" version of the S. Morgenstern classic. Or so the story goes.

What's needed with Herodotus, it occurred to me, is a "good parts" version of *The History*, a book for the everyday reader who's unlikely to slog through all the "begats" to get to the juicy bits. Hence this volume, a loose retelling of Herodotus' account, with obscure references explained and the boring bits left out. Here's an example of what you'll be missing, Herodotus' description (indeed, only part of it!) of the steps taken by Croesus, the king of Lydia, to propitiate the god Apollo prior to his sending a delegation to the Delphic oracle:

> After this Croesus, having resolved to propitiate the Delphic god with a magnificent sacrifice, offered up three thousand of every kind of sacrificial beast, and besides made a huge pile, and placed upon it couches coated with silver and with gold, and golden goblets, and robes and vests of purple; all which he burnt in the hope of thereby making himself more secure of the favour of the god. Further he issued his orders to all the people of the land to offer a sacrifice according to their means. When the sacrifice was ended, the king melted down a vast quantity of gold, and ran it into ingots, making them six palms long, three palms broad, and one palm in thickness. The number of ingots was a hundred and seventeen, four being of refined gold, in weight two talents and a half; the others of pale gold, and in weight two talents. He also caused a statue of a lion to be made in refined gold, the weight of which was ten talents. At the time when the temple of Delphi was burnt to the ground, this lion fell from the ingots on which it was placed; it now stands in the Corinthian treasury, and weighs only six talents and a half, having lost three talents and a half by the fire. (1.50, trans. Rawlinson)

This sort of thing is great if you're a historian looking for information about ancient metallurgy or the treasures housed at Delphi, but it's unlikely to interest most laymen.

This book, necessarily, is very subjective. Lock a hundred classicists in a room filled with typewriters, and each one of them could write a version of a "good parts" Herodotus. But the hundred resulting manuscripts would be very different from one another, each imprinted with its author's writing style, interests, and editorial decisions. While there would certainly be considerable overlap in the material covered—no one in his right mind would omit the Croesus story, for example, from a retelling of Herodotus—the set of passages each author discussed might well be unique. A look at the table of contents of this version suggests that my own interests tend to the scatological, sexual, and sophomoric—whatever that may say about me. In other words, lengthy descriptions of dedicatory gold ingots? Out. But stories about medicinal urine and retaliatory cannibalism and historically significant flatulence were keepers.

I would stress here that this book does not claim to be a history of the period covered by Herodotus. It's an introduction to the author and his rich subject matter, which includes folktales and myths and ancient propaganda along with more reliable historical information. While I sometimes allude to the scholarly debate surrounding passages under consideration, I do not do so in all cases, and my discussions are by no means exhaustive. That sort of detailed work would be the subject of a very different sort of book—or a number of them. An academic paper or two or ten could probably be written (in some cases they have already been written: the bibliography on Herodotus is vast) on virtually every section of Herodotus' *History*—examining his prose style, sniffing out his sources, picking apart his chronology, comparing what he tells us with the evidence of other ancient sources, mining his account for information on a myriad of topics: barbarian appeals to the Delphic oracle or Scythian funeral practices or Athenian constitutional history. There is a lot of meat in *The History* to chew on, in other words. But in this book we'll only be taking a taste of Herodotus, skimming along the surface of *The History* by way of introduction to the work. Readers interested in digging deeper can start by seeking out a translation of the text and by delving into some of the more serious scholarship listed in the bibliography.

The passage about dedicatory gold ingots quoted above is taken from George Rawlinson's translation of Herodotus, which was originally published in the mid-nineteenth century. I have used Rawlinson's translation also for the quotes from Herodotus that appear as epigraphs throughout this book. Unless otherwise noted, however, translations from the Greek that appear within the text are my own.

Rawlinson's text has been reissued, with minor changes, in editions published in the 1990s by Wordsworth and Everyman's Library. See the translations section at the end of the book for a more complete list of translations that are readily available in bookstores or on the internet. I have provided sample text from each to aid readers in selecting a translation that suits their needs.

Greek words have often made their way into English via Latin, and in the process their spellings were Romanized: thus the Lydian king with whom Herodotus starts his story is more familiar to us as Croesus than Kroisos, and the Persian who conquered him appears in English more often as Cyrus than Kuros. In transliterating proper names from the Greek, I have followed the style of the *Oxford Classical Dictionary*, third edition (Oxford University Press, 1999), which uses the more familiar Latinate spellings (with *c* for *k*, *oe* for *oi*, *us* for *os*, etc.).

There are two units of currency mentioned in the text. A talent was both a unit of weight, equal to about 57 pounds, and the corresponding value of that weight of precious metals. There were 6000 drachmas in a talent. To get a sense of the value of a drachma, consider the following. In the late fifth century B.C. it cost one talent of silver to pay the wages for the crew of one trireme for one month: 200 men at a drachma a day apiece (Thucydides 6.8.1). Around the same time, skilled workers and laborers who were employed by the Athenian state on the construction of the Erechtheum, a temple on the Acropolis north of the Parthenon, were paid between one and one and a half drachmas per day.

Herodotus' account of Persia's expansion under four kings—Cyrus, Cambyses, Darius, and Xerxes—and its eventual collision with the city-states of Greece was divided up sometime after his death into nine books (what we would call chapters), each book in turn divided into some unequal number of sections (paragraph-sized chunks). Here is an overview of what the books of *The History* contain:

Book 1
1–5. The origins of the enmity between East and West (the Trojan War).
6–94. King Croesus of Lydia and the conquest of his kingdom by Persia under Cyrus the Great.
95–216. The childhood and rise to power of Cyrus the Great, his various conquests, and his death in battle.

Book 2

1–182. The geography, history, marvels, and customs of ancient Egypt.

Book 3

1–66. Cambyses' expeditions against Egypt and Ethiopia, his madness and death.

67–160. Darius' rise to power and the first years of his reign.

Book 4

1–125. Darius' expeditions against the Scythians and the Persian expansion into Libya.

Book 5

1–126. Persia's conquest of Thrace and the Ionian Revolt, with digressions on Athens and Sparta.

Book 6

1–32. The Ionian Revolt.

33–93. Miltiades, Mardonius' expedition against Greece, the Spartan kings Cleomenes and Demaratus, and Athenian hostilities against Aegina.

94–120. The Persian advance and the battle of Marathon.

121–131. The history of the Alcmaeonidae.

132–140. Miltiades' expeditions to Paros and Lemnos.

Book 7

1–239. The invasion of Greece to the Battle of Thermopylae.

Book 8

1–39. The battles at Artemisium and the Persian advance to Attica.

40–125. The battle of Salamis and the retreat of the Persians.

126–144. Greek and Persian actions in late 480 and early 479.

Book 9

1–89. The battle of Plataea.

90–113. The battle of Mycale.

114–122. The siege of Sestus.

How to Destroy a Mighty Empire

The Story of Croesus of Lydia

CHAPTER TIMELINE

716?	Gyges kills Candaules
594/3	Solon's archonship
585	Total solar eclipse
	End of war between Lydia and Media
561–556	Pisistratus in power in Athens (first time)
560–546	Reign of Croesus
555?–?	Pisistratus in power in Athens (second time)
550	Cyrus defeats Astyages
550–?	Croesus plans to challenge Persia
548–547	Spartans ally with Croesus
547?	Croesus crosses the Halys River and attacks
	Persian territory
547–546?	Persian invasion of Lydia and the fall of Sardis
546–528	Pisistratus in power in Athens (third time)

GYPTIAN WOMEN URINATED STANDING UP. The Persians learned pederasty from the Greeks. The Massagetae, who lived to the east of the Caspian Sea, drank milk. Herodotus tells us all this and much besides in his *History of the Persian Wars*. The book is a font of ancient trivia, famous for its digressions, with too-good-to-be-true stories and cultural, geographic, and historical factoids shoehorned into the narrative. The author's highly readable, chatty prose style contributes to one's sense that his *History* is undisciplined, even frivolous. But Herodotus is a far more organized and intelligent writer than a careless read of his *History* might suggest. For all his digressions, the stew of miscellanea that he couldn't bear to leave out, Herodotus always circles back to his main storyline, the inexorable expansion of Persia that led to its collision with Greece and the two Persian Wars of the early fifth century B.C. And he deftly weaves through this historical scaffolding his main theme, the instability of human affairs, which is evidenced in the fates of both individuals and whole civilizations.

Herodotus doesn't start his discussion of the conflict between East and West with either Persia or Greece, however, but with the last king of Lydia, Croesus, who was the first barbarian to demand tribute of Greeks (1.6.2). (The Greeks called non-Greek speakers *barbaroi*, perhaps because, as the standard explanation has it, their unintelligible foreign speech sounded like "bar-bar" to the Greek ear. Ancient "barbarians," then, were simply non-Greek speakers and may or may not have been barbaric in the modern sense.) The kingdom of Lydia, with its capital at Sardis in western Asia Minor, was at the height of its power under Croesus' reign.

Croesus' family was called the Mermnadae. They had seized power four generations and some 150 years earlier from the Heraclidae (the "descendants of Heracles"), whose last king was an ill-starred fellow named Candaules. Candaules' downfall, as Herodotus tells it, was a direct result of his infatuation with his own wife.

Gyges and Candaules (1.8–13)

Now it happened that this Candaules was in love with his own wife; and not only so, but thought her the fairest woman in the whole world.   (1.8.1)

Candaules, the Heraclid king of Lydia, had fallen in love with his own wife.[1] The arousal of this sort of passionate affection within marriage may or may not have been unusual, but certainly the way that Candaules dealt with his infatuation was rather strange. (At least from my perspective. One [male] scholar, writing in the early twentieth century, says of Candaules' behavior that it is "highly characteristic of a certain type of man.")[2] Candaules used to brag about his wife's good looks to his bodyguard Gyges. Gyges presumably made whatever noises were appropriate in response, but even so, Candaules was not convinced that Gyges really appreciated just how good-looking his wife was. So—and this is where Candaules went overboard—he suggested that Gyges take a look at the queen while she was naked.

Gyges wasn't interested. In fact, he was downright scandalized. He argued with Candaules, begging the king not to make him do this: it would rob the queen of honor, he said, and traditional wisdom suggested that a man should not be looking at other men's wives. He may also have had some concerns about where precisely Candaules was going with this, given that the king felt it necessary to assure him he wasn't being tested. Gyges had nothing to fear from either him or his wife, Candaules said. In fact, she wouldn't even know she was being watched: Candaules' plan was for Gyges to hide behind the open door of their bedroom and watch the queen get ready for bed; when her back was turned, he could slip out of the room. What could possibly go wrong?

That night, as ordered, Gyges hid behind the door and watched the queen get undressed, but as he was sneaking out, she saw him. Strangely, she didn't scream or say anything to her husband. Perhaps, we might rationalize, she was too embarrassed: according to Herodotus, public nakedness was a source of great shame among the barbarians. Or maybe the incident would have tainted her by the same sort of logic that leads to the stoning of rape victims in Candaules' neck of the woods to this day. But in fact, as Herodotus tells the story, the queen kept quiet because she knew at once that her husband was behind the offense, and she became determined to punish him for it. Why, though, should she immediately assume that Candaules was complicit in Gyges' voyeurism? Herodotus leaves us in the dark, but there is an alternate version of the story that suggests a possible explanation. A brief fragment—only sixteen recoverable lines—has survived from a tragedy based on the Gyges story. In it the queen herself explains what happened in her bedroom. Initially she feared that the man she saw in the shadows had murder in mind, but, she says, "when I saw Candaules still awake, | I knew what had been done and what man had done it."[3] (Unfortunately the date of the tragedy is unknown: it may or may not antedate Herodotus' version of the story.) Perhaps we are to understand that Candaules likewise lay awake and watchful in Herodotus' version, even if he doesn't say as much, and that the queen saw Candaules watching Gyges watch her.

The next morning the queen let the household servants who were faithful to her in on her plans, and she summoned Gyges. When he showed up, unaware there was anything amiss, she told him he had two choices: either he had to kill Candaules and take her and the kingdom for himself, or else he was the one who was going to die. Presumably she had the muscle in the room to make the latter option a reality. Gyges tried to talk her out of this, but he wasn't any more persuasive with her than he had been with her husband. In the end he chose self-preservation over loyalty to the king. The queen had Gyges hide behind the same door he'd watched her from the previous night, and after Candaules fell asleep Gyges came out of hiding and stabbed him to death.

Thus Gyges gained the kingdom, and the Lydian throne passed from the Heraclid dynasty to the Mermnadae, though the succession was not as smooth as it might have been. Some of the Lydians took Gyges' usurpation of power poorly. It was decided to ask for advice from the oracle of Apollo at Delphi. If the oracle proclaimed Gyges king, he was in; if not, Gyges agreed to hand the throne back to the Heraclids.

This is the first of many oracles that will figure in Herodotus' *History*. As we will see, the oracles give some of Herodotus' stories their bite, but the appeal to oracular authority was no mere literary trope. (Though not all of the oracular pronouncements preserved in our sources are historical: some may have been fakes written after the fact.) In the ancient Greek world both states and individuals habitually sought the counsel of oracles when undertaking important actions—founding colonies, for example, or beginning military campaigns. A number of oracles studded the Greek world, but the preeminent one was at Delphi, on the slopes of Mount Parnassus in central Greece. There the priestess of Apollo, in response to an inquiry, would issue a cryptic prophecy, apparently while intoxicated by vapors rising from a fissure in the ground. The prophecy was then delivered to the person requesting it through an intermediary, a "prophet," who may have modified the form of the prophecy by, for example, turning it into verse. That the priestess's oracular pronouncements were authoritative may seem strange to us millennia after the fact, but the persistence of superstition in the modern day should quell any surprise the ancients' gullibility might inspire. (Seeing the image of a religious icon in a grilled cheese sandwich, for example, would await our own enlightened age.)[4] Besides, the oracles often knew what they were talking about. They attracted emissaries from around the ancient world. The shrine precincts were abuzz with gossip and news. The prophetic output of the god's spokeswoman will have been informed by real-world knowledge.

So it was not strange for the Lydians and their now unstable leadership to appeal to Delphi for help with their political situation. In the end, the oracle confirmed Gyges in his kingship. The Mermnadae were to keep the throne. But the priestess had added a caveat: the Heraclids would have their vengeance on the Mermnadae in the fifth generation.

The Temple of Apollo at Delphi, on the slopes of Mount Parnassus in central Greece.
Photograph courtesy of Clare Dudman.

The Historicity of *The History*

> There is charm, vigor, and beauty in his narrative, but he "tells his tale like a
> poet," not with understanding, in this case, but mellifluously and with a honeyed
> tongue.   (Plutarch, *On the Malice of Herodotus* 43 = *Moralia* 874B,
>   trans. Walter Blanco)

At this point you'll be wondering about the historicity of Herodotus' account.
Is that *really* how Gyges took over the kingship of Lydia? Or has Herodotus
preserved a bit of political propaganda, a story that Gyges or his supporters told
to justify the new king's murder of his predecessor?

Certainly it is not the only ancient account of Gyges' usurpation of the
throne. The philosopher Plato, writing in the mid-fourth century B.C., tells an
even more fantastic story (*Republic* 359a–360d). In his account, which is remi-

niscent of the story of Aladdin in *Arabian Nights,* Gyges finds a magic ring in a cave and discovers that it renders him invisible if he twists it on his finger. This Gyges is a shepherd in the service of the Lydian king, and he sometimes reports to the king on the state of the royal flocks. On one such occasion Gyges becomes invisible, seduces the queen, and, with her help, assassinates the king. Note that Gyges is invisible in Plato's story, but in Herodotus he is merely hidden from view. Herodotus' account may in fact be a rationalization of an original Gyges story involving a magic ring that Plato has preserved. Herodotus, that is, may have taken out the magic bits in the popular story of Gyges' rise to power and explained the same events as the result of purely human action.

In another account, by Nicolaus of Damascus (who wrote during the Augustan period but was relying on earlier sources), Gyges is a trusted bodyguard of the king, sent to fetch the king's fiancée (*Die Fragmente der griechischen Historiker* [hereafter *FGH*] 90 F 49). En route to the palace, Gyges tries to have his way with her. She tells the king, who plans to kill Gyges. But instead Gyges kills the king and gets the girl. The Delphic oracle confirms Gyges in his kingship.

Plutarch, a Greek historian who wrote during the first century A.D. but likewise relied on earlier sources, offers a more believable if less entertaining, bare-bones account of the story, that Gyges overthrew the Lydian king with the help of a certain Arselis of Mylasa—a city in southwestern Asia Minor, near Halicarnassus (*Greek Questions* 45 = *Moralia* 301F–302A).

A third-century A.D. abridgment by Justin (1.7) of a first-century B.C. history by Pompeius Trogus (who will have been relying on earlier sources himself) suggests that Herodotus has telescoped events and cleaned up the story by having the queen and Gyges kill Croesus on the day after the door incident. According to Justin/Trogus, some time in fact elapsed between Gyges' voyeurism and his regicide, during which period Gyges and the queen became lovers.

The underlying facts of the various accounts, whatever their particulars, seem to be that the kingship of Lydia was usurped by this Gyges, who won the queen as well, and that with his ascent there was also a dynastic shift, power passing from the Heraclid dynasty to the Mermnadae. The queen may or may not have been complicit. The Delphic oracle was apparently consulted in the wake of the transition.

Herodotus uses the story of Candaules and Gyges to introduce a theme to which he will return later in his *History*: autocrats who transgress societal norms—as Candaules did by displaying his wife naked to Gyges—tend to fare poorly. The story also serves as a lead-in to Herodotus' account of King Croesus of Lydia, providing as it does an explanation for the fate that would befall the Mermnad dynasty in the fifth generation. To suit his purposes Herodotus molded the story that had built up around the bare facts of Gyges' ascension to the Lydian throne, dropping details and introducing dramatic elements and making use of stock narrative motifs. (Some aspects of the Gyges story have parallels in other folktales, both Greek and non-Greek.) Not for nothing has Herodotus, called the Father of History since Cicero's day (Cicero, *On Laws* 1.5), been known for almost as long as the Father of Lies (Plutarch, *On the Malice of Herodotus*).

Herodotus' account of Gyges' usurpation, then, cannot be taken at face value. But here, as elsewhere in his *History*, Herodotus does preserve kernels of historical truth. I will address the question of Herodotus' historicity from time to time in what follows, but determining how much of each story is fact and how much embellishment is not the business of this book.

The Wisdom of Solon (1.29–33)

But in every matter it behoves us to mark well the end: for oftentimes God gives men a gleam of happiness, and then plunges them into ruin.   (1.32.9)[5]

Croesus was the fifth Mermnad king of Lydia. He expanded the kingdom through conquest and made strategic alliances so that under his reign Lydia was at the height of its power. As a burgeoning metropolis, Sardis became an attractive destination for travelers. One of the people who came to visit Croesus' court, according to Herodotus, was Solon, an Athenian who was so famous for his wisdom that his name has become an English noun: a *solon* is a wise lawgiver or respected statesman. Solon had been elected by the Athenians to an extraordinary office in 594 B.C. and given authority to enact reforms that would solve Athens' socioeconomic crisis. He accomplished a great deal during his tenure—abolishing enslavement for debt, for example, and reforming the justice system. The Athenians agreed to abide by his laws for a period of time after they were enacted—probably ten years—but there was a lot of grumbling over what he'd done and hadn't done, a classic case of not being able to please everybody. To get away from it all, to avoid being pestered at every turn to amend his enactments, Solon went abroad. It was during this voluntary period of exile, Herodotus tells us, that Solon visited Sardis.

After Solon had been at Croesus' palace for a few days, the king had his servants give the Athenian a tour, pointing out all their master's vast stores of treasure as they went. (Croesus' legendary wealth explains why Montgomery Burns, the resident billionaire on *The Simpsons*, lives on the corner of Croesus and Mammon—the latter another ancient word for or personification of wealth.) Croesus wanted Solon to see how much good stuff he owned in preparation for asking him something. When he got the chance, Croesus put the question to his guest. You've traveled the world and seen a lot of things, he said. Who in your opinion is the happiest of men?

Croesus expected Solon to name him, given the grand tour he'd just sent his guest on, so he was shocked when Solon instead named some nobody, Tellus the Athenian. Solon explained his selection: Tellus had lived in a prosperous community and had healthy sons. His sons gave him grandchildren, all of whom survived (hardly a foregone conclusion in the ancient world). And finally, Tellus died heroically in battle and was honored by the Athenians in death.

Croesus was a little perturbed at this point, but he figured he'd be a shoe-in for the second-place slot. So, he asked Solon, who's the second happiest?

Not Croesus, it turns out. Solon gave second place to a pair of brothers, Cleobis and Biton, prize-winning athletes who were literally as strong as oxen. Their mother had to get to an important religious festival, but the oxen for her cart were out in the field. So Cleobis and Biton harnessed themselves to her wagon and pulled it more than five miles to the temple of Hera. When they got there the brothers' feat caused a stir. Men were crowding around the boys congratulating them. Women were complimenting the boys' mother on what fine sons she had. In her joy the mother prayed to a statue of Hera asking that the goddess bestow on her sons whatever was the best thing for a man to receive, and her prayer was answered: Cleobis and Biton took a nap after lunch and—perhaps you'll have guessed it by now—died in their sleep. (Herodotus tells us that the Argives dedicated statues of Cleobis and Biton at Delphi. These appear to have survived: A pair of statues dating to the early sixth century B.C. and believed to be representations of Cleobis and Biton were uncovered in excavations at Delphi in the late nineteenth century.)

After hearing this, Croesus was nearly sputtering with rage. Look at me, he said to Solon. I'm as rich as Croesus, for heaven's sake! Does all my wealth mean nothing to you? And Solon finally explained his point, which is obvious to us but wasn't at all obvious to Croesus. You're still alive, he said. You never know what's going to happen. Don't count your chickens before they've hatched.

Solon's explanation for this truism was much, much longer than what I just wrote, however, and it involved math: Solon did an on-the-spot calculation of the length of the average lifetime (not forgetting to factor in the ancient equivalent of leap days) and concluded that there are 26,250 days, give or take, during which something bad can happen to a person. And, he went on, sure, a rich guy beats a poor guy, assuming he dies well. But it's better to be poor and lucky than rich and unlucky. Because if you're rich you can buy stuff, but if you're lucky. . . . You get the idea. Maybe if Solon hadn't been so long-winded and scientific about it, Croesus would have taken what he said to heart.[6] Or maybe not: Croesus was so blinded by his own good fortune at the time that he couldn't imagine how things could ever be otherwise. He sent Solon away, thinking him a fool and scoffing at his ideas.

Croesus' meeting with Solon makes for a great story, the wealthy king given a lesson in priorities by the Athenian wise man. The story introduces themes that will be important throughout *The History*, and it establishes a standard against which Croesus' behavior and that of other tyrants can be gauged. Unfortunately, the story is too good to be true: Croesus came to power more than thirty years after Solon instituted his reforms in Athens. So the meeting Herodotus describes between the two men appears to be pure invention.

The Misfortunes of Adrastus (1.34–45)

It chanced that at this very same time there was in the Mysian Olympus a huge monster of a boar, which went forth often from this mountain country, and wasted the corn-fields of the Mysians. (1.36.1)

Croesus had two sons. One was deaf and dumb, and Croesus didn't pay much attention to him. But the other, Atys, was a strapping fellow, the finest young man of his generation. After Solon left Sardis, Croesus had a dream about Atys, one that he feared might be prophetic. Herodotus tells us the dream "stood over" the sleeping king and showed him that Atys would be struck by an iron spear point and die. When Croesus woke up he was worried, naturally, and he immediately took steps to prevent the dream from coming true. He found a wife for Atys and got him married off. (The purpose of this isn't entirely clear. Perhaps as a married man Atys would be expected to live a more tranquil, less risky life.) And Croesus would no longer allow Atys to take part in military exercises. He also had all the spears and javelins taken down from the walls lest something fall on Atys and the dream be fulfilled.

It was reasonable for Croesus, as a concerned parent, to take these precautions. Still, anyone who's ever read *Oedipus Rex* or watched *Sleeping Beauty* knows how futile it is to try to elude fate by leaving home, for example, or by removing dangerous objects from the vicinity of someone fated to be harmed by them. Taking the javelins off the walls, in other words, was unlikely to do Croesus much good. And it is indeed an act of arrogance on Croesus' part for him to assume that he would be able to alter fated events or even that he has fully understood the purport of his dream.

Around this same time a man with blood on his hands (figuratively speaking) showed up at Croesus' palace and begged the king to perform a ritual purification ceremony for him. Croesus performed the rite, which involved pouring the blood (the literal kind) of a suckling pig over the man's hands. Once this was done, the two got down to introductions: the man who had needed purification was Adrastus, a member of the royal family of Phrygia. (The Phrygians were one of the many peoples in Asia Minor whom Croesus had subdued.) Adrastus had unintentionally killed his brother and thus been driven out by his father. He had lost everything and had nowhere to go, but Croesus proved to be the perfect host. No worries! he said. You're among friends. Stay in the palace as long as you like and you'll want for nothing. Hospitality was a big deal in the ancient world, and Croesus knew how to do it right.

Now, Herodotus doesn't point this out, but his original audience would have known at once that the name "Adrastus" in Greek could be taken to mean "unable to escape"—as in, unable to escape one's fate. Bad things are wont to happen to someone with a name like that. So having Adrastus show up at Croesus' door, given the implications of the man's name, is like putting a loaded gun on the mantel in a play's first act: if the story's any good, the gun is eventually going to go off.

Thus, with Adrastus' introduction, the pistol is cocked, and we and Croesus have reason to fear for Atys' safety.

Act two. There's another knock on the palace door, so to speak. Some of Croesus' subjects, Mysians, from northwest Asia Minor, arrived to ask for help in hunting a wild boar (the Greek literally calls it "a great thing of a boar") that was regularly coming down from the mountains and trampling their fields. David Grene's translation of Herodotus' text here is particularly charming: "He [the boar] made his headquarters on that mountain and would issue from it and ravage the tilled fields of the Mysians." Then, I suppose, it was back to headquarters.

The Mysians had tried and failed to kill the boar. Now they asked that Croesus send his son out with a hunting party to get the job done. Croesus was happy to help, but there was no way he was sending Atys out boar hunting. He told the Mysians he'd send some men to help them, but his son was too busy with his new marriage to take part. The Mysians were happy with this, but Atys happened to walk in just then and he heard what his father had said. He had been annoyed by his father's precautions before, but this was the last straw. He demanded to know why his father had been mollycoddling him. What must the guys think, he asked, what must my new bride think when all I do is go back and forth to the marketplace and you won't let me go hunting or go out on maneuvers? Did his father think he was a coward?

Finally, Croesus told Atys about his dream. He explained that he didn't want to lose Atys, particularly as he considered him to be his only son: the other one, because of his deficiencies—he was, you'll remember, deaf and dumb—was to Croesus' mind no son at all. The king's explanation appeased Atys, but he really wanted to go hunting, and he didn't think the dream should prove such an obstacle. He pointed out to his father that boars don't carry spears. They've got teeth and claws, he said, but the dream didn't say anything about him dying by tooth or claw: he should be allowed to go. His logic was persuasive enough that Croesus changed his mind.

But Croesus was still worried, and reasonably so, since the hunting party might have a run-in with bandits. He summoned his houseguest Adrastus and asked him to go along on the hunt and act as his son's bodyguard. After all, Croesus reminded him, you owe me, since I purified you after your misfortune and I've been feeding you all this time. Adrastus didn't want to go, but he knew he owed Croesus. He agreed to accompany Atys and told Croesus that his son would return home without a scratch—at least as far as he was concerned.

You may have already guessed how the story ends. Because it's perfect, really: any other ending would be disappointing. The men went out to hunt the boar. When they found it they encircled it and started throwing spears at it. And in a longish sentence Herodotus tells us what happened next, delaying the punch line by separating the subject of the sentence from its verbs with a pair of clauses that reintroduce Adrastus:

Then the stranger, this man who had been purified of blood guilt, whose name was
Adrastus, threw his spear at the boar and missed, but he hit the son of Croesus.

A runner went ahead to tell Croesus what had happened, which gave the
king time to bewail his son's fate before the corpse was borne back to the palace. Croesus called on Zeus in his various manifestations to bear witness to
what he had suffered at Adrastus' hands. Adrastus' betrayal, such as it was, was
particularly odious because of Croesus' relationship with him: they were *xenoi*,
"guest-friends," a relationship that was taken very seriously in the Greek world
and implied mutual obligation. The power of the relationship is evidenced in
Homer's *Iliad*, already centuries old by Herodotus' day: when the enemies Diomedes and Glaucus meet on the battlefield in Book 6 and they chat before
trying to kill one another, they discover that Diomedes' grandfather had once
hosted Glaucus' grandfather for twenty days, and they'd exchanged presents.
Their grandsons had inherited the guest-friend relationship. Thus the two warriors not only resolve not to kill one another, but they embrace and exchange
suits of armor (6.212–236).

Failing to live up to the more quotidian obligations of one's guest-friendship
was frowned upon. But killing the son of one's host was arguably on a par with
antiquity's most famous example of hospitality poorly returned: when the Trojan prince Paris stayed with Menelaus in Sparta back in the day, he repaid his
host's kindness by stealing his wife, Helen. That led to an epic clash of civilizations, ten years' worth of fighting, and countless spears plunged into countless
necks.

Soon enough the rest of the hunting party made its way back to the palace
with Atys' body. Adrastus, when he came in, stood over the corpse and surrendered himself to the king, urging Croesus to cut his throat over the dead
boy's body. Croesus, as we know, had been ranting in his misery, calling on the
gods to witness what he'd suffered from his guest-friend, but seeing Adrastus
like this and hearing him pronounce a penalty of death on himself, Croesus was
moved to pity. He refused to punish Adrastus, who, he realized, was not the
cause of his troubles: some god was behind it, as his son's death by spear point
had long before been prophesied in a dream.

Herodotus reports that Croesus buried Atys in accordance with Lydian custom. He then concludes his story of Adrastus with a sentence that is arresting both for its content and its length—thirty-eight words long in the original Greek. As with his sentence describing Adrastus' accidental killing of Atys,

Herodotus here builds suspense by injecting a series of phrases between the subject and the verb. And then his finale punches us in the gut:

> Adrastus—the son of Gordias, the son of Midas, this man who had become the murderer of his own brother, and the murderer of the son of his purifier, when there was no bustle of men around the tomb, being conscious that, of all the men of whom he was aware he was the most unfortunate—slit his throat over the grave.

Adrastus fulfilled his destiny when he killed the son of Croesus, and in the perfect coda to the tragedy, Adrastus, that most unfortunate of men, kills himself as well. (The Greek word Herodotus uses for "most unfortunate" is an aptly ponderous seven syllables long, *barusumphorotatos*, lending further weight to his sentence.) Close curtain.

Consulting the Oracles (1.46–55)

> Both the oracles agreed in the tenor of their reply, which was in each case a prophecy that if Croesus attacked the Persians, he would destroy a mighty empire.... (1.53.3)

Croesus mourned the death of his son for two years until he was roused into action by Persia's conquest of Media. Media, which bordered Lydia to the east, on the other side of the Halys River, had been ruled by a man named Astyages, who, according to Herodotus, was Croesus' brother-in-law. (It is not certain that Croesus was in fact related to Astyages: other ancient sources disagree with Herodotus on this point.)

The marriage between Astyages and Croesus' sister, Herodotus tells us a little later in his narrative (1.73–74), had been arranged to solidify a peace between the Median and Lydian kingdoms after five years of war. The war began when a group of Scythian nomads staying at the Median court were slighted by the king, Astyages' father Cyaxares. To punish the king the Scythians killed one of the Median boys they'd been entrusted to teach. They chopped him up and dressed him up like wild game, delivered him to Cyaxares, and then high-tailed it out of Media. They wound up in Lydia as suppliants of the king, Croesus' father Alyattes. Alyattes' refusal to hand over the Scythians when Cyaxares demanded he do so started the war, which ended when a total eclipse of the sun interrupted a battle they were fighting and shocked the combatants into making peace. (One may doubt the historicity of Cyaxares' cannibalism, but the battle-

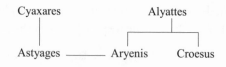

Croesus' Family Tree According to Herodotus

ending eclipse may have been historical: a total solar eclipse that would have been visible from the likely battle site occurred shortly before sunset on May 28, 585 B.C.)

Media's conquest by Persia was alarming both because of Croesus' familial connection with Astyages and because an expanding empire now lay on his border, implicitly threatening his own kingdom. Croesus thought it might be wise for him to make a preemptive strike against Persia, to weaken the Persians before they became too powerful. But not wanting to rush into anything, he determined first to seek the advice of an oracle. And not wanting to trust just any oracle—Croesus really was trying very hard to be careful—he sent messengers to seven different oracles, in Greece and Libya and Asia Minor, to test their prophetic powers. He sent his men off on the same day, instructing each to ask his oracle, precisely one hundred days later, what Croesus was doing right at that moment.[7]

The messengers did as instructed and returned to Lydia with the answers they'd received. In the end, only two of the seven oracles knew what they were talking about, Amphiaraus in Greece—though we're not told what that oracle's response was—and the Delphic oracle. The latter correctly answered that on the day in question Croesus had been boiling turtle and lamb in a bronze cauldron. (Croesus is unlikely in fact to have tested the oracles as Herodotus describes. The Delphic oracle took questions only one day a month at most. The other oracles probably had similarly restricted schedules. Croesus could not have guaranteed that his messengers would all have access to the various oracles consulted on the date he'd specified.)

You may remember reading in this book's introduction a passage from *The History* in which Herodotus writes about sacrificial animals and purple cloaks and goblets and gold ingots that measured six by three by one palm length each. This is the point where those gold ingots and goblets enter the story. Croesus burned a lot of stuff by way of sacrificing to Apollo. Then he got a bunch of loot together—not just the ingots and so on already mentioned, but other treasures as well, most interestingly a statue of a woman who was believed to be his baker.

(There is a story in other sources that Croesus' baker saved his life when his stepmother tried to have him poisoned [Plutarch, *On the Pythian Responses* 16 = *Moralia* 401E].) Croesus then sent all these treasures off to Delphi as dedicatory gifts to Apollo's temple, and he sent other things to Amphiaraus: the point, of course, was to butter up the oracles in preparation for asking another question.

The Lydians who were sent to bring these gifts to Delphi and Amphiaraus were instructed to ask the oracles whether Croesus should make war against Persia and whether, to that end, he should form any alliances. Both oracles agreed in their response: if Croesus should make war upon Persia, they predicted, he would destroy a mighty empire. The oracles also advised Croesus to ally himself with whichever Greek city was the most powerful.

Reading the oracles' response just now, I bet you caught the ambiguity at once: ah, but *which* mighty empire would be destroyed? Croesus, though, however careful he was being in some respects, was yet too blind to appreciate that the oracle he received was capable of a darker interpretation than the one he gave it. In this case and on subsequent occasions when he consulted the oracle, Croesus went into the experience expecting to receive a prophecy favorable to himself. He finds in the oracles what he expects to find and ignores information that doesn't fit his preconceived notions. Croesus, then, was delighted with this prophecy. In his mind it clearly signaled that he would be victorious over the Persians. He was so pleased, in fact, that he sent even more gifts to Delphi and asked another question. Would his monarchy be lengthy? This time the oracle's response pleased Croesus even more:

> When a mule becomes king of the Medians, then, tender-footed Lydian, flee along the River Hermus with its many pebbles and don't loiter, nor be ashamed to be a coward.

In short, the oracle advised, if a mule ever takes the Median throne, *run away!* A more insightful man might have wondered longer at the oracle's purport, but our Croesus was nothing if not literal-minded. One can imagine him reading a copy of the prophecy with a snort, crumpling it up, and tossing it over his shoulder: when a mule becomes king of the Medians indeed! Like *that's* ever going to happen. He figured he was in for a long reign. Success would be his. All signs pointed to go. And he promptly turned his attention to another piece of divine advice, figuring out which of the Greeks he should approach about an alliance.

Athens and Sparta (1.56–70)

Afterwards he turned his thoughts to the alliance which he had been
recommended to contract, and sought to ascertain by inquiry which was the
most powerful of the Grecian states.   (1.56.1)

Croesus' search for allies gives Herodotus the opportunity to introduce Athens
and Sparta into his narrative. They were the two preeminent Greek city-states
during the fifth century, when Herodotus was writing, and they will figure
prominently in Herodotus' *History* when he finally gets around to discussing
the Persian Wars, the conflicts toward which everything else in his *History* is
leading. According to Herodotus, Athens and Sparta were likewise the two
main powers in Greece in the mid-sixth century, when Croesus was in the mar-
ket for allies, though as we'll see, Sparta seems to have had more going for it at
the time than Athens.

"City-state" is a translation of the Greek word *polis*, plural *poleis*, from which
derive our English words *metropolis* and *politics*, for example. A *polis* was, briefly
put, an independent state comprising an urban center and its surrounding territory. Greece was divided into hundreds of these *poleis*, which employed different forms of government and varied greatly in population and size. (Athens was
one of the largest *poleis* in the Greek world. Attica, the territory it controlled,
was about 1,000 square miles in area, roughly the size of Rhode Island.) When
Aristotle famously stated in his *Politics* (1253a2) that "man is by nature a political animal," what he meant was that man's natural state—that is, the state in
which he is most fully developed—is to live in a *polis*. The Greek city-states
shared a common culture, but they were often openly hostile to one another.
There was no Greek nation per se.

Croesus learned that Athens at the time was under the rule of the tyrant
Pisistratus. (A "tyrant" in sixth-century Greece was not necessarily tyrannical
in the modern sense: the term didn't have negative connotations until later. A
tyrant was simply someone who had seized power for himself extra-constitu-
tionally. He might be a very effective and even a popular leader, or he might
not.) Pisistratus first seized power in Athens around 560 B.C., but he was driven
out not long afterward. To regain his position he entered into an alliance with a
certain Megacles, a prominent Athenian of the day, from a prominent family—
the Alcmaeonids, whom we'll hear more about in chapter nine. Their compact
was sealed with Pisistratus' marriage to Megacles' daughter. But neither Pisi-

stratus' hold on power nor, apparently, his marriage were to last long. The trouble was, Pisistratus didn't want to have children with his new wife. He had sons already, and he didn't want to get mixed up with the Alcmaeonids. So he had sex with her, but "not in the conventional way"—you can take your guesses as to what that might mean. Eventually, his wife complained to her mother (there's a conversation one would like to have on tape), and the mother complained to her husband (ditto), who, indignant, started looking for allies elsewhere. Seeing the writing on the wall, Pisistratus left Athens for the second time.

Pisistratus' second exile lasted some ten years, after which he returned and took Athens by force. This time Pisistratus remained in power for almost twenty years, until his death in 528 or 527. It was during Pisistratus' third period in power that Croesus allegedly made his enquiries with a view to finding an ally.[8]

When Croesus inquired about the state of affairs in Sparta, on the other hand, he learned that the *polis* was well-governed and that the Spartans were enjoying a period of military success. Earlier in the century, however, things had not gone so smoothly for them. The Spartans had had it in mind to conquer Arcadia, a region to the north of Sparta, smack dab in the center of the Greek Peloponnese. They sent to Delphi to ask for advice, and the response they received seemed to them reasonably favorable:

> You ask me for Arcadia? You ask me for a big thing. I will not give it to you. There are many acorn-eating men in Arcadia who will stop you. But I will not begrudge you. I will give you Tegea as a floor to dance on, a fair plain to measure out with a rope.

Fair enough, the Spartans figured. We can't have Arcadia because of the acorn eaters. (What Herodotus means is that the Arcadians were so primitive they subsisted on acorns.) But Tegea (a town in Arcadia) is ours for the taking: march on Tegea and we'll be dancing in the Tegeans' streets and dividing up their land for ourselves in no time.

Except that's not quite how things turned out. The Spartans advanced against the Tegeans, so confident they'd be victorious that they carried shackles with them to use on their future prisoners. But instead of dancing the night away, the Spartans were defeated. Those who were captured were bound in their own shackles, and they measured out the Tegean plain not for their own benefit but, Herodotus' implication seems to be, with the ropes that bound them together, chain-gang style.

A more insightful man than Croesus might have pondered the implications of the Spartans' experience for his own situation. The Spartans had received an oracle that seemed promising yet had a sting in its tail. Croesus had likewise received a pair of oracles that he considered favorable but which, for anyone with eyes to see it, were ambiguous at best. Mightn't he meet with the same kind of ironic fate the Spartans had suffered?

If the Spartans' history gave Croesus pause, we never hear about it. Besides, by the time Croesus made his enquiries, the Spartans' luck had turned. Following the advice of yet another oracle, they'd found and dug up the bones of Orestes, which had been buried in Tegea, and brought them to Sparta. (Orestes was the son of Agamemnon, one of the leaders of the Greek forces at Troy. Agamemnon was the younger brother of Menelaus, the Spartan king whose wife, Helen, was abducted by Paris. Orestes famously killed his mother Clytemnestra because she'd killed Agamemnon when he got back from the war. And she'd killed Agamemnon because he had killed their daughter Iphigenia to appease the goddess Artemis when the Greek fleet was ready to sail to Troy.) Once they got their hands on Orestes' bones, whatever protective power the hero had been offering the Tegeans was translated to Sparta, which subsequently became the preeminent power in the Peloponnese—just the sort of potential ally Croesus was looking for.

Croesus sent messengers to Sparta to ask for an alliance, and the Spartans were happy to oblige. By forging an alliance with the strongest power in Greece, Croesus had now done as Apollo's prophecy suggested, but in the event it wouldn't do him much good.

The Capture of Sardis (1.71–85)

Meanwhile Croesus, taking the oracle in a wrong sense, led his forces into Cappadocia, fully expecting to defeat Cyrus and destroy the empire of the Persians.   (1.71.1)

After Croesus had obtained an alliance with Sparta, and while he was making further preparations for war against Persia, he was approached by a man named Sandanis, a Lydian, who tried to change his mind about the invasion. Sandanis pointed out that while the Lydians lived in comfort, the Persians had nothing: they lived hard lives in a rock-strewn country without wine or figs. Croesus thus had nothing to gain by conquering their territory, while the Persians had everything to gain should they conquer Lydia. Sandanis, like Solon before him, is one of a number of characters in Herodotus' *History* who play the role of the wise advisor, a sage who comes on the scene and offers practical advice or tries to alter a leader's actions with his insight. As a literary device, the advisor also serves to foreshadow future events. The wise advisor is usually right, but his efforts are often in vain.

As we've seen, Croesus was not necessarily the brightest bulb in the chandelier. His preconceptions blinded him to the alternate interpretations possible for the oracles he'd received, and he was too unimaginative to recognize the wisdom in what Solon had told him, that the fortunes of man are subject to change. Croesus didn't get it—despite Solon's lecture, despite his son's death at the hands of Adrastus, despite the example of the lovesick Candaules, whom his own ancestor had slain. Still, Croesus had shown on at least one occasion that he was capable of being influenced by argument. After he had subdued the Greeks in Asia Minor earlier in his reign, he had it in mind to build a navy so that he could extend his influence over the islands off the coast as well. Another wise man approached him at that time—either Bias of Priene, Herodotus says, or Pittacus of Mitylene—and convinced Croesus that it would be foolhardy for him to try to defeat the islanders at sea, given that their naval capabilities so surpassed his. Croesus was persuaded and gave up the project, and he made alliances with the islanders instead (1.27). But the king was not so easily persuaded this time. Sandanis' advice went unheeded.

When his preparations were complete, Croesus brought his army across the Halys River, which separated Lydia from Cappadocia—territory that had been subject to Media but was now under Persian control. At once Croesus set to ravaging the countryside and capturing cities and towns and driving people out of their homes and enslaving them. In response, the Persian king, Cyrus, assembled his host and marched to confront the invaders. When the armies met they fought a fierce but inconclusive battle, disengaging at nightfall. The next day neither side advanced against the other, and Croesus withdrew to Sardis—back across the Halys and some 350 miles southwest—figuring he would winter there and invade Persia again in the spring after he'd assembled a larger force. Once he was back in Sardis Croesus dismissed his mercenaries and sent messengers to his allies—among them the Spartans—requesting that they send forces in time for his next expedition. And then, one imagines, he sat back with his feet up, looking forward to an uneventful winter, and imagined himself to be still, all things considered, among the most fortunate of men.

But the winter would not be as relaxing as Croesus had supposed. First, there were the snakes. Of a sudden the suburbs outside the city gate were swarming with them, and horses pasturing nearby came over and started to eat them. Croesus saw this as a portent and sent an embassy off to a famous bunch of seers in Telmessus, in southwest Asia Minor, to ask what it signified. The seers' interpretation of the incident amounted to another warning to Croesus—though in the event it arrived too late to do him any good. What they allegedly said (though this interpretation was presumably invented after the fact to correspond to what happened) was that Croesus should be on the lookout for a foreign army that would come into the country and defeat the indigenous population—just as the horses had come from their pastures to destroy the autochthonous snakes.

Worse for Croesus by far was the invasion that the snakes had portended. Cyrus decided he would preempt any future trouble with Croesus by crossing the Halys River himself and marching against Sardis. He assumed, correctly, that Croesus would disband his army once he'd arrived back at his capital and would thus be unprepared for an attack. When Cyrus arrived before the city, Croesus was forced to meet him with what forces he still had—without mercenaries or allies.

Interestingly, one of the first things we are given to understand about Cyrus is that—unlike Croesus much of the time—he was able to take and benefit from advice. At the recommendation of Harpagus, a Mede whom we'll be hearing more about in chapter two, Cyrus' first move in the battle at Sardis was to send a preliminary wave of camels against the Lydians, having equipped their riders as cavalrymen. Horses are afraid of camels, so the Lydian cavalry on which Croesus was relying was rendered impotent by the tactic. Their horses bolted, and the Lydians were compelled to meet the Persian onslaught on foot. And things just got worse for Croesus from there. The Lydians were routed in battle and forced back behind their walls, and the siege of Sardis was begun.

Croesus, fenced in by the Persians, sent out a second batch of messengers to his allies telling them that Sardis was besieged and asking that they come at once to relieve him. Croesus had good reason to think his allies would make it in time. In ancient times, sieges tended to be drawn-out affairs. Besieging armies often took cities not by breaching their walls—a difficult business that was likely to entail heavy casualties—but by trickery or with the assistance of some treacherous party inside the city or by, very slowly, starving out the inhabitants. So there was a chance that Croesus could hold out until the Spartans or his other allies came to the rescue. But, as you'll likely have guessed by now, that's not how things worked out.

Two weeks into the siege, according to Herodotus (other sources tell different stories about how the city was taken), Cyrus announced to his men that he would give a prize to whoever first scaled the city's acropolis (its citadel, a high, fortified area). Now, the walls of Sardis had an interesting history. Herodotus tells us that an earlier king, Meles, had a concubine who had given birth to a lion. The Telmessians—the same group of seers Croesus had consulted about the snakes—had announced that if the lion cub were carried around the city's walls, Sardis would be impregnable. So Meles carried the lion around the city, but he didn't complete the circle. He figured that the southern wall of the acropolis was so sheer that it was impregnable anyway, so he gave up the job at that point and called it a day.

Meles should have gone the extra mile, of course, because this gap in the circle is precisely where the citadel proved vulnerable—or so the story goes. (I really can't stress enough the importance of being thorough when you're trying to do this kind of thing—to render a city impregnable by making a magic circle around it, or to make your child invulnerable by dipping him in the River Styx, as Thetis did with Achilles. If you don't take the time to do the job right, it will come back to bite you in the heel.) A Persian by the name of Hyroeades happened to see one of the city's defenders climb down the cliffs to retrieve his helmet. Hyroeades thus learned where and how the acropolis could be scaled. He climbed up, followed by other Persians, and the acropolis was taken.

Back in the palace, or wherever it was Croesus was holed up during the assault, a funny thing happened. You'll remember that Croesus had two sons. One was killed by Adrastus on that boar hunt, and the other was deaf and dumb and relegated by Croesus to a distant second place in his affections. Some years earlier Croesus had sent to Delphi to ask about this second son. As often, the oracle's response was cryptic:

> Lydian, king of many men, Croesus you great fool, do not wish to hear the much prayed for sound of your son speaking in your home. It would be far better for you not to get what you want. For you will first hear his voice on a luckless day.

The oracle was also rather worrying, one would think, but Croesus had a habit of ignoring doom-and-gloom prophecies. He probably paid this one no heed until the prediction came to pass.

Cyrus had given the order to his men to take Croesus alive, but a Persian soldier came upon the king in the melee and, not recognizing him, was about to kill him. Croesus was past caring at this point and didn't make any move to save himself. But Croesus' formerly speechless son saw what was happening and of a sudden cried out, "Sir! Don't kill Croesus!" thereby saving his father's life. For the time being, at least: Croesus was about to make the proverbial leap out of the frying pan and into the fire.

The Wisdom of Croesus (1.86–91)

When this thought smote him he fetched a long breath, and breaking his deep silence, groaned out aloud, thrice uttering the name of Solon.   (1.86.3)

The fire into which Croesus leapt was a real one. He was captured and bound in chains, and Cyrus heaped up a pyre and set Croesus on top of it along with fourteen Lydian children, all of whom he planned to burn alive. At this point— a little late in the game—Croesus remembered what Solon had said to him, and he understood the wisdom of it. And having been impassive before, he now began lamenting, and he called out the name "Solon" three times. This got Cyrus' attention. He had his interpreters ask Croesus what he was talking about, and after some prodding, Croesus told the story: how the Athenian Solon had visited Sardis and had thought so little of Croesus' riches, and how things had turned out for Croesus as Solon had suggested they might. Croesus recognized too that Solon's wisdom was not relevant to himself alone but pertained to everyone, particularly those who are convinced of their own good fortune.

The Persian king turned out to be quicker on the uptake than Croesus, prepyre, had been. He recognized at once the wisdom of Solon's words and their relevance to his own life, and he understood the similarity between himself and the Lydian king. He changed his mind about killing Croesus—figuring also that it was the kind of act that might bring retribution (just as Gyges' murder of Candaules had come with a price tag)—and he ordered his minions to douse the fire, which had already been set. Unfortunately, this was easier said than done. Cyrus' men tried to put the fire out, but it had gotten out of control. It looked like Croesus would burn to death after all.

Croesus, from atop the pyre, saw the men trying to put out the fire, and he realized that Cyrus had changed his mind. His instinct for self-preservation kicked in, and he called upon Apollo to save him, reminding him of the very

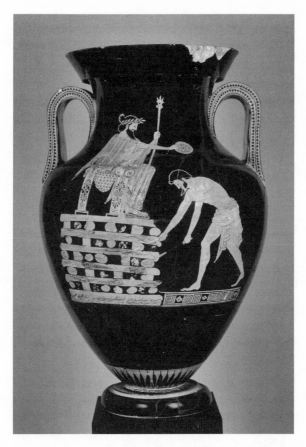

Croesus seated on his funeral pyre. The red-figure amphora by Myson dates to the early fifth century B.C. Réunion des Musées Nationaux / Art Resource, NY

many gifts he had dedicated to the god in the past. Croesus was hoping for some payback in his hour of need, that is, and he got it. Out of a clear sky there came a sudden, violent rain, which quenched the flames and impressed the Persian king. Here, Cyrus realized, was a good man who was beloved by the gods. He got Croesus down from the pyre and, with all that unpleasantness behind them, the king and the former king got to talking. It was the start of a mutually beneficial relationship that would last another sixteen years, until Cyrus' death in 530—the event with which the first book of Herodotus' *History* comes to a close.

Actually, it may not have been the start of anything. We can't be sure what happened to Croesus after the fall of Sardis in 546. Reports vary. According to the third ode of Bacchylides, a Greek poet born in the late sixth century (thus some twenty to thirty years older than Herodotus), Croesus is the one who ordered a pyre built. He sought to kill himself on it together with his wife and daughters. He had his servants light the fire, but because of Croesus' piety and his earlier largesse toward the temple at Delphi, Zeus quenched the flames with rain. Apollo showed his appreciation in turn by carrying the king and his family off to live among the Hyperboreans—a people thought to inhabit northern Europe. Nicolaus of Damascus, whose evidence for the Gyges story we discussed above, reports that Croesus in fact died on the pyre (*FGH* 90 F 68). The Greek historian Xenophon (c. 431–355 B.C.), in his biography of Cyrus, omits altogether any reference to attempted immolation (*Cyropaedia* 7.2). Rather, in his version of events Croesus and Cyrus skip right to the talking stage, the point where we left off in Herodotus' narrative. Other sources suggest that Croesus lived on as a sort of vassal to Cyrus.

In short, Croesus either died or he did not die after the fall of Sardis. He was killed by his own hand or was executed by order of the Great King (as the Persian kings styled themselves). And he may or may not have lived on as an advisor to Cyrus. Herodotus probably didn't know what really happened to the Lydian king. But from among the various stories circulating in his day, he will have selected and tweaked the one which best suited his narrative. We're unlikely ever to know the truth either. Chances are good, however, that Croesus was not spirited off by Apollo to northern Europe. While divine intervention may have been perceived in the event by onlookers, the gods are unlikely to have been involved in fact.

Back to the story. When Croesus came down from the pyre, Cyrus asked the king what had possessed him to attack Persia. Herodotus has already told us Croesus' reasons for making war: he wanted to check the growth of Persia and avenge his brother-in-law Astyages, he wanted additional territory, and he was relying on the oracles he'd received, which had implied (or so he thought) that he was destined to destroy Persia (1.46.1, 73.1). But when Cyrus asked him why he did it, Croesus omitted the practical and personal reasons behind his attack and lay the blame squarely at Apollo's door: "The god of the Greeks is responsible," he said, "who urged me to go to war. For no one"—and this is an oft-quoted remark that readers may have encountered before—"no one is so foolish as to prefer war to peace: for in the one sons bury their fathers, but in the other fathers bury their sons. I suppose it was divine will that things turned out this way."

As his response suggests, Croesus emerged from his near-death experience a changed man, with a clear appreciation of the role of the gods in his personal drama and a healthy respect for the horrors of war. He has in fact turned into the sort of wise advisor by whom he was himself counseled in the past, able to dish out advice both philosophical and practical. And he was ready to jump into his new job immediately. Once his chains were removed and Cyrus and his courtiers had gazed at him in admiration for a while[9]—Croesus himself sitting silently, in thoughtful contemplation—the Lydian king-turned-wise-man spotted something amiss in Cyrus' administration of his affairs. Specifically, Croesus noticed that the Persian soldiers were pillaging Sardis—not an unexpected sight after the fall of an ancient city, but Croesus thought it unwise for Cyrus to allow it. In the conversation that followed, the two men essentially hammered out the terms of their new relationship:

> Croesus: Your majesty, can I tell you what I'm thinking about, or should I keep quiet?
>
> Cyrus: Say what you want.
>
> Croesus: What's that excited mob up to?
>
> Cyrus: Plundering your city and stealing your stuff.
>
> Croesus: Um. . . . It's not *my* stuff, anymore, it's yours.
>
> Cyrus: D'oh!

Okay, I admit it: I added the "D'oh!" But Cyrus may well have let loose with the Persian equivalent. He was, at any rate, impressed once again with what his prisoner had to say. He ordered everybody else out of the room and then asked Croesus what he should do about the pillaging. Croesus suggested that he confiscate the loot from the soldiers, telling them that a tenth of it had to be dedicated to Zeus. Your soldiers, he said, will willingly hand over what they're carrying because they'll know it's the right thing to do.

It's a stupid idea, or at least an incomplete one. The tithing of spoils to the gods was itself not unusual: later in his *History* Herodotus will describe how the Greeks apportioned booty collected after the battle at Plataea in 479, dedicating 10 percent of it to Delphi (9.80–81). But in that case the collection of the spoils was an orderly affair. Nothing had to be wrested from the soldiers. Croesus doesn't say anything here about how (or whether) what remained of the booty from Sardis after tithing would be redistributed—evenly? in proportion to how much each man turned over in the first place? The first option would almost certainly leave some of the soldiers dissatisfied. The second would be a bookkeeping nightmare.

Cyrus, however, was again impressed. Indeed, Croesus' practical advice had pretty much secured his position as a royal hanger-on. Because of Croesus' willingness to help, Cyrus told him to ask for anything he wanted. Rather than requesting some practical comfort, what Croesus asked for was the chance to reproach Apollo for having misled him. He told Cyrus all about the oracles he'd received, and Cyrus granted his request to send messengers to Delphi to question the god, adding that he would give Croesus anything else he needed as well. (If you had to lose your kingdom and your throne to someone, you really couldn't ask for a better conquering foe than Cyrus.)

Thus Croesus sent a final embassy to Delphi, instructing his messengers to put the fetters he'd been bound in on the threshold of the temple. They were to ask the god whether he was ashamed of himself for urging Croesus to make war and whether the Greek gods were wont to be ungrateful. Like the drawing room scene at the end of a murder mystery, Croesus' confrontation of Apollo allows Herodotus to tie his story up neatly, to reveal the hidden—or previously unappreciated—meanings of the oracles to his principals and his audience. When Croesus' messengers posed their questions, the priestess of Apollo provided a lengthy response that made everything clear. As to the meanings of the oracles, the priestess explained that the first—which said that Croesus would destroy a mighty empire should he invade Persia—had been ambiguous: Croesus should have asked *which* empire was destined to be destroyed. The oracle that warned Croesus to flee should a mule become king of the Medians, on the other hand, referred to Cyrus: the Persian king was a "mule" because his mother was a Mede and thus of higher station than his Persian father—the Persians being subject to the Medes—just as a mule's mother (a horse) is of a higher breed than its father (a donkey). Croesus had misunderstood both oracles and thus had no grounds for complaint against the god.

Further, the priestess explained that Croesus was fated to pay the price for his ancestor's regicide. It was now the fifth generation since Gyges' murder of Candaules, when the kingship of the Medians had passed to the Mermnad dynasty. Even Apollo couldn't help him out there, though the god had managed to buy Croesus a little more time: he had somehow postponed the capture of Sardis by three years. On top of that, Apollo had saved Croesus from burning to death on the pyre. When Croesus heard the priestess's response, he recognized that the responsibility for the fall of Sardis was his and not the god's. His education was complete.

Torture and Prostitution (1.92–94)

The daughters of the common people in Lydia, one and all, pursue this traffic, wishing to collect money for their portions.   (1.93.4)

With Sardis captured and Croesus' status dramatically altered, Herodotus' Lydian story is effectively finished, but the historian still has a few juicy things to tell us about Croesus and Lydia before moving on to his discussion of Cyrus and Persia. He mentions, for example, that before he was king Croesus' succession to the throne was contested by his half-brother Pantaleon. Croesus later executed Pantaleon by having him dragged across a carding comb—that is, by having his skin ripped to shreds over the long, sharp teeth of an instrument used to prepare fiber for spinning. (Imagine something along the lines of a steel brush or a board with rows of nails sticking out of it.) This probably won't be the first time that events described in *The History* will remind readers of the tactics employed more recently by the likes of Saddam Hussein. But as repugnant to us as it may be, Croesus' torture and execution of his disloyal half-brother is not an occasion for moralizing in Herodotus. It's just another interesting piece of information the historian came across in his travels that was too good to leave out of his narrative.

Herodotus tends to wrap up his discussions of various peoples by describing their customs and by noting any geographical points of interest in their countries. In this way Herodotus has preserved a great deal of fascinating, almost random information—some of it credible, some more dubious. At the close of his Lydian section Herodotus mentions that the Lydians were the first shopkeepers and the first to use gold and silver currency. He also says it was customary among the Lydians for the daughters of commoners to earn their own dowries by prostituting themselves. But apart from that, Herodotus says, the Lydians' customs were pretty similar to those of the Greeks.

Lydia was just one of the kingdoms the Persians rolled through on their seemingly inexorable march toward confrontation with the Greeks of the mainland. Thus Lydia and Croesus might well have been treated as a footnote, but Herodotus starts his *History* with Croesus because, as he explains at 1.6.2, the

Lydian king was the first barbarian to demand tribute of the Greeks. This is justification enough for its primacy, but Croesus' story also serves as a microcosm of Herodotus' work as a whole, which makes it an ideal introduction to *The History*. Croesus is the prototype of Xerxes, the hubristic Persian king whose invasion of Greece in 480 is the subject of the second half of Herodotus' work. Both men transgressed the natural limits of their power and marched blindly to their fates, ignoring warnings from gods and men, speeding their destruction through recklessness. On a grander scale, the defeat of Lydia at the hands of the Persians foreshadows the later defeat of the Persians by the Greeks.

In the Croesus story we are also introduced to the main theme of Herodotus' *History*, the mutability of human affairs: fortune does not always reside in the same place; great empires are sometimes toppled; only a fool counts himself blessed before he is dead. Before we're finished with Herodotus we'll meet more kings and tyrants who could have benefited from Solon's wisdom.

We'll encounter Croesus a few more times in Herodotus' *History* too, dutifully offering sage advice in his capacity as wise advisor to the Persian king. But with the Lydian kingdom now subsumed by the Persian Empire, Herodotus turns his attention from the newly wise Croesus to the history of Persia and the rise of Cyrus the Great.

CHAPTER TWO

Cannibals and Conquests

The Story of Cyrus the Great

O NE OF THE REASONS BEHIND Croesus' decision to attack Persia—what in fact got him thinking along those lines in the first place—was that the Persians under Cyrus had conquered the kingdom of Media, which lay just across the Halys River from Lydia. It was bad enough that an aggressive, expanding empire now lay on his border, but the king of Media, Astyages, was also (supposedly) Croesus' brother-in-law: the possibility of avenging Astyages made a preemptive strike against Persia that much more attractive.

It's interesting that this familial connection should have been a factor in Croesus' decision to attack Persia, given that he and Astyages weren't the only relatives involved in this clash of civilizations. Astyages—at least as Herodotus tells the story—was also Cyrus' grandfather.[1]

The Birth and Exposure of Cyrus (1.107–113)

He dreamt that from her such a stream of water flowed forth as not only to fill his capital, but to flood the whole of Asia.   (1.107.1)

Astyages had a daughter named Mandane. When she was young, he dreamt that she urinated so copiously that she flooded his city and all of Asia besides. The king consulted some dream interpreters among the Magi about it. (The Magi were a tribe or caste within Median society whose members served as priests and seers. The name is the root of our word *magic*. The three wise men who are said to have visited Jesus bearing gifts were likewise Magi.) Herodotus doesn't record their response, but the purport of it, given Astyages' subsequent actions, seems to have been that Mandane's child would one day become king, but the succession would not be a peaceful one.

As Croesus had after he'd dreamt of his son Atys' death, and with equally unsatisfactory results, Astyages took steps intended to prevent what his dream predicted from coming to pass. When his daughter was old enough, he married her off to someone of inferior station, a Persian by the name of Cambyses. (The Persians, who inhabited part of what is modern-day Iran, had been subjugated by the Medes in the seventh century. Herodotus does not mention it, because it doesn't fit in well with the story as he tells it, but Cambyses was in fact the king of the Persian city Ansan—a vassal-king to be sure, as the Medes had dominated the Persians, but royalty nonetheless.) Apparently Astyages assumed that any son issuing from this marriage would be, by virtue of his father's status, intrinsically incapable of usurping the throne in the manner portended by the dream. This was not a safe assumption.

When Mandane was in her first year of marriage Astyages had another alarming vision. This time he dreamt that a vine grew out of Mandane's vagina and shaded all of Asia. Again Astyages consulted the Magi. This time we're explicitly told that they interpreted the dream to mean that Mandane's child would become king in Astyages' stead. Clearly, the steps Astyages had taken to prevent this from happening had been insufficient. And in fact, in trying to make things better, Astyages had only made them worse. Even if handing his throne over to Mandane's son would have been a natural and desirable thing to do under other circumstances, Astyages had now married Mandane off to a Persian, so any son she bore would be Persian rather than Median. In giving his throne to a grandson, then, Astyages would at the same time be surrendering the Medians' authority to a subject people. This he was not prepared to do.

Astyages summoned Mandane, now pregnant, from Persia. When she arrived, Astyages kept her under guard, waiting until the baby was born so that he could have it destroyed. (Herodotus doesn't tell us if Mandane knew what her father was up to.) When the time came, Astyages gave the job of killing the baby to Harpagus, the guy who would later advise Cyrus to use camels during the battle for Sardis. Harpagus was a Mede to whom Astyages entrusted all his affairs, and he was related to Astyages in some unspecified way (and thus also related to Mandane and her baby). Astyages ordered Harpagus to take the baby home and kill it, then bury it however he liked. He warned Harpagus to take care of the problem and not to deceive him and "choose others" (that is, apparently, not to elect to serve anyone else's interests), lest in the future he "trip himself up." The threat may not have been specific, but Astyages' purport was clear enough: there would be hell to pay if Harpagus failed him.

Harpagus agreed to do as he was told, but he wasn't happy about it. He brought the baby home, weeping as he went, and when he got there he told his wife what had happened and what he was planning to do. He had no intention of doing what Astyages wanted, he said, "not even if Astyages were to lose his mind and go crazier than he is now." There were a bunch of reasons why he wouldn't—the baby was related to him, for one thing—but self-preservation was near the top of the list: if Mandane should inherit the throne from Astyages, what do you suppose would happen to the trusted minister who'd murdered her child?

So—big sigh of relief—Harpagus wasn't going to kill the baby.

On the other hand, he said, somebody had to do it. Otherwise Harpagus would suffer whatever horrible consequences Astyages had in mind. He decided to delegate the responsibility to one of Astyages' herdsmen, a fellow named Mitridates, who pastured his cows in the foothills of some mountains to the north, just the place for exposing an infant. Harpagus summoned Mitridates and ordered the poor man to take the baby and expose it, threatening him with death should he not comply. Harpagus would himself inspect the corpse once the baby was dead.

The story is probably beginning to sound familiar. There are a great many tales in different cultures in which infants who were exposed or were supposed to have been exposed somehow survive and, in adulthood, find themselves heir to a kingdom. As David Asheri explains in his commentary on 1.113.1, this story type "is sometimes used to provide a pseudo-historical legitimation for controversial usurpation, change of dynasty, foundation of a kingdom, a cult, etc."[2] When the twins Romulus and Remus were infants, for example, the king of Alba Longa, their mother's uncle, ordered that they be left to drown in the Tiber River so that in adulthood they couldn't challenge his sovereignty. (He had stolen the throne from his brother Numitor, the twins' maternal grandfather.) But the basket in which the babies were placed floated to shore, and they were nursed by a she-wolf and eventually discovered by a shepherd. When they grew up, they killed their great uncle, returned their grandfather to the throne of Alba Longa, and, most famously, went on to found the city of Rome.

A similar story was told about Paris, the Trojan prince who would grow up to steal Helen from her husband and thus spark the Trojan War. Before Paris was born, his mother, Hecuba, dreamt that she'd given birth to a flaming torch. The dream—very similar to Astyages' dream about his daughter's vaginal vine—was interpreted to mean that the baby would somehow destroy Troy. Thus, after Paris was born, Hecuba and her husband, Priam, reluctantly handed the baby over to a shepherd so that he could kill it. The shepherd exposed the baby on Mount Ida. Unfortunately for Troy, a she-bear suckled the infant, Paris survived, and the shepherd, finding the baby still alive after a number of days, took him home to raise as his own.

The story of Oedipus is also very close to what we find in Herodotus' account of Cyrus' infancy. Before Oedipus was born, a prophecy suggested that he would grow up to kill his father. His parents, thinking (like Croesus, like Astyages) that they could prevent the prophecy from being realized, gave the baby to a shepherd when it was born and ordered him to expose it. The shepherd instead gave the baby to another shepherd, who gave Oedipus to the king and queen of Corinth, who raised him as their own. When Oedipus was grown he heard a rumor—spat out by a drunk at a public feast—that he was not the legitimate son of the king and queen. He went to the oracle at Delphi to find out the truth, and he learned not only that he was destined to kill his father but that he was also slated to have sex with his mother. He attempted (like Croesus, like Astyages, like his parents) to circumvent his fate by leaving home—because he supposed the king and queen of Corinth to be his real parents. But en route from Delphi to Thebes he had a run-in with his biological father (whom he of course didn't recognize) and killed him. Shortly thereafter, Oedipus unwittingly married the dead man's widow, his own mother.

The herdsman Mitridates, as it turned out, was no better at following directions than the shepherds in Oedipus' story.

When Mitridates got home, his wife—although she had news of her own to share—asked him at once what had happened. (It's not every day that the king's right-hand man orders you to come to his house, and it's not necessarily a good sign when he does, so she'd been worried.) Mitridates told her the whole story, including what he'd found out from a servant on the way home: the doomed baby was not, as he had first supposed, the child of one of the servants; it was in fact Astyages' grandson. When he finished his story Mitridates uncovered the baby and showed it to his wife, who burst into tears, grabbed hold of her husband's knees, and begged him not to kill it.

It was all very affecting, but Mitridates was in the same boat Harpagus had been in: if he didn't kill the baby, then Harpagus was going to kill *him*. He wasn't happy about it, but there was no way out of it. The baby was a goner.

Unlike Harpagus' wife, however, who'd merely acted as a sounding board when her husband came home with the baby, Mitridates' wife—whose name was Spako—had an ace up her sleeve. The conversation went something like this:

> Spako: You can't kill it! You just can't!
>
> Mitridates: I must!
>
> Spako: You mustn't!
>
> Mitridates: If I don't, Harpagus will kill me.
>
> Spako: Okay, okay, I've got a plan. It turns out that while you were gone I had a baby.
>
> Mitridates: Oh right, I'd been meaning to ask about that....
>
> Spako: But the baby was stillborn.
>
> Mitridates: Damn.
>
> Spako: So I say, let's switch babies! We'll keep Astyages' grandson, and you can show Harpagus the body of our dead son.
>
> Mitridates: Brilliant! I'll go and dress the corpse in the royal baby clothes now.

Herodotus does tell us early in his description of the scene at the herdsman's house that Spako had given birth that day—so it's no surprise to us when she suggests this morbid but eminently sensible plan to her husband. Herodotus also tells us that Mitridates had been worried about his wife all day, given that her labor was imminent, but he doesn't come across as particularly concerned in Herodotus' narrative: when Mitridates gets home he doesn't notice anything that would suggest his wife had given birth, nor does he ask about her, so full is he of the story he has to tell. The lapse is comical, but it's also understandable: it would have made for a weaker story had Spako told Mitridates her news first.

As my dramatization above suggests, Mitridates went along with Spako's idea, and the plan worked perfectly. Mitridates dressed his dead son's body in the clothes in which Astyages' grandson had been swaddled and left the corpse on the mountain. After three days Mitridates went back to Harpagus and told him the body was ready for viewing, and Harpagus sent some of his men to inspect and bury the corpse.

The infant Cyrus, meanwhile, heir to the Persian throne, survived and grew up safely and secretly in the care of the herdsman Mitridates and his wife.

The Recognition of Cyrus (1.114–119)

Harpagus, on hearing this, made obeisance, and went home rejoicing to find that his disobedience had turned out so fortunately, and that, instead of being punished, he was invited to a banquet given in honour of the happy occasion.

(1.119.1)

It seems that Cyrus was genetically endowed with a healthy sense of entitlement. This became clear one day when he was ten years old. He and a bunch of other boys were playing outside, and the group chose Cyrus to act as their pretend king. Cyrus in turn divvied out various offices and responsibilities to his friends, but one of them refused to do what he was told. Cyrus, acting in his capacity as king, whipped the boy by way of punishment.

The boy was outraged, and his fury was exacerbated by the fact that Cyrus, who was ostensibly just the son of a cowherd, was his social inferior. This boy's father, by contrast, was a distinguished Median who was held in high regard by Astyages himself. The boy went home and complained to his father, Artembares, and the two went off to tell Astyages what his cowherd's son had done. After hearing their complaint Astyages summoned Mitridates and Cyrus to court. Astyages too was struck by the audacity of Cyrus' attack on a boy of higher station. He asked Cyrus to explain himself, and again Cyrus' haughtiness was clear in his response, the purport of which was that the boy had deserved what he got because he had disobeyed Cyrus during their game. "But," Cyrus added, "if I deserve punishment for this, here I am."

It was an unusual response from the son of a cowherd, from whom one might have expected fawning servility. But despite having grown up mucking out cow stalls, Cyrus had maintained the nobility that was his birthright. He submitted to Astyages' authority in his response but in no way surrendered his dignity. Cyrus' outspokenness was not lost on Astyages, who was temporarily dumbstruck while the pieces fit together in his head—Cyrus' noble bearing, his age, his appearance. Suspecting the truth, he quickly dismissed Artembares and his son, assuring them he'd take care of the matter. Then he interrogated Mitridates, who spilled the beans about Cyrus' true identity as soon as Astyages threatened to have him tortured.

Once Astyages had gotten the truth out of Mitridates, he lost interest in him, but he was furious with Harpagus and sent his bodyguards to fetch him. When Harpagus arrived, Astyages asked him to describe precisely how Mandane's baby had died. Harpagus saw the cowherd in the room, so he understood that lying wasn't an option, and he told Astyages everything he had done. His story jibed with what Mitridates had said: as far as Harpagus knew, the baby had been exposed, and Harpagus' men had seen the corpse. Astyages was angry, but he hid his feelings from Harpagus and said he was actually glad things had turned out this way: he had felt bad about killing his grandson, and it had caused a rift between him and Mandane, so it was just as well that the baby had lived. He proposed they celebrate Cyrus' survival with a feast. He invited Harpagus to dinner and suggested he send his son over early: the boy was about thirteen, so he would make good company at court for the ten-year-old Cyrus.

Harpagus was enormously relieved. He went home and sent his son to the palace, and he told his wife the good news. Then, presumably, he got cleaned up for the feast.

Meanwhile, when Harpagus' son arrived, Astyages got *him* ready for dinner. That is, as Herodotus tells us, "he slit the boy's throat and chopped him up, limb from limb, and some of the flesh he roasted and some he boiled, and he made him ready for the table." Astyages had pretended otherwise, but he was still miffed about Harpagus' failure to take care of the Cyrus business ten years earlier. Killing and cooking Harpagus' only son (who was, remember, in some way related to Astyages himself) was his way of expressing his disappointment with Harpagus. There was some precedent for Astyages' brand of revenge in the Median court: you may remember that Astyages' father had been tricked by some offended Scythians into eating an unrelated Median boy—an incident that had led to a five-year war between Media and Lydia. Astyages took his re-taliatory cannibalism to the next level by slaughtering the flesh and blood of the man he was punishing, but this too was not a new idea. The prototype for Astyages' gruesome dinner was the infamous feast of Thyestes, part of the mythical backstory to the Trojan War.

We mentioned Agamemnon and his wife and kids in chapter one, a nuclear unit famous for its chain reaction of intra-family murder: Orestes killed Clytemnestra because she killed Agamemnon because he killed Iphigenia. But they weren't the first murderous members of the clan. Agamemnon and his brother Menelaus were the sons of Atreus. This Atreus had a brother named Thyestes with whom he squabbled over the throne of Mycenae. Atreus eventually won the kingship (it's a long story, involving divine intervention, a golden ram, and the sun going backwards in its course), and he banished Thyestes from the kingdom. But when he subsequently discovered that his wife had been having an affair with Thyestes, Atreus pretended he wanted to reconcile with his brother. He prepared a feast very much like the one Astyages served: Atreus slaughtered his nephews, Thyestes' sons. "And having cut them limb from limb and boiled them, he served them up to Thyestes without the extremities; and when Thyestes had eaten heartily of them, he showed him the extremities, and cast him out of the country." (The quotation is from the epitome to Pseudo-Apollodorus' *Library* [2.13], a summary of Greek mythology compiled in the second century A.D., trans. J. G. Frazer.)

Just so, when dinner was served at Astyages' court, everybody else ate mutton, but Harpagus was given his own son to eat, "except for the head and the hands and the feet, which were kept separate, covered up in a basket." When Harpagus had finished eating, Astyages asked him whether he'd enjoyed the meal. "Very much!" he said, and Astyages had his servants bring the covered basket over to his guest. They stood next to Harpagus and told him to lift the cover and take what he wanted.

Harpagus was remarkably cool. When he saw his son's severed head and hands and feet, he betrayed no sign that anything was wrong. Astyages asked him if he knew what wild beast it was whose flesh he'd been eating. "I know," Harpagus said. "Whatever the king does is best." Then Harpagus gathered up what was left of his son and went home. "I suppose," Herodotus writes, "he was going to gather the pieces together and bury them."

Harpagus' Revenge (1.120–130)

But truly we are persuaded that the dream has had its accomplishment in this
harmless way; and so our own fears being at rest, we recommend thee to banish
thine.   (1.120.6)

Having dealt with Harpagus, Astyages turned his attention to Cyrus, considering what he should do with the boy now that he'd survived. He consulted the
Magi again, and they reiterated their opinion that Astyages' dreams signified
that Cyrus would become king. The message was the same as before, but this
time Astyages was less concerned. He told the Magi that Cyrus had acted as king
while playing with his friends, that he'd done everything kings do, appointing
bodyguards and messengers and so on. In effect he had ruled. This changed the
Magi's interpretation of the dreams as well: sometimes, they explained, portents
are indeed fulfilled in trifling ways. If Cyrus had served already as king, then he
no longer represented a threat to Astyages. The Magi were quite confident of
this and suggested that Astyages send the boy off to live with his biological parents. Astyages agreed and did as they suggested, but he would come to regret
his leniency (as would the Magi): Astyages and his seers were wrong to think
that Cyrus, having played the king as a boy, would not grow up to do so again.

Astyages' decision to spare his grandson and send him to Persia is reminiscent of the story of Croesus and his son Atys. Both Croesus and Astyages
had frightening dreams that portended disaster, and both took pains to try to
prevent those dreams from being realized. Both were subsequently persuaded
to slacken their precautions, and both unwittingly took actions that led to the
disaster they were attempting to prevent: Cyrus sent the ill-fated Adrastus off
on the boar hunt with Atys, and Astyages married Mandane off to Cambyses,
thus assuring that the grandson he was afraid would wrest the kingdom from
him would be Persian.

So it was that Cyrus went to live in Persia with Mandane and Cambyses.
Cyrus told them everything that had happened, and he talked about his adop-
tive mother Spako a great deal while describing his life as the son of a cowherd.
According to Herodotus, this gave Cyrus' parents an idea.

In Herodotus' day there was a legend that Cyrus had been suckled by a dog
as an infant. (Note the similarity to the myths of Paris and Romulus and Remus.) A version of this story is preserved in Justin's abridgment of Pompeius
Trogus' history:

The herdsman, by chance, had a son born at the same time; and his wife, hearing of the exposure of the royal infant, entreated, with the utmost earnestness, that the child might be brought and shown to her. The herdsman, overcome by her solicitations, went back into the wood, and found a dog by the infant, giving it her teats, and protecting it from the beasts and birds of prey. Being moved with pity, with which he saw even a dog moved, he carried the child to the cattle-folds, the dog vigilantly following him. (Justin 1.4, trans. John Selby Watson)

Herodotus explains what he imagines is the genesis of this myth. *Spako* is the Median word for "dog." When Mandane and Cambyses heard Cyrus had been raised by Spako, they put it about that he had been suckled by a dog. That way his survival would seem to the Persians to have been divinely contrived. Herodotus' rationalization of the myth suggests that Cyrus' parents had big plans for him. If so, they weren't the only ones.

Harpagus may have held his tongue while he gathered up his son's body parts after Astyages' banquet, but he was not about to forget what the king had done to him. He figured his best hope for revenge lay in Cyrus, and so he cultivated the prince's loyalties by sending him gifts as he got older. Harpagus also prepared the way for a potential coup by meeting secretly with Median noblemen and urging them to transfer their allegiance to Cyrus. Finally, some years after the banquet, Harpagus sent Cyrus a message via rabbit: he slit open a hare and sewed a letter inside it, then dispatched a trusted servant to Persia with the rabbit and some nets, in the guise of a hunter. The servant was instructed to tell Cyrus to slit the animal open when no one else was around.

In the letter Harpagus urged Cyrus to lead the Persians in revolt against the Medes. He told Cyrus that he and other Median noblemen stood ready to desert Astyages and join him. Cyrus, who had inherited the throne of Ansan from his father by this time (in 559, at the age of 16 or 17), was open to the possibilities Harpagus was suggesting. He gave some thought to how he might persuade the Persians to revolt against the Medes, and he came up with a plan. He announced to the Persians that Astyages had named him their general—a lie, of course—and he ordered them to report for duty, each man armed with a scythe. When they showed up, he put them to work, ordering them to clear an area some two miles square in a single day. Afterwards he sent them home to get cleaned up, with orders to return in the morning.

The next day Cyrus entertained the Persians with a feast. (He'd slaughtered a bunch of sheep and goats and cattle overnight by way of preparation.) The men reclined in a meadow and ate and drank, and when they were done Cyrus asked them which activity they'd preferred, clearing the land all day or feasting. The Persians were no dummies and replied as Cyrus had expected, at which point he urged them to follow him and revolt against the Medes. If they did, he said, there would be an end to slavish work, and they would enjoy an abundance of good things—just as they had that day. A vote for Cyrus, that is, was a vote for idle luxury. Cyrus' object lesson did the trick: the Persians were eager to slough off their Median overlords under his leadership.

The struggle for dominance that ensued is much abbreviated in Herodotus' account. What must have taken years to accomplish is summarized in two brief sections. The hostilities, we're told, were preceded by a brief exchange between Astyages and his grandson. The Median king, having somehow learned what Cyrus was up to, sent a messenger to summon Cyrus to his court. Cyrus responded that he would come, but sooner than the king wished. When that gauntlet had been thrown down, Astyages armed the Medes. And he was delusional enough to appoint Harpagus as their general—forgetting that he'd killed and cooked Harpagus' son, which a reasonable person would understand made handing Harpagus an army a dangerous proposition. Harpagus, remember, had long been plotting Cyrus' takeover, and his work paid off: during the battle, although some Medes fought, many deserted to the Persians, and others deliberately broke ranks and fled.

Astyages took out his fury over what was happening on the battlefield by seizing the Magi, who had suggested years earlier that he send Cyrus to Persia, and having them impaled. That is, they were not crucified in the more familiar sense—nailing people to boards was a Roman practice—but actually skewered and hung out to die. We'll see more impalements in Herodotus before we're done. (This is the sort of thing that Vlad the Impaler—one of the influences behind Bram Stoker's character Dracula—would become famous for in the fifteenth century. He reportedly made an art of impalement, carefully inserting a stake into his victim through the anus and driving it upward so as to avoid the major organs and thus delay his victim's death. The skewered, hoisted aloft on their impalement sticks, might also be arranged in attractive geometrical patterns for the pleasure of those watching their death throes. Vlad is said to have sometimes executed thousands of people at a time by this means.)

In a final battle, the Medes were soundly beaten by the Persians, and Astyages himself was captured. Harpagus visited the Median king in his captivity and taunted him, claiming responsibility for having brought about his defeat.

Astyages insulted Harpagus in turn, saying he was stupid because he'd missed the chance to become king himself, and that he was wrong to surrender the kingdom to the Persians. But Harpagus doesn't seem to have been unhappy with his new Persian master. It was he, as we've seen, who helped win Lydia for Cyrus by suggesting he send camels against Croesus' cavalry. And as we'll see, he served as general in Cyrus' campaigns against the Ionians. As for Astyages, he suffered no further harm and lived at his grandson's court until his death. Herodotus makes no further mention of him in his *History*.

Vomit and Pederasty (1.131–140)

As soon as they hear of any luxury, they instantly make it their own: and hence, among other novelties, they have learnt unnatural lust from the Greeks.

(1.135)

As he did at the conclusion of his Lydian story, Herodotus closes his account of Cyrus' early career with a summary of Persian customs. He tells us, for example, that among the Persians it is not permissible to vomit or urinate in front of anyone.[3] He claims too that the Persians—who were in the habit of adopting pleasant pursuits from other peoples—began engaging in pederasty after learning about it from the Greeks. Plutarch, writing a screed against Herodotus some four hundred years later, objected that Herodotus got this wrong: the Persians can't have learned pederasty from the Greeks, he says, because they were practicing castration long before they ever laid eyes on the Aegean (*On the Malice of Herodotus* 13 = *Moralia* 857B–C.) Why castration should imply the practice of pederasty in Plutarch's view, however, is unclear.

The Persian Conquest of the Asiatic Greeks and the Revolt of Lydia (1.141–177)

"If I live, the Spartans shall have troubles enough of their own to talk of, without concerning themselves about the Ionians."   (CYRUS, at 1.153.1)

Having filled us in on the Persian king's backstory—Cyrus' childhood and the conquest of Media—Herodotus picks up his narrative where he left it at 1.91: Cyrus had conquered Lydia and taken Croesus prisoner, and he'd learned from his captive the wisdom of Solon. At this point the Greeks who lived along the coast of Asia Minor, just west of Lydia, and who had been paying tribute to Croesus, became nervous. Understandably so: they needed to know what Cyrus had in mind for them.

The Greek cities in Asia that were now threatened by Persia's expansion had been colonized by the Greeks in the preceding centuries, various city-states on the mainland founding and serving as the sponsors of self-governing *poleis* across the Aegean. The cultural differences among the founding cities were thus transplanted to Asia Minor. There were three different linguistic/cultural groups within ancient Greece, the Aeolians, the Ionians, and the Dorians. The three groups spoke different dialects of Greek and differed in their religious practices, for example, but they could understand one another perfectly and had more in common than not. The Athenians spoke Ionic Greek, the Spartans Doric. The poems of Sappho, whose erotic writing prompted the association between female homosexuality and Sappho's home island of Lesbos, are written in Aeolic. On the coast of Asia Minor, the Aeolian Greek cities were in the north (Herodotus lists eleven of them), the Dorian cities (five) were in the south, and the Ionian cities (twelve, nine in Asia Minor) were between the two. Herodotus' hometown of Halicarnassus was a Dorian colony, but the city's population was a mix of Dorians and native Carians who had inhabited Asia Minor prior to the Greeks' colonization. In the fifth century the dominant dialect spoken in Halicarnassus was Ionic, however, rather than Doric. Herodotus, surely the most famous product of this multicultural stew, wrote his *History* in Ionic.

After Persia's conquest of Media, the Aeolians and Ionians in Asia Minor sent messengers to Cyrus asking if they might become subject to Persia under the same terms that had been granted by Croesus. The embassy is noteworthy because it is the first recorded encounter between the Persians and the Greeks. And it is memorable because of the response Cyrus allegedly gave: he told the Greeks a story—one that would later be included in a collection of fables attributed to the sixth-century Greek slave Aesop.[4]

A flute player saw fish in the water and started to play, thinking they would come out onto the land. But when he was disappointed in this, he took a fishing net and threw it around a great many of the fish and he dragged them out. Seeing them flapping about on the land he said to the fish, "Stop dancing, since you didn't want to come out and dance when I played my flute."

Prior to his conquest of Lydia, Cyrus had sent messengers to the Ionians asking that they desert Croesus (1.76.3). The Greeks hadn't listened to him then (with one exception), so now he was in no mood to offer lenient terms.

Cyrus' image of fish flapping on dry land, writhing in their death throes, can't have been a comforting one to the Greeks. They took the hint and began fortifying their cities, and the Aeolians and Ionians—most of them—decided to send messengers to Sparta to ask for help. The citizens of Miletus, however, the southern-most Ionian city, did not take part in the embassy. They alone had come to an agreement with Cyrus earlier and thus enjoyed the same relationship with the Persian king that they'd had with Croesus.

The Spartans listened to what the Ionians and Aeolians had to say when they arrived, but they decided against sending help. They did, however, send an embassy to Sardis to issue a warning: "Do not harm a Greek city," they told the Persian king. "The Spartans will not allow it." Cyrus wasn't very concerned about the Spartans' threat. He told the messengers that if his health held up they'd have more to worry about than the Ionians' troubles, things a lot closer to home. Then Cyrus marched off to Ecbatana, the Persian capital in Media, taking Croesus with him. He had more important things to worry about himself than the Ionians. He would delegate the conquest of the Asiatic Greeks to an underling.

Cyrus left Sardis in the hands of a Persian named Tabalus, but he put a Lydian, Pactyes, in charge of the Lydian treasury. This turned out rather badly. Pactyes immediately revolted from Persia, hired mercenaries, and laid siege to the Sardian acropolis, where Tabalus had holed up. The episode gives Herodotus the opportunity to tell a story about the origin of Lydian effeminacy: the Lydians had a reputation for being soft. (You may remember that in its response to Croesus warning about a mule becoming king of the Medes, the Delphic oracle addressed the king as "tender-footed Lydian." It's not the sort of epithet one applies to a Charles Bronson type.)[5] When he heard about the revolt, Cyrus asked Croesus for advice, saying that perhaps he should just enslave the Lydians and be done with it since they were causing such problems. But Croesus managed to talk him out of it. He argued that the whole thing was Pactyes' fault and not the Lydians' per se. He advised Cyrus to punish the ringleader of the revolt and at the same time to impose certain behaviors on the Lydians:

> Pardon the Lydians and issue these orders, so that they neither revolt nor remain a threat to you. Forbid them from possessing weapons and bid them wear

tunics under their cloaks and soft boots. Tell them to play the lyre and the harp and to raise their children as shopkeepers. Soon, my Lord, you'll see they've become women rather than men, so that they will neither be a threat to you nor revolt.

Croesus' idea was to effeminize the Lydians—to turn them into a "nation of shopkeepers," as Napoleon famously said of England—so that they would no longer be capable of rebellion: Cyrus would surely destroy the Lydians if they revolted again. Croesus, that is, was attempting to save his former subjects—or so the story goes, at least. It was interesting advice coming from Croesus, because it's reminiscent of the strategy he'd adopted when trying to save the life of his son: emasculating Atys hadn't saved him from Adrastus' spear point, but it seems to have done the trick with the Lydians, who did not rebel again.

Cyrus approved of Croesus' advice and sent a general, Mazares, to disarm the Lydians and instruct them in their new lifestyle. Mazares was also tasked with capturing Pactyes and enslaving his followers. Pactyes fled before Mazares got there, and the Persians had some trouble getting their hands on him. But in the end he was captured, and Mazares and his army did some damage in the area by way of penalizing Pactyes' supporters. Shortly afterwards, Mazares took sick and died.

Mazares' replacement was none other than Harpagus, who had taken his revenge against Astyages by helping Cyrus revolt against the Medes. Unfortunately, there are no good stories attached to this part of Harpagus' career. He attacked the Ionian cities in Asia Minor, with the exception of Miletus, and subdued them, and the Aeolians also either surrendered or were subdued. Then Harpagus marched south and reduced the populations there, both the Doric Greek cities and the native populations who had inhabited the area before the Greeks colonized the coast.

While Harpagus was still busy in Ionia, the people of the Dorian city-state of Cnidus attempted to make their city safe from attack. Cnidus was on a peninsula, and the Cnidians wanted to turn it into an island by digging through the peninsula's neck, which was a little more than a half mile wide. The problem was that the people working on the project were sustaining a surprising number of injuries from the splintering of the stone, principally to their eyes—so many injuries that it seemed a god might be behind the trouble. The Cnidians sent an embassy to Delphi to ask what the problem was. For once the priestess's reply was unambiguous:

Neither wall off nor dig through the isthmus.
Zeus would have made it an island if he'd wished.

The Cnidians knew when they were beat. They gave up the project at once and surrendered to Harpagus when he advanced against them.

In discussing the Cnidians and their abandoned canal, Herodotus introduces a theme to which he will return repeatedly in his *History*: attempting to alter the physical landscape is a transgression of the natural order of things and can only bring trouble. Even attempting to extend one's power beyond certain natural boundaries—rivers, for example—can be problematic: the boundaries are not merely geographic but somehow morally significant and divinely ordained. Disregarding these natural limitations on one's authority is a sign of arrogance. Croesus was able to extend his kingdom to the west coast of Asia Minor, remember. But once he crossed the Halys River, which separated Lydia from Media, his days were numbered.

With Harpagus' victories over the coastal populations of western Asia Minor complete, Cyrus now controlled most of the peninsula. He turned his attention to Assyria, in the northern half of Mesopotamia, a region that straddles modern Iraq, Syria, and Turkey. As for Harpagus, who played such an important role in Cyrus' early life, his successful campaigns against the Asiatic Greeks are the last we hear of him in Herodotus' *History*.

Crossing the Gyndes River (1.189)

Cyrus, enraged at the insolence of the river, threatened so to break its strength that in future even women should cross it easily without wetting their knees.

(1.189.2)

Herodotus' account of Cyrus' conquest of Babylon (1.191–192), the most important city in Assyria and the site of the royal palace, is not particularly interesting. Suffice it to say that Cyrus took the city by a clever stratagem, lowering the height of the Euphrates, which flowed into it, by diverting some of its water, thus allowing his troops to enter along its path. The men who did the grunt work of digging were, Herodotus tells us, the "useless" part of Cyrus' army: we'll see what happens to them a bit later in Herodotus' narrative. (Herodotus, by the way, does not mention that after his conquest of Babylon Cyrus allowed the Israelites who had been in exile there to return to their homeland, thus effectively ending the fifty-odd-year period of the Babylonian Captivity. Cyrus' stratagem of lowering the height of the Euphrates, meanwhile, was allegedly prophesied in the Bible, at Isaiah 44:28.)

More interesting than Herodotus' account of the capture of Babylon is an incident that occurred prior to Cyrus' arrival at the city. When Cyrus was some fifty miles north of Babylon he came upon the Gyndes River, which empties into the Tigris from the northeast. The river wasn't fordable and had to be crossed by boat. While Cyrus was working on getting his army across, one of his horses plunged into the river and was carried off by it. Now, admittedly the animal was special, a white horse that was sacred to the Persian sun god. Still, Cyrus' reaction to the loss, as Herodotus tells the story, seems over the top: in his fury at the river's insolence Cyrus threatened to make the water so weak that even women would be able to cross it without getting their knees wet. Then, rather than marching on Babylon immediately, he set his army to digging 360 canals alongside the river—one for each day of the Egyptian solar year (a symbolic number, used because of the sun god connection)—thereby lowering the water's height significantly and making good on his threat.

It seems unlikely that Cyrus really wasted the better part of a year having his men dig canals just to punish the river for killing his horse. The Persians' work did make the Gyndes fordable, but surely diverting the water for that purpose could have been done more quickly and with less drama. One scholar has suggested that the diversion of the water was part of a substantial irrigation project undertaken by Cyrus in advance of his capture of Babylon.[6] On the face of it, this seems a likely explanation for the digging. But taken as a literary device alone, the story suggests that Cyrus was flirting with insolence himself, transgressing boundaries both geographic and moral. There is no immediate punishment for the canal digging: Cyrus succeeded in taking Babylon—and he in fact did so by lowering the water level of a river. But Herodotus' account of Cyrus' final campaign, against the Massagetae, suggests that Cyrus' behavior toward the Gyndes was an early sign of his descent into ruinous arrogance.

There are more such incidents of monarchic excess to come in Herodotus' *History*: indeed, Cyrus wouldn't be the last Persian monarch to punish a body of water.

Sex and the City of Babylon (1.196–199)

For the custom was that when the herald had gone through the whole number
of the beautiful damsels, he should then call up the ugliest—a cripple, if there
chanced to be one—and offer her to the men, asking who would agree to take
her with the smallest marriage-portion.   (1.196.3)

Having described Cyrus' capture of Babylon, Herodotus goes on to discuss Assyria in some detail—remarking on its geography and weather, its boats and
crops and clothing and customs. In this context he mentions a number of interesting Babylonian practices.

First is a custom that Herodotus says is in his opinion "the wisest." Each
village in Assyria used to hold an annual auction of marriageable girls. The
auction would start with the best-looking girls, who would go for the highest
prices. Once the pretty girls were disposed of, however, the rules of the auction
changed. Now the Assyrians would auction off the ugly and crippled, starting
with the least objectionable, who would go to whomever would *take* the least
money to have her. And it went on from there, the girls getting uglier and
uglier, so that the worst of the lot brought the highest dowry. The money fund-
ing these "ugly auctions" came from the earlier auctions of pretty girls, so that
these events also served as a means of redistributing wealth in the village. After
the conquest of Babylon, however, the annual auctions were discontinued. In
his day, Herodotus says, if any of the common people wanted for money, they
simply prostituted their daughters.

Herodotus wasn't fond of all the Babylonians' customs. The worst of them,
he says, was that every woman in Assyria was obliged to go once in her lifetime
to the Temple of Aphrodite and stay there until she'd had sex with a stranger.
The women who showed up for duty at the temple would sit in the sacred
precincts waiting to be picked while men walked around checking out the mer-
chandise. When a man had made his selection he'd throw a coin in the woman's
lap and the two would go off and have sex somewhere outside the temple precincts. (The woman had no choice in the business. She was not allowed to reject
anyone who tossed a coin to her.) Once this was done, the woman's obligation
was fulfilled and she could go home. For some women, this was easily done.
The pretty ones were in and out of the temple in no time. But the uglier ones
had a much harder time of it. According to Herodotus, some of them would
have to remain at the temple for as long as three or four years.

Cyrus' Campaign against the Massagetae (1.204–214)

"Refuse, and I swear by the sun, the sovereign lord of the Massagetae, blood-thirsty as thou art, I will give thee thy fill of blood." (Tomyris, at 1.212.3)

The first book of Herodotus' *History* ends with the story of Cyrus' campaign against the Massagetae, who lived to the east of the Caspian Sea. Herodotus introduces his account of the campaign by explaining the Great King's motivation in undertaking it: "Many great reasons were inducing him, first his birth—that he seemed to be more than a man—and second the good fortune he had had in war." By contrast, Herodotus introduces his account of Cyrus' campaign against the Assyrians with a simple statement of fact, devoid of editorializing: "When Cyrus had subdued all the people of the mainland, he attacked the Assyrians" (1.178.1). That Cyrus was thinking of himself, according to Herodotus, as being "more than a man" is a sign of trouble to come. Back in the day, Croesus had been blinded by his good fortune to the fact that he was at base human and thus subject to reversals of fortune, as all humans are. He learned his lesson the hard way, and Cyrus seemed to have learned from Croesus' mistakes. At least, he appeared to understand Solon's wisdom and its applicability to his own life back when he had Croesus on the pyre. But Cyrus' military successes and his own propaganda machine—the stories circulating about the extraordinary circumstances of his birth and survival—had apparently clouded his vision. Cyrus, that is, was poised at the brink of a reversal of fortune when he undertook his campaign against the Massagetae.

Cyrus' first step in his attempt to attach the Massagetae to his growing empire was not a military one. He sent a message to their widowed queen, Tomyris, with a view to getting her to marry him. But Tomyris wasn't interested in Cyrus' courtship: she knew he wasn't wooing her so much as her kingdom. So Cyrus moved to Plan B, gaining the kingdom of the Massagetae through naked aggression. He advanced as far as the Araxes River, which separated the two kingdoms, and started building bridges to get his army across. (The Araxes empties into the Caspian Sea from the west. But Herodotus seems to have confused his rivers: he may be referring to the Oxus River, for example, which is to the east of the Caspian and empties into the Aral Sea.) The Araxes River, as it turned out, defined the natural border of Cyrus' kingdom in the same way that the Halys had defined Croesus' kingdom—not that this would have been obvious to the players except in retrospect. Cyrus had gotten away with his treatment of the Gyndes prior to conquering Babylon, distorting its natural path by digging channels alongside it. He would not be allowed to bridge the Araxes with impunity.

While Cyrus was working on his bridges, Tomyris sent a herald with a proposition for him. She first suggested that Cyrus simply not attack her country, that he remain content with the status quo, ruling over his people as she ruled hers—like that was going to happen. She knew he wouldn't back down, however, so she also suggested, more practically, that they agree to one of two possibilities: either she would withdraw a three days' journey from the river and allow the Persians to cross unharassed, at which point they would fight in her territory; or Cyrus could withdraw, and the Massagetae would cross the Araxes and fight on Persian turf. Cyrus put the question to his advisors—calling a council for the first time in his career that we hear of in *The History*—and all but one of them agreed that the Persians should choose the latter option: they wanted the Massagetae to come to them.

Croesus was the exception. In a lengthy speech he explained to Cyrus why he should instead take the fight to the enemy. Croesus began by reiterating what he'd told Cyrus in their first conversation, when they had hammered out the terms of their wise advisor/advisee relationship, that he would do what he could to keep Cyrus from making a mistake that would be injurious to his kingdom. And then he gave Cyrus a refresher course in Solonic wisdom—apparently recognizing, as we have, that the Great King was no longer acting appropriately. If you're immortal, Croesus said, you don't need my advice. But if you know that you and your subjects are human, understand this: human affairs are cyclical, and the same men are not always fortunate. And then Croesus gave his advice about the matter at hand. He made two arguments in favor of crossing the Araxes. The first and more substantial is summed up in the diagram below. In short, Croesus argues, there is more to be gained and less lost by crossing into the territory of the Massagetae. The alternative leads to negative results whether the Persians win or lose.

Croesus' argument is good as far as it goes, but as the diagram makes clear, he fails to mention a fourth possible outcome, the one that actually came to pass, that Cyrus would cross the Araxes and lose. In that case, Croesus might have said, the Persians' withdrawal would be complicated by the fact that they were in enemy territory and had to cross a river to get back home. Croesus probably didn't want to weaken his argument for crossing the Araxes by pointing out potential negatives, but even so they were not lost on Cyrus, as we'll

Massagetae cross ➡ Persians win: Persians still have to cross river to get additional

the Araxes   territory (BAD)

                   ➡ Persians lose: Massagetae will press on and Cyrus will lose his

                      empire (BAD)

Persians cross   ➡ Persians win: Cyrus gets additional territory (GOOD)

the Araxes   ➡ Persians lose: ???

Crossing the Araxes

see. Croesus' second argument, meanwhile, was that it would be disgraceful for Cyrus to yield to a woman.

Croesus further suggested a specific stratagem Cyrus could use to win the battle. He advised Cyrus to have a great banquet prepared, with plenty of strong wine set out, and to leave the dregs of his army behind with the food while the rest of his men retreated to the river. The Massagetae, Croesus said, because they were relatively impoverished and unused to luxuries, would be attracted to the spread. And when they'd eaten and drunk to excess, the bulk of the Persian army could return and rip them to shreds.

Cyrus took Croesus' advice and gave Tomyris his answer. Then he put his affairs in order. He entrusted his kingdom to his son Cambyses. He also put Croesus in Cambyses' hands, ordering him to treat the Lydian well in the event that things went badly in the coming battle. In other words, Cyrus prepared for the eventuality that Croesus had neglected to mention, that having crossed the Araxes the Persians might be defeated or, at least, that they might lose their king. That done, Cyrus sent Cambyses and Croesus back to Persia, and he and his army crossed the river.

During the Persians' first night in enemy territory, before they had engaged the Massagetae, Cyrus had a disturbing dream about a man named Darius, who was the eldest son of Hystaspes. This Hystaspes was in the Persian army—and he would later serve as a governor under Cambyses—but Darius, who was only about twenty years old, was back in Persia. Cyrus dreamt that Darius had wings, one of which overshadowed Asia, and the other Europe. Clearly, this wasn't a good omen. Cyrus' dream is reminiscent of the disturbing visions his grandfather had seen years before—his daughter Mandane's urine flooding Asia, and then a vine growing out of her vagina to overshadow the continent. Those dreams had signified that Astyages' grandson—the issue of the womb he was dreaming about—would come to power in his grandfather's stead. And Astyages had nearly killed Cyrus in an effort to prevent his dream from being realized. Now Cyrus was in a similar position.

Cyrus reacted to the dream by summoning Hystaspes and telling him his son Darius was plotting against the crown. He told Hystaspes how he knew this: "The gods," he said, "take care of me and show me in advance everything that will happen." As far as Cyrus was concerned, his dream was certain evidence of Darius' guilt. He ordered Hystaspes to go back to Persia as quickly as possible and prepare things so that Cyrus could interrogate Darius as soon as he had defeated the Massagetae and returned home.

This wasn't a smart move. Having supposedly uncovered a plot against his regime, the last thing Cyrus should want to do is take the plotter's father into his confidence. He should have anticipated that Hystaspes would either protect his son or perhaps even assist Darius in his designs on the throne—assuming he had any. But Cyrus, blinded by overconfidence, took the dream as evidence of the gods' especial concern for him—despite what the dream appeared to signify—and he was insufficiently worried about the alleged plot itself. Cyrus, moreover, was too quick to assume that he understood the dream's meaning. Herodotus himself thinks Cyrus got it wrong. "The god," he writes, "was showing Cyrus that he was going to die there, and that his kingdom would pass [eventually] to Darius."

Cyrus' reaction to the dream could have been disastrous, but in the event it didn't matter much. Hystaspes responded as one facing those circumstances would have to, saying that anyone who plotted against the king should be killed. And he promised that he would surrender his son to Cyrus "to do to him whatever you wish." Hystaspes then returned to Persia. We can't know whether he would in fact have handed Darius over to Cyrus, because he was never called upon to do so. Cyrus never made it back home.

After his talk with Hystaspes, Cyrus turned to the second part of Croesus' advice. He advanced a day's march into Queen Tomyris' territory, and he left the "useless" part of his army at this forward position with food and wine. (These useless fellows were presumably the same bunch, more or less, whose digging had lowered the water level of the Euphrates before Cyrus' conquest of Babylon.) Then Cyrus and the rest of his army withdrew to the Araxes to await events. It wasn't pretty. The Massagetae, with only a third of their army, attacked and butchered the men Cyrus had abandoned to an almost certain death. Then, just as Croesus had predicted, they ate and drank what Cyrus had left behind and, glutted, fell asleep. The Persians came back and butchered the Massagetae in turn, though they also took a great many of them prisoner. Among those they captured was Spargapises, who was the general of the Massagetae and also Tomyris' son.

A lesser warrior queen might have pleaded for her son's release, but Tomyris was a fearsome woman. She sent a herald to the Persian camp to rebuke Cyrus for having gotten the better of her army through deception rather than force of arms—military victory gained through trickery had been frowned upon in the Greek world since at least Homer's day. And she issued an ultimatum: "Return my son and leave this country unharmed—even though you have outraged a third of the army of the Massagetae. But if you do not, I swear by the sun, master of the Massagetae, I will give you who are insatiate of blood your surfeit." Cyrus, however, was not intimidated by the queen's threats. There would be no turning back.

Note that Herodotus has told us more than once now that the Persians had defeated one third of the army of the Massagetae. Two thirds of the army, in other words, had yet to take the field against the Persians, and they were surely itching to do so after what had happened to their comrades.

Before the two armies could meet in their final battle, something else happened to make Tomyris that much more formidable an enemy. Spargapises, when he'd sobered up, realized how bad his situation was. He asked to be unchained, which his Persian captors allowed, and once he had use of his hands he killed himself. From our comfortable position on the other side of Herodotus' pages this seems premature: he might at least have waited to see if the Massagetae would ultimately prevail and gain the release of the captives. But perhaps Spargapises thought it was better to kill himself than to face his scary mother again after his shameful defeat. At any rate, Spargapises' death made Tomyris even more furious with the Persian king.

The battle that followed was, in Herodotus' view, the fiercest ever fought among barbarians. And when it was done, the better part of the Persian army lay dead, including Cyrus himself. Tomyris was true to her word. She sought out Cyrus' corpse, had his head cut off, and stuck it in a wine sack filled with human blood. "I am alive," she said, "and I defeated you in battle, but you have destroyed me, having taken my son by deceit. But as I threatened, I will give you your fill of blood!"

This, Herodotus tells us, was the most credible story about Cyrus' death that he came across, but there were others. He doesn't tell us what they were, but we know of a few alternative endings from other sources: Cyrus died after being wounded in battle by an Indian, for example (Ctesias, *FGH* 688 F 9); or he was crucified by the queen of the Scythians (Diodorus 2.44.2); or he died in his own bed when he was a very old man (Xenophon, *Cyropaedia* 8.7). But for sheer drama and visual appeal, I think Herodotus selected wisely: you can't beat a crazed queen carrying a bloody head around in a bag.

Granted, things ended poorly for Cyrus, but was Croesus' advice about crossing the Araxes for that reason bad? Scholarly opinion on the question is divided. Arguments can be made for fighting in Persian territory, but Croesus' reasons for bringing the fight to the Massagetae were certainly valid. And as Christopher Pelling points out, Croesus' own experience informed his opinion: he had crossed the Halys River to fight the Persians, it's true, but the crucial battle occurred after he had withdrawn into his own territory, the Persians following on his heels.[7] Croesus was attempting to prevent Cyrus from suffering the same fate. Some have argued that if Croesus were in fact still wise, he would have recommended—as Tomyris in fact did—that Cyrus forego the battle and go back home, that he not expand his empire beyond its divinely sanctioned boundaries. Cyrus, however, had his heart set on conquering the Massagetae (1.201). There may have been nothing Croesus or anyone else could have done to dissuade him from the course he'd decided on. Still, Croesus was blamed in some quarters: as we'll see, he would one day catch hell from Cambyses for causing Cyrus' death (3.36).

Is He Soup Yet? (1.216)

Milk is what they chiefly drink.   (1.216)

Herodotus ends his discussion of the Massagetae with a brief ethnographic section. Most interestingly, he tells us about the tribe's funeral practices:

There is no limit to their lifespan but this: when someone is very old, all his relatives get together and sacrifice him along with some sheep, and they stew the meat and feast. This is considered the most blessed means of death for them. But they do not eat anyone who has died from disease. They bury him in the ground and lament that he did not get to be eaten.

Presumably, the Massagetae washed down their old people with refreshing glasses of milk, because Herodotus sees fit to tell us also, in one of the briefest sentences of *The History*, that the Massagetae were milk drinkers (*galaktopotai de eisi*).

Cyrus was dead. In his thirty-odd years as king, he had raised Persia from a backwater into an expanding world power, subjecting first the Medes and then Lydia and Assyria to Persian sway. With Cyrus' death the kingdom passed to his son Cambyses, whose reign would be briefer and less successful than his father's. But Cambyses did succeed in expanding his father's empire yet further through his conquest of Egypt.

CHAPTER THREE

Horny Goats and Medicinal Urine

The Egyptian *Logos*

664–610	Reign of Psammetichus
589–570	Reign of Apries
570–526	Reign of Amasis
530–522	Reign of Cambyses

T HE FIRST BOOK OF HERODOTUS' *History* is divided into two distinct stories, or *logoi*: the Croesus *logos* and an account of Cyrus' life and reign. As we've seen, these stories are punctuated by brief ethnographic sections. Herodotus concludes his accounts of any particular people—in his first book, the Lydians, Persians, Assyrians, and Massagetae—with a discussion of their noteworthy customs and the geography or natural wonders or the great buildings of their respective countries. This is in keeping with Herodotus' stated purpose for writing his *History*. In his first sentence, Herodotus tells us that he is publishing his research so the "great and wondrous things done—some by Greeks, some by barbarians—not be forgotten, both other things and in particular why they fought one another." Herodotus' account of Persia's expansion and inevitable clash with Greece—the "why they fought one another"—provides the skeleton onto which he packs his ethnographic material—the "great and wondrous things done."

Herodotus' second book is very different from the first in that it is virtually all ethnographic digression. It is a lengthy account of Egypt's geography, history, marvels, and customs. The unusual length of the section is warranted, Herodotus tells us, because Egypt has more wonders in it and more works that defy description than any other country (2.35). The *logos* is shoehorned into his narrative, attached only tenuously to his larger story of Persia's expansion. That is, Herodotus' Egyptian account reads like it was written independently of *The*

History—and it may well have been—and then wedged into the narrative at the point where the Persians first encounter the Egyptians. The subject of Egypt's relationship to Persia is introduced briefly in the book's first section: after his father's death, we are told, Cambyses came to the throne and made war against Egypt. Cambyses then goes unmentioned for the rest of Book 2. His story is picked up again at the beginning of Herodotus' third book.

As with the ethnographic discussions in book one, Herodotus' Egyptian account does contain some juicy nuggets of information, and there are some lengthier *logoi* in the book that will merit our attention. But much of the book would likely be of interest only to specialists. While nearly all of Herodotus' first book made its way into our "good parts" version of *The History*, I'm afraid much of book two will be left on the cutting room floor.

Herodotus' Methodology

Thus far I have spoken of Egypt from my own observation, relating what I myself saw, the ideas that I formed, and the results of my own researches.

(1.99.1)

Much more so than in his first book, Herodotus gives readers a sense of his methods in the Egyptian *logos*, hinting at how he conducted his research and referring to his sources. He repeatedly mentions talking to people to obtain information: priests, priestesses, scribes, interpreters, miscellaneous Egyptians or Libyans or Greeks (for example, sections 2, 10, 13, 28, 53, 123, 125, 147); he weighs and dismisses evidence (20); he distinguishes his opinion from those of his sources (18, 53, 99, 131); he mentions traveling to various places and seeing things for himself (29, 44, 49, 148); he tells us when his descriptions are based on hearsay rather than his own observations (148). He also explains that his general rule is to write down what he hears from his sources, whether or not he believes the information himself: a story's inclusion in his *History*, in other words, does not imply its credibility (2.123; cf. 4.195.2, 7.152.3). For scholars interested in Herodotus' methodology, Book 2 is a rich source of information. His references to his informants are interesting to the casual reader as well, however, because they somehow breathe life into the historian and his *History*:

Regarding the sources of the Nile, no one of the Egyptians or Libyans or Greeks I spoke with professed to know except for the scribe of the holy things of Athena in

the Egyptian city of Saïs. And he seemed to me, at least, to be pulling my leg when
he said he knew for sure. But he said this: there are two mountains with sharp peaks
lying between the city of Syene, in the Thebaid, and Elephantine. . . . (2.28.1–2)

It's hard to know for sure what sort of interaction Herodotus is describing here.
Was the scribe making a friendly joke that Herodotus was in on? Was his asser-
tion that his knowledge was accurate delivered with a wink? Or was Herodotus
unsure—given that his interlocutor probably spoke Greek poorly or not at all—
whether his source was being serious? It's lost to us. But still, one has the sense
reading this of a real moment captured, that if you set your time machine to
just the right moment and made your way to the office of the scribe of the holy
things of Athena in the Egyptian city of Saïs, you'd interrupt a conversation between a dusty Greek and an Egyptian scribe about the Nile's sources. And then
you could judge the nature of their interaction for yourself.

Egyptians Do It Backward (2.35–36)

Not only is the climate different from that of the rest of the world, and the
rivers unlike any other rivers, but the people also, in most of their manners and
customs, exactly reverse the common practice of mankind.   (2.35.2)

After a lengthy discussion of Egypt's geography, much of it having to do with
the Nile (its sources, the reasons for its inundation, and so on), Herodotus
discusses the customs of the Egyptians in sections 35 through 98 of his second book. They were, he tells us, given to doing things backwards from the
norm—the norm, that is, as exemplified by the Greeks. For example, in Egypt
the women ran the markets while the men stayed home weaving, and while
weaving they pushed the woof down rather than up. They kneaded dough with
their feet but mixed mud with their hands, and they wrote from right to left
rather than left to right. And Egyptian women urinated standing up while men
did so sitting down.[1]

Herodotus also mentions in this context that the Egyptians "eased themselves" in the house—because one should take care of things that are necessary
but shameful in private—but ate outdoors. We are not to imagine, however,
that the Greeks, by contrast, were defecating willy-nilly in the streets of Athens: the Greeks used chamber pots in Herodotus' day, and they presumably
didn't drag them out in the street for the purpose.

Pigs, Goats, and Satanism (2.38–47)

The Mendesians hold all goats in veneration, but the male more than the female, giving the goatherds of the males especial honour.   (2.46.3)

The Egyptians sacrificed bulls if they were worthy of the honor. They revered cows and would not eat beef. Greeks, in fact, were considered tainted because they were cow eaters: no Egyptian would kiss a Greek on the mouth, Herodotus says, or use a Greek's knife or spit or cauldron. Pigs were considered unclean. If an Egyptian happened to touch a pig he would immerse himself in the Nile to wash off the contamination. As for swineherds, who would have been touching pigs all the time, they were a sort of outcast group, prohibited from entering shrines and, because of their stigma, unable to contract marriages outside of their swineherd circle.

The Egyptians' religious practices were not standardized. Herodotus tells us that only the gods Isis and Osiris were worshipped by all the Egyptians in the same way. Some Egyptians, for example, refused to sacrifice sheep, while another group, those who worshipped Mendes (identified by Herodotus with the Greek god Pan) or who lived in the province of Mendes (the eastern Nile delta), were fine with sacrificing sheep but refused to sacrifice goats. This Mendes was represented with the head and legs of a male goat, though why he was thus depicted Herodotus refuses to say. Herodotus very often shows his religious scruples by refusing to mention things it would be unholy to mention (for instance, 2.61, 2.86.2), but whether his silence here is an example of scrupulousness or disgust is not clear. Certainly there were aspects of the Mendesians' goat worship that may have troubled him.

Indeed, Herodotus tells us that in his day something strange occurred in the province of Mendes. A goat had sex with a woman out in the open, in front of an audience. Substantiating evidence suggests that Herodotus wasn't making this up or falling for some tour guide's tall story: the fifth-century lyric poet Pindar (fragment 201) wrote about he-goats mounting women in Mendes, for example, and there is a plaster cast from the province that depicts a goat mounting a human female *a tergo*. (Apparently, Egyptian women also sometimes exposed themselves to goats because goats were thought to bestow fertility.) Regarding this interspecies goat coupling, one appalled nineteenth-century commentator, Pierre-Henri Larcher, writes: "Nothing is more certain than the infamous custom of enclosing women with the goat of Mendes. The same thing was done at Thmuis. A thousand authors speak of it; but we will draw a veil over these horrors."[2]

By a strange twist, the sacred goats of Mendes have come to be associated with the occult and Satanism. In 1854 the occultist Eliphas Lévi published *Dogme et Rituel de la Haute Magie*, in which he included his own drawing of a goat-headed human figure, with cloven feet and wings, that represented Baphomet, an idol allegedly worshipped by the Knights Templar. Lévi called the figure the "Baphomet of Mendes"—an apparent reference to Herodotus' discussion of goat worship in Mendes. Satanists adopted Lévi's image in turn:

> The goat-headed Baphomet drawing of Eliphas Levi has now morphed into our stereotypical depiction of Satan, and modern Satanists have adopted him as one of their symbols. The icon they use for him is an inverted pentagram with the details of a goat's face drawn into it—an image which is also based on a drawing by Eliphas Levi. They call this symbol the "Goat of Mendes," linking Baphomet to the goats that were used for fertility rites at the temple of Ammon, in the ancient Egyptian city of Mendes. In these rites, the goat copulated with the temple priestesses, an appropriately sinister heritage for a Satanic symbol.[3]

Lévi's image of Baphomet may be familiar to readers because it is also the source of the devil card in one of the most popular tarot decks (the Rider-Waite deck).

And now, having made our way from goat-on-human sex to Satanism, let us take our cue from Mr. Larcher and indeed draw a veil over these horrors. . . .

Bring in Your Dead (2.86–90)

> It is not till they have been dead three or four days that they are carried to the embalmers.   (2.89.1)

The Egyptians were renowned for embalming their dead, so it's no surprise that the practice attracted Herodotus' attention. Happily, Herodotus gives us a rundown of the various options that faced the newly dead. There were, he says, three different price plans available for embalmment—the deluxe, regular, and economy versions. When a body was brought in to the embalmer's shop, the embalmer would show the dead man's relatives samples of his handiwork, wooden models of embalmed corpses. (Anyone who's been led on a tour of caskets in a funeral parlor will find this process familiar.) The grieving party would agree on a price and leave the embalmer to it.

Eliphas Lévi's drawing of the Baphomet of Mendes (*Dogme et Rituel de la Haute Magie,* 1854)

The Deluxe Package

Customers who purchased the deluxe package got the full treatment. First the embalmer pulled the dead man's brain out through his nostril using an iron hook. In his commentary on the passage, Alan Lloyd adds that the body's nose would first have been broken and the brain sliced up with one implement and extracted with another. The procedure was, as he describes it, a "violent operation which often resulted in considerable damage to the face." After the brain was removed, the brain cavity was filled in with drugs. (Lloyd provides further gory descriptions of the embalmment procedure that Herodotus does not get into. For example, the Egyptians "took precautions to prevent the nails falling off. The skin was cut around the finger-tips, drawn thimble-wise over the finger-tips and then tied down.")[4]

The embalmer next sliced open the body's abdomen, washed it out, and replaced its contents with crushed spices. That done, he immersed the body in natron (natural soda) and left it to dry—rather like drying a fish in salt—for (Herodotus claims, though he may have exaggerated the time) precisely seventy days. Afterwards, the body was wrapped up mummy-style in linen and handed over to its relatives, who would encase it in a wooden coffin and stand it up against a wall in a burial chamber.

The Regular Package

Customers who couldn't afford the deluxe package could opt for a less expensive, less invasive method of embalmment. In the "regular" version, there were no incisions, the brain was left intact, and there was no nostril penetration. There was, however, penetration via another orifice. The embalmer filled a syringe with oil of cedar and injected it into the corpse's bowels via the anus. Then he stopped up the anus to prevent the liquid from flowing back out and left the body to dry in natron for the requisite period. When the body was ready, the embalmer would remove his stopper and drain the bowels, withdrawing the oil together with dissolved bits of viscera. The body was then returned to its family, presumably after it was bandaged up, though Herodotus doesn't mention this step.

The Economy Package

If you were short of funds you could get your dead bodies embalmed on the cheap. The least expensive method of embalmment involved rinsing the stomach of its contents—presumably this was another turkey-baster-up-the-anus situation—using oil of radish: no dissolved bits of viscera expelled from the anus this time. The body was then dried out in natron, bandaged up (though again Herodotus skips this step), and returned to its relatives.

Having detailed the various methods of embalmment, Herodotus adds this titillating detail:

> They do not bring the wives of prominent men to be embalmed right away when they die, nor those who are very attractive or illustrious. Rather, they bring such women in after three or four days. They do this for this reason: so that the embalmers don't have sex with the women. They say that someone was caught having sex with the fresh corpse of a woman, and that his co-worker told on him.

Alan Lloyd takes some of the fun out of the passage, however, by suggesting that any delay in beginning the embalmment process likely had a more pedestrian explanation:

> The most plausible explanation is that pressure of work often prevented the mummifiers from giving a body their immediate attention. This is not to say that the iniquities described by H. are a complete fabrication but the account smacks not a little of Gk. scandal-mongering and has probably gained much in the telling.[5]

Psammetichus and the Antiquity of Egypt (2.2)

> He took two children of the common sort, and gave them over to a herdsman to bring up at his folds, strictly charging him to let no one utter a word in their presence, but to keep them in a sequestered cottage, and from time to time introduce goats to their apartment, see that they got their fill of milk, and in all other respects look after them.   (2.2.2)

Herodotus follows his discussion of the Egyptians' customs (2.35–98) with a history of Egypt (2.99–182) from its first king, who ruled around 3200 B.C., to Amasis, against whom Cambyses was to lead his troops. But Herodotus does tell a story about one of Egypt's kings, Psammetichus, earlier, at the very beginning of his Egyptian *logos*.

Prior to Psammetichus' reign, Herodotus says, the Egyptians used to think that theirs was the oldest civilization. Psammetichus sought to verify this, first by inquiry and, when that didn't bring him any closer to the truth, by scientific experiment. He took two newborn babies from their parents and gave them to a shepherd to raise with his flocks. They were to be housed by themselves, with as little human company as possible, though they would be fed and cared for to the necessary extent. The important point was that no human who came in contact with the children was to speak in their presence. (Herodotus reports that the Greeks say, "among other foolish things," that they were instead housed with women whose tongues had been cut out.) Psammetichus wanted to find out what language the babies would speak when they stopped babbling and uttered meaningful speech. The idea was that the children, raised in a linguistic vacuum, in a pre-civilized state, would naturally begin speaking a sort of proto-language, the language of the world's oldest civilization.

After two years with the sheep, the toddlers finally said something meaningful: they grabbed the shepherd's knees when he came to take care of them, reached out their hands, and called out, "Bekos!" It turns out that *bekos* was the Phrygian word for "bread." Thus Psammetichus was forced to concede that the Phrygian civilization was the oldest. The Egyptian civilization was assumed to be the second oldest, though this conclusion of course does not follow from the experiment's results.

Interestingly, Psammetichus' peculiar brand of child abuse has been repeated by other rulers over the years. (As Deborah Levine Gera notes in her discussion of these later experiments, "It surely is not a coincidence that autocratic rulers are the ones to execute such heartless trials."[6]) In the thirteenth century, Frederick II of Germany tried it, but in that case all the experimental subjects died before they uttered meaningful speech:

> Like Psammetichus in Herodotus, he made linguistic experiments on the vile bodies of hapless infants, "bidding foster-mothers and nurses to suckle and bathe and wash the children, but in no wise to prattle or speak with them; for he would have learnt whether they would speak the Hebrew language (which had been the first), or Greek, or Latin, or Arabic, or perchance the tongue of their parents of whom they had been born. But he laboured in vain, for the children could not live without clappings of the hands, and gestures, and gladness of countenance, and blandishments."[7]

James IV of Scotland likewise tried the experiment in the fifteenth century. The babies in his case allegedly spoke Hebrew. In the sixteenth century the Mogul emperor Aqbar the Great, having conducted a similar trial, wound up with children who communicated only by sign language.

The Vengeance of Nitocris (2.100)

> The gorgeous trumpery of banquet invaded by howling waters of death! Gayly dressed merrymakers caught suddenly in the grip of terror! Gasps and screams of the dying amid tumult and thickening dark!
>
> (TENNESSEE WILLIAMS, "The Vengeance of Nitocris")

Herodotus tells us that a woman, Nitocris, came to power after the Egyptians killed her brother, the king (who, this being ancient Egypt, may also have been her husband). Once in power, Nitocris devised an elaborate plan for taking vengeance on her brother's murderers. She had a large subterranean chamber built and, to inaugurate its use, she invited the Egyptians she thought most responsible for her brother's death to a feast. During the dinner, Nitocris somehow diverted water from the Nile so that it flooded the chamber. (This sounds like something out of an old Vincent Price film: pulling a lever that would seal his guests' fate, Vincent slips up a staircase, cape billowing behind him, and drowns out their cries for help with a few dirges on the organ.)

Unfortunately, Herodotus doesn't tell us anything about how this was accomplished—clearly the construction of the underground room would have been a complicated affair—nor about how Nitocris managed to be elsewhere when the water came rushing in. But however she did it, Nitocris did survive the flood, if only briefly: she committed suicide, apparently not long afterward, by throwing herself into a room filled with hot ash. (Not the most pleasant means of disposing of oneself, I should think, and complicated by the necessity of finding a room full of hot ash for the purpose.) She did this, Herodotus reports, so that her murders would not be avenged in turn.

In 1928, when he was still in high school, Tennessee Williams earned $35 for his first published piece of fiction, a well-imagined if melodramatic short story entitled "The Vengeance of Nitocris" in which he fleshes out Herodotus' bare-bones account. In his story the king's death is a punishment for sacrilege—an angry mob rends his body, but his death is technically accidental. Nitocris, once in power, has her chamber built in secret by Ethiopian slaves who can't speak the Egyptian language. When it's ready, she hosts a banquet, her guests gorging themselves and drinking and dancing into the night. Hours into the debauch, no one notices as she slinks away up the stairs. No one notices when a great slab of rock is lowered over the chamber's entrance. And Nitocris makes her way to a pier by the river, where she pulls a series of "fantastic, wandlike levers" that control the flow of water into the banquet room. The resulting "howling waters of death" lead to the "gasps and screams of the dying" mentioned in this section's epigraph.

Urinating for the Blind (2.111)

He must find a woman who had been faithful to her husband, and had never preferred to him another man. (2.111.2)

During the reign of a king Herodotus calls Pheros—the name simply means "pharaoh" and possibly does not refer to a historical sovereign—the Nile River flooded higher than it ever had before. The fields were flooded and it was windy and stormy, and the whole thing really got Pheros' goat in the way only a misbehaving river can: he threw a spear into the river's eddies, presumably to punish it, or maybe just because he was so angry. Whatever the case, we've seen before that abusing bodies of water is not the way for a tyrant to get ahead in the world. Pheros' impudence was punished on the spot: he was immediately struck blind.

After ten years of blindness Pheros received an oracle—not from Delphi but from the sanctuary of Leto in Buto, a city in the Nile delta. The oracle informed Pheros that the period of his punishment was over and that he would be able to see again once he'd washed his eyes in the urine of a woman who had had sex only with her own husband and was "without experience of other men." Naturally, the first woman he asked to produce a urine sample was his own wife. She must have gone off with her collection cup with some misgivings, though, because—you guessed it—she was more experienced than her husband had supposed. He washed his eyes in her urine but remained as blind as ever. Still, Pheros wasn't about to let one setback stop him. He tried again with the urine of another woman, then another, and another, and . . . well, it went on for quite a while. As our friend Mr. Larcher wrote more than 150 years ago, "We may thence conclude that the corruption of morals had attained a dreadful pitch in Egypt."[8] Dreadful indeed! But finally Pheros washed his eyes with the urine of a woman whose morals were unsullied—Diodorus adds the detail that she was the wife of a gardener (1.59)—and of a sudden his sight was restored.[9]

And what of Pheros' morally bankrupt wife and her sisters in shame? Pheros herded up all the women whose urine had proved ineffectual, deposited them all in one city, and then burned that city to the ground. Then he married the gardener's wife. No word on what the gardener had to say about it.

An Egyptian version of the Pheros story that dates to about 100 A.D. and is only partially preserved shows some interesting variations from the tale as recorded by Herodotus. In both stories the pharaoh is blinded after throwing a spear, and the restoration of his sight is dependent on his locating a virtuous woman. But in the Egyptian account, the pharaoh throws his spear not into a river but into a man's chest, and he is cured by a virtuous woman's tears, not her urine.

Helen in Egypt (2.112–120)

> After this friendly treatment Menelaus, they said, behaved most unjustly towards
> the Egyptians; for as it happened that at the time when he wanted to take his
> departure, he was detained by the wind being contrary, and as he found this
> obstruction continue, he had recourse to a most wicked expedient. (2.119.3)

In discussing the reign of Pheros' successor, Proteus, Herodotus mentions a
sanctuary in Egypt named after the "foreign Aphrodite." Herodotus believes
this is a reference to Helen of Troy, that most beautiful of mortal women,
whom Paris allegedly stole from Sparta and carted off across the Aegean. It may
seem strange that Helen should be the namesake of an Egyptian sanctuary—assuming that Herodotus' identification is correct. But alongside the standard
Helen myth preserved in Homer—that she lived in Troy with Paris while the
Greeks and Trojans fought over her—there was another, less known story told
about her: Helen, as this story has it, never made it to Troy.

This alternative version of the Helen myth goes back at least as far as the
eighth century B.C. But our first reference to the story that has any meat on
it—that is, one that is more than the briefest of fragmentary references—dates
to the late seventh or early sixth century. In his dialogue *Phaedrus* (243a–b),
Plato mentions that the lyric poet Stesichorus (c. 640–555 B.C.) was struck
blind after writing a poem disparaging Helen. Somehow recognizing the cause
of his blindness, Stesichorus issued a retraction in the form of a poem—the *Pal-
inode*, or ode of reversal—and immediately regained his sight. Plato preserves
the only fragment we have of the poem: "This story is not true | You did not go
in well-rowed ships | Nor reach the citadel of Troy."

Euripides, writing in the late fifth century B.C., took this theme and ran
with it. In his play *Helen*, the gods spirited the real Helen off to Egypt and
replaced her with a phantom before she could meet Paris. Paris ran off to Troy
with the phantom, so the Greeks and Trojans fought their decade-long war
over nothing while the real Helen waited out events, protected by Egypt's King
Proteus. When the war was won, Menelaus happened to come ashore in Egypt
and was finally reconciled with his wife, though not without difficulty. By this
point, he'd been living with the Helen he'd retrieved from Troy for some time.
He was not easily convinced that she wasn't the real deal.

Herodotus' version of the Helen story, which he heard from some Egyptian
priests, differs both from Homer's and from this alternative version involving

a phantom—though in this story too, Helen never made it to Troy. Herodotus was told that Paris and Helen were blown off course by strong winds while en route from Sparta to Troy. They came ashore in Egypt near a sanctuary of Heracles. This sanctuary was by custom a refuge for servants. Any servant who wished could become a suppliant there, and if he did, no one could lay a hand on him. When Paris' servants heard this, they deserted their master, and they told the priests of the place that Paris had stolen Helen from her husband. Word of Paris' impiety was forwarded to the Egyptian king, who had Paris arrested and brought to his court. Proteus was disgusted that Paris had repaid his host's hospitality by stealing his wife, and he gave him a stern talking-to. The king would gladly have killed Paris for the offense, in fact, but he refrained from doing so. Instead, he confiscated the property Paris had stolen from Menelaus. (Paris had apparently pocketed the silverware, so to speak, on his way out the door in Sparta.) And Proteus kept Helen with him as well, safeguarding her for Menelaus in case he ever showed up to claim her. As for Paris, he was given three days to leave the country.

The Greeks, meanwhile, sailed to Troy and demanded the return of Helen. The Trojans told them they didn't have her and that she was in Egypt, but the Greeks didn't believe them. So the war was fought, and when the Greeks won they found out that the Trojans hadn't been lying to them after all: Helen wasn't in Troy and never had been. So Menelaus sailed to Egypt and was finally reunited with his wife. Proteus had done him a great service. It would have been a happy ending—Menelaus and Helen choosing to put that Paris business behind them, sailing off across the Mediterranean against a cerulean sky, maybe doing that "I'm the king of the world!" thing on the prow like Leonardo DiCaprio in *Titanic*.

Except for the damned winds. The winds were against Menelaus, and he couldn't get out of port, and he didn't much fancy hanging around Egypt any longer. This sort of thing had happened before, of course, more than a decade earlier. The Greek fleet had been stuck at Aulis, on the east coast of Greece, unable to set sail for the big campaign against Troy. Menelaus' brother Agamemnon had done what he had to do in that case: he'd slit his daughter Iphigenia's throat to appease the goddess Artemis. The winds had changed and the fleet sailed, but Agamemnon had bought his own destruction, as we've seen: his wife stabbed him to death when he got back home from the war. So, with the winds against him there in Egypt, Menelaus did what he had to do too. He grabbed a couple of Egyptian kids and sacrificed them—handsome repayment of Proteus' hospitality. Apparently the winds changed for Menelaus too, because when the Egyptians found out what he'd done and came after him, he was able to flee by sea to Libya. He escaped them, and that's where the story ended for the Egyptians: they didn't know what happened to Menelaus and Helen once they'd outstripped the Egyptians' boats.

Herodotus concludes his account of the Egyptians' version of the Helen story by arguing for its credibility. The Trojans, he explains, cannot have had Helen in their possession, because if they had, they would surely have handed her over to the Greeks. Troy's King Priam and the rest of the royal family would not have risked the kingdom and the lives of their children just so Paris could sleep with his Greek tart. And even if they had refused to hand her over at first, they would surely have done so once the Trojans—and in particular the princes of Troy—started dying in large numbers. Thus the Trojans were telling the truth when they said they didn't have Helen. As for why the Greeks didn't believe them, Herodotus thought the gods were behind it: the utter destruction of Troy in war would be a clear sign to mankind that the gods would impose great penalties as punishment for great offenses.

Rhampsinitus and the Wily Thief (2.121)

He sent his own daughter to the common stews, with orders to admit all comers, but to require every man to tell her what was the cleverest and wickedest thing he had done in the whole course of his life.   (2.121ε2)

Proteus was succeeded in the kingship by Rhampsinitus, about whom Herodotus tells a story that is, as Alan Lloyd puts it, "a veritable string of folk-motifs, in particular that of the wily thief."[10] This Rhampsinitus was enormously wealthy, and he decided that he needed a secure place to store his riches. He had a treasury built for the purpose, a stone chamber that abutted his house. The architect who built the chamber, thinking to provide his sons with financial security, fixed it so that one of the heavy stones of the chamber wall could easily be pulled out by a pair of men—or even by one man. Thus anyone who knew the secret of the removable stone would be able to access the king's treasure at will. The workman himself seems not to have made use of the secret entrance, but when he was on his deathbed he told his two sons about it. They were more eager to get their hands on the money than their father had been, and it wasn't long before they were making a late-night run to the royal bank.

The sons, in fact, made rather a large withdrawal, so much so that the next time the king entered the treasury, he saw at once that some of his money was missing. This happened a second time as well, and a third, as the boys kept coming back for more. The king was at a loss to understand how someone was stealing from him, since there was no sign that the chamber's regular entrance had been compromised. To try to catch the thief, the king had traps set around the money jars in the treasury. Sure enough, the next time the thieves came, one of them was caught. There was apparently no way of extracting him, so the thief who was caught persuaded his brother to cut off his head and take it away with him. That way his body could not be identified, and his brother would not be implicated in the crime. The free brother did as he was told.

When Rhampsinitus found the headless corpse in his treasury the next day, he was as confused as before, but again he had a plan. He had the corpse hung out in public, and he ordered the sentries guarding the body to arrest anyone who showed signs of mourning when they saw it. The king's plan didn't work, but it did make an impression on the dead thief's family. The thief's mother was unhappy about her son's corpse being strung up, and she demanded that her other son somehow bring the body home. She in fact threatened that if he didn't retrieve his brother's body she would tell the king herself that her son had stolen the money. And so the surviving son came up with a plan. He loaded up a donkey with wineskins, drove them along in front of the sentries, and invented a reason to interact with the guards: he opened a few of the skins so that they leaked on the road. The thief pretended to be upset by the loss and upset as well when the guards came over and collected some of the wine for themselves. But his mood gradually improved as they joked with him—or so he pretended. He buddied up to the guards, giving them more and more of his wine, and in the end he got them so drunk they fell asleep on the job. When it was dark, he cut down his brother and loaded the body on his wagon. By way of mocking the guards, who were both bearded, he shaved the right cheek of each of them before he left.

The king was furious. The thief had repeatedly made a fool of him, and now he wanted nothing so much as to catch the man. He laid another trap, using his daughter as bait. He put her in a room and ordered her to have sex with any man who came by, provided he first tell her what were the most clever and the most wicked things he had ever done. If someone happened to mention that he had stolen from the king's treasury, she was to grab him and not let go until help arrived.

The king's daughter did as instructed, and somehow word got out that she was available. Somehow, too, the thief knew what the king was up to—perhaps he heard about the questions the princess posed by way of foreplay—and he figured out how to avoid getting caught by her. He went to the princess's room with an arm he'd severed from a fresh corpse concealed under his cloak. When the princess asked him what the cleverest and wickedest things he'd ever done were, the thief answered honestly: he'd cut off his brother's head in the king's treasury—that was the wickedest thing—and he'd cut down his brother's body after getting the king's guards drunk. The princess, hearing this, made a grab for him but got the dead man's arm instead. She held onto it, thinking she had her man, and the thief handily escaped, having once again outwitted her father.

Rhampsinitus was impressed. He announced that the thief would be given immunity and a great reward if he showed himself. This time, the thief did not suspect a trap. He came forward, and the king, who admired the thief for his cleverness, gave him his daughter's hand in marriage. The Egyptians, the king explained, were superior to the rest of humanity, but this man was superior to the rest of the Egyptians.

Herodotus doesn't find this final episode of the Rhampsinitus story plausible. His objection seems to be that the king is unlikely to have thus prostituted his daughter. Fair enough, though the very next Egyptian king Herodotus mentions, Cheops, is said to have done just that: when he was short of money due to the cost of building his great pyramid, Cheops allegedly set his daughter up in a brothel and specified the price she was to charge per client (2.126). But Rhampsinitus' prostitution of his daughter is, at any rate, certainly not the only element of Herodotus' story that beggars belief.

Amasis, the Flatulent Revolutionary (2.162)

> Patarbemis, on arriving at the place where Amasis was, called on him to come
> back with him to the king, whereupon Amasis broke a coarse jest, and said,
> "Prythee take that back to thy master." (2.162.3)

We discussed Psammetichus above, the Egyptian king whose cruel experiment in the language adoption of feral children is a staple of linguistics textbooks. Psammetichus' great-grandson was Apries, who took the throne about a century after Psammetichus and ruled for some twenty-five years. After a disastrous campaign against Cyrene, in Libya, for which they held Apries responsible, some of the Egyptians revolted against the king, eventually elevating a man named Amasis to serve as their leader. Apries sent an envoy to Amasis, a distinguished Egyptian by the name of Patarbemis, who was ordered to bring Amasis back alive. But Amasis was not about to surrender himself. When Patarbemis ordered Amasis to show himself before the king, "Amasis (for he happened to be sitting on a horse) rose up and broke wind, and he bid Patarbemis bring *that* back to Apries."

In the modern era Herodotus' brief account of the flatulent Amasis has caught the attention of respected writers from Uncle John (author of *Uncle John's Absolutely Absorbing Bathroom Reader*) to Jim Dawson (*Who Cut the Cheese?: A Cultural History of the Fart*) to Mark Twain. The last of these referred to the Herodotean passage in an essay published anonymously (though he later copped to writing it) in 1880: *(Date: 1601.) Conversation, as It Was by the Social Fireside, in the Time of the Tudors*, known more briefly as *1601*. Twain's essay purports to be a record of a conversation in which, among other topics, instances of historical flatulence were discussed. The speakers were eminent personalities such as Queen Elizabeth, Ben Johnson, and Walter Raleigh:

> Nay, worthier names than those of any yet mentioned have discussed the matter. Herodotus tells of one such which was the precursor to the fall of an empire and a change of dynasty—that which Amasis discharges while on horseback, and bids the envoy of Apries, King of Egypt, catch and deliver to his royal master. Even the exact manner and posture of Amasis, author of this insult, is described.

Amasis couldn't know it when he issued his insult, but his flatulence—despite its ephemerality—would echo for millennia.

Amasis made it clear to Patarbemis that he intended to march against the Egyptian king. Patarbemis thus hurried back to tell Apries what was going on, but the king, seeing that his man had failed to return with Amasis—and without giving Patarbemis a chance to explain himself—ordered that Patarbemis be punished by having his ears and nose sliced off. This turned out to be a mistake, because Apries' cruelty resulted in his losing support among those Egyptians who had still sided with him. Now everybody hated the king, and they joined Amasis in revolting. In the ensuing battle Apries was defeated and taken prisoner. Later he was strangled to death, at least according to Herodotus (2.169).

(An Egyptian source, the so-called Amasis stele, indicates that Apries was killed in battle.) Once Apries had been removed from power, Amasis succeeded to the throne.

As we will see in the next chapter, it was this Amasis, the flatulent revolutionary, against whom the Persian King Cambyses, son of Cyrus, was to make an expedition.

Madness and Mummies

The Reign of Cambyses

AFTER SPENDING THE WHOLE OF HIS SECOND BOOK describing the marvels and mores of Egypt, Herodotus finally gets back to the subject of Persian expansion, specifically Cambyses' invasion of Egypt in 525. It all started—at least according to one story Herodotus tells—with an ophthalmologist.

Eye Doctors and Other *Casus Belli* (3.1–3)

His adviser was a physician, whom Amasis, when Cyrus had requested that he would send him the most skilful of all the Egyptian eye-doctors, singled out as the best from the whole number. (3.1)

The Egyptians were renowned in antiquity for their medical skill, so when Cyrus of Persia was suffering from an affliction of the eye, it was only natural that he would try to get ahold of an Egyptian specialist. He asked Amasis to send over the best eye doctor Egypt had to offer. Amasis complied, but the doctor, who was forced to leave his family behind in Egypt, was not happy about going. After Cyrus died, the doctor, who was still stuck in Persia, came up with a plan to get back at Amasis. He urged Cambyses to send to Amasis and ask him for his daughter as a wife. If Amasis agreed, he would be separated from his child and would experience the same sort of anguish the doctor had. If Amasis refused, he would make Cambyses his enemy: a win-win situation as far as the doctor was concerned.

Per his doctor's suggestion, Cambyses sent to Egypt with a view to hooking up with the Egyptian princess. Cambyses' request put Amasis in a difficult position. He was loath to get on the Persian king's bad side, but he also wasn't thrilled about sending his daughter off to Persia. He decided to trick Cambyses instead. The former Egyptian king, Apries, had a daughter named Nitetis who was tall and beautiful and just right for the purpose. Amasis dressed her up in nice clothes and sent her to Cambyses. Presumably, he also told her that when she got there she should pretend to be his daughter. But Nitetis' father had lost his kingdom because of Amasis, and Nitetis herself was probably not in the mood to do him any favors. Sometime after her arrival in Persia, when Cambyses greeted her as the daughter of Amasis, she spilled the beans. The result was Cambyses' invasion of Egypt.

The above account, which Herodotus got from Persian sources, is the first of three stories he tells about the genesis of Cambyses' Egyptian campaign, and it is the one to which he gives the most credence. He tells the Egyptians' version of the story next. According to them, it was Cambyses' father who asked Amasis to send his daughter to Persia. Amasis sent Nitetis to Cyrus, and the son of their union was Cambyses. Thus Cambyses, in invading Egypt, was simply claiming his maternal inheritance. But Herodotus makes it clear that this second account is not to be believed for a number of reasons, among them that Cambyses was certainly the son of Cyrus by the Persian Cassandane, not by Nitetis.

Herodotus doesn't believe the third story he tells either. According to this last version, Cambyses was the son of Cyrus by Cassandane, but Nitetis was also on hand as Cyrus' concubine. One day Cambyses' mother expressed her resentment of Nitetis in front of her son, and he promised her that when he became a man he would "make the top of Egypt its bottom and the bottom its top." His expedition years later was undertaken in memory of this vow.

Nitetis is the common element in all three of the stories Herodotus tells. Since this is so, and since she has a name, as Mabel Lang argues—that is, her name is a concrete particular unlikely to have been conjured out of thin air—it may be that Nitetis is "the one kernel of fact in a tissue of adapted folktale motifs, interpretation, rationalization and justification."[1] It may be, that is, that there really was an Egyptian princess by the name of Nitetis in the Persian court around the time of the invasion. Her presence may have been connected with the expedition. Or, perhaps more likely, a story developed around the bare facts of the expedition and her presence at court to explain how the two might have been connected.

Meanwhile, Cambyses' invasion of Egypt can be explained easily enough without blaming it on a personal motive. Back when Croesus was looking for allies for his war against Persia, he came to an agreement with Amasis (1.77.2). This alliance, coupled with Cambyses' lust for conquest, is sufficient to explain his attack on Egypt.[2]

Cambyses may have invaded Egypt with a view to dethroning Amasis, but by the time he got there Amasis was past caring. The king had died some six months earlier—of natural causes, of all things—having ruled without incident for forty-four years (3.10). He was succeeded by his son Psammenitus. Amasis' death feels almost anticlimactic: the Egyptian *logos*—the whole of Herodotus' second book—had built up to and concluded with the reign of Amasis, the point being that he was the king of Egypt when, finally, Egyptian civilization collided with—or got in the way of—the expanding Persian Empire. And in the first sentence of his third book Herodotus writes that it was "against this Amasis" that Cambyses made his expedition. But it makes sense for Herodotus to have introduced the Egyptian expedition as if Amasis were king rather than his son. For one thing, Herodotus' account suggests that Cambyses hadn't heard the news about Amasis prior to his arrival in Egypt, so that he had indeed intended to campaign against Amasis. More importantly, the first story Herodotus tells about the reason for Cambyses' campaign—the story that Herodotus finds most credible—has to do with a trick pulled by Amasis, his substitution of Apries' daughter for his own. Introducing the expedition with a reference to Psammenitus and then backtracking to Amasis' reign to explain the campaign would have made for a less coherent narrative.

Thick-Skulled Egyptians (3.11–12)

The same cause prevents baldness in Egypt, where you see fewer bald men than in any other land.   (3.12.3)

Cambyses invaded Egypt with the help of a certain Phanes, who had been one of Amasis' bodyguards. Phanes had run away from Egypt for some reason and made his way to Persia, where he provided Cambyses with information about how best to cross the Egyptian desert. But Phanes would soon have cause to regret his treachery. When the Persians were encamped near the Egyptians and were preparing for battle, the Greek mercenaries in the Egyptian army decided to punish Phanes for having led an army against his homeland. They brought Phanes' children out in view of their father and slit the kids' throats over a mixing bowl. Then they mixed the blood with water and wine, and all the mercenaries enjoyed a hearty beverage prior to battle. Despite this fortification, the Egyptians and their mercenaries were defeated.

In Herodotus' day, the bones of some of the men who died in this battle were allegedly still strewn about. Herodotus tells us he saw them himself, and there were distinct piles of them, the Egyptians on one side, the Persians on another, still lying right where they were killed. What was odd about the skeletons, though, was the relative thickness of their skulls. Herodotus says the skulls of the Egyptians were thick and hard, but the Persians' skulls were brittle: if you threw a pebble at one of them it was enough to shatter it. The natives told Herodotus why this was so, and he believed them. They said that the Egyptians shaved their heads routinely, as a consequence of which their scalps were exposed to the sun and their skulls grew thick. For the same reason, they explained, there was very little baldness among the Egyptians. The Persians, on the other hand, tended to wear hats, and their pampered skulls were the weaker for it.

In his discussion of the passage David Asheri notes that the fragility of the skull and other bones is a common symptom of rickets, which may explain the weakness of some of the skulls Herodotus saw.[3] But we may doubt that Herodotus was right in his identification of the skeletons as either Egyptian or Persian, because their bodies are likely to have been either buried or embalmed after the battle. The bones, if they in fact dated to this occasion, were instead probably those of mercenaries fighting on both sides in the battle. Decades of exposure to the weather and the predations of wild animals are likely, too, to have displaced at least some of the bones, so that their organization into ethnic groups was probably not as neat as Herodotus suggests.

The End of Psammenitus (3.14–15)

> He therefore had him set in one of the suburbs, and many other Egyptians with
> him, and there subjected him to insult. (3.14.1)

After their defeat in battle the Egyptians holed up in Memphis, not far south of the Nile delta. The Persians laid siege to the city and eventually reduced it, after which a number of the Egyptians' neighbors—the Libyans, Cyrenaeans, and Barcaeans—came to terms with the Persians without a fight. The dirty business of conquering the place thus finished, it remained only for Cambyses to conduct cruel psychological experiments on his royal captive.

Ten days after the siege, Cambyses stationed Psammenitus and some Egyptian nobles in the outer part of the city. Then he dressed the king's daughter and the daughters of the other Egyptians in rags and gave the princess a pitcher with which to fetch water—a menial task far beneath her previous station. The girls were paraded past their fathers, and they cried because of their plight, and their fathers cried to see the girls being treated like servants. But Psammenitus maintained his dignity and merely bowed his head when his daughter passed by.

Cambyses next rounded up Psammenitus' son and some two thousand other young Egyptians. The boys were bound together by the neck with ropes, and bits were placed in their mouths, and, like the girls, they were herded past Psammenitus and the nobles. Again there was weeping and great lamentation all around, except that Psammenitus kept quiet and, as he had previously, merely cast his eyes downward.

That was all Cambyses had up his sleeve, but soon something else occurred that managed to pierce Psammenitus' stoic exterior. An old friend of his, a drinking buddy who had now lost everything, happened to walk by, begging from the soldiers. When Psammenitus saw him, he burst into tears and beat himself in the head and generally made the sort of scene he'd been expected to make when he saw his children paraded past. Cambyses heard about this and was shocked by the dethroned king's ostensibly misplaced grief. He sent a messenger to Psammenitus and asked him, in essence, What gives? Why the tears for the old guy when you kept quiet at the sight of your own children? Psammenitus explained that his own griefs were too great for tears, but seeing his old friend brought low was something he could cry about.

Psammenitus' answer may not strike the modern ear as particularly pathetic, but it made our old friend Croesus cry when it was reported to Cambyses in his presence, and it moved Cambyses himself to pity. He ordered his henchmen to spare the life of Psammenitus' son, who'd been led off in shackles with the other Egyptian youths, but it was too late: the prince had been the first of the two-thousand-odd boys to be killed. Still, Cambyses did what he could for Psammenitus. He allowed the former king to live in his household, and Psammenitus could have done so indefinitely—one imagines him playing mah jongg of an afternoon with his fellow ex-king Croesus. But after a while Psammenitus was caught trying to raise the Egyptians in revolt, and when his plot was revealed to Cambyses he drank—or was made to drink—bull's blood. Naturally, he dropped dead right away, since bull's blood congeals so rapidly that upon drinking it, one chokes to death at once (see Aristotle, *History of Animals* 5206; Pliny, *Natural History* 11.91).

But hold! I hear you cry. I had a cup of bull's blood with my breakfast this morning and I'm just fine! And so you are. Because in fact bull's blood isn't poisonous and does not cause death by virtue of the speed at which it coagulates—or by virtue of anything else, for that matter. But there was in antiquity a widespread belief that drinking it was lethal. Psammenitus is not the only ancient figure alleged to have died from a quaff of it. The Athenian statesman Themistocles[4] and Midas, the legendary king of Phrygia (Strabo 1.61), were both said to have offed themselves in this way. (Midas, of course, is famous for another story, that he was granted his wish that everything he touched should turn to gold. But Midas managed to get that decidedly mixed blessing rescinded. Otherwise, suicide by bull's blood would not have been possible for him. Or rather, anything Midas tried to drink would have choked him to death at least as effectively as coagulated blood.) Given the reputation of bull's blood, Herodotus' account of Psammenitus' mode of death does not surprise, but we also shouldn't take it very seriously.

This, at any rate, was the end of Psammenitus, whose misfortune it was to assume the Egyptian throne mere months before Cambyses' invasion.

Mummy Whacking (3.16)

Egyptian mummies, which Cambyses or time hath spared, avarice now
consumeth.   (SIR THOMAS BROWN, *Hydriotaphia*)

Cambyses' treatment of Psammenitus after the siege of Memphis was arguably unkind. He had Psammenitus' son killed, after all, and the Egyptian king's daughter was made at the least to fetch water in front of an audience. Still, nothing in Cambyses' behavior—even his execution of the two thousand Egyptian boys—suggested there was anything amiss with the Persian king. Back in the day, mass executions were simply what one did after a military conquest. It's what Cambyses did *next*, however, that gives one pause: the king, we begin to think, was nuts.

Cambyses went to the palace of Amasis in Saïs and had his men take Amasis' mummy out of its burial place. He ordered them to "whip it and pull out its hair and stab it and commit all other outrages upon it." They did their best, but Cambyses wasn't satisfied with the results: whipping and stabbing the mummified Amasis was like whacking a particularly stubborn piñata. Cambyses' men weren't getting to the candy innards as quickly as their king would have liked. Cambyses then ordered his men to burn the mummy, and that seems to have done the trick, as it was apparently the final indignity heaped upon the corpse.

It seems like a crazy thing to do, but Cambyses' outrage of Amasis' corpse may have been a canny political move, a calculated attempt to diminish Amasis by treating his corpse as if it were that of a criminal: for the ancient Egyptians, "burning a corpse branded the dead person as a criminal at the terrestrial and divine level."[5] Thus we should not be so quick to brand Cambyses a madman just because he went postal on a mummy. There are plenty of other reasons to think he was crazy, as we'll soon see.

The Ethiopian *Logos* (3.17–26)

So long as the earth gave them anything, the soldiers sustained life by eating the grass and herbs; but when they came to the bare sand, a portion of them were guilty of a horrid deed: by tens they cast lots for a man, who was slain to be the food of the others.   (3.25)

After his successful siege of Memphis, Cambyses made plans for three expeditions—against the Carthaginians, the Ammonians, and the Ethiopians. The first campaign never got off the ground, and the second went poorly: the army of fifty thousand men that marched west against the Ammonians, who lived near the modern border of Egypt and Libya, was lost en route; after it had reached the halfway point, it was never heard from again. The story told by the Ammonians was that the Persian army was buried in a sandstorm. The fate of Cambyses' lost army is a great archaeological mystery. Herodotus' spare account, our only evidence for the expedition, has inspired romantic adventurers and treasure seekers to try to locate the army, including attempts made by Count László Almásy, the Hungarian aviator and desert explorer on whom Michael Ondaatje's *The English Patient* was based. More recently, a tourism company has been bringing tourists to Egypt's Western Desert to hunt for remains of the army.[6]

Herodotus' account of the Ethiopian campaign is the most extensive of the three he mentions at 3.17, and it is introduced by a brief ethnographic section. Prior to making his expedition against the Ethiopians, Cambyses sent spies to the country, men from the city of Elephantine (modern-day Aswan), whose people apparently ate a lot of fish (Herodotus calls them the Ichthyophagi, or "Fish-Eaters"). They were sent off to scope out the situation in Ethiopia, but they pretended merely to be bringing gifts to that country's king. The Fish-Eaters gained an audience with the king and handed over their gifts, and they fed him a story about Cambyses wanting to be his guest-friend.

The Ethiopians, Herodotus says, were said to be the tallest and the most attractive of all men, and their king was the strongest and tallest of all of them. He was, moreover, no dummy: he saw through Cambyses' men at once, and he said as much. You've come as spies, he told them, and your king is interested in conquest, not friendship. Cambyses, he said, is not a just man: "for if he were, he would not desire lands other than his own, nor would he lead into slavery men from whom he has suffered no injustice." And then the king unstrung a great bow and gave it to the spies, and he told them to bring Cambyses a message:

> The king of the Ethiopians advises the king of the Persians, when the Persians can draw a bow as big as this one this easily, *then* make an expedition against the long-lived Ethiopians, and come in great number. Until then, give thanks to the gods, who haven't put the idea of adding new lands to their own into the heads of the sons of the Ethiopians.

The king's remarks may sound familiar. His suggestion that Cambyses should be content with the current size of his kingdom is reminiscent of the message Tomyris sent Cyrus (1.206) prior to his ill-fated foray into the territory of the Massagetae. In that case too the message had been preceded by an ostensibly friendly gesture from the Persian king—Cyrus' offer of marriage—the ulterior motives behind which were transparent. Cyrus, to his detriment, didn't listen to Tomyris, and his son wasn't any more likely to heed this warning.

The Ethiopian king's message is also reminiscent of the challenge Odysseus' long-suffering wife Penelope issues in book 21 of the *Odyssey*: unaware that her husband has finally returned from Troy after twenty years, she pledges to give herself to whoever of her unwanted suitors is able to string Odysseus' bow and shoot an arrow through twelve aligned axe heads. But while Odysseus' son Telemachus is almost able to string the bow, none of the suitors can. Odysseus then steps forward in his disguise as a beggar, strings the bow easily, and sends a shaft through the axe heads—a prelude to the bloodbath that will follow, when Odysseus rids his home of the suitors once and for all.

As it turns out, there was no one among the Persians who was able to string the Ethiopian king's great bow. But there was one man who, like Telemachus, could *almost* do it. We'll hear more about him shortly.

Given what we know already of Cambyses' anger management problems, his reaction to his spies' report on their trip to Ethiopia is hardly surprising. Herodotus describes him as "raving and being out of his mind"—the first explicit reference in *The History* to his madness. According to Herodotus, Cambyses was so enraged that he set off on an expedition against the Ethiopians without giving any thought to how he was going to supply his army. One-fifth of the way there, his provisions ran out, but Cambyses kept marching, his men surviving by eating first the pack animals and then grass. Eventually, even that failed. The army hit the desert and they resorted to cannibalism, the men casting lots to see which of them would be for dinner. This proved to be too much even for Cambyses, and he finally abandoned the expedition and returned with what was left of his army to Memphis.

Cambyses and the Apis Bull (3.27–29)

Apis, wounded in the thigh, lay some time pining in the temple; at last he died of his wound, and the priests buried him secretly without the knowledge of Cambyses.   (3.29.3)

When Cambyses returned to Memphis following his unsuccessful campaign, the Egyptians started celebrating. They weren't reveling because of his misfortunes, but that's how it looked to Cambyses. He summoned the leaders of Memphis and asked them why they just happened to throw a party after he'd lost most of his army. They tried to explain that it had nothing to do with the king's campaign: the Egyptians were celebrating a religious festival. Their god appeared to them irregularly, they said, and when he did, as now, they celebrated. But Cambyses, assuming that the men were lying, had them killed.

Cambyses next sent for the priests, and they told him the same thing. This time Cambyses apparently believed the story—tough luck for the first wave of messengers, but at least the priests were spared—and he bade them bring the god to him in its current earthly incarnation.

The Egyptians believed that the god Ptah manifested himself in the form of the so-called Apis bull, an animal distinguished from his peers by various markings. Specifically, the Apis bull was black with a white triangle on its forehead and an eagle-shaped mark on its back, and it had double hairs on its tail and a beetle-shaped mark under its tongue. When an Apis bull died—the typical lifespan was about 20 years—it was embalmed and buried. At some point after the death of the old bull, a new Apis bull was born, and that calf was installed as the official bull in the Ptah temple at Memphis after the old bull was buried. When Cambyses returned to Memphis, the Egyptians were celebrating because the god had "appeared" to them, which is to say that a new Apis bull had either just been born or had been installed in office.

It was this newborn or newly installed calf that was brought to Cambyses, no mere bull but a god translated into bovine form. Given the animal's status among the Egyptians, Cambyses could not have committed any greater sacrilege in his subjects' eyes than what he did upon meeting the animal: he drew his dagger and stabbed it in the thigh, then laughed maniacally because the Egyptians' god was a weak thing of flesh and blood. The whole business ended badly. The Apis bull died and was buried in secret by the priests. The priests themselves were whipped. And the Egyptians were ordered to abstain from celebration on penalty of death.

Herodotus' story of the Apis bull's murder makes for good reading, but it may not be true. Inscriptions found at the Serapeum, the burial place of the Apis bulls, do refer to a succession of bulls occurring around the time of Cambyses' conquest of Egypt—one bull was buried in October or November of 524 B.C., and its successor was born in May of 525[7]—but neither can be Herodotus' calf: the former bull was almost twenty when it died, and the latter died in 518 at the age of seven. Still, the archaeological evidence does not preclude the possibility that Herodotus' report is accurate: there may have been another Apis bull sandwiched between the two mentioned in the Serapeum inscriptions, a calf whose death at Cambyses' hand went unrecorded there. According to Herodotus, after all, the bull Cambyses killed was buried secretly. On the other hand, the humiliation of priests and the slaughter of sacred animals by an outsider are traditional elements of a type of Egyptian literature, a tradition that may have shaped the stories about Cambyses that were preserved and ultimately told to Herodotus by his Egyptian informants. In other words, the story of Cambyses' murder of the Apis bull may be complete hogwash.

The Smerdis Affair, Part I: Prexaspes' Secret Mission (3.30)

And now Cambyses, who even before had not been quite in his right mind, was
forthwith, as the Egyptians say, smitten with madness for this crime.   (3.30.1)

The Egyptians said it was because of his slaughter of the Apis bull that Cambyses went mad. But truth be told, as Herodotus adds, the king hadn't been
a paragon of sanity even before this incident. Herodotus himself is not sold
on the Egyptians' explanation for Cambyses' insanity: at 3.33 he suggests that
Cambyses' madness may have had a physical cause. He tells us that the king
suffered from the so-called "Sacred Disease"—epilepsy—and reasons that it
wouldn't be surprising, given his physical problems, if Cambyses suffered men-
tally as well. But whatever the cause of his madness, Cambyses, having (allegedly) gone off the deep end with his sacrilegious bovicide, turned his attention
next to his own kin.

We mentioned earlier that there was only one man among the Persians who
even came close to being able to string the Ethiopian king's great bow. The
strongman in question was Smerdis, Cambyses' brother. Herodotus tells us that
Cambyses was jealous of his brother because of the bow, and he consequently
sent Smerdis back to Persia. Given what followed, it appears that Cambyses
understood his brother's ability with the bow to constitute some vague threat
to himself—not enough to warrant a more permanent solution to the problem,
but enough that he wanted Smerdis out of the way. This may seem a stupid
move. If Smerdis was in fact likely to turn against Cambyses, then sending him
home where he could foment rebellion behind the king's back was not a good
idea. But Cambyses wouldn't be the first king in Herodotus' *History* to respond
unwisely to a suggestion of trouble. (Cyrus, for example, when he suspected
that Darius was plotting against him, sent Darius' father, of all people, back to
Persia to keep an eye on the boy.)

After Cambyses sent Smerdis to Persia, he had a dream that validated his
earlier concerns. He dreamt that a messenger came to him from Persia and
told him Smerdis was sitting on the royal throne, touching the heavens with his
head. The implications of the vision were clear enough, and Cambyses didn't
waste any time before taking decisive action. He sent a particularly trusted servant off to kill his brother. This servant, Prexaspes, took care of the problem,
though precisely how he killed Smerdis is unknown. Herodotus heard different
versions—that he killed Smerdis during a hunting trip, that he drowned the

king's brother in the Red Sea. But however Prexaspes did it, Smerdis was dead. Maybe. As it turns out, there came to be some cause for doubt about that point.

Lettuce, Puppies, and Sororicide (3.31–32)

The two were sitting at table, when the sister took a lettuce, and stripping the leaves off, asked her brother "when he thought the lettuce looked the prettiest— when it had all its leaves on, or now that it was stripped?"   (3.32.3)

Marrying one's full sister was not the done thing among the Persians, but Cambyses—at least as he's portrayed in Herodotus' pages—was not above transgressing moral boundaries. The king had a number of wives, and among them were two of his sisters. One of these was Atossa, about whom we'll be hearing more later. The name of the other sister may have been Meroe (Libanius, *In Praise of Antioch* 59), though Herodotus doesn't record it.

Herodotus tells us that after having his brother Smerdis killed, Cambyses murdered this second sister. He recounts two different stories about her death. According to his Greek sources, the royal couple was watching a fight between a lion cub and a puppy. When the dog was losing, its brother broke its chain and ran to help, which prompted Cambyses' wife to cry. Asked why she was upset, she explained that it was because Smerdis would no longer be available to defend Cambyses, as the puppy had its brother. Cambyses didn't like having his nose rubbed in this Smerdis business, so he killed her.

The Egyptians told a different story. Cambyses and his sister-wife—who was pregnant, in this version—were sitting at the dinner table when she picked up a head of lettuce, pulled off some of its leaves, and asked her husband whether it was better plucked or full. When Cambyses said it was better full, she drew the parallel you likely see coming. You did the same thing, she said, when you stripped bare the house of Cambyses. The queen's analogy would probably have annoyed far better men than her husband. *Him* it enraged. He threw himself at her and she wound up having a miscarriage and dying.

The two stories Herodotus reports differ in detail, but the kernel of the story is the same in both: Cambyses' sister confronted him about his murder of Smerdis, and he responded by killing her. But is it in fact true that Cambyses killed his sister, whether provoked by animal, vegetable, or anything else? In short, we don't know. Herodotus' account is not substantiated elsewhere. Ctesias, a physician and historian who wrote in the fifth century B.C., doesn't mention the murder in his history of Persia, for example, as we might expect him to—though he does tell us that Cambyses' wife Roxanne (not Meroe in this story) gave birth to a headless baby (*FGH* 688 F 13). (Ctesias' work survives only in fragments and in a ninth-century A.D. abridgment by Photius.) It's not hard to imagine how the story of a sororicide might have arisen, if it wasn't in fact true. Given the headless baby and the miscarriage mentioned in our sources, we might guess that Cambyses' sister died in childbirth rather than at her husband's hand. Rumors about the fate of Smerdis can have suggested a juicier explanation for the woman's death, which sources hostile to Cambyses would have been happy to promulgate.

Trial by Fire: Cambyses and Prexaspes' Son (3.34–35)

I pray thee tell me, sawest thou ever mortal man send an arrow with a better aim?   (CAMBYSES, at 3.35.4)

Cambyses' madness in the wake of his slaughter of the Apis bull was not manifested only in the murder of his siblings. He did other crazy stuff too. In particular, there was an incident involving Cambyses' trusted advisor Prexaspes—the guy he'd sent to Persia to kill Smerdis—that calls to mind Astyages' unpleasantness back in the day toward *his* minion, Harpagus. Cambyses was sitting around with Prexaspes one day and fell to talking about, well, Cambyses. "What do the Persians think of me?" Cambyses asked, and Prexaspes—foolishly, we understand in retrospect—told him the truth. "Master," he said, "they praise you highly, except for one thing: they say you're excessively fond of wine."

Upon hearing this, Cambyses became furious and raged at Prexaspes, exaggerating the criticism his minister had related. They think I'm deranged from drinking? said the king, and he sought to demonstrate to Prexaspes that he was as sane as he'd ever been. Prexaspes' son was standing in the doorway—the boy was Cambyses' cupbearer—and Cambyses took aim at him with his bow. "If I hit the boy's heart," Cambyses said, "then the Persians don't know what they're talking about. If I miss, then they're right and I'm out of my mind."

Cambyses may or may not have been thinking clearly—the test he allegedly devised doesn't strike the modern ear as a meaningful diagnostic tool—but at least he was a good shot. Prexaspes' son collapsed, and when he was cut open Cambyses' arrow was shown to have indeed struck the heart. Cambyses laughed in his delight and said to Prexaspes, "So is it clear to you now that I'm not crazy and the Persians are? Tell me, do you know of anyone else who could shoot so accurately?" Prexaspes was now terrified for his own sake, and like Harpagus before him—when he was shown the remains of his son and asked if he recognized the wild beast he'd just eaten—he sought to placate the lunatic who'd just killed his flesh and blood. "I think the god himself could not shoot so well," he said.

The difference between Prexaspes and Harpagus, of course, is that the former was not guilty of offense, and the murder of his son was not, at least as Herodotus presents it, a calculated form of revenge. Also, while Harpagus went on to formulate his own brand of revenge against Astyages—his smoldering hatred resulting eventually in Cyrus' usurpation of his grandfather's throne—we'll see that Prexaspes' response to Cambyses' slaughter of his son was rather different.

Croesus: The Final Act (3.34, 36)

"But thou shalt not escape punishment now, for I have long been seeking to find some occasion against thee."   (CAMBYSES, at 3.36.3)

The above episode wasn't the first time Cambyses had sought feedback from his courtiers. He once asked a bunch of them how they thought he compared to his father. The Persians in the group were quick to compliment the king, saying he was a better man than his father because he had all of Cyrus' possessions and had added Egypt to the Empire besides. A pretty answer, and it doubtless pleased Cambyses, but there was one dissenting voice. Croesus was also present—the former Lydian king Cambyses had inherited as an advisor from his father. Croesus, disagreeing with his fellow sycophants, took a more nuanced approach to sucking up to the king. "I do not think that you are the equal of your father," he said, "for you don't have a son such as that man left behind." Croesus' answer might have offended Cambyses if he'd been in a worse mood: he could have taken it as a reminder that he not only had a succession problem but that he'd caused it himself, since he'd killed his pregnant sister over a head of lettuce. But Cambyses took Croesus' remark at face value and was pleased with it.

Herodotus hasn't had much to say about Croesus since the last time the Lydian king had a minority opinion to offer, back when he advised Cambyses' father to cross the Araxes and take the fight to the Massagetae. That, as you'll remember, had ended badly, with Cyrus' head marinating in a bag. When we next hear of Croesus offering his advice to a Persian king, the result is likewise unpleasant. Among the imprudent things Cambyses did in his madness—in addition to killing Prexaspes' son and his brother Smerdis and his pregnant sister and the Apis bull—was an act that was likely to lose him popular support. Cambyses punished twelve noble Persians for some insignificant offense by burying them alive up to their necks. Croesus tried to talk some sense into him at this point. You can't go around acting on your whims, he said. You have to restrain yourself and think ahead. You're killing your own citizens on trivial charges. You're killing kids. If you keep that up, the Persians will revolt against you. Croesus closed by reminding the king that Cyrus had asked him to offer Cambyses advice should he need it.

Croesus' advice was of course perfectly reasonable. Anyone this side of Caligula could see that. But unfortunately his interference on this occasion was too much for Cambyses, who had apparently been harboring some ill will toward his advisor for some time. You're advising me?! he spat out. Like you did such a great job running your country? Plus you told my father to cross the Araxes when the Massagetae would have crossed over to Persia. You lost your own country because you governed it poorly, and your advice got my father killed!

Croesus didn't have time to defend his thinking on the Araxes question—we discussed the pros and cons of that strategy back in chapter two—because once Cambyses finished his harangue—and with a cry of "I've been waiting a long time for this!"—he grabbed his bow. He was about to shoot Croesus down, but the old king managed to run away and thus evade death at the hands of a Persian king for the second time in his life.

Cambyses, in his rage, ordered his people to kill Croesus, but they were used to living under the thumb of a fickle tyrant and knew how to hedge their bets. They hid Croesus instead, figuring Cambyses would eventually change his mind and would applaud them at that point for their prescience. They were right, at least in part. Cambyses did come to regret ordering Croesus to be killed, and when they heard this the men who had hidden him told Cambyses the good news that Croesus was still alive. The king was happy with the result, but he couldn't countenance his attendants' disobedience, and he had them killed.

So Croesus lived to bestow his advice another day. Or so the story goes. Unfortunately, whatever wisdom he had to impart in future years has gone unreported. Herodotus does mention Croesus a few more times in his *History*, but only in passing and with reference to events that antedated the conquest of Lydia by Persia. The spat between Croesus and Cambyses—the undignified chase scene and the monarchs' subsequent reunion, about which we hear very little—is, chronologically, the Lydian king's final appearance on Herodotus' stage. Admittedly, these stories about Croesus' days in the Persian court are likely pure fiction. (This final episode may in fact have been modeled on a story about Assyrian court life that was current in Herodotus' day, the *Story of Ahiqar,* to which it bears some resemblance.) Croesus may well have died immediately after the fall of Sardis, burnt on a pyre lit at either his or Cyrus' direction. But the fiction of the defeated monarch living on after the conquest of his kingdom and counseling the victor is for some reason hugely appealing. Now that Croesus has been chased off the scene, I, for one, am going to miss the guy.

Cambyses' Madness and Cultural Relativism (3.37–38)

Unless, therefore, a man was mad, it is not likely that he would make sport of such matters.   (3.38.2)

Herodotus concludes his account of Cambyses' madness with a brief reference to the king's further impieties. Cambyses opened coffins in Memphis and looked at the dead bodies. He mocked the sacred images in the temple of Hephaestus. He entered another shrine that was off-limits to anyone who wasn't a priest and mocked and burned the sacred images there. Herodotus takes Cambyses' mockery of the Egyptians' religion and customs as a sure sign that the king was deranged. Otherwise, he explains, Cambyses would not have done it. He goes on to discuss cultural relativism. Herodotus explains that all people think their own customs are the best, and he offers a juicy anecdote to illustrate the point. The Persian king Darius (Cambyses' successor) once asked some Greeks in his retinue what it would take to get them to eat their dead fathers rather than burn the bodies. The answer: nothing could make them do it. Darius next asked some Indians—who *were* accustomed to eating their dead fathers—the reverse question: how about burning dad's corpse rather than scarfing it down? The Indians were aghast at the suggestion.

Custom is king, Herodotus concludes, quoting (and putting a different spin on) Pindar's famous phrase to that effect.[8] Herodotus himself displays in his *History* an almost shocking degree of tolerance for unfamiliar cultures. He doesn't bat an eye at necrophagy (1.216) or making clothes out of human skin

(4.64) or any of the other bizarre customs he ran across in his travels—though he does wince at the idea of people having sex in temples (2.64). His multiculturalism is to be applauded. Still, he hasn't offered any support for his position that Cambyses' mockery of the Egyptians' customs implies that the king was mad. It might be proof enough for Herodotus, but what are we to think? Was Cambyses crazy?

The answer, as it so often is, is that we don't know. It's entirely possible that, as Herodotus surmised, Cambyses suffered from some mental illness in addition to being an epileptic (if Herodotus is in fact correct about that detail). Alternatively, Cambyses' alleged madness may have been an invention by sources hostile to the king, part of an anti-Cambyses tradition that Herodotus picked up from his Egyptian informants. Whatever the truth about the historical king's mental state, however, the Cambyses who strides across Herodotus' pages was to enjoy one final, impressive moment of lucidity prior to his dramatic exit from the scene.

The Smerdis Affair, Part II: I'm Not Dead Yet (3.61–63)

And not only was this brother of his like Smerdis in person, but he also bore the selfsame name, to wit Smerdis.   (3.61.2)

Cambyses had left a steward behind in Persia to take care of his household. Herodotus calls the man "Patizeithes," but it may be that the Persian title for his position—something like *pati-khayathia*—was transformed into his name, either by Herodotus or his source (rather like mistakenly calling a manservant Butler). This Patizeithes knew that Cambyses' brother Smerdis was dead, and he knew that his death was being kept secret. He figured he could use this secrecy to his advantage. Patizeithes happened to have a brother named Smerdis, and this Smerdis happened to look a lot like Cambyses' brother—with one enormous exception, which we'll get to in a bit. Patizeithes convinced his brother to assume the throne in the guise of the real Smerdis. Once that was done, Patizeithes sent heralds to various parts of the empire to announce that the Persians were now to obey Smerdis, the son of Cyrus, rather than Cambyses. In particular, a herald was sent to Egypt to make this proclamation before the Persian army and Cambyses himself.

The announcement was troubling, to say the least. Smerdis was *supposed* to be dead, but here he was trying to wrest the throne from his brother. Cambyses rounded on Prexaspes, whom he'd sent to kill Smerdis, and accused him of not doing his job. But Prexaspes swore that he had, that Smerdis was dead and he'd buried him with his own hands. He suggested Cambyses interrogate the herald. The king—surprisingly, given his temper—was persuaded to do so. He asked the herald whether he'd gotten his orders directly from Smerdis, and the herald admitted he hadn't actually seen Smerdis but had been instructed by Cambyses' steward. Hearing this, Cambyses was convinced of Prexaspes' innocence (that is, innocent insofar as he had not failed to murder Smerdis). The picture became clearer yet when Prexaspes suggested it was Cambyses' steward Patizeithes and his brother Smerdis who had risen in revolt.

Cambyses must have let slip a "D'oh!" or its Persian equivalent when he heard the name Smerdis, slapping his forehead as the horrible truth hit him. It was a dream, remember, that had prompted Cambyses to have his brother killed. He'd dreamt that a messenger told him Smerdis was sitting on the royal throne, his head touching the heavens. Importantly, Cambyses had not seen this dream Smerdis himself. But he had assumed—naturally enough—that the Smerdis whom the dream implicated was his brother, the guy he'd sent back to Persia because he was almost able to string the Ethiopian king's bow. (If that didn't make him suspect, what would?) It simply hadn't occurred to Cambyses that there could be a second Smerdis who would challenge his authority. But real life had again taught that, where fate is concerned, resistance is futile. Understanding now the horror of his fratricide, Cambyses wept for his dead brother.

Cambyses: The Final Act (3.64–66)

As he made his spring, the button of his sword-sheath fell off, and the bared point entered his thigh, wounding him exactly where he had himself once wounded the Egyptian god Apis.   (3.64.3)

But Cambyses didn't waste too much time crying, and once he'd finished, he jumped on his horse. He was going to hightail it back to Persia to teach the False Smerdis a thing or two about messing with Cambyses. Once again the Persian throne would be securely in the hands of a legitimate son of Cyrus. Alas, when Cambyses leapt on his horse, the cap fell off his scabbard and the blade pierced his thigh (precisely where he'd stabbed the Apis bull, Herodotus says). The wound seemed to Cambyses quite serious, and so—another horrible possibility pricking at his brain—he asked someone what city they were in. "Ecbatana," came the response.

"D'oh!" again! The oracle in Buto had once prophesied that Cambyses was destined to die in Ecbatana. Naturally, he'd assumed he would die in the Ecbatana in Media, back home in Asia. It made sense: it's like a European assuming that the Paris he's slated to die in is in France rather than Texas. You can't blame Cambyses for thinking as much. Still, he'd made the same mistake his advisor Croesus had made long before, assuming he fully understood the implications of a prophecy. Too late, the terrible truth was clear to him—this last shock having brought him to his senses—and he announced to his company: "This is where Cambyses, the son of Cyrus, is fated to die."

Twenty days later Cambyses called together the more important Persians who were with him in Egypt with a view to putting his affairs in order. He told them everything: that he'd dreamt about Smerdis and ordered Prexaspes to kill his brother; that it was Patizeithes and his brother Smerdis who had seized power back in Persia, not the real Smerdis. Cambyses charged his nobles with taking the throne back from the usurpers by whatever means necessary, as they were—Herodotus now mentions—Medes. Just as the throne had passed from the Medes to the Persians when Cyrus had led a successful revolt against Astyages, so the Medes now threatened to recapture the reign. The Persians, Cambyses insisted, couldn't let that happen.

Cambyses, during his talk, was appropriately self-effacing. Like Croesus before him, he too had learned from suffering. His murder of his brother had been impetuous, he explained, "for it turns out that it is not in the nature of man to escape what is destined to happen." Cambyses concluded his moving speech—reading it, one can almost forgive him his more unpleasant excesses—by crying again, which got the Persians crying and rending their garments, moved as they were by his tears.

Sometime after his tell-all chat with his minions, the wound in Cambyses' thigh gangrened and he died, having ruled the Empire for about seven and a half years. Fortunately the king's protracted illness had given him a chance to settle things with the nobles, to set them straight about the False Smerdis so they'd be sure to prevent the Medians' grab for power from succeeding. He must have died reasonably confident that things would work out okay as far as the Persian Empire went.

Unfortunately, Cambyses' nobles—for all their garment-rending—didn't believe a word he'd said. As far as they were concerned, the Smerdis who was on the throne back in Susa, Persia's capital, was Cambyses' brother, the son of Cyrus. They figured Cambyses had lied about Smerdis in order to make the Persians rebel against him. As for Prexaspes, who alone knew the truth, he denied having killed the real Smerdis: when the king has just died without issue, it's not safe to admit you're the guy who murdered the rightful heir to the throne.

As we pull back from the scene—Cambyses lying dead from his putrefied thigh—affairs in Persia are looking poorly. There is no legitimate heir, since Cambyses had ordered the death of his brother Smerdis, the only one who could have continued the dynasty begun by Cyrus. An impostor sits in Smerdis' place, and though warned, the Persian nobility aren't buying Cambyses' contention that their new king isn't the real deal. And Prexaspes, the one man who could prove that the Smerdis who sits on the throne is a fake, isn't talking. We'll leave the Persians stewing in their dynastic troubles for a time while we direct our attention to the island of Samos in the Aegean, where another tyrant found that he too was incapable of averting his fate.

CHAPTER FIVE

Meanwhile, Elsewhere in the Mediterranean

The Stories of Polycrates and Periander

625–585	Tyranny of Periander
617–560	Reign of Alyattes
570–526	Reign of Amasis
c. 532–517/6?	Tyranny of Polycrates
525	Spartan campaign against Samos

W HILE CAMBYSES WAS CAMPAIGNING and going crazy in Egypt, the Spartans made an expedition against the island of Samos, off the coast of Asia Minor. Herodotus has mentioned the Spartans before: Croesus made an alliance with them back when he was looking for help against Persia. They're the ones who misunderstood the purport of an oracle they'd received and wound up measuring the fields of the Tegeans with their fetters (1.66–68). About seven years before the Spartans attacked, Polycrates had installed himself as tyrant in Samos. For a time he enjoyed remarkable military success, plundering neighboring states willy-nilly, such that he was the talk of Ionia. But in the world of Herodotus' *History*, undiluted fortune is rarely a good thing.

Polycrates and the Ring (3.39–43)

Now it happened five or six days afterwards that a fisherman caught a fish so large and beautiful that he thought it well deserved to be made a present of to the king. (3.42.1)

Polycrates had a guest-friendship with Amasis, the flatulent king of Egypt who died shortly before Cambyses' invasion. Amasis turns out now to be one of those wise advisors who pop up in Herodotus' *History* from time to time, offering good advice that goes unheeded. Watching Polycrates' string of successes from afar, Amasis grew concerned, and he dashed off a letter that could have come from Solon's own stylus, so wise was it.

The gods, Amasis wrote to Polycrates, are jealous, wont to strike down mortals who are too successful. If someone enjoys unmitigated success, their downfall will likewise be complete. The idea would have been familiar to Herodotus' audience. Croesus springs to mind as an example of a man whose good fortune didn't last, of course. But there are other famous examples of gods punishing mortals whose good fortune or pride exceeded appropriate human limits and thus offended them. Niobe, for example (the daughter of that Tantalus who was punished by being forever "tantalized"—the word finds its origin in his name—by food and drink placed just beyond his grasp), once bragged that she had borne more children—twelve, by some accounts—than the goddess Leto, mother of Artemis and Apollo. This didn't sit well with Leto, who sent her kids down to slaughter Niobe's children. Artemis and Apollo did as they were told, and Niobe, in her grief, was turned to stone (Homer, *Iliad* 24.602–617; Ovid, *Metamorphoses* 6.165–312). Similarly, the satyr Marsyas (satyrs were randy half-horse men—in the Roman tradition they would be portrayed as goatlike) was so confident in his ability as a pipe player that he challenged the god Apollo to a musical contest: whoever pleased the Muses most with their playing would get to do whatever they wanted to the loser. Marsyas lost the duel, and he was flayed alive by Apollo. His skin, Herodotus tells us, hung in the marketplace of Celaenae in Asia Minor (7.26).

The point is that the gods are apt to destroy men whose good fortune catches their attention. So it's better not to do quite so well in life—to fly under the radar, so to speak, and thus live to enjoy one's more moderate successes another day. In his letter to Polycrates, Amasis wrote that in his own life he hoped to alternate success with failure. Since Polycrates' successes had been consistent, Amasis urged him to impose a sort of failure on himself, to diminish his fortune before the gods did it for him. Amasis' advice was two-pronged. Think about what it is that you most value, he wrote, something which, if you lost it, "would cost you most agony of soul." (That translation of the phrase, by David Grene, captures the purport of the original Greek well.) Once you've identified what that thing is, throw it away in a way that is irrevocable, "such that it will no longer come among men." And if that doesn't work, if you're still enjoying one success after another, try again. (Amasis, that is, wanted Polycrates to keep throwing stuff away in order to offset the successes he was enjoying in other respects.)

Polycrates thought Amasis' advice was sound, so he looked for something among his treasures that it would particularly annoy him to lose. He settled on a gold signet ring, and he resolved to throw it away irrevocably, just as Amasis had prescribed. He went out in a penteconter—a big ship manned by some fifty men; this wasn't some rinky-dink operation—and in full view of the crew he threw the ring into the sea. And then he went home and grieved for his loss.

Five or six days later a fisherman caught a really big fish and decided that rather than sell it, he would give it to Polycrates as a gift. Polycrates was pleased with the present and invited the man to come for dinner. We're not told how the evening went, however, because the meal itself was overshadowed by what happened during its preparation: Polycrates' servants cut open the fish and— you guessed it—found the ring the tyrant had thrown into the sea. They were thrilled and brought the ring to Polycrates, but the coincidence made him un- easy: the gods seemed to have had a hand in it. He promptly wrote a letter to Amasis explaining everything that had happened.

Amasis, when he heard the news, severed his guest-friendship with Poly- crates. He recognized at once that, for all his success, Polycrates was doomed, and it was not in Amasis' power to deliver him from his fate. By breaking his ties with the tyrant now, Amasis saved himself the grief he would otherwise have felt when the inevitable downfall happened. (Apparently, Amasis' emo- tional ties were as easily severed as his diplomatic ones.) Polycrates, as far as Amasis was concerned, would go guest-friendless into whatever dark future awaited him, the path to his destruction paved with military success. (In fact, it seems not to have been Amasis who broke off relations with Polycrates, but the reverse. Herodotus' story, which he will have gotten from his Samian sources in the fifth century B.C., hides the uglier truth that Polycrates medized—that is, allied with Persia—and in fact supported Cambyses in his campaign against Amasis [3.44].)

So what went wrong? Why was Polycrates' attempt to avert the jealousy of the gods rejected? Herodotus offers a clue. Amasis had suggested that Poly- crates appease the gods by getting rid of whatever was most important to him, something—and not necessarily a physical object—the loss of which would cause him mental anguish: the verb Herodotus uses here is *algein*. But in seek- ing to comply with his guest-friend's advice, Polycrates went to his store of treasures and selected a physical object the loss of which would "annoy" (*asast-*

hai) him: the verb has changed. Polycrates was indeed fond of his ring: he went home and mourned after he dropped it in the sea. But was it what mattered most to him in all the world? Did its loss cost him "agony of soul"? If the threat from the gods had been more immediate and concrete, if someone had pushed a spear against Polycrates' temple and told him to identify what mattered most to him or be run through, would his signet ring have come to mind? Probably not. Polycrates' attempt to neutralize the jealousy of the gods was half-hearted. His forfeiture of the ring was not sufficiently wrenching to placate the gods, so it was rejected.[1] Polycrates had accomplished nothing with his great show of sacrifice. He was—as Amasis was quick to realize—utterly doomed. We have only to sit back and watch how his inevitable downfall was to play itself out.

The Siege of Samos (3.44–47, 54–56)

Accordingly at this first sitting the Spartans answered them that they had forgotten the first half of their speech, and could make nothing of the remainder. (3.46.1)

Some seven years after Polycrates had first become tyrant in Samos, the Spartans attacked the island, having been called in against Polycrates by a group of Samian exiles. Herodotus tells us that the exiles had gone to Sparta and made a long speech to the authorities there to recruit them to their cause. But the meeting was unproductive. When the exiles finished speaking, the Spartans said they'd already forgotten what the Samians had said at the start of their speech, and they hadn't understood what they'd said at the end. To appreciate why the Spartans reportedly couldn't follow the Samians' argument, you have to understand that they were famous in antiquity for their terseness of expression. They were men of action, not words. Indeed, the word *laconic*—meaning brief and to the point—comes from Laconia, the area of the Greek Peloponnese in which Sparta was the principal city-state. (The Spartans were also regularly referred to as Lacedaemonians.)

The Samian exiles, having gotten nowhere with the Spartans when they harangued them with a lengthy speech, tried a different approach. They met with the Spartans a second time, carrying an empty sack, and made their point more briefly. Gesturing to the sack, one imagines, they said simply, "The sack needs grain." *This* the Spartans understood, even if the significance of the sack isn't immediately obvious to us. Still, the Samians might have expressed themselves even more concisely. The Spartans pointed out that they hadn't needed to use the word *sack* in the sentence: "Needs grain" would have sufficed. But they determined to help the Samians against Polycrates anyway.

The Spartans sailed off to Samos in 525 and laid siege to the island, but after forty days, having failed to accomplish anything, they sailed off, leaving Polycrates as firmly in control as ever. The Samian tyrant's comeuppance would not be delivered by the Spartan horde. It would come instead, some eight years later, at the hands of a Persian.

The Crucifixion of Polycrates (3.120–125)

Then was the dream of the daughter of Polycrates fulfilled; for Polycrates, as he hung upon the cross, and rain fell on him, was washed by Jupiter; and he was anointed by the sun, when his own moisture overspread his body.   (3.125.4)

While Cambyses was in Egypt, the Persian capital Sardis was in the hands of a governor named Oroetes. Around the time that Cambyses became sick, this Oroetes decided to do something wicked. He'd never met Polycrates or been injured by him in any way, but he got it into his head that he wanted to kill the Samian tyrant. Herodotus heard two explanations for Oroetes' bloodlust. Most people believed he had targeted Polycrates after the governor of another Persian province mocked him for not having conquered Samos and added it to the Persian Empire. But according to another account, Oroetes was angry with Polycrates because an ambassador he'd sent to the island had been snubbed by the tyrant. In either case, Oroetes' targeting of Polycrates was unwarranted and consequently shocking.

Oroetes established himself in the city of Magnesia on the Maeander (a winding river whose name gives us the word *meander*), which was on the Ionian mainland across from Samos. He had heard that Polycrates was hoping to expand his rule to other islands in the Aegean and to Ionia itself. For such an enterprise Polycrates would need money, and Oroetes used that to his advantage, baiting his trap with the promise of financial backing. He sent someone to Polycrates with the following message:

Oroetes says this to Polycrates: I understand that you are planning great actions, but you don't have the money needed for what you have in mind. If you act as I suggest you will do right by yourself, and you will also save me. For King Cambyses wishes me dead. This has been made clear to me. Get me and my money safely away from here and you can have some of the money, but let me keep some. With the money you will rule all of Greece. If you don't believe what I'm saying about the money, send someone whom you particularly trust and I'll show it to him.

Polycrates was pleased with Oroetes' offer, and he sent his secretary Maeandrius to Magnesia to make sure the satrap's money was good. Oroetes didn't actually have as much as he'd alleged, but he pulled a Potemkin Village trick on Maeandrius. He filled eight chests with stones but laid gold on top of them so that it looked like he had a substantial treasury. Maeandrius saw the gold and was tricked, and he reported back to Polycrates that Oroetes' money was there for the taking.

Polycrates now determined to travel to Magnesia himself, but the decision was met with horror in some quarters. Oracles were advising him against it and his friends were urging him not to go. His daughter dreamt she saw her father aloft in the air, being bathed by Zeus and anointed by the sun. This vision terrified her, and she begged him not to make the trip, even chasing him down and saying ominous things as he was boarding his ship. Annoyed by her at this point, Polycrates threatened that if he did come back safely she would stay a virgin for a long time. But she said she'd rather be an old maid than lose her father.

Polycrates, of course, was not destined to survive the trip. When he arrived in Magnesia, Oroetes had him killed. We're not told how, but Herodotus underscores the horror of his death. Polycrates "died badly," Herodotus writes, "in a manner not worthy of himself or of his ambitions." And after Oroetes killed him "in a way not worthy to be told," he had Polycrates impaled. The vision Polycrates' daughter had seen was thus realized: skewered on a stake as he was and raised aloft, Polycrates was washed by Zeus when it rained and anointed by the sun when his body yielded moisture in the heat. Just as his onetime guest-friend Amasis had foreseen, Polycrates, for all his previous good fortune and however worthy a man he may have been, came to a horrible end. The story is meant as further proof, as if we needed it, of the veracity of what Herodotus is continually telling us, that fortune does not long reside in the same place.

Periander's Dynastic Troubles (3.48–53, 5.92)

"If there has been a calamity, and thou bearest me ill will on that account,
bethink thee that I too feel it, and am the greatest sufferer, in as much as it was
by me that the deed was done."   (PERIANDER, at 3.52.4)

Another Peloponnesian city-state, Corinth, also took part in the Spartan expedition against Samos in 525, back before Polycrates was killed so dramatically by Oroetes. Herodotus explains at some length what motivated the Corinthians' involvement in the campaign, but he tells the story in reverse chronological order. It will be easier to follow if we start from the beginning.

Between 625 and 585 Periander was the tyrant of Corinth, which lay at the western end of the Isthmus of Corinth, the strip of land that separates central Greece from the Peloponnese. Periander had a wife, Melissa, who was the daughter of Procles, the tyrant of Epidaurus. (Epidaurus was about sixty-five miles to the southeast of Corinth, on the shore of the Saronic Gulf.) The whole thing started because Periander killed Melissa. Herodotus doesn't tell us how, but Diogenes Laertius, writing in the third century A.D., says that Periander either kicked her or threw her down a flight of stairs when she was pregnant. Periander was angry because of false accusations his concubines had made, but he showed his regret for the deed later by having the concubines burnt alive (Diogenes Laertius 1.94).

Herodotus tells another story about Melissa that isn't related to the expedition against Samos but is too good to pass up. Sometime after her death Melissa appeared as a ghost to some messengers Periander had sent to an oracle. But she refused to give them the information they sought because she was cold and naked: her clothes hadn't been burnt with her corpse. The ghost gave the messengers proof that she was indeed Melissa, telling them something only she could know, that after she'd died Periander had "put his loaves into a cold oven," if you catch Herodotus' drift. Periander knew full well what he'd done with his "loaves," so when he heard the report from his messengers, he knew the ghost they'd encountered was the real article. He therefore had all the women of Corinth herded together and stripped, and he burnt their clothes by way of propitiating his dead wife.

But back to the story. Periander and Melissa had two sons, aged seventeen and eighteen. Sometime after their mother's death, the boys went to visit their maternal grandfather in Epidaurus. They weren't aware of their father's role in

Melissa's death, but their grandfather was. When they were about to leave for home again, he hinted at the horrible truth. "Do you know, boys, who killed your mother?" he asked them. The older boy didn't think anything of the remark, but the younger son, Lycophron, put two and two together. When he got back to Corinth he refused to speak to his father. Lycophron must have been particularly good at the silent treatment, because he managed to infuriate Periander, who finally kicked him out of the house.

Periander had his suspicions, but he wasn't sure why his son was so upset with him. So after he kicked Lycophron out, the tyrant quizzed his older son about what had happened in Epidaurus. The older boy was somewhat dull-witted, and he hadn't paid attention to his grandfather's remark at the time. But after a lot of prodding he managed to remember what was said—though he may not have understood its significance—and he told his father. Thus Periander knew that Lycophron knew what he'd done. And, sure, Lycophron might have had a legitimate beef, but that didn't mean Periander was going to get all emotional about it. He was very much an advocate of tough love. Periander not only didn't beg Lycophron for forgiveness and ask him to come back, he made a proclamation that anyone who received his son into their home or even talked to him would be fined, effectively turning Lycophron into an outcast.

After only three days the proclamation had taken its toll. Periander happened to run into Lycophron, and he was unwashed and hungry and generally miserable-looking. Periander took pity on the boy and made a little speech, the purport of which was that Lycophron, now that he knew how much better it was to be a tyrant's son than a beggar, should submit to his father and come back home. But Periander also addressed the topic of his wife's death—if only indirectly, his almost comic egocentrism and tortuous logic sounding like something O. J. Simpson might have come up with. Periander explained that he was the last person Lycophron should be angry at. "For if some misfortune happened in our family," he said, "for which you hold me under suspicion, this misfortune happened to me and I have a greater share of it insofar as I did it."

Lycophron's response in turn was priceless, a typical teenager's retort. Referring to Periander's proclamation outlawing interaction with him, he said only that Periander himself would now have to pay a fine.

Since Lycophron wouldn't come home and wouldn't talk to him, Periander sent him off to Corcyra, an island off the west coast of Greece—modern-day Corfu—which was a Corinthian colony. He also made war on Epidaurus, because he believed his father-in-law Procles was chiefly responsible for the situation. (Note again how Periander fails to accept responsibility for his wife's death and the subsequent breach with his son.) Periander captured Epidaurus and took Procles prisoner, and that's the last we hear of the old man.

Years went by with no improvement in Periander's relationship with Lycophron, but eventually Periander came to realize he could no longer govern Corinth on his own. His older son wasn't up to the task of succeeding him, so Periander sent a messenger to ask Lycophron to return home and take over the tyranny. Lycophron ignored him. Periander then sent another messenger, his daughter, who said what she'd been coached to say, that Lycophron shouldn't allow the rule of Corinth, his patrimony, to fall into anyone else's hands. Lycophron answered that he would not return to Corinth while Periander was still alive. But with a third messenger an agreement was reached: Periander would pack up and move to Corcyra, and Lycophron would move back to Corinth. The two men wouldn't even have to see each other, but Lycophron would succeed his father in the tyranny, and any unpleasantness connected with a change in dynasty would be avoided. It was a good plan, but Periander might have guessed it wouldn't work. His father Cypselus, before he became tyrant of Corinth, had received an oracle from Delphi suggesting that while he and his children would reign in Corinth happily, his children's children would not. Not surprisingly, then, Periander's plans came to nothing. The Corcyraeans, hearing what was in store for them, decided they didn't want Periander living among them, so they nixed the deal by killing Lycophron.

And that's why Periander was upset with the Corcyraeans.

To get back at the Corcyraeans for killing his son, Periander carefully selected three hundred Corcyraean boys, the sons of leading men on the island, and sent them off by sea to Media to be castrated. The ship bearing these unfortunates crossed the Aegean and finally put in at Samos. The Samians, when they found out what the Corinthians were going to do with their cargo, told the boys to take sanctuary in the temple of Artemis, and they subsequently refused to hand the boys over to the Corinthians. The Corinthians tried various means of getting the boys back, including starving them out, but nothing worked, and in the end they gave up and sailed away. When they had gone, the Samians returned the boys intact to Corcyra, having robbed Periander of his due meed of revenge.

And that's why Periander was upset with the Samians and allegedly why the Corinthians joined in the Spartan attack on Samos some decades later.

Arion and the Dolphin (1.23–24)

His strain ended, he flung himself, fully attired as he was, headlong into the sea.

(1.24.5)

We took no note of it at the time, but Herodotus has already mentioned Periander in his *History*, in his first book, while describing the Lydians' siege of Miletus during the reign of Alyattes, Croesus' father. Periander, Herodotus says, helped out Thrasybulus, the tyrant of Miletus, by giving him a heads-up about an oracle Alyattes had received (1.20–22). The reference to Periander is not strictly necessary to the story of the siege, but it does provide an excuse for Herodotus to launch into his story of Arion and the dolphin. The connection between the Arion story and the surrounding narrative is very thin—a "gossamer thread connects this story to its immediate context," as one scholar writes.[2] A lot of ink has been spilt on the question of how the story fits into Herodotus' first book. But for our purposes it makes sense to have delayed the discussion of the digression until now.

Arion was a famous singer and musician who spent much of his time at Periander's court. But wanting to see the world, he traveled from Corinth to Italy and Sicily. He made a lot of money performing there and then decided to head back to Greece. He hired a ship with a Corinthian crew—because he trusted Corinthians particularly—and he set sail from Tarentum, a city in the instep of the Italian boot that had allegedly been founded by Taras, the son of Poseidon. Unfortunately, the Corinthians manning the ship turned out to be less trustworthy than Arion had supposed. When they were out to sea the sailors began plotting to throw Arion overboard and take his money. Arion got wind of this and pleaded with them to take the money and spare his life, but they would not be persuaded. They gave him two options, either to kill himself on board—in which case they'd bury him when they got back to land—or to jump into the water. Neither option was particularly appealing, but Arion opted for the second, asking only that the sailors allow him to give a final performance before he jumped to his death, to sing while decked out in what he usually wore when performing.[3] The sailors were happy to agree. They'd get Arion's money, they'd not have to take the trouble of killing or burying him, and they'd get a free show from a famous singer besides. They retreated while he prepared for his performance, and when he was dressed in all his gear Arion stood on the deck, took out his lyre, and sang the *nomos orthios* to them, a traditional song usually sung in honor of the god Apollo. That done, he leapt into the sea as promised, and the Corinthians sailed off.

But Arion's leap wasn't fatal. A dolphin picked him up and carried him safely to Taenarum, on the southern coast of the Peloponnese, where (although Herodotus doesn't mention this) there was a famous sanctuary of Poseidon. From there he traveled to Corinth, where he told Periander what the Corinthian sailors had done to him. Periander, to his credit, was suspicious, and he detained Arion until the sailors returned: Arion had beaten them back to Greece despite traveling first by dolphin and then overland across the Peloponnese. When the sailors returned, Periander summoned them and asked if they had word of Arion. They said he was presumably safe and sound in Italy, as they'd left him prospering in Tarentum. At that point Arion leapt out of hiding, dressed again in his singing regalia, and put the lie to their story. We don't hear what ultimately happened to the sailors beyond that they were astonished at Arion's appearance and were unable, given this proof, to continue in their falsehood. As for Arion, Herodotus says that when he was at Taenarum he saw a small bronze statue, dedicated by Arion, of a man riding on a dolphin.

Two questions about the Arion story suggest themselves. First, why did Arion, when given the Sophie's Choice of two types of death, elect to jump into the sea? It's ostensibly the worse choice, because it implied that his corpse would remain unburied, and the Greeks took the subject of the proper burial of corpses very seriously. A quick read of Sophocles' tragedy *Antigone* makes this clear enough: it is her uncle Creon's determination to leave the body of one of her brothers unburied that gets Antigone in such a lather early in the play. Nor was this concern with burial merely a tragic topos. Ancient Greek armies took great pains to recover the corpses of their fallen so as to bury them. And according to Aelian's *Varia Historia* (5.14), a miscellany of anecdotes and maxims written in the third century A.D., the Athenians had a law that bid "anyone who happens upon an unburied corpse to throw earth upon it, and to bury it while facing the setting sun." Given that your average Greek would shudder at the prospect of remaining unburied and that burial at sea didn't count as a proper burial, why opt for a watery grave? The second question that leaps to mind is, what was the point of the singing? Did Arion want to put a brave face on things and go out as he'd lived, or was there a more practical reason for his behavior?

Herodotus doesn't make a link between Arion's singing and his subsequent rescue, but the dots are there to connect. Arion performed a song tradition-ally sung to the god Apollo who, as it happens, had been known at least once before to change into a dolphin. *The Homeric Hymn to Pythian Apollo* describes the mythical foundation of Delphi: Apollo, appearing in the form of a dolphin, leapt aboard a Cretan ship and led the sailors to shore; then (after turning first into a star and then into a guy with long hair) he bade the sailors hike up a mountain and build a temple in honor of "Apollo Delphinios"—Apollo the dol-phin god. Delphi, that is, home of the oracle whose advice was sought by kings and paupers throughout the Mediterranean, was the site of a sort of dolphin cult, despite being some two thousand feet above sea level. Given this back-story, Arion's decision to jump into the water makes sense. If he killed himself on the boat, he was a dead man. But if he jumped overboard after singing to Apollo, well, he just might have a shot.

That Apollo was behind Arion's rescue is an attractive suggestion because it was he who would allegedly save Croesus from the pyre a little bit later in Herodotus' *History*. (The Arion story comes at the tail end of his brief account of Croesus' father's reign. So we launch almost immediately after Arion into the story of Croesus, with the dolphin rescue fresh in our minds.) Alternatively, the dolphin may have been sent by Poseidon, the god of the sea. There were other stories in antiquity about people connected to Poseidon being rescued by dol-phins, including Poseidon's son Taras. And Arion was, after all, traveling from one city with a Poseidon connection to another. As Vivienne Gray writes, "It is entirely appropriate that Arion, who began his journey at Taras, a place named for the son of Poseidon, should then land at Poseidon's sanctuary on Taenarum. As Poseidon's agent, the dolphin would naturally bring him to this sanctuary, and Arion followed the usual procedures of the Greeks in his dedication, thank-ing Poseidon for salvation from the sea."[4] But whoever the divine agent may have been, we can, as we've seen, make sense of the choices Arion made by con-necting his singing to his rescue, something that Herodotus himself elected not to do. He may have assumed that an audience of his contemporaries wouldn't need the extra help.

Having caught up with what's been happening elsewhere in the Mediterranean, we can return now to the goings-on among the Persians. When we left them, at the end of chapter four, Persia was in a perilous state: Cambyses was newly dead, a Median imposter was on the throne, and the Persian nobles whom Cambyses had warned about the False Smerdis weren't taking his concerns seriously. Will Prexaspes save the day by telling the world he killed the real Smerdis? Will the Persian nobles realize they've been duped? Or will the throne slip back into Median control with hardly a murmur of protest? Stay tuned for the exciting developments. . . .

CHAPTER SIX

Earless Imposters and Randy Mounts

The Early Reign of Darius the Great

C AMBYSES, AS WE LEARNED IN CHAPTER FOUR, had had his brother Smerdis killed. Alarmed by a dream he'd had that suggested that Smerdis was plotting against him, Cambyses sent his loyal servant Prexaspes to Persia to take Smerdis out. Prexaspes completed his mission secretly, such that very few knew of Smerdis' death. But two Median Magi were in the know, Patizeithes, whom Cambyses had left behind as steward of his household, and Patizeithes' brother Smerdis. Taking advantage of the secrecy surrounding the real Smerdis' death, they somehow installed the Median Smerdis on the throne. This False Smerdis not only shared Cambyses' brother's name, but he looked a lot like him as well—with one big exception, which would prove his undoing.

The Smerdis Affair, Part III: The False Smerdis Revealed (3.67–69)

"If thou findest him to have ears, then believe him to be Smerdis the son of Cyrus, but if he has none, know him for Smerdis the Magian."

(OTANES, at 3.69.3)

The so-called False Smerdis ruled the Persian Empire for about seven months in 522, although for some of that period he was ruling simultaneously with Cambyses. (Cambyses died in July of 522, and Smerdis would rule until

September.) It was Otanes, Herodotus tells us, who was the first to doubt that Smerdis was in fact Cambyses' brother. Otanes was a Persian aristocrat and the father of one of the wives the False Smerdis had inherited from Cambyses when he took over the throne. Otanes sent a message to his daughter, Phaedyme, and asked her whether the man she was sleeping with was in fact Smerdis, the son of Cyrus and brother of Cambyses. Phaedyme, however, couldn't say for sure: she'd never met Smerdis, son of Cyrus, and really had no idea who it was she was married to.

Otanes sent another message to Phaedyme asking her to ask Atossa with whom the two of them were sleeping. Atossa was another wife Smerdis had inherited from Cambyses. But she was also the daughter of Cyrus, sister of Cambyses and Smerdis. If the man she was married to wasn't her brother, Atossa would know. Unfortunately, Phaedyme wasn't able to contact her. Smerdis, when he became king, had scattered his wives so that they were housed separately. When Otanes heard that the king had taken this precaution, he became even more suspicious.

Since they were unable to determine the identity of the king by easier means, Otanes asked his daughter to do some undercover work. When he's in bed with you, he told Phaedyme, and sound asleep, feel his head and see if he's got any ears. If he has ears, he's the real Smerdis. But if he's earless, he's an imposter: Smerdis the Magian, Otanes remembered, had once been punished by Cambyses by having his ears cut off.

Reading this, one is at first surprised that Phaedyme didn't know right away whether her husband had ears. But this wasn't a twenty-first-century marriage between affectionate equals. Smerdis, as we've seen, had multiple wives, and he reportedly bedded them in rotation, presumably one wife per night. So Phaedyme didn't see much of her husband. Beyond that, we must imagine that Smerdis' head was well covered at all times, whether by hair or headgear, and that preliminary embraces of the sort that might have revealed his ears were not the done thing.

Later authors report that Darius, Smerdis' successor, had 360 concubines servicing him, so that each girl's turn would have come roughly once per year (Athenaeus 13.557b). Happily, our Phaedyme didn't have to wait that long to put her father's plan into action. Although she was concerned about what would happen to her if she was caught—certainly Smerdis, if he was in fact earless, would respond violently if he woke up to find her feeling his head—she did as she was told. One can imagine the scene: she waits in bed for the sound of his heavy breathing, her heart pounding in her chest. And finally, in the dead of night, she reaches hesitantly to the mat of hair that frames his face. Careful not to wake him, she slips her hand beneath the tangles, expecting him to jolt awake at her touch. . . .

And nothing bad happens: Smerdis doesn't wake up and grab her hand in the dark. He sleeps peacefully through the night, and Phaedyme lives to see another day and to report to her father in the morning: the man she'd slept with the night before, she told him, did *not* have ears.

The Conspiracy of the Seven and the Fate of Prexaspes (3.70–79)

Such was the end of Prexaspes, a man all his life of high repute among the Persians.   (3.75.3)

When his suspicions about Smerdis were confirmed, Otanes told two trusted friends what he'd discovered, and then the three of them each brought another man into their confidence to form a core group of six conspirators: Otanes, Aspathines, Gobryas, Intaphernes, Megabyzus, and Hydarnes. (Some of the names of the conspirators, though not their number, differ in other sources.) They were joined by a final conspirator, Darius, the son of Hystaspes, who was the current governor of Persia. Darius is the guy Cyrus dreamt about back in 530, shortly before he lost his life fighting against the Massagetae. In the dream Darius had wings that overshadowed both Asia and Europe, a vision Cyrus took to mean that Darius was plotting against him. He wasn't, so far as we know, but with Cyrus' successor dead and an imposter on the throne, the time had come for Darius to enter the world's stage and spread his wings.

The conspirators met and discussed their strategy for disposing of the Magian usurpers, and at once a difference of opinion arose between Darius and Otanes. Otanes preferred a slow approach and suggested they bring in additional conspirators. But Darius wanted them to act immediately. He argued that any delay or addition to their numbers would increase the likelihood that they would be found out. He threatened to turn them in himself, in fact, if they didn't act at once. Otanes asked Darius how he intended to get into the palace to kill the usurpers, since it was well fortified and guarded. Again, Darius advised a bold approach: they would gain entry with a lie, pretending they had a message for the king. It was a simple plan, but Darius couched his suggestion in a lengthy defense of lying: liars are no different from truth tellers, he explained, because both seek to gain advantage from what they say.

It was Gobryas who got the rest of them to go along with Darius' plan. When, he asked, would there be a better time for them to win back the throne or die? They were Persians who were being ruled by a Mede, and an earless one at that! He reminded the other conspirators of Cambyses' deathbed scene, when the king had urged them not to allow the usurper to remain long on the throne. (They knew better now, of course, but at the time no one had believed him.) Gobryas then cast his vote for Darius' plan and urged them not to dissolve their council before they made an attack on the Magi. And so saying, he won the rest of the conspirators over: they would proceed to the palace at once and restore the throne to Persian rule or die in the attempt.

But it so happened that at the very time the seven were conspiring against the Magi, matters in the palace had taken a momentous turn. The False Smerdis and his brother had hoped to gain the support of Prexaspes, Cambyses' old henchman. He would be a valuable ally for a couple of reasons: he was well respected among the Persians, for one thing, but more important, he knew the truth about the Smerdis who now sat on the Persian throne. Then too, Prexaspes must have looked like he'd be amenable to an alliance. Cambyses, after all, had cruelly killed Prexaspes' son, shooting him with an arrow as a sick "proof" of his sanity. The Magi met with Prexaspes, and the thing was agreed: Prexaspes would not tell anyone about the usurpers, and the Magi would reward him with great riches. Smerdis and his brother asked that Prexaspes make an announcement from the palace tower to a throng they would gather for the purpose, that he declare once and for all that the real Smerdis, son of Cyrus and brother of Cambyses, was alive and well and on the Persian throne. Again, Prexaspes was more than happy to comply. He'd been saying as much, anyway, since Cambyses died, seeking to assure the Persians that, despite the old king's rants, Prexaspes had not in fact murdered the royal heir. One more announcement couldn't hurt.

But when Prexaspes mounted the tower before the assembled masses to say his piece, he changed his tune. He made a long speech about the history of the Achaemenid dynasty, tracing the ancestry of the Persian kings from the dynasty's founder, Achaemenes, through Cyrus and Cambyses. And then he told them the truth, that despite his earlier denials, he had in fact obeyed Cambyses' orders and killed Smerdis, the true son of Cyrus. The Smerdis who was on the throne was a usurper, Prexaspes said, and he called upon the Persians to over-throw the Magians and win back the throne. And then Prexaspes threw himself off the tower and fell to his death, "a worthy man all his life," Herodotus tells us, "and he died thus as well."

The seven conspirators were en route to the palace to kill the Magi when they heard what had happened with Prexaspes. They pulled aside for a huddle and debated their plan anew. Again, Otanes and his supporters among the seven were in favor of postponing the assassinations while the situation was so un-certain. And again, Darius wanted the conspirators to act without delay. In the end, the matter was decided by an omen whose interpretation is so obvious that the least superstitious of us might be swayed by it to act: seven pairs of hawks suddenly flew into view, in hot pursuit of two pairs of vultures, whom they tore at and ripped into and generally savaged. The decision was easily made: the conspirators continued on their way.

When they got to the palace, things initially went smoothly. The guards manning the outer doors admitted them without question, the seven being some of Persia's chief men. But the conspirators were stopped in the inner courtyard by a bunch of eunuchs, royal messengers, who wouldn't let them get any closer to the king. And so the seven drew their daggers and stabbed the eunuchs and advanced at a run to the men's quarters.

Smerdis and his brother were in the palace discussing the Prexaspes business when they heard the commotion. One of them—Herodotus doesn't specify which—grabbed a spear and the other his bow. When the seven attacked, the Magus with the spear managed to wound two of his assailants, hitting Aspa-thines in the thigh and stabbing Intaphernes through the eye. (Neither man died from his wounds, but Intaphernes lost his eye.) The other Magus wasn't as successful, however, since his bow was ineffectual at close quarters. He fled into another room and tried to shut the door behind him, but Darius and Gobryas rushed in after him. Gobryas was soon locked in combat with the Magus while Darius stood nearby, hesitating to strike lest he wound his fellow conspirator, but Gobryas urged him to kill both of them if he had to. So Darius struck, and he managed to stab and kill the Magus without injuring Gobryas. The other Magus, too, was killed, though we're not told by whose hand.

Having killed the Magi, the conspirators cut off their heads, and the five of them who weren't injured ran off, heads in hand, to spread the news of what they'd done to the Persians. And while they were at it, they decided to start a massacre. They killed any Magians they came across, and the other Persians joined in the fun, and their killing spree was stopped only by the onset of nightfall: "If night had not fallen," Herodotus writes, "they wouldn't have left any Magians alive." In later years the Persians would celebrate this massacre as a public holiday—*magophonia*, "the murder of the Magians"—a day on which any Magians living in the Empire were wise not to show themselves in public.

Thus were the Magian usurpers routed and the throne returned to Persian control—though which Persian would wind up sitting on it was yet to be determined.

Was the False Smerdis Really False?

Says Darius the King: Afterwards there was a certain man, a Magian, named Gomates. . . . To the state he thus falsely declared: "I am Bardes the son of Cyrus, the brother of Cambyses."

(BEHISTUN INSCRIPTION, column 1 section 11, trans. Henry Rawlinson)

Before we move on to the selection of Smerdis' successor, however, we should consider another issue connected with his brief regime, one that has long exercised ancient historians. That is, was the False Smerdis really an imposter, as Herodotus' account has it?

Herodotus' version of events, to recap, is as follows: While Cambyses was on campaign in Egypt he sent Prexaspes back to Persia to secretly kill his brother, Smerdis, who he thought was plotting against him. Prexaspes did as instructed and returned to Egypt. Later, two Magian brothers who knew about the murder took advantage of the situation and installed one of them on the throne. The usurper, also named Smerdis, not only shared a name with Cambyses' brother but happened to look like the real Smerdis as well, except insofar as his ears had been cut off. It was this usurper whom Darius and his six fellow-conspirators later killed.

Although there are some differences, Herodotus' version agrees in many respects with the official account of the Smerdian business as it was promulgated by Darius. Shortly after he assumed the throne (we'll discuss how he became king in the next section), Darius had a record of his achievements engraved in three languages—Old Persian, Elamite, and Babylonian—on an imposing limestone cliff at Behistun, in what today is western Iran. (The inscription was transcribed and translated in the first half of the nineteenth century by Henry Rawlinson, a British army officer and the older brother of George Rawlinson, whose translation of Herodotus is excerpted in many of the epigraphs found in this book.) According to the Behistun inscription, Cambyses killed his brother before he left for Egypt. (The brother's name in this account is Bardiya: Herodotus transcribed the Iranian name into Greek and came up with "Smerdis.") While Cambyses was in Egypt, a Magian named Gaumata pretended to be Bardiya and took over the empire. Darius later killed Gaumata and took the throne himself.

Prexaspes does not appear in Darius' account, and the murder of Smerdis/Bardiya occurred before the expedition to Egypt rather than during it, as Herodotus has it. Further, the Magian usurper in Darius' version, Gaumata, does not share the name of Cambyses' dead brother. But the accounts of Herodotus and Darius agree on the most important question, that Darius killed an imposter, not the legitimate son of Cyrus and heir to the throne of Persia.

Still, that both Herodotus and Darius agree on this particular is no guarantee that it was true. Darius, new to the kingship and looking to publicize a version of events that emphasized his legitimacy, had every reason to claim the man he'd killed to get to the throne was an imposter. And Herodotus, traveling in Persia about a century later, may simply have adopted the official story of the execution of Smerdis/Bardiya, then massaged the bare facts of that account into a more exciting story that better fit his narrative.

If we accept that Smerdis/Bardiya was an imposter, we must believe that Cambyses had his brother killed—not inherently implausible—and that the murder remained enough of a secret that the imposter could credibly assume the dead man's identity. Then too, the imposter's true identity had to be kept secret for some time, not only from the public but also from people who had been close to the real Smerdis/Bardiya—his hangers-on, his sister Atossa, and so on. According to Herodotus, this cover-up was achieved in part by the remarkable similarity in appearance between the imposter and the real Smerdis. The story is a little hard to swallow, but one can imagine ways that such a deception might be made to work. People who had been close to the son of Cyrus could have been silenced. (In Herodotus' account, remember, the imposter's wives were separated from one another. And Darius says in the Behistun inscription that Gaumata killed many people who had known the real Bardiya.) And the False Smerdis/Bardiya would naturally have limited his public exposure. Still, the story smells fishy.

Alternatively, it's possible that Cambyses never killed his brother and that it was the real Bardiya who assumed power in Persia. Darius, in that case, will have murdered the legitimate heir to the throne, then whitewashed his actions by making up the story we're now familiar with: the secret murder of the real Smerdis/Bardiya and his replacement by an imposter, with Darius cast as the hero who restored the throne to legitimate rule. On the face of it, this understanding of events seems the more likely, but in the end we can't say for sure whether the Smerdis—or Bardiya—Darius killed on his way to power belonged on the Persian throne or not.

The Constitutional Debate (3.80–84)

What government can possibly be better than that of the very best man in the whole state?   (3.82.2)

Five days after their assassination of the Magian usurpers, the conspirators got together and—or so Herodotus would have us believe—debated the merits of various constitutional types. We may doubt that such a debate ever took place, though Herodotus twice insists it is true (3.80.1 and 6.43.3; his insistence is itself unusual). The debate probably tells us more about the conversations going on in the Greek world in Herodotus' day than it does about the politics of late sixth-century Persia. But Herodotus' account of the so-called Constitutional Debate is noteworthy, since it is, as Mogens Hansen writes, "the earliest substantial piece of political theory we have in Greek prose."[1] It is the first explicit appearance of the classification of constitutions into three types—rule of the one, rule of the few, and rule of the many—a system that would be further developed by Aristotle in the fourth century B.C. (The tripartite classification appears some decades before Herodotus, in fact, in a poem by Pindar [*Pythian Odes* 2.86–88], but Herodotus offers the first extended discussion of the typology.)

Three of the seven conspirators spoke in the debate. Otanes—the father of Phaedyme, who had felt for the ears of Smerdis in bed—argued at length that Persia should no longer be a monarchy: the outrages of Cambyses and Smerdis were in themselves an argument against maintaining that type of regime, and absolute power, he explained, breeds excesses even in the best of men. He argued instead in favor of the rule of the many. A democracy—though Otanes doesn't use the word to describe his proposed government—had two advantages over a monarchy: first, under a democracy the Persians would enjoy equality under the law (*isonomia*), and second, a democracy wasn't a monarchy.

That is, it was free of the many negatives that were associated with a monarchy.

Megabyzus spoke next. He agreed with Otanes on the subject of monarchies, but he was no fan of democratic rule. He derided rule by the mob because the many are uneducated and given to outrage. At least a tyrant knows what he's doing, he said. The mob is untrained and acts without intelligent purpose. Megabyzus preferred handing over the rule (*kratos*) of Persia instead to an oligarchy composed of the best men (the *aristoi*, which is the root of our word *aristocracy*), including the conspirators themselves. The best men, he reasoned, would likewise probably be the best in counsel.

Darius was the third to speak. He agreed with Megabyzus on the deficiencies of democratic rule, but he was opposed to instituting an oligarchy. He offered several arguments in favor of maintaining a monarchy in Persia. First, he said, given the best government of all three types—the best monarchy, the best oligarchy, and the best democracy—the monarchy would be superior to the others: since the best single man would inherently be the best, his judgment and administration would naturally be blameless; since he is one man, he would best keep his plans for evil-doers secret. Second, Darius argued, both oligarchies and democracies are inherently flawed systems that ultimately lapse into tyranny. Oligarchies lead inevitably to factional fighting and murder, and from that despotism arises. In democracies, on the other hand, the corrupt conspire together in running affairs until someone, some single man, steps forward to put a stop to it. And there again you have your despot. Finally, Darius argued that the Persians should keep the type of government they had inherited from their ancestors: they had been freed from the rule of the Medes by a single man, Cyrus; they should likewise maintain their sovereignty through a single man.

In the end, Darius' speech proved the most persuasive, and the four conspirators who had not spoken gave their support to his position. The decision thus made, Otanes, who had advocated establishing a democracy, addressed the group for a second time. It was clear that one of the conspirators would wind up becoming king, he said, however that man should be selected. But Otanes wanted neither to rule nor to be ruled. He proposed that he withdraw from the running on the condition that he and his descendants not be ruled by any of the other conspirators. The other six agreed to the plan, and Otanes thenceforth enjoyed a singular position in Persian society. Even in Herodotus' day, he tells us, Otanes' household was the only free one in Persia, his descendants submitting to the authority of the state only insofar as they wished (although they did not transgress the laws of the Persians).

Before one of them was elevated to the kingship, the conspirators also established some ground rules for the future relationship between the king and the rest of the group. First, they decided that, whoever the king might be, the other conspirators would be allowed to enter the palace without formal announcement *unless* the king happened to be sleeping with a woman at the time. (It is somehow very easy to imagine this conversation as a Monty Python sketch, with the troop members cackling out what-ifs—What if the king's taking a bath, can we come in then?—until they agree that the king was not to be disturbed during intercourse.) The seven also decided that the king would not be allowed to marry outside of the families of the seven conspirators.

All this done, it remained only to decide which of them would rule.

The Neighs Have It (3.85–87)

They say that in the morning he stroked the mare with his hand, which he then
hid in his trousers until the sun rose and the horses were about to start, when
he suddenly drew his hand forth and put it to the nostrils of his master's horse,
which immediately snorted and neighed.   (3.87)

The conspirators settled on a strange means of selecting which of them would sit on the throne. They decided they would all get on their horses before daybreak and ride outside of the city. The one whose horse was the first to whinny as the sun rose would be the next king of Persia. Now, Darius was no dummy. He had agreed with the others to leave the selection of the new king up to the horses—for all we know, it was Darius' idea—but he wasn't above giving fate a hand in making the right decision. He spoke to his groom, Oebares, explaining how the selection of the king was to proceed, and he asked Oebares if he knew some trick that would ensure Darius' horse neighed first the next morning.

Oebares was a crafty fellow and knew just what to do. He tied up a mare at a spot the six would-be kings would pass in the morning, and he brought Darius' horse there and let him mount her. When the conspirators went on their morning ride and came to the site of the previous evening's debauch, Darius' horse rushed forward and neighed. According to another account Herodotus mentions, Oebares was actually present in the morning, standing alongside Darius and his horse at sunrise. He had earlier rubbed his hand around the mare's privy parts, and at just the right moment he took his hand from his pocket and let Darius' horse smell it, which is what prompted the neighing. But however the horse was made to cooperate, its neigh was accompanied by a second omen. At that very moment there was a flash of lightning in the cloudless sky and a roll of thunder, as if the gods were confirming the sign that Darius had brought about through trickery. And that was enough. The other conspirators leapt off their horses and made obeisance to their new king.

Cannibals, Flying Snakes, and Gold-Digging Ants: The State of the Empire (3.88–117)

Here, in this desert, there live amid the sand great ants, in size somewhat less than dogs, but bigger than foxes.   (3.102.2)

Herodotus says that one of the first things Darius did after coming to power was to set up a monument. On it was an engraving of a man on a horse and an inscription: "Darius, the son of Hystaspes, with the excellence of his horse . . . and of his groom Oebares, won the Persian kingship." The relief hasn't survived, if it ever existed, and Darius does not mention Oebares' alleged role in his acquisition of power in the Behistun inscription. Instead, Darius attributes his royal authority to the patronage of the god Ahura-Mazda and to his own distinguished heritage. There were eight kings among his ancestors, he says in the inscription, but he doesn't do us the favor of naming them, and it's not clear who they can have been. We know that his father and grandfather were not kings. Darius says that his great-great-grandfather was a certain Teispes, and we know that Cyrus had a great-grandfather named Teispes, but it's not clear if they were the same man. So when Darius alleges that he gained the throne by virtue of his lineage, it seems that he's not being entirely truthful.

Whatever the basis of his power, however, Darius was well and truly king as of 521, and he set about buttressing his royal credentials with a series of marriages. He married Atossa, the daughter of Cyrus, who had previously been married to her brother Cambyses and to the Magian Smerdis; he married Artystone, another daughter of Cyrus; he married Parmys, who was the daughter of the real Smerdis and thus the granddaughter of Cyrus; and he married Phaedyme, the daughter of Otanes, who had been married to both Cambyses and the False Smerdis.

Having settled all this at home, Darius set about organizing the empire into twenty satrapies, or provinces. Herodotus describes the organization of the empire at some length, including detailed information about each province's annual contribution in taxes. For our purposes, much of Herodotus' discussion can be ignored, but he does include a few items of interest. For example, he mentions a nomadic Indian tribe called the Padaei who, like the Massagetae (1.216), would kill and eat anyone among them who became sick or was very old. This makes a lot of sense from a reduce-reuse-recycle standpoint: no point in letting good meat go bad if the guy's on his way out anyway. What's funny, though, is that if the person who was about to be eaten claimed he wasn't sick, his fellow Padaei would ignore him and eat him anyway. This was a society in which you didn't dare sneeze in public, lest the kinfolk show up with lobster bibs tied around their necks.

The Padaei and other Indians were also in the habit of copulating in public, like animals. Herodotus says that "their semen, which they ejaculate into their women, is not white like that of all other men but black, like their skin. The Ethiopians likewise have black semen." It's not clear where our historian got this idea—firsthand knowledge would seem to be ruled out—but to his credit Aristotle pooh-poohed the report about a century later:

> All blooded animals emit semen. We shall state elsewhere what is its contribution to generation, and the method of it. For his size, man emits more than any animal. The semen of hairy animals is sticky, but that of others is not. In all animals it is white. Herodotus is mistaken when he writes that the Ethiopians emit black semen. (*History of Animals* 523a17, trans. A. L. Peck)

Herodotus writes about how another Indian people, the Pactyes, used a fabulous animal to help them find gold in what would now be the upper Indus area of northern Pakistan. There were ants there, Herodotus explains, who were a bit bigger than foxes. (Bigger than foxes and smaller than dogs, he says, not very helpfully, since the upper size limit will depend on what kind of dog one has in mind.) These animals burrowed underground, and in digging out their homes they threw up sand that had gold in it. The Pactyes would collect this gold-infused sand during the hottest time of the day, when the animals were likely to be underground. It was necessary to avoid the gold-digging ants, Herodotus says, because they were vicious. If they smelled the Indians or their camels they would chase after them, and they were strong enough to take out both the men and the camels they rode in on if they caught up to them.

The story of the gold-digging ants of India was repeated and embellished in antiquity. By the third century A.D. the creatures had become lion-like animals, with gold-scooping talons (Solinus, *De Mirabilibus Mundi* 30.23), or they were like griffins, ant-lions with wings and an eagle's beak (Aelian, *De Natura Animalium* 4.27). Herodotus' description wasn't quite so fantastic, but his account of the ants is the sort of thing that gave him a reputation as a teller of tall tales.[2] The story might never have seemed so incredible and been embellished so dramatically, however, if Herodotus had not described the animals as "ants." If he had written instead that they were dog-sized animals who threw up gold-infused sand as they burrowed and were fiercely protective of their homes, the passage would hardly have attracted notice. In modern times scholars have attempted to identify the animals. French ethnologist Michel Peissel, for example, has argued that Herodotus' "ant" was a mistranslation of an old Persian word for "marmot." He suggests that the animals Herodotus describes were in fact marmots, and he's located a species of the rodent in the Dansar Plain of modern Pakistan that seems to fit the bill. These modern marmots throw up gold-rich sand as they burrow, and like Herodotus' Pactyes the villagers living nearby have historically collected the gold that the animals bring to the surface. Herodotus, it turns out, may not have been so credulous after all.

In Arabia, Herodotus says, the frankincense bushes are guarded by dappled, winged snakes, animals that migrate to Egypt every spring and are eaten in great numbers there by ibises. Herodotus says he saw piles of their bones in Egypt, near where the ibises catch them (2.75). (Aelian, writing in the second century A.D. but citing an earlier source, adds the detail that the flying snakes appeared only by night and emitted urine that would produce a festering wound on any body with which it came into contact [*De Natura Animalium* 16.41].) Herodotus conjectures that the number of winged snakes worldwide is relatively low (probably why you haven't seen one) because the female kills the male during intercourse and the babies eat their way out of their mother's womb by way of being born, killing her in the process. It's been suggested, however, that the snakes Herodotus is describing weren't snakes at all but insects, specifically locusts, which have plagued Egypt intermittently since Biblical times. The creatures' sloughed-off exoskeletons, "the exuviae of the last pupal stage of the locust before it emerged as the perfect imago," may have suggested to locals that the creatures were eaten away from the inside, as Herodotus suggests.[3]

Having discussed these and other wonders from the farthest reaches of the world, Herodotus returns to Persia proper, closing off his tour with a discussion of more banal matters, Darius' administration of water resources. But the subject need not concern us here. We turn next to the death of Intaphernes, one of Darius' co-conspirators.

Intaphernes and His Wife (3.118–119)

The doorkeeper, however, and the chief usher forbade his entrance, since the
king, they said, was with his wife.   (3.118.1)

The trouble started when Intaphernes showed up at the palace one day to talk
to Darius. As one of the seven conspirators, he had the right to enter without
announcing himself unless the king was having sex with a woman. But as it happened Darius *was* with a woman when Intaphernes showed up. Two of Darius'
lackeys told Intaphernes as much, but he didn't believe them. In his anger at
being lied to, as he thought, he sliced off their ears and noses, threaded them
through his horse's bridle, wrapped the bridle around their necks, and released
them. The two men promptly ran off to complain to Darius about the humiliat-
ing treatment they'd suffered.

Intaphernes had not come up with this bizarre form of abuse on his own.
Cutting off the nose and ears was a standard punishment for rebels in Persia.
Darius mentions inflicting the punishment himself several times in his Behistun
inscription. The Egyptian king Apries likewise sliced off the nose and ears of
his messenger, Paterbemis, when he failed to bring the revolutionary Amasis
back with him as ordered. The business of tying the severed appendages on a
string and wrapping it around the victim was also not unheard of in antiquity.
It's reminiscent of the practice of *maschalismos*, the ritual severing of a corpse's
extremities, which might then be strung together and tied around the neck and
under the armpits of the body. The idea was to hamstring the corpse—particularly the corpse of someone wrongfully killed—so that its ghost would be
unable to take vengeance on the living. The practice was, as one writer puts
it, "the fifth-century equivalent of being staked and wreathed with garlic."[4]
Most famously, Clytemnestra reportedly did this to her husband Agamemnon's
corpse after she'd murdered him (Aeschylus, *Libation Bearers* 439–443).

When Darius heard what had happened, he immediately suspected that Intaphernes' action was the first step in a coup against him and that Intaphernes
had acted at the behest of or with the approval of the other conspirators. He
brought in the others and questioned them individually, but in the end he was
satisfied that Intaphernes had acted alone. Darius then had Intaphernes and the
rest of his family—though apparently just the males—arrested and imprisoned
pending their execution.

After the men in her family were arrested, Intaphernes' wife went regularly to Darius' door and cried and lamented, day after day, until finally Darius broke down and made her an offer. He sent a messenger to the woman to say she could save one member of her family: he would release whomever she selected. The woman gave the matter some thought. Intaphernes was in custody, of course, but also her sons and a brother. Finally she announced her decision: "If the king offers the life of one, I choose out of all of them my brother."

When Darius heard the woman's answer he was as surprised by it as you probably are. He sent another messenger to ask her to explain her choice: "The king asks you why you have abandoned your husband and sons and chosen that your brother survive; he is less close to you than your children and less dear than your husband." The woman's response is striking: "My Lord," she said, "I could have another husband, if the god wills it, and other children, if I lose these. But as my mother and father are no longer alive, it is not possible for me to have another brother." Darius was impressed by her argumentation, and by way of rewarding her for it, he released not only her brother but also her oldest son. Intaphernes and the rest of the woman's male relatives were put to death.

While it's not impossible for individuals or societies to favor fraternal connections over those between a mother and her children or a wife and her husband, the choice made by Intaphernes' wife, given Darius' reaction to it, does not seem to have been a natural one in her world. She had approached the problem posed by the king with cold logic, using her head instead of her heart, as we—and Darius—had expected. In her clinical worldview, "husband" and "child" were job descriptions, positions that could be filled by others, should those currently holding the titles not work out. The same idea is expressed earlier in Herodotus' *History*: a number of Egyptians who were in revolt from their king were urged by him not to desert their wives and children. One of them pointed to his penis in response and said that wherever *that* went, he'd have a wife and kids (2.30.4).

Intaphernes' wife had impressed the king with her choice. She also apparently impressed Herodotus' contemporary Sophocles, the tragic playwright, who adopted her reasoning for use in his play *Antigone*. (Or he may have adopted it: some scholars argue that the passage in question was not written by Sophocles but was a later interpolation, a note that was accidentally inserted into the text at some point when the manuscript was being copied by a scribe.) Antigone was the daughter of Oedipus and his mother Jocasta, the king and queen of Thebes. (So Jocasta was Antigone's mother and grandmother, and Oedipus was his own step-father, and Antigone was Oedipus' daughter and half-sister, and so on.)

As we saw already in chapter two, Oedipus and his mother had gotten married and had children without being aware of their biological connection. When the truth finally came out—the revelation and its immediate consequences are the subject of Sophocles' play *Oedipus Rex*—things rapidly went downhill: Jocasta killed herself, and Oedipus blinded himself and was banished from Thebes. He lived miserably for the rest of his life. (After his death he turned into a sort of divinity, with the power to bring good fortune to the country where his corpse lay, so it wasn't all bad.) In the end, Antigone was left without parents, though she did have two brothers—Polynices and Eteocles—and a sister. Before the action of *Antigone* begins, however, Polynices and Eteocles have both been killed in battle. Polynices had marched on Thebes in an attempt to wrest power from his brother. After their deaths Antigone's Uncle Creon became the new king of Thebes. He gave Eteocles a fitting burial but declared that Polynices, as a traitor to Thebes, would lie unburied.

We mentioned in the last chapter that the Greeks were very keen on proper burials. Second to none in her respect for burial rights, Antigone disobeyed Creon's order and "buried" her brother Polynices by tossing some dirt on his corpse, an act that landed her in serious trouble. Eventually Creon ordered that she be walled up in a cave. Still, Antigone defended her actions, explaining herself using the argument Sophocles had borrowed from Herodotus: I never would have defied the law, she says, if it had been my child or my husband who'd died. "I could have another husband, if mine died, and a child from another man, if I lost the one I had. But with my mother and father both lying in Hades, a brother could never burst forth into life" (Sophocles, *Antigone* 908–912). Sophocles, however, has transferred the Herodotean argument to a very different situation. Intaphernes' wife had a real choice to make among living relatives—a husband and sons and a brother. Since she was tasked with deciding which of her relatives would live, it made sense for her to rank them by some criteria as part of her selection process. Her method may have been coldly calculating, but it was not unreasonable.

Antigone, on the other hand, is considering whether she would bury a dead child or husband in defiance of the state in the same way that she had elected to bury her brother. But the situation she describes is entirely hypothetical: she has not been made to decide between burying one or another family member, and she doesn't have a husband or children. Still, Antigone's use of the argument makes a sort of sense. By burying her brother, she has in effect made the same choice that Intaphernes' wife made: she has preferred her brother—or the act of burying her brother—to the husband and children she might have had if she had not chosen to defy the law. Whether or not her brother was replaceable does not, on the face of it, have anything to do with her decision to bury him: he was lost to her whether she buried him or not. But that he was irreplaceable can explain why he was so dear to her, and thus why she made the decision she did.[5]

Democedes of Croton (3.129–138)

These were the first Persians who ever came from Asia to Greece; and they were sent to spy out the land for the reason which I have before mentioned.

(3.138.4)

The Persian satrap Oroetes, who had killed Polycrates of Samos pretty much just to watch him die, was executed by order of Darius in about 516 (3.126–128). Some time later, after the satrap's possessions (including his slaves) had been brought to Darius' court in Susa, the king jumped off his horse and twisted his ankle rather badly. The Egyptian doctors in his retinue tried treating it, but they weren't any help, and after a week Darius was no better off than before. He heard about a Greek doctor named Democedes who had been with Oroetes in Sardis and was reportedly very skilled. Darius' men tracked Democedes down, locating him among the slaves that had been taken from Oroetes, and brought him to the king in rags and chains.

Democedes had not started out as a slave. He was originally from the Greek city of Croton in Italy (in the instep of the Italian boot), and he had practiced also in Athens and Aegina (an island in the Saronic Gulf, southwest of Athens). Polycrates of Samos had then hired him, so he sailed east to work with the tyrant. But when Oroetes killed Polycrates he enslaved the foreigners in Samos (3.125), and Democedes' days as a free, itinerant professional were over. Democedes had been caught up in the political events of the day and had lost his freedom through no fault of his own. But he still harbored some hope of one day making it back to Greece.

When Democedes was brought to see the king and Darius asked him whether he knew about medicine, he lied. If he wound up serving Darius as a doctor, he figured, he'd never see Greece again. It wasn't an unreasonable fear: we mentioned in chapter four the Egyptian eye doctor who was stuck in Persia indefinitely after treating Cyrus. But Darius had ways of making people talk.

When he ordered his men to get the whips and goads ready, Democedes backed down and admitted that maybe he knew a little something about medicine after all, since he had once been associated with a doctor. It was enough. Darius submitted to Democedes' care, and after a while he was completely cured. By way of reward Darius gave the doctor a gift, ill conceived, perhaps, if surely valuable: a pair of gold fetters. Darius' wives, too, plied Democedes with bowls filled with gold coins. Indeed, after healing Darius, Democedes' position was enviable. He had a huge house, and he ate at the royal table, and he had influence at court: Darius was going to impale the Egyptian doctors who had failed to cure him, and Democedes convinced him to let them live. Democedes was given everything he could possibly want, in fact—except his freedom.

Later, Darius' wife Atossa came to Democedes with a problem. She had some kind of growth on her breast that had burst and spread. (It won't have been cancer, but some kind of benign tumor or mastitis.) Democedes said that he would cure it, but he made her swear that she would do him a favor in return (though nothing dishonorable). She did so, and after Democedes cured her Atossa held up her end of the bargain. She talked to her husband one night, as Democedes had asked, and suggested that it was high time he tried to conquer somebody. There were good reasons to do it, she said: it would keep the Persians busy; he would seem virile to his people; and if he was going to do it, he should do it sooner rather than later, while he was still young. Darius had been thinking along these lines himself, and he told her he had it in mind to attack the Scythians, who lived in Europe, to the north of the Black Sea. But Atossa pooh-poohed the suggestion, again in accordance with Democedes' instructions. The Scythians could wait, she said. Better to attack Greece first: she could get some Greek servants out of the deal—warfare was a great source of slave labor—and their resident doctor, Democedes, could provide Darius with crucial intel about his homeland. Atossa's suggestion made sense to Darius, and he agreed to send some spies and Democedes himself over to Greece to scope out the situation.

Darius acted quickly. The next day he summoned fifteen Persian nobles and told them to sail along the coast of Greece with Democedes, and he made it very clear that they were not to allow the doctor to escape. Darius summoned Democedes as well and told him to give the Persians a tour of Greece, but by all means to return again to Persia. The doctor pretended that escape was the furthest thing from his mind.

Democedes and the Persians sailed around as ordered, surveying the coast and making maps. Eventually they landed at Tarentum in Italy, the city from which Arion is said to have set sail on his return trip to Greece. The tyrant of the place, Aristophilides, hobbled their ships by removing their rudders—rather like swiping someone's distributor cap nowadays—and he arrested the Persians, alleging that they were spies (which, of course, they were, even if they weren't necessarily spying on him). It's not clear from Herodotus' Greek text whether Aristophilides detained the Persians in order to give Democedes a chance to escape or if Democedes was merely the lucky beneficiary of his act: Herodotus' version is ambiguous, stating that Aristophilides acted "to the advantage" of Democedes. But wittingly or no, Aristophilides provided Democedes with a window of opportunity, and the doctor grabbed it. He hightailed it back to his hometown of Croton, across the instep of the Italian boot from Tarentum. Afterwards, Aristophilides released the Persians and gave them back their rudders.

After their release, the Persians tracked Democedes down in Croton. (It was a good bet he'd head home after his escape.) They grabbed him and tried to drag him back to their ship, but some of the Greeks who witnessed the incident prevented them, and the Persians were forced to leave Italy without their man. They can't have been looking forward to telling Darius what happened. Their king was the sort of guy, after all, who would impale a doctor for failing to mend his ankle. But their reckoning with Darius was delayed. Shortly after they'd set sail, they were shipwrecked, sold into slavery, and finally ransomed by a guy who brought them back to Persia in the hope of earning a reward. Herodotus is silent about what happened to them after that. Perhaps their trials on the return trip will have counted as sufficient penalty for their failure to guard the doctor adequately.

Fashion and the Fall of Samos (3.139–149)

"Give me Samos, I beg; but give it unharmed, with no bloodshed—no leading into captivity." (SYLOSON, at 3.140.5)

Back before Darius was king, when he was serving in Egypt as one of Cambyses' spearmen, he went shopping one day in the marketplace in Memphis. While he was there he saw a man by the name of Syloson who was wearing a red cloak Darius just *had* to have. He approached Syloson and offered to buy the cloak off him, but Syloson didn't want to sell it. Instead—in a moment of divinely inspired fortune, as Herodotus describes it—Syloson decided to give the cloak to Darius. Darius took the cloak and went away happy, and Syloson went away thinking he'd been a bit foolish.

Time passed and Cambyses died and Darius took the Persian throne, and when Syloson realized who the king was, suddenly his impulsive generosity didn't seem so foolish anymore. Syloson made his way to Darius' court at Susa and announced himself to the gatekeeper as a benefactor of the king. The gatekeeper announced Syloson to the king in the same terms, surprising Darius because he wasn't aware of having any Greek benefactors. But Syloson reminded Darius of the gift of his cloak back in Egypt. Darius, remembering the incident, was extremely grateful to Syloson, who had done him this kindness when he was a nobody, and he offered Syloson countless sums of gold and silver by way of reward.

Now, it so happened that Syloson wasn't exactly a nobody himself. He was the younger brother of the Samian tyrant Polycrates. For a short time at the beginning of his tyranny Polycrates had shared power with his brothers, but finally he'd killed one of them and forced Syloson into exile. What Syloson wanted from Darius, far more than gold and silver, was to be restored to the Samian tyranny. He asked Darius to give him his country back, with the one proviso that his restitution not result in any bloodshed or enslavements.

After Polycrates was so dramatically executed by the Persian satrap Oroetes, the tyranny had passed to Maeandrius, Polycrates' old secretary: Maeandrius was the guy who had been tricked into reporting to Polycrates that Oroetes had chests full of gold on hand. (You'd be forgiven for thinking there was something fishy about Maeandrius' sudden rise to power after convincing Polycrates that Oroetes was on the up and up: there was a tradition hostile to Maeandrius in antiquity that claimed he had in fact betrayed Polycrates to Oroetes [Lucian, *Charon* 14].)

In reintroducing Maeandrius to his readers, Herodotus writes, "It was not granted to him, who wished to be the most just of men, to be [what he wished]"—a pithy, rather sad epitaph. Shortly after coming to power, Maeandrius set up an altar to Zeus the Liberator, a move that suggests he was announcing a new era of freedom for Samos after Polycrates' tyranny. He also proposed that the Samian political system be democratized. He had not liked the fact that Polycrates ruled over men who were as good as he was, and he didn't want to head that sort of government himself. In return for stepping down from power, Maeandrius asked only that the Samians give him six talents of Polycrates' money—a small fortune—and that the priesthood of Zeus the Liberator be given to him and his descendants in perpetuity.

The offer was not well received. A man named Telesarchus stood up and challenged Maeandrius' authority, saying he was baseborn and unworthy to rule and demanding that he give an account of the money he'd had in his control. Telesarchus' opposition made the situation clear to Maeandrius: the democratic reforms he had in mind would not work, and if he stepped down from the tyranny, someone else would step in to fill the power vacuum. Maeandrius didn't want that to happen, so in order to save Samos from someone else's tyranny, he resolved to be tyrant himself.

It's not clear whether Maeandrius had been serious about establishing a democracy on Samos, but in any case he gave up on the idea and embraced autocratic rule awfully quickly. Sometime after this meeting he had his opponents among the citizenry imprisoned, and while they were in prison he fell sick. Maeandrius' brother Lycaretus, thinking the tyrant was going to die and hoping to take his place, ordered that the prisoners be executed, thus removing an obstacle to his own rise to power when the time came.

This was the situation in Samos when Syloson asked Darius to restore him to the Samian tyranny. Darius agreed to send an expedition to Samos under the leadership of Otanes, who was told to do as Syloson wished, that is, to restore Syloson without resorting to bloodshed or enslavements. Otanes, you'll remember, was one of the seven conspirators. Indeed, he was the first conspirator: he had brought friends in with him to form a core group of six, to which Darius was finally added as the seventh. After the execution of the False Smerdis, when the conspirators were considering the form Persia's government should take, Otanes had argued for a democracy. And when it was decided that Persia would remain a monarchy, Otanes had removed himself from consideration for the kingship. In other words, Otanes was similar to Maeandrius in that both had advocated the democratization of their respective countries. But when democracy had proved unworkable in each case, Otanes had withdrawn from power, whereas Maeandrius had clung to it.

When the Persians got to Samos, they met with no resistance whatever. Maeandrius agreed to surrender the island to them and evacuate under truce. But then he changed his mind. Maeandrius had another brother, Charilaus, who was reportedly half-mad and was being held in a dungeon for some offense Herodotus doesn't name. Charilaus heard about what was going on in Samos, and, peeking out from a hole in his dungeon, he was able to see some Persians sitting around unmolested, which irked him. He demanded that his brother speak to him, and when Maeandrius complied he raved about the situation: here he was rotting in a dungeon, while the Persians could just walk in and take Samos without anyone raising a finger against them. Charilaus asked that Maeandrius give him an army of mercenaries. Maeandrius could leave if he wanted to: Charilaus would take care of the Persians himself.

Maeandrius agreed to do as Charilaus asked. Herodotus says he didn't really expect his brother to beat the Persians. Instead, he wanted Samos to be weakened, and he wanted the Persians to be angry with the Samians, so that Syloson's takeover would not be a tidy affair. Herodotus' explanation doesn't make a lot of sense, but neither does Maeandrius' decision to give his brother what he wanted. At any rate, Maeandrius gave Charilaus his army, and he himself fled Samos, slipping out a secret passageway that led from the citadel to the sea. He made his way to Sparta, probably wanting the Spartans to help restore him to power, but they eventually kicked him out after he tried to bribe the Spartan king, Cleomenes. That's the last we hear of him.

Charilaus, meanwhile, led his army against the Persians and enjoyed some success, but in the end the Persians overwhelmed the Samians and drove them back into the citadel. The Persians had gained the upper hand quickly enough, but Otanes was angry about the losses the Samians had inflicted on his army, and with good reason: the Persians hadn't been expecting an attack, since Maeandrius had already agreed to terms. Because he was angry, Otanes—who had been ordered by Darius not to kill or enslave anyone, and who was opposed to monarchy in part because unchecked power leads kings to do outrageous things like killing people without trial (3.80)—ordered his men to slaughter the Samians, any man or child they could get their hands on (women seem to have been given a free pass). The Persians did so with gusto, cutting down anyone they found, even if they had taken refuge in a sacred place.

Later on, the Persians supposedly depopulated the island completely, "trawling it with a net," as Herodotus describes it: imagine an army of men walking at arm's length from one another, sweeping up the population, like searchers combing an area for remains during a crime scene investigation. Thus Syloson's impulsive gift of a cloak to the man who would be king of Persia led to the slaughter of innocents and the desolation of a countryside. Darius rewarded Syloson's generosity with an island that was bereft of men.

Later yet, the Persians resettled Samos with the help of Otanes, who had proved under pressure of circumstances to be as liable as the most brutal tyrant to engage in indiscriminate slaughter. Otanes was prompted to undertake the repopulation of Samos by divine signs—a dream and some unspecified disease of the genitals. Apparently, these indicated to him or perhaps to his soothsayers that in ordering the slaughter of the Samians (or possibly in condoning the murder of people who had taken refuge in sacred spaces), he had committed a fault.

The Babylonian Revolt (3.150–160)

"Till mules foal ye will not take our city."

(A BABYLONIAN SOLDIER, at 3.151.2)

While all this was going on in Samos, and even before that, before Darius became king, the Babylonians had been secretly preparing to revolt from Persia.[6] The Babylonians were able to make preparations without anyone noticing for some time, but when it became obvious that they were up to something, they acted with more dispatch. Each man set aside his mother (Herodotus may mean that the mothers were sent away from Babylon) and selected some other woman from his family who would serve as bread maker. The rest of the women were herded together and strangled to death so they wouldn't be a drain on the food supply should it come down to a siege. (It's difficult to imagine a mass execution by strangulation. I suppose the victims would have to be inordinately cooperative for it to go at all smoothly.)

Darius duly laid siege, but the Babylonians made light of his efforts from their walls, dancing around and mocking the Persians. In particular, one of the Babylonians called out that the Persians would only take Babylon "when mules bear young." It's an expression that meant the same thing—or was intended to mean the same thing—as our "when pigs fly," but there's a big difference between the two: pigs really can't fly, but mules—very, very rarely—can foal. (A mule gave birth to a foal in Colbran, Colorado, in April of 2007, for example. The foal's parentage was confirmed with genetic testing.)[7] Twenty months after the siege of Babylon had begun, Zopyrus—the son of Megabyzus, one of the seven conspirators—was astonished to learn that one of his mules had indeed given birth, and it got him thinking: if, as that Babylonian had said, the city would be taken only when a mule foals, and since Zopyrus' mule had now done just that, then it followed logically that. . . .

Excited at the implications of the birth, which he took to be a divine omen,

Zopyrus went to Darius and asked if he was really serious about capturing Babylon. You'd think, twenty months in, that he wouldn't need to ask, but presumably he wanted to be quite sure that what he was about to do was worth the trouble. Darius assured Zopyrus that he was very keen on capturing Babylon, and Zopyrus went off and put his plan into action: he cut off his nose and ears, chopped off his hair, and whipped himself. Then he reported back to Darius.

Darius was appalled when he saw Zopyrus, thinking that someone else had done this to him. But Zopyrus explained that the self-mutilation was part of his plan to take Babylon: he intended to go over to the Babylonians, posing as a deserter who had been cruelly disfigured by Darius. Since he'd been so abused by his king, the Babylonians would trust him and, Zopyrus assumed, put him in charge of an army. He'd gain their trust further with a series of increasingly impressive military successes that would, however, be prearranged between him and Darius. Ten days after Zopyrus' arrival in Babylon he would defeat an army of one thousand expendable, lightly armed Persians. A week after that he would defeat an army of two thousand. Twenty days after that, an army of four thousand. At that point the Babylonians would trust Zopyrus completely and would rely on him so extensively that he'd be given supreme command. And then Zopyrus would open the gates of Babylon.

On the face of it, Zopyrus' plan seems impossibly optimistic. Its success depends on too many things happening just so for it to be likely to succeed. But in the event, it worked. Zopyrus told the Babylonians that Darius had punished him for saying the Persians had no hope of capturing Babylon. (That must have been a crowd pleaser.) And as he'd predicted, Zopyrus was given an army when he asked for it. He led the Babylonians against the Persians three times—killing all or most of the seven thousand expendable souls Darius had abandoned as cannon fodder. Finally, when Darius made an assault on the walls, Zopyrus threw open the gates. The Persians rushed in, and Babylon was taken for the second time.

After the siege, Darius pulled down the walls of Babylon and impaled three thousand of its leading citizens. Then, concerned about repopulating the city after so many of its women had been strangled, he ordered the surrounding peoples to contribute prescribed numbers of women to join its population. Zopyrus, meanwhile, was greatly honored for his sacrifices, and was in fact given Babylon to rule for the rest of his life. In the latter half of the fifth century, his grandson, also named Zopyrus, would desert from Persia to Athens.

It's not impossible that he was Herodotus' source for the stories of the elder Zopyrus and Megabyzus the conspirator.

Thus Darius came to power through brawn and daring and guile. He strengthened his position through a series of marriages, reorganized the kingdom, and put down the revolt of the Babylonians. The expedition to Samos—allegedly undertaken as repayment to Syloson for his earlier kindness—was Darius' first campaign outside of Persian territory. With its conquest under his belt, Darius turned his attention to the Scythians.

CHAPTER SEVEN

The Trouble with Nomads

Darius' Scythian Campaign

513	Darius' Scythian expedition

THE SCYTHIANS WERE A NOMADIC PEOPLE who lived in tribal groups to the north and east of the Black Sea. Darius, so Herodotus tells us, had had it in mind to attack them for some time, since before he sent Democedes and some trusted Persians off to reconnoiter Greece. Sometime after his capture of Babylon, Darius took the plunge, leading his army against the Scythians over the objections of his brother, Artabanus. But Herodotus delays his brief account of the campaign for nearly half of his fourth book while he discusses the history, geography, and ethnography of Scythia.

Golden Flasks and Serpentine Seductresses: The Origins of Scythia (4.5–13)

He looked at her wonderingly; but nevertheless inquired, whether she had chanced to see his strayed mares anywhere.   (4.9.2)

Herodotus relates four stories he'd heard about the origins of the Scythian nation. The Scythians themselves said they were descended from a man named Targitaus, the son of Zeus by the daughter of the river Borysthenes. Targitaus was king in Scythia a thousand years before Darius' expedition. He had three sons who succeeded him and ruled the land jointly. During their reign, some objects made of gold fell from the sky, a plow, a yoke, a sword, and a flask. First the eldest son tried to retrieve them, but they burst into flame when he approached. The middle son tried next, and the same thing happened. But when the youngest son approached the fire went out, and he was able to take up the objects and bring them home. His older brothers, recognizing this as a divine sign, surrendered the sovereignty of the kingdom to him. The various tribes of Scythia were descended from these three brothers.

The Greeks around the Black Sea, however, said Scythia was founded by the Greek hero Heracles (a.k.a. Hercules). (Note how the history of a barbarian people was thus assimilated into Greek mythology.) Heracles is famous for being given a series of twelve labors to undergo as punishment for having killed his family in a fit of madness. One of the tasks he had to perform was stealing the cattle of Geryon. Geryon lived more or less at the end of the world, to the west of the Mediterranean Sea. As one version of the story has it, Africa and Europe were connected at the time, but Heracles smashed through a mountain on his way to Geryon's place, thereby forming the strait of Gibraltar. He also created the so-called Pillars of Hercules that now stand on either side of the strait. Retrieving Geryon's cattle thus involved a lot of travel and discomfort, and the task was further complicated by the fact that Geryon was a three-headed, six-legged monster. He was in fact the grandson of Medusa, the snake-haired Gorgon whose gaze could turn a man to stone, so it's not surprising that Geryon was a bit irregular in appearance. (When Medusa was beheaded by the hero Perseus, two sons popped out of her neck. One of them was Geryon's father.)

Despite the difficulties, Heracles managed to kill Geryon and steal his cattle. He was en route to deliver them to King Eurystheus in the Greek Peloponnese—herding the cows the long way, looping around the Black Sea before heading back west—when he wound up falling asleep in the area later known as Scythia. When Heracles woke up he discovered that his horses were missing, and he began to search the country for them. (The cows Heracles was driving are conveniently forgotten at this point.) Finally he came upon a half-woman, half-snake creature—the snake part was the bottom half—living in a cave. She had the horses, it turned out, and was willing to hand them over if he had sex with her. Heracles complied, but the snake woman held off on returning the animals for quite some time—until, in fact, she and Heracles had three sons. When Heracles finally got his horses back and was ready to leave, the snake woman asked him if she should send the boys to him when they were older or keep them with her. Heracles, in reply, gave her one of his bows and his belt and told her to wait until the boys were grown and see which of them was able to draw the bow in the right way and girdle himself with the belt. The one who did these things properly should stay in his mother's country, and the others should be sent away. When the boys had grown to manhood their mother carried out Heracles' instructions. The older two failed at the tasks and were sent away. But the youngest son, Scythes, was successful. He stayed in the country, which came to be named after him, and the Scythian people were descended from him.

The third story Herodotus tells about the origins of Scythia, to which he gives the most credence, is a prosaic one. The Scythians, he says, under pressure from the Massagetae, crossed into the territory of the Cimmerians and displaced them. A fourth story has the Scythians being forced out of their land instead by another people, the Issidones.

Gilded Skulls and Merry-Go-Rounds: Scary Scythian Customs (4.16–82)

To effect this, a second stake is passed through their bodies along the course of the spine to the neck; the lower end of which projects from the body, and is fixed into a socket, made in the stake that runs lengthwise down the horse.   (4.72.5)

Herodotus has a lot to say about the geography of Scythia—particularly its rivers (4.47–58)—and the various tribes, both Scythian and non-Scythian, that inhabited the country and surrounding areas. But his information only extends so far. He regularly remarks that he has no trustworthy information about the people living beyond the Scythians, or beyond the tribes with whom the Scythians came in contact. These unknown entities are sometimes rumored to have fantastic qualities or habits: they're goat-footed or one-eyed or they hibernate for six-month stretches. He is more surefooted when it comes to describing the Scythians themselves and their customs. They were, it must be said, a rather scary bunch.

Every time a Scythian king died, there was a great to-do. His body was embalmed and covered in wax and borne around to all the subject peoples. The mourners would wound themselves as a sign of their loss—cutting off part of an ear, for example, or stabbing themselves through the hand with an arrow. A number of people and animals who were to accompany the king in the afterlife were strangled to death: a concubine, his cupbearer, his groom, his cook, his message-bearer, a servant, some horses.

That last part is a bit gruesome, but not very shocking: a dead king needed his dead servants, after all, and the number of people killed for the purpose apparently wasn't very large. Besides, the sacrifice of a king's retainers upon his death is the sort of thing we're used to hearing about in other societies. The ancient Egyptians practiced retainer sacrifice, for example, as did the Vikings and Incans and a number of other cultures. More impressive was what happened on the first anniversary of the king's death, when the Scythians arranged a grisly sort of stick puppet display to honor him. Specifically, fifty of the dead king's male servants were strangled to death, and fifty of his horses were killed. The horses and men were then gutted and cleaned out, stuffed with plant husks, and sewn back together. Then the Scythians erected a hundred wooden supports: wheels were cut in half and each half affixed, concave side up, to two wooden posts so as to form a stand.

The dead horses were skewered lengthwise on long stakes—we'll see why in a minute—and each horse was placed on two of the wooden stands, one wheel half supporting its shoulders, the other its hindquarters, with its legs on either end hanging free. The horses were given bits and reins so as to look realistic.

Finally, the fifty dead servants were mounted on the dead horses. Now, if you've ever done anything like this yourself, you'll know there's no way a human corpse is going to stay mounted on a dead horse without a little help. Happily, the Scythians had an ingenious way of dealing with the problem. They drove a stake through the servant's body up to its neck, but left some of the stake sticking out below, lollipop-like. This protruding bit was then plunged down through the horse's back and fit into a hole that had been made in the stake that was driven through the horse's body earlier. The fifty dead riders, pinned to their fifty dead mounts, and the fifty pairs of wooden stands that supported the horses were then arranged in a circle around the old king's tomb, a macabre merry-go-round that Vlad the Impaler would have appreciated.

The Scythians did unpleasant things to the bodies of enemy combatants as well. The heads of enemy dead were brought to the king as proof of a kill: turning in a head earned the warrior a share in whatever loot had been obtained in the current hostilities. Those enemy heads were also routinely scalped, the scalps scrubbed clean with an ox rib and kneaded until soft. Herodotus describes the resulting patch of flesh as being "like a hand towel." Scalps might be hung on a warrior's bridle as evidence of his prowess, or they could be sewn into coats, which presumably were just as effective at advertising one's status as a killer. The hands of the dead were sometimes flayed as well and the skin used, with fingernails intact, to make covers for their quivers. A Scythian would drink the blood of the first man he killed. If a Scythian killed a particularly bitter enemy, he might turn the man's skull into a drinking cup by sawing the top of the head off below the eyebrows and gilding the inside.

An enemy combatant who was taken alive stood some chance of being sacrificed to the god Ares: one out of every hundred POWs had their throats slit and their right arms cut off as part of an annual offering to the god. No word from Herodotus on what happened to the other 99 percent, but one suspects it wasn't pretty.

The Scythians, with their fierce warrior ethos and penchant for turning people they didn't like into clothing and dinnerware, were not an enemy to be taken lightly. As Darius was about to find out, they also had an ingenious way of responding to foreign invasions that rendered them all but invincible.

Crossing the Bosporus (4.83–119)

They are the aboriginal people of the country, and are nomads; unlike any of the neighbouring races, they eat lice.   (4.109.1)

Darius' brother Artabanus was worried about the Scythians and tried to talk Darius out of making an expedition against them, but he failed to persuade the king. (As we'll see, Artabanus would likewise fail to talk his nephew Xerxes out of attacking Greece a generation later.) Darius, heedless of his brother's concerns, prepared his army, collecting contingents from across his empire, and he marched from Susa to the Bosporus—the strait that links the Black Sea to the Sea of Marmara and separates Asia from Europe. According to Herodotus, Darius had amassed an army some seven hundred thousand men strong and he had a fleet of six hundred ships, but the historian's numbers when reporting on the strength of Persian armies should not be taken as gospel.[1]

During this buildup to the campaign, a Persian by the name of Oeobazus approached Darius. He had three sons, all serving with the army, and he asked that one of them be allowed to remain behind in Persia. Oeobazus was overjoyed when Darius responded, with apparent sympathy, that he would in fact leave all three of the boys behind. But anyone who's read this far in Herodotus' *History* will likely suspect the catch: the boys remained behind, to be sure, but with their throats slit by Darius' henchmen. We'll see a parallel to this grisly episode, too, when we discuss the buildup to Xerxes' invasion of Greece in 480.

(The Greek word used to describe Oeobazus' great joy at Darius' response—*perichares*—is in fact an ominous one, regularly used by Herodotus when the delight of a character is to be short-lived. Harpagus, for example, was overjoyed—*perichares*—when Astyages invited him to dinner, ostensibly having forgiven him for not killing the infant Cyrus when he'd been ordered to [1.119].)

Darius had had a bridge constructed over the Bosporus—presumably a bridge of boats and rafts that were tied to one another and anchored at the opposing shores. (See chapter eleven for a description of the bridges Darius' son Xerxes would build across the Hellespont in the late 480s.) Darius' land army thus crossed into Europe. His fleet, meanwhile, sailed through the Bosporus to the Black Sea, then north to the Ister River (the modern Danube). While the men of the fleet built a bridge across the Ister, Darius led the land army north from the Bosporus to meet them, subjugating people as he went and adding them to his forces.

Finally Darius arrived at the Ister, and his army crossed the bridge the fleet had constructed. Darius ordered the sailors to cross as well and then to destroy the bridge and follow the army on land, but he soon changed his mind. A general from Mytilene by the name of Coës advised Darius to leave the bridge standing: that way the army would have an exit route ready in case they couldn't find the Scythians and needed to leave the country. (Coës was careful to say he wasn't worried the Persians would be defeated by the Scythians, but I bet he was.) Coës suggested leaving the Ionians behind to guard the bridge, and Darius, persuaded, did just that. He left them with orders to withdraw to their homes if he and the Persians had not returned after sixty days, and he gave them a rudimentary device with which to reckon the passage of time, a leather strap with sixty knots tied in it, one of which was to be unraveled each day. Once that primitive time-keeping piece is brought into Herodotus' narrative, the clock starts ticking on Darius' campaign: the longer he tarries in middle-of-nowhere Scythia, the more perilous his situation will become, since he's foolishly imposed an expiration date on his safe return to Asia.

In response to the Persians' advance into Europe, the Scythians sent messengers to their neighbors, whose kings were in fact already meeting to discuss the invasion. Herodotus gives a quick summary of the various tribes represented at the meeting. The Neuri, for example, were rumored to be sorcerers, and every year one of their tribe was said to turn into a wolf for a few days. The Taurians displayed their enemies' heads on stakes. Those whom Herodotus calls the "Man-Eaters" (*androphagoi*) were—you guessed it—cannibals. The Budini, meanwhile, were nomads and, Herodotus says, "the only ones in this country who eat lice." (The verb in Greek for "eat lice" is *phtheirotragein*, and it unfortunately admits of a more banal definition as well: that is, the Budini may have been eaters of fir-cones rather than parasites. But the practice of lice-eating is surprisingly widespread in both ancient and modern cultures,[2] which makes the more disgusting definition of *phtheirotragein* by no means impossible.)

The Scythians urged the kings of these neighboring states to join them in resisting the invaders, arguing that the Persians would come after them too once they'd finished with Scythia. But they managed to convince only three of the other tribes to join them in alliance.

Chasing the Scythians (4.120–133)

"Thou strange man, why dost thou keep on flying before me, when there are two things thou mightest do so easily?"   (IDANTHYRSUS, at 4.126)

Since the Scythians did not have the support of many of their neighbors, they decided against meeting the Persians in a pitched battle. They sent their women and children and animals north, out of harm's way, and divided their forces (including those of their allies) in two. Their strategy would be to withdraw before the Persians so that they were always a day's march ahead. They would devastate the countryside as they went, destroying the wells and springs and grassland so that the Persians would be unable to support themselves from the land. And eventually they would attempt to force their neighbors to join the fight against the Persians, those tribes that had refused to ally with them previously, by leading the Persians into their territory.

Herodotus' discussion of what happened next is likely inaccurate. It's been argued, for example, that his account is a conflation of two separate Persian expeditions into Scythia. But as he tells the story, one division of the Scythians, appearing to retreat before the Persian host, led the enemy eastward across the northern shore of the Black Sea. Then, while Darius was busy with the construction of a series of forts, the Scythians slipped away. The Persians, assuming that the Scythians had fled for good, turned around and went back the way they'd come. But the Scythians had in fact doubled back and met up with the second division of their army, and they were now in front of the Persians as they marched west.

The Scythians now put the second part of their plan into action. Again, they withdrew before the Persians, but this time they led the enemy into the territory of their neighbors. They expected by this means to involve the neutral tribes in the fighting, but their plan failed. The other tribes either fled or else opposed the entry of both armies into their territory. But none of them joined the Scythians' fight.

The trouble with nomads, Darius was coming to appreciate, is that they don't stay put long enough for you to kill them. Darius was fed up with chasing the Scythians back and forth across eastern Europe. He sent a messenger to the Scythian king, Idanthyrsus, suggesting he either stand and fight or submit and recognize Darius as master. In the latter case, Darius said, Idanthyrsus should send along the standard tokens of submission—gifts of earth and water—which would symbolize the Scythians' surrender. Rather than packaging up a box of dirt, however, Idanthyrsus sent off a plucky response by return messenger. The Scythians weren't running away from the Persians out of fear, he said. They were just doing what nomads did, moving from one place to another. (This is disingenuous, of course. In leading the Persians around as they were they were hardly following an established pattern of travel.) As a nomadic people, the Scythians did not have cities or crops to protect, so there was no need for them to stop for battle. But if the Persians wanted to speed things up, he said, they should find the graves of the Scythians' ancestors and try to destroy them: they'd have a fight on their hands then. As for gifts of earth and water, the Persians shouldn't expect them anytime soon, but he'd be sending along some gifts that were more appropriate. And Darius would be sorry he'd ever said anything about being the Scythians' master.

Soon after this exchange, the Scythians adopted a more aggressive strategy. They began harassing the Persians with their cavalry, attacking them day and night, whenever they were out gathering supplies. They were attempting to exhaust the Persians, but at the same time they'd sometimes throw Darius a bone, leaving some of their flock behind where the Persians could capture the animals. By such means they hoped to encourage the Persians to stay longer in Scythian territory. The clock was ticking, remember.

The Scythians also sent a contingent to the Ister River, where the Ionians were still guarding the bridge, unraveling a knot a day while waiting for Darius' return. The sixty days they had been required to remain had not yet elapsed, but the time was running short. The Scythians approached the Ionians and suggested they simply do as Darius had instructed: go back home when the time was up. They'd be blameless as far as Darius was concerned, since they would have adhered to his orders, and they'd get no trouble from the Scythians either. The Ionians agreed to this, and the Scythians withdrew, leaving the Greeks to guard the bridge in peace for the remainder of their allotted time.

Idanthyrsus had said he would send Darius gifts that were more fitting than the earth and water he'd demanded. The Scythians did finally send a messenger bearing an assortment of gifts—a bird, a mouse, a frog, and five arrows. These weren't simple presents but a form of symbolic communication, just as the gift of earth and water, in the Persian culture, symbolized surrender. The purport of the gifts would probably have been immediately apparent to a Scythian, but the Persians were perplexed. Darius, whose interpretation was almost laughably optimistic, assumed the Scythians' were offering the equivalent of earth and water: the mouse was a creature of the land, after all; the frog lived in water; the bird, Darius thought, symbolized the Scythians' horses (perhaps because both animals were swift); and the arrows represented the Scythians' valor, which they were now surrendering to the Persians.

Gobryas, one of the seven conspirators who had killed the Magi, offered a different interpretation:

> If you do not become birds and fly up to the sky, Persians, or become mice and dig into the ground, or become frogs and jump into the lakes, you will not return home but will be struck by our arrows.

Needless to say, Gobryas was closer to the mark than Darius.

The Persian Withdrawal from Scythia (4.134–142)

> And hence the Scythians are accustomed to say of the Ionians, by way of reproach, that, if they be looked upon as freemen, they are the basest and most dastardly of all mankind—but if they be considered as under servitude, they are the faithfullest of slaves, and the most fondly attached to their lords.   (4.142)

It didn't take long for Darius to realize Gobryas' interpretation was the correct one, though the event that changed his mind seems an unlikely one. The Scythians and Persians were ranged against one another, about to fight a pitched battle, when a hare ran between the two armies. This got the Scythians excited, and a bunch of them started chasing the hare and hollering it up. Darius heard the commotion and found out what was going on. You might think that the

Scythians' lack of discipline would please him, but the opposite was true: the Scythians' apparent insouciance in the face of battle disturbed him. He turned to his advisors and said that Gobryas had been right: the Scythians were utterly contemptuous of them. What the Persians needed, he said, was a plan to get themselves home safely. Happily, Gobryas was once again ready with a solution.

> I suggest that as soon as night falls we light our fires like we usually do. But then we deceive those of the soldiers who are least able to endure hardship and we tie up all the donkeys and we leave before either the Scythians go to the Ister and destroy the bridge or the Ionians decide to do something that could destroy us.

In other words, Gobryas was suggesting that the Persians sneak off in the middle of the night, which would not only pull one over on the Scythians but also cruelly deceive some of their own men, who would wake up in the morning to find themselves abandoned. It's a cold-blooded plan, the sort of thing a commander would agree to only in the most dire of circumstances. A century later, for example, the Athenians fighting in Sicily against the Syracusans would be forced to leave their wounded behind while they fled overland in a vain attempt to save their own lives. Thucydides' description of the scene is one of the more heart-wrenching in his *History of the Peloponnesian War* (7.75). But Athens was a society in which the individual was valued. In Persia, individuals were expendable. Darius didn't have a problem with Gobryas' suggestion.

When night fell, Darius put the plan into action. He told the soldiers who were being left behind that they were to guard the camp while the rest of the army made an assault on the Scythians. Then he and his army of able-bodied men hightailed it out of there.

Gobryas' plan worked perfectly. The Scythians were deceived and the men Darius abandoned were deceived and no one realized what Darius was up to until morning, when the Persians woke up to find they'd been betrayed. Having no other option, they surrendered to the Scythians and told them what had happened. At once the Scythians gathered their whole force and went off toward the Ister in pursuit of the Persians. Darius had a head start of some hours, but even so, the Scythians beat them to the bridge: they were on horseback and knew the most direct route to the river, while the Persians, being less familiar with the country, had been taking a more circuitous route. When they got to the Ister the Scythians found that the Ionians were still there, after their allotted time on guard duty, despite their earlier promise to abandon the bridge after sixty days. The Scythians told the Ionians to break up the bridge and go home. They need no longer fear Darius: when the Scythians were through with him, they said, he wouldn't be leading an army against anyone ever again.

The Ionians had been quick to agree to the Scythians' demand that they abandon the bridge the first time they'd met. Herodotus, at least, does not report there being any debate over the matter at the time. In the event, of course, the Ionians had not complied, and it may be that they had never intended to. Now, however, the Scythians' repetition of their demand prompted a debate. Miltiades spoke first. He was the tyrant of the Thracian Chersonese (the modern Gallipoli peninsula), which had been colonized by Greeks in the seventh and sixth centuries B.C. Miltiades was a citizen of Athens, but he had inherited the tyranny of the Chersonese from his uncle, also named Miltiades, about ten years before Darius' Scythian campaign. We will be hearing much more about the younger Miltiades in chapter ten. For now, in his first appearance in Herodotus' pages, Miltiades' role is a minor one. Herodotus tells us that he urged the Ionians to do as the Scythians wished, to withdraw to their homes, leave Darius to his fate, and thereby free Ionia from Persian domination. For a brief time Miltiades had the crowd on his side, but then Histiaeus, the tyrant of Miletus, spoke. He said that the Ionians should remain at their posts, not out of loyalty to the Persian king, but because it was in their interest to do so. None of the Ionian tyrants, he said, would be able to hold onto power without Persian backing, since the men they ruled would all prefer to be governed democratically. We'll see soon enough that the tyrannies of Ionia were indeed ripe for a democratic revolt, as Histiaeus implies. For now, his reminder to the tyrants of the fragility of their power was sufficient to sway their decision. They voted to remain at the bridge, thus preserving their positions as vassals to Darius—assuming he made it past the Scythians.

The Ionians, however, were wily when it came to telling the Scythians their plans. They agreed to break up the bridge, and indeed they started dismantling it on the Scythian side of the river, making a show of their cooperation. They were eager for their freedom, they said, and urged the Scythians, while they were taking care of things at the Ister, to go off and look for Darius' army so that they could wreak their vengeance. The Scythians were taken in by the Ionians' lies. Trusting, for the second time, that the Ionians would do what they said, the Scythians rode off to look for the Persians. The Ionians, meanwhile, having dismantled only a part of the bridge, remained where they were and waited for Darius.

The Scythians couldn't find the Persians. They rode along the route they thought the Persians were most likely to take, where the land was well provided with forage for horses. But the Persians, since they were unfamiliar with the country and didn't know what the best route was, traveled instead along the path they'd taken into the country. The Scythians, in the end, completely missed them. The Persians made it to the Ister unmolested, in the middle of the night, and must have felt great relief over their narrow escape until they took a good look at the river. As far as they could see in the dark, the Ionians were gone, the bridge had been destroyed, and they were trapped inside Scythia, sitting ducks for the wild nomads who so far had outmaneuvered them at every turn. Morning, when it came, would have put their fears to rest: they'd see that the Ionians were waiting for them on the other side of the river and that much of the bridge was still in position. But as it happened they didn't have to wait that long. There was an Egyptian in the army who had the loudest voice in the world, Herodotus says, and Darius had him stand on the river bank and yell for Histiaeus. Histiaeus heard the call and ordered the ships that had pulled out of formation to move back into position. With the bridge thus rebuilt, the Persians crossed to safety.

As for the Scythians, when in the future they talked about the Ionians, who had twice deceived them, they said that if you judged them as free men, they were the basest and least manly of all. But if you judged them as slaves, they were the most submissive and loyal. They were, that is, really good slaves. It's not the most flattering of compliments, but the Scythians' assessment of the Ionians is an interesting one. The question of the Ionians' status as free men or slaves or something in between and their determination not to revolt from Persia on this occasion look forward to what is to come in Herodotus' fifth book (our chapter nine).

Darius' bridging of the Bosporus and the Ister and his cruel slaughter of the three sons of Oeobazus during the buildup to the Scythian campaign were the sort of hubristic acts we might expect to signal imminent catastrophe in Herodotus' pages. It thus comes as no surprise that Darius' campaign was unsuccessful. The expedition was not ruinous, however: unlike Cyrus before him, whose crossing of the Araxes led to his death and decapitation, Darius and his army lived to fight another day.

The Scythian campaign was Darius' first expedition into Europe. As such it prefigures the two campaigns the Persians would later wage against Greece, the subject of the second half of Herodotus' *History*. In particular, the Scythian campaign anticipates Xerxes' expedition of 480: like Darius in 513, Xerxes would ignore the counsel of Artabanus; he would disappoint a father begging for his son's discharge from service; he would bridge the strait between Europe and Asia; and ultimately, like his father before him, he would fail.

CHAPTER EIGHT

Stuttering Kings and Lousy Deaths

The Libyan *Logos*

c. 630	Founding of Cyrene
513	Persian expedition to Libya

A T ABOUT THE SAME TIME AS THE SCYTHIAN CAMPAIGN, the Persians who were based in Egypt launched an expedition against Libya. ("Libya," in Herodotus' parlance, was not the country known by that name today but the African continent as a whole. He refers to the northern Africans who lived west of Egypt as "Libyans" and those to the south as "Ethiopians.") Herodotus introduces his account of the expedition at 4.145, and in the same sentence introduces the digression that will preempt that account for fifty-five sections: "At the same time there was another great expedition, against Libya; I will explain the cause of it after I have first related the following." Herodotus goes on to discuss the colonization and subsequent history of the city of Cyrene in Libya, then Libyan ethnography. The Libyan expedition proper, when it finally comes at the very end of Book 4, is a mere five sections long, about two pages in translation. The bulk of Herodotus' Libyan *logos* is thus not pertinent to his main theme of Persian expansion. But it does allow him to include some nice examples of misinterpreted oracles and immoderate behavior.

The Colonization of Libya (4.145–158)

This girl's mother having died, Etearchus married a second wife; who no sooner took up her abode in his house than she proved a true step-mother to poor Phronima, always vexing her, and contriving against her every sort of mischief.

(4.154.2)

Herodotus tells two stories about the founding of the Greek colony of Cyrene on the northern coast of Africa (it happens to be in modern Libya). He heard the first from sources on the island of Thera (modern Santorini), which is about seventy miles north of Crete in the middle of the Aegean. Thera had been colonized by the Spartans. It was named after the leader of the Spartan expedition to the island, Theras, who was reportedly a great-great-great-grandson of Oedipus. (Yes, *that* Oedipus, the guy who married his mother and killed his father.) Among the colonists who accompanied Theras were a number of Minyae. The Minyae were descendants of the crew of Jason's Argo. (Yes, *those* Argonauts, who sailed off to find the Golden Fleece and were immortalized in stop-motion splendor in the 1963 film *Jason and the Argonauts*.)

Some untold number of generations after Thera was founded, Grinnus, the king of Thera at the time and a descendant of Theras, went to consult the oracle at Delphi. He was accompanied by a man named Battus, who was a descendant of those Minyae who'd gone to Thera with Theras. Grinnus was consulting the oracle about an unrelated matter when the priestess of Apollo told him that he should found a city in Libya. Grinnus, when he received the command, begged off from the task. He was too old to undertake a project of that sort, he said, and he suggested, pointing at Battus, that the assignment be given to a younger man instead. Then he and Battus went back to Thera and promptly forgot about the whole thing. Libya, wherever it was, was a big unknown to them, and they weren't about to send a colony off to some place they'd barely heard of.

After Grinnus and Battus got back from Delphi, Thera suffered a seven-year drought. It was so severe that every tree on the island but one died. The Theraeans again sent to Delphi for guidance, and again the priestess of Apollo told them to establish a city in Libya. This time, the Theraeans listened . . . sort of. They got a Cretan fisherman to help them find the place, and they wound up founding a colony on the island of Platea, just off the African coast. Battus was chosen to serve as the new colony's king.

The Cyrenaeans told a different story. There was a city on Crete named Oaxus whose king was Etearchus. He had a daughter named Phronime, and after her mother died, he remarried in order to give the girl a stepmother. His new wife, however, acted like a stepmother in the worst sense of the word. (Herodotus says she "thought it appropriate to be a stepmother to Phronime in deed": stepmothers had a bad reputation already in antiquity, long before Cinderella and Snow White came along.) The stepmother's various cruelties culminated in her claiming that Phronime was a wanton. Unfortunately, Etearchus believed the lie, and his response was unforgiving. In short, he arranged to have Phronime murdered—the ancient equivalent of a modern honor killing.

Etearchus did not try to kill his daughter himself. Instead, he took a Theraean trader named Themison as his guest-friend—a ritualized relationship, you may remember, that was taken very seriously in the Greek world and implied mutual obligation. Etearchus then had Themison swear he would do whatever Etearchus asked of him. Once that was done, Etearchus gave Themison his assignment: he was to take Phronime out on his boat and drop her into the sea.

Themison was furious about being tricked into promising to kill the girl. He dissolved the guest-friendship, but he was still bound by the terms of the oath he had sworn. He thus took Phronime away with him and, once they were at sea, he satisfied the letter of the oath, if not its intent: he dropped the girl into the sea but pulled her up again with a rope. And then they sailed off together to Thera.

Later on, the Cyrenaeans say, Phronime became the concubine of a Theran named Polymnestus, and they had a son named Battus who stuttered and spoke with a lisp. (*Battus* means "stutterer" in Greek.) When he grew to manhood Battus went to the oracle to ask about his voice, and the priestess of Apollo responded: "Battus, you came for your voice. But Lord Phoebus Apollo sends you to sheep-feeding Libya as founder of a colony." Like Grinnus in the Theraeans' version of the story, Battus was not thrilled at the prospect of following the god's order. Grinnus had objected that he was too old to found a colony. Battus argued that the task was impossible for him, that he simply was not in a position to accomplish something on that scale. But the oracle ignored his objections and repeated its injunction, and Battus, not bothering to wait for the priestess to finish, turned on his heel and went back to Thera.

As we might expect, ignoring the instructions of the oracle did not work out well, either for Battus or the Theraeans. We're not told the specifics, but things went badly for them, and the Theraeans sent to the oracle to find out what the problem was. They were told they should help Battus found Cyrene in Libya. (As Herodotus tells it, this is the first time the oracle named the colony the Theraeans and Battus were to found.) This second oracle moved the Theraeans to action. They sent Battus and a bunch of colonists off to Libya in two ships. When the colonists got there, they didn't know what to do. They tried returning to Thera, but the Theraeans wouldn't let them land. So the colonists were forced to turn around and head back to Africa. They wound up establishing a colony on the island of Platea.

The Theraean and Cyreneaen versions of the story differ in some of their particulars, but in both accounts the foundation of the colony is ordained by the god Apollo. This is not surprising: the Greeks regularly consulted the oracle in important matters related to warfare and colonization. Both stories, too, end at the same point: the Theraeans have established a colony on the island of Platea off the coast of Libya. But as we'll see, that wasn't exactly what Apollo had in mind.

Two years after colonizing Platea, Battus and his colonists weren't faring any better. They decided to consult the oracle yet again. They left one man behind on Platea and the rest of them sailed off to Delphi, where the god let them know, if only indirectly, where they'd gone wrong: "If you who have never been to sheep-feeding Libya know it better than I, who have, I greatly admire your wisdom." We've seen before that the interpretation of an oracle is not always clear cut, and it was never a good idea to approach an oracular response with preconceived notions: Cambyses, for example, had been too quick to assume that the city named "Ecbatana" in which he was destined to die was located in Asia. It may seem obvious to us that colonizing an island off the coast of Libya doesn't cut it when a god commands you to colonize Libya proper, but the Theraeans had failed to question their assumptions. With this third oracle, however, they were finally on the right track. They sailed back to Africa, picked up their man in Platea, and founded a city named Aziris on the mainland. Six years after that, they were persuaded to move again: some Libyans led them to a better place where, they said, "the heavens are pierced," so abundant was the rainfall. Finally, after three oracles and fifteen or so years, the Theraeans succeeded in founding Cyrene per the god's instructions.

Arcesilaus III and Pheretime (4.159–199)

If, however, thou heatest the oven, then avoid the island else thou wilt die thyself, and with thee the most beautiful bull.   (4.163.3)

Herodotus gives us a thumbnail sketch of what happened in Cyrene over the next hundred-odd years. Battus ruled for forty years and his son Arcesilaus for sixteen. During the reign of Arcesilaus' son Battus II, there was an influx of colonists to the city. The dramatic increase in Cyrene's population led to hostilities with the neighboring Libyans and their allies, the Egyptians. We've heard about this before, in Herodotus' second book (2.161): The Egyptians were badly beaten by the Cyrenaeans, which prompted them to revolt against their king, Apries. He was replaced on the throne by Amasis.

Next was Arcesilaus II. (If it's not clear by now, the kingship in Cyrene would pass for generations between fathers and sons named Battus and Arcesilaus.) Hostilities between this Arcesilaus and his brothers led to the latter's abandonment of Cyrene—they founded a nearby city called Barca, which we'll hear more about shortly—and eventually to open warfare. After a Cyrenaean defeat, Arcesilaus was strangled to death by one of his brothers (or, in other versions of the story, by a friend), and his killer was in turn murdered by Arcesilaus' wife.

During the reign of Battus III the government of Cyrene was democratized to an extent and the power of the monarchy correspondingly decreased. While Battus ruled, the reduction in royal authority was apparently not problematic, but his son Arcesilaus III balked at the diminution of authority once he came to power. His demand that the king's ancestral privileges be restored led to civil strife, as a result of which he was forced to flee to the island of Samos. His mother, Pheretime, fled to the city of Salamis on Cyprus, where she did her best to get her son restored to the Cyrenaean throne. Specifically, she kept badgering the king of Salamis, Euelthon, repeatedly asking him to give her an army. Euelthon gave her lots of things other than what she asked for, plying her with gifts, and each time she said that what he'd given her was nice but it wasn't what she wanted. Finally, Euelthon gave her a golden spindle, a distaff, and some wool, and told her these were more appropriate gifts for a woman than an army would be. But if Euelthon thought Pheretime would be pleased with his presents, he didn't know what kind of a girl he was dealing with. He's lucky she didn't put his eyes out with the spindle. As we'll see, she was capable of that and a whole lot more.

Meanwhile, Arcesilaus was in Samos, likewise working on getting himself restored to power. He was gathering Samians to his cause by promising them land in Cyrene. He also went to Greece to consult the oracle of Delphi, which returned the following less than pellucid response:

Loxias Apollo [fittingly, the epithet "Loxias," applied to Apollo in his manifestation as god of prophecy, means "obscure"] grants to you to rule Cyrene for the reigns of four kings named Battus and four named Arcesilaus. More than that he recommends that you not attempt. Return to your country in peace. If you find a

kiln full of pots, do not bake them but send them off on a fair wind. If you do fire
the kiln, do not enter the place that is surrounded by water. If you disobey, you
yourself will die along with the prize bull.

The first part of the oracle is transparent enough, and Arcesilaus must have
taken it as an all clear to go ahead and take the throne of Cyrene back. He
was, after all, the third Arcesilaus, which meant that things would go well for
his family in Cyrene for another two generations. (I know, I know: the oracle
Herodotus quotes was surely written after the fact, and thus described events
after they had occurred, when the nicely symmetrical reigns of the four Bat-
tuses and four Arcesilauses was a done deal. But we're reading *The History* as
a story, remember, more superficially than we would if we wanted to dissect it
and expose its failings as a strict historical narrative. Some suspension of dis-
belief is called for.) As far as the business of the pots and the prize bull was
concerned, Arcesilaus apparently had no more of a clue about it than we would
without the benefit of hindsight. But events were to teach him, too late, what it
was the oracle was forbidding him to do.

Arcesilaus returned to Cyrene with the men he'd gathered in Samos, and he
dealt harshly with the opposition. He sent some of them off to Cyprus to be
killed. (These men wound up being rescued along the way, however, and sent
to Thera.) Others fled to a tower, and Arcesilaus piled wood up around it and
burned them alive. It occurred to him afterwards that the men he'd burnt to
death must have been the pots the oracle had mentioned, and here he'd gone
and fired the kiln, as it were. Having disobeyed this injunction of the oracle,
he determined not to enter the land surrounded by water where, according
to Apollo, he was destined to meet his death. Arcesilaus assumed that this was
Cyrene, so he went instead to nearby Barca to ask the king, his father-in-law
Alazir, for help. But Arcesilaus was wrong in his identification of the seagirt
place the oracle spoke of, and he'd unwittingly gone to the very place he was
destined to die. Some of his enemies found him walking in the marketplace in
Barca and killed him. They killed Alazir as well: he was apparently the prize
bull mentioned in the oracle, though it's not clear why he was referred to in this
way.

Pheretime, meanwhile, had moved back to Cyrene from Cyprus, and she
was running things there in her son's absence. When she heard that Arcesilaus had been killed, however, she fled to Egypt and did the same thing there

that she'd done in Salamis. She asked the Persian governor in Egypt—Aryandes, who'd been left in charge by Cambyses—for an army. Unlike Euelthon, however, Aryandes was happy to oblige. He sent an expedition against Libya, ostensibly to punish the murderers of Arcesilaus, but more likely, Herodotus suggests, because he had in mind the conquest of Libya. As for what happened next, the Persian expedition to Libya that we've all been waiting for, Herodotus keeps us in suspense for another thirty-two sections while he discusses the geography and fauna of North Africa and the customs—the diet and sexual practices and hair styles—of its inhabitants.

Certainly there are some interesting tidbits in Herodotus' digression on Libyan ethnography. He says, for example, that many of the nomadic Libyans cauterized the veins of their children's scalps when they were four years old, a practice they believed would save the children from being harmed later on by phlegm running down their heads—evidently more of a concern back then than it is now. (If a child convulsed during the procedure, goat urine was poured on the wound as a remedy.) He describes the polyandrous women of the Gindanes, who wore an anklet for each man they'd slept with. Whoever had the most anklets was considered the best, as I suppose she must have been. The Adyrmachidae, meanwhile, were the only Libyans who showed their virgins to their king prior to the girls' marriages. The king would get to deflower whichever of them he liked best. When the Adyrmachidae had lice, they'd pull the parasites off their scalps and bite them back before tossing them away. In this practice too, Herodotus sees fit to tell us, the Adyrmachidae were unique among the Libyans.

As usual, then, Herodotus' account is peppered with the strange and strangely specific. But nothing in this section need detain us any further from the Persian expedition against Libya toward which Herodotus' narrative has been building.

Severed Breasts and Wormy Deaths: The Persian Expedition to Libya (4.200–205)

Her body swarmed with worms, which ate her flesh while she was still alive.

(4.205)

The Persian army that Aryandes sent from Egypt arrived outside Barca in Libya and demanded the surrender of the murderers of Arcesilaus. Pretty much everyone in Barca claimed responsibility for the killing, however, so the Persians' request came to nothing. The Persians next laid siege to Barca, a time-consuming prospect in antiquity because it was difficult to take a fortified city by force. One hoped to starve out the inhabitants or to have the gates opened by fifth columnists. There were tricks one might try, too, to breach an enemy's walls. The Persians, for example, attempted to undermine the Barcaeans' fortifications by digging tunnels under the city's walls, but they were detected in the act: the Barcaeans went around the inside perimeter of their city banging the ground with a shield, hollow side down. They were able to tell from the sound whether they were above a tunnel. When they were, they dug down and killed the tunnelers.

The Persians besieged Barca for nine months, and in the end they took the city by a clever if dishonorable stratagem. By night, undetected by the Barcaeans, they dug a huge trench outside the city's walls, then covered it over with planks and sand so it looked like firm ground. The next day they invited representatives of Barca out to parley, and they wound up negotiating a treaty while standing over the trench. The Barcaeans said they would pay an indemnity to the Persian king, and the Persians said they wouldn't make any political changes within Barca. And they swore to abide by these terms with an oath that would remain intact "as long as the earth beneath them was in place." The Barcaeans, not suspecting a trick, opened their gates to the Persians. And the Persians broke the supports they'd built over the trench so that the ground gave way and they were absolved of the oath they'd just sworn. Barca was theirs for the taking, and they didn't have to feel any moral qualms about going back on their word.

The result was ugly. The men who were responsible for the murder of Arcesilaus were handed over to Pheretime, who had them impaled on posts erected around the walls. As for the wives of those implicated in the murder, Pheretime had their breasts cut off, and she hung these up around the city walls as well. She told the Persians to leave the Battiads in charge in Barca—descendants of the founders of the city—and pretty much everyone else was enslaved. Then the Persians, having finished with Barca, marched toward Cyrene.

Given the attention Herodotus has lavished in his account on the foundation and history of Cyrene, one would expect the Persian invasion of Libya, when it finally comes, to center on an assault on that city. Instead, the focus is on Barca, and Herodotus' account of what happened between the Persians and Cyre-

naeans is confusing and inconsistent. Herodotus reports that the Persian commanders on the scene disagreed about whether they should capture Cyrene,
but the opinion of the general of the army, Amasis, won out: they had not been
tasked with capturing the city, he argued, and so should leave it be. The Cyrenaeans, meanwhile, opened their gates to the Persians and allowed them to pass
through the town. After the Persians had left, however, both sides seem to have
had a change of heart. The Persians regretted not having taken Cyrene, and
they went back and tried to gain access to the city a second time, but this time
the Cyrenaeans wouldn't let them in. The Persians then reportedly panicked—
we're not told why—and fled for more than six miles before setting up camp. At
this point Aryandes sent word that they were to return to Egypt. They packed
up, asked for and were given supplies by the Cyrenaeans, and marched back to
Egypt. The Libyans followed the army and killed and despoiled any stragglers.
Pheretime, meanwhile, decided not to remain in Cyrene, and she returned to
Egypt as well.

As it stands, Herodotus' account doesn't make a lot of sense. It hints at Cyrenaean resistance to the Persians—that business of Cyrene's gates being closed
when the Persians showed up the second time. This evidence of opposition may
have been tacked onto the story in later years, however, to exonerate Cyrene
from complicity in the Persian expedition against Barca. Certainly Battus IV
came to rule in Cyrene at some point after this, though it's not clear whether
he came to power before or after Pheretime's removal to Egypt. Nor is it clear
why Pheretime elected not to remain in Cyrene. Perhaps she didn't feel secure
there: given the impalements and mutilations she had ordered in Barca, she was
probably not a popular figure on the Cyrenaean street.

Pheretime, however, did not live to enjoy a comfortable retirement in
Egypt. She contracted a disease that made her body "swarm with worms." She
died a horrible death that was, Herodotus suggests, a fitting punishment for
her behavior: excessive vengeance, he moralizes, earns the gods' resentment.
Pheretime is not alone among the ancients in being reputed to have died from
an infestation of worms. Herod the Great (Acts 12:20–23), the Roman dictator Sulla (Plutarch, *Sulla* 36), and the Greek poet Alcman (Aristotle, *History
of Animals* 556b–557a), among others, were all alleged sufferers. Pheretime
may or may not have died as Herodotus describes, but the disease he seems
to be describing—phthiriasis—is real, an infection caused by the infestation of
mites. "What is common to all accounts," Thomas Africa writes in his paper on

wormy deaths, "is a fatal corruption of tissue in the lower abdomen, swarming with worms or 'lice' and emitting a terrible stench. An object of loathing, the victim of phthiriasis dies horribly and painfully."[1]

So much for Pheretime, and so much for the Persians' rather disappointing—from a dramatic standpoint—campaign to Libya. These hostilities would be followed soon enough, however, by warfare on a grander scale: Darius would spend the better part of the 490s putting down a revolt of the Greek colonies in Ionia. The bloodshed in Ionia, meanwhile, would lead directly to the Persian invasion of Greece in 490 and to the heroics of Marathon.

CHAPTER NINE

Tattooed Slaves and Ousted Tyrants

The Ionian Revolt and Post-Pisistratid Athens

W HEN DARIUS WITHDREW FROM EUROPE after his unsuccessful campaign against the Scythians, he left his general Megabazus behind with an army (4.143–144). Megabazus was given the task of subduing part of Thrace, the area of southeastern Europe that lay to the north and east of Greece. In Herodotus' day Thrace extended as far north as the Ister, and it was bounded to the south and east by the Aegean and Black

Seas. Thrace, in other words, was the area through which a Persian army would march if it were intent on invading Greece by land.

Herodotus' fifth book begins with a brief discussion of Megabazus' operations in Thrace and the Hellespont. But at section 28 the story moves to Ionia and the revolt of the Ionian Greek colonies against Persia. The revolt would ultimately be unsuccessful, but the uprising would lead directly to Persia's later expeditions against the Greek mainland, in 490 and 480. And those wars would in turn shape the history of Greece over the next century as surely as the two world wars sculpted the twentieth century.

Megabazus and Macedon and Murder (5.17–22)

And these men, when the Persians began to be rude, despatched them with their daggers.   (5.20.5)

Herodotus doesn't go into much detail about Megabazus' Thracian campaign, but he does say that Megabazus concentrated on the coastal areas of the region, apparently in an attempt to secure a route across Thrace to northern Greece. He captured a number of the cities of the Paeonians, who lived near the western edge of Thrace. Their populations were subsequently driven to Asia, where they were settled in their own village in Phrygia.[1] Megabazus also sent a party of seven ambassadors to Macedon, which lay to the west of Thrace, demanding that the Macedonians give earth and water as tokens of submission to the Persian king.

As Herodotus tells the story, Amyntas, the king of Macedon, complied with the Persians' demand with little or no hesitation and then invited the envoys to a banquet. He entertained them lavishly, and afterwards, when they were all sitting around drinking, the Persians asked the Macedonians to bring in women— not prostitutes but the Macedonians' wives and concubines. This, they claimed, was the custom among the Persians. Amyntas wasn't thrilled with the request, which by Greek and Macedonian standards was wholly out of line: in ancient Greece, respectable women were rarely seen by strangers, and they certainly did not dine with men to whom they weren't related. But Amyntas was nothing if not conciliatory that evening, so he had the women brought in, and they sat down opposite the Persians.

This wasn't what the ambassadors had in mind. What was the point of having girls in the room if they were to be kept out of reach? So they asked that the women be allowed to sit next to them. Amyntas allowed the change in seating, but, again, he wasn't happy about it. He was less happy still when the Persians started groping the women. The ambassadors had an army at their back, however, and Amyntas wasn't suicidal: he was prepared to swallow his humiliation in the interest of self-preservation. Amyntas' hotheaded son Alexander wasn't as accommodating, however. Alexander—who would rule as Alexander I after his father's death and who was the great-great-great-grandfather of Alexander III (a.k.a. "the Great")—suggested that his father go to bed and leave him to play host. It was clear to Amyntas that his son had something other than entertaining in mind. Alexander was on fire with anger, as Herodotus puts it, and wanted Amyntas out of the way. Amyntas warned his son that he shouldn't do anything rash: violence committed against the ambassadors could result in their own destruction. However obnoxious the envoys' demands, the Macedonians would simply have to endure it. But with his dire warning delivered and the fate of his monarchy and his country at stake, Amyntas decided that maybe it was time for bed after all, and so he left things in the hands of his son.

When his father had left, Alexander suggested to the Persians that the women be sent off to bathe. They would be brought back in when they were ready, he said, and the envoys could do what they liked with them—all of them, some of them, whatever they preferred. Alexander's fury may have been obvious to his father, but the Persians didn't pick up on it: they blithely watched the women leave and waited, unsuspecting, for their return. Alexander, meanwhile, sent the girls off to the women's quarters, and he replaced them with boys, beardless youths who were dressed like women and armed with daggers.[2] Alexander led the boys into the dining area and passed them out, one to each envoy. What's ours is yours, he told the Persians, including our mothers and sisters. The Persians were thoroughly deceived and ready to enjoy themselves, but when they got grabby, the boys pulled out their daggers and killed them. The Persians' servants were killed as well, and all evidence of what had happened to the delegation was disposed of. Later on, the Persians sent out a party to search for the missing envoys, and Alexander—so the story goes—paid hush money to the Persian in charge of the search, Bubares, to whom he also married his sister.

Scholars have long doubted Herodotus' story about the Persian embassy. Certainly some of the details of the account are inherently implausible. It's hard to believe, for example, that Amyntas would have entrusted a delicate diplomatic encounter to his son if he suspected Alexander intended to murder the envoys. But at least one part of the story is true: though the nuptials may not have been used to buy Bubares' silence, Alexander's sister was in fact married to the Persian nobleman. Alexander may have spread the story of the slaughter of the envoys himself later on, when hostilities between Persia and Greece had heated up, to explain away this familial connection and to bolster his reputation as a philhellene and foe of Persia.

In closing his account of the Persian embassy to Macedon, Herodotus says that the Macedonian royalty were in fact Greek. Alexander, Herodotus explains later in his *History*, was seventh in descent from the first Macedonian king, Perdiccas, who had settled in Macedon after being banished from Argos in Greece. (The story of Perdiccas' rise to power, at 8.137–139, is a typical folktale of the "clever youngest son makes good" variety.) As proof of his claim that the Macedonian kings were Greek, Herodotus says that Alexander was once allowed to compete in a footrace at the Olympics. Objections to his participation were raised at the time by some of his competitors on the grounds that the Olympics were open only to Greeks, but Alexander was able to prove his Greekness to the satisfaction of the marshals of the games. (We're not told what proof he offered.)

There are reasons to be skeptical of this Olympic evidence. Herodotus tells us, for example, that Alexander tied for first place in the race he entered, but his name does not appear in the lists of Olympic victors for the footrace, which survive in full for the relevant period. It could be argued that Alexander lost the race in a run-off, or that he did not compete in a regular race but in some special event, or that despite what Herodotus says, Alexander did not win at all. But even if we were to accept Herodotus' story as it stands, it would not so much prove that Alexander was Greek (the Olympic officials may have been wrong in their judgment, after all, or bribed) as establish that he was not considered to be Greek by at least some of his contemporaries. It would not be the last time that the Greekness of the Macedonian royal house would be questioned in antiquity. In the fourth century B.C., when Macedon was looming as a threat to the Greek states, the Athenian orator Demosthenes would repeatedly denounce its king, Philip II, as a barbarian—that is, as non-Greek (*Third Philippic* 31, *Third Olynthiac* 16, 24). The question of the Greekness or not of the Macedonians and the Macedonian royal house has inspired a great deal of scholarly debate, and it's a matter of fierce controversy to this day. We needn't get into it here. Suffice it to say that whatever the Macedonians' ethnic and linguistic ties to Greece may have been in fact, they do not seem to have been uniformly perceived as Greek. Still, it was sometimes politically useful for the

Macedonian kings to promote themselves as philhellenic, and Alexander in particular tended to emphasize his Greekness and his role as a benefactor to the Greeks: we'll hear more about the services he performed for the Greeks during the Persian Wars in subsequent chapters.

Aristagoras and the Failed Expedition to Naxos (5.23–34)

Full of anger at such carelessness, he bade his guards to seek out the captain, one Scylax by name, and thrusting him through one of the holes in the ship's side, to fasten him there in such a way that his head might show outside the vessel, while his body remained within.   (5.33.2)

After the Persians' failed Scythian expedition, a number of cities in northern Asia Minor revolted. Darius appointed a man named Otanes (not Darius' co-conspirator against the Magi) to succeed Megabazus as general in the area. Otanes put down the revolts and also captured the nearby islands of Lemnos and Imbros, which had not been in Persian hands before. Herodotus tells an interesting story about this Otanes. The general's father, Sisamnes, had been a judge during Cambyses' reign. He was caught taking a bribe, however, and Cambyses ordered that his throat be slit and his body flayed. Sisamnes' skin, once removed, was cut into strips and stretched across the chair he'd sat in while rendering judgments. After Sisamnes' execution, Cambyses appointed Otanes to the position his father had vacated. The chair went with the job, which meant that Otanes had to sit on strips of his father's skin while he worked—a constant reminder that he should refrain from taking bribes himself.

While Otanes was mopping things up around the Hellespont, Darius left his half-brother Artaphernes in charge in Sardis and withdrew to the Persian capital of Susa. He took Histiaeus, the tyrant of Miletus, with him, ostensibly to serve as a sort of advisor. Histiaeus is the guy who convinced the other Ionians to remain at the Ister and wait for Darius after the Scythians told them to leave. After the Scythian expedition, Darius had rewarded Histiaeus by giving him an area in Thrace to govern, Myrcinus (5.11). Now, however, Darius recalled Histiaeus from Thrace. Herodotus suggests that Darius wanted to keep a closer eye on the tyrant: his general Megabazus had suggested Histiaeus could use Myrcinus as a base from which to cause Persia trouble. Histiaeus thus accompanied Darius to Susa, apparently without complaint, but as we'll see, he would soon grow unhappy with his stay there.

While Histiaeus was in Susa with Darius, trouble was brewing back home. In his absence, Miletus was being governed by Aristagoras, who was Histiaeus' cousin and son-in-law. Some exiles from the island of Naxos arrived looking for help from their guest-friend Histiaeus. Since he wasn't there, they asked Aristagoras if he could help get them reinstated in Naxos. Aristagoras couldn't provide them with an adequate army himself, but he wanted to help: if he got them restored in Naxos, he figured, he would effectively control the island. (He must have imagined Darius would reward him by installing him as tyrant once Naxos was subdued.) Aristagoras told the exiles he would try to get them an army from Artaphernes. Then he went to Sardis and made his case for the campaign. The Naxians intended to pay for the maintenance of the army, but Aristagoras offered to give Artaphernes money on top of that. And he said that once the Persians had taken Naxos, the rest of the Cyclades would fall to them. From there it was just a hop, skip, and a jump to Euboea (just off the coast of Greece), which they could easily take as well. In short, Aristagoras made a campaign against Naxos sound like an enormously attractive proposition, and Artaphernes, after consulting with Darius, was sold on the idea. He gave Aristagoras a fleet of two hundred ships and an army, and he gave the command of the army to his cousin Megabates. Aristagoras sailed off with Megabates to Naxos, but, as Herodotus puts it, the island wasn't destined to be destroyed by this particular fleet: the Naxians had about nine years left before the Persians would come back and do the job right. This time around the attack was foiled because of a disagreement between the two leaders of the expedition.

The disagreement arose over a disciplinary matter. While the ships were beached on the island of Chios, Megabates made his rounds and discovered that there was no guard posted on one of them. By way of punishment, he ordered that the captain of that ship, Scylax, be tied up and his head shoved through an oar hole of the boat. Since the ships weren't under sail, there wouldn't have been any waves crashing against the hull, so Scylax may not have been in any real danger, but the punishment can't have been pleasant. Aristagoras was incensed when he heard about it, at least in part because Scylax was his guest-friend. He demanded that Megabates release the man, and when Megabates refused, Aristagoras freed Scylax himself. Megabates, not surprisingly, was furious at this public subversion of his authority, but when he argued with Aristagoras about it he was quickly reminded of the pecking order: Megabates may have been general of the army and the fleet, but Aristagoras was in charge of the campaign.

Since Aristagoras wasn't subordinate to him, Megabates couldn't respond by, for example, jamming *his* head through an oar hole, though he doubtless wanted to. Instead, Megabates got back at Aristagoras—so Herodotus tells us—by sabotaging the operation against Naxos. That night he sent some men in a boat to warn the Naxians that they were about to be attacked. The Naxians supposedly had been unaware that they were the target of the Persians' expedition. But once they were told, they immediately jumped into action, bringing supplies into their fortifications and shoring up their walls in preparation for a siege. When the Persians arrived, they found the city barricaded against them. They laid siege for four months without accomplishing anything, then built a fort on the island for the Naxian exiles to operate from before they sailed back to Ionia with nothing to show for their troubles.

It's not easy to swallow Herodotus' story of the Naxian expedition whole. Scholars have long doubted that Megabates, a high-ranking Persian official and cousin of the king, would sabotage a military expedition over a petty argument. And if he did, it's hard to believe that he would remain in favor afterward. Yet we know that Megabates would later serve as governor of Phrygia under Xerxes (Thucydides 1.129). It's hard to believe, too, that the Naxians were so clueless about the intentions of the fleet that was bearing down on them across the Aegean. As Macan writes in his commentary at 5.34, "The Naxians are represented as little better than simpletons, paying no heed to the intrigues of their exiled fellow-citizens abroad, suspecting nothing of the two hundred triremes at Miletus, taking no thought of the fate of Samos, Chios, Lesbos, Lemnos; yet able withal on the shortest notice to make all things ready for a siege."[3] It's quite possible that Megabates in fact bears no responsibility for the failure of the expedition and that the story of his sabotage was a later smear. The Naxians, meanwhile, could have gotten wind of the expedition against them by other, less dramatic means and made their preparations for a siege over a longer period. But whatever the reason for it, the Persian expedition to Naxos failed, and Aristagoras returned to Miletus in sorry straits.

The Ionian Revolt, Part I: Histiaeus and Aristagoras (5.35–38)

For Histiaeus, when he was anxious to give Aristagoras orders to revolt, could find but one safe way, as the roads were guarded, of making his wishes known; which was by taking the trustiest of his slaves, shaving all the hair from off his

head, and then pricking letters upon the skin, and waiting till the hair grew
again.   (5.35.2)

The failure of the Naxian campaign had Aristagoras worried about his future.
Specifically, given his spat with Megabates—who was the king's cousin, after
all—and given that all his grand plans for Persia's easy subjugation of the Aegean Islands had come to naught, he was concerned that the tyranny of Miletus would be taken from him. He was mulling over the idea of revolting from
Persia when he received a message from Histiaeus in Susa urging him to do
just that. The form of Histiaeus' communication was an unusual one: he had
tattooed a note on the scalp of one of his slaves and, after the man's hair grew
back, sent him off to Miletus with directions to have Aristagoras shave his head.
According to Herodotus, Histiaeus urged Aristagoras to revolt purely for personal reasons. He was sick of Susa and wanted to return home, but the chances
of Darius releasing him were slim. If Miletus revolted, however, he figured he'd
be sent to the coast to suppress the uprising. What Herodotus says about Histiaeus' motivation in sending his message is hard to believe, since the plan seems
too far-fetched for Histiaeus to have hung his hopes on. Probably the story was
invented after the fact by sources wishing to implicate Histiaeus in the revolt.
But we'll get into the veracity of Herodotus' portrayal of the tyrant below.

Aristagoras, when he got the message, talked to his people—Herodotus calls
them "conspirators," which has suggested to some that Aristagoras had already
been conspiring for some time—and with one exception they were in favor
of revolting. The holdout was Hecataeus, who advised against the insurrection because of the power and size of the Persian Empire. Hecataeus is another
one of those wise advisors whom we see throughout *The History*: they come on
the scene and give good advice that nobody listens to. Hecataeus' participation in the deliberations may not be historical, but it's not impossible on geographic or chronological grounds: he was a native of Miletus and lived during
this period. Hecataeus was also the author of a geography of the known world,
which included Asia and the countries bordering the Mediterranean. (Herodotus was not only familiar with Hecataeus' work, he twice explicitly names him
as a source of information.) Hecataeus, that is, knew his geography, and he was
acutely aware of what the Milesians would be up against if they revolted. He
was thus peculiarly suited to play the wise advisor in this instance. Not that
anyone listened to him: Aristagoras and his cronies decided to revolt.

The rebels' first act was to arrest the generals of the Persian fleet, men whom

Darius had installed as puppet tyrants in their various cities. These tyrants were handed over to their subjects to do with as they wished. Most were allowed to go into exile, but the people of Mytilene so disliked their tyrant that they stoned him to death. (This was Coës, who had advised Darius to leave the bridge over the Ister River standing during the Scythian expedition. Afterwards, Darius had rewarded Coës with the tyranny of Mytilene, just as he rewarded Histiaeus with Myrcinus.) Other tyrants who had not been with the fleet were likewise driven out of their cities. Aristagoras, meanwhile, abdicated the tyranny of Miletus, and he advised the rebelling Ionians to install military governors in their tyrants' stead. Then Aristagoras sailed off to Greece to look for allies.

Aristagoras Visits Sparta (5.39–51)

"Father," she said, "get up and go, or the stranger will certainly corrupt thee."

(GORGO, at 5.51.2)

Croesus' search for Greek allies to join his ill-fated campaign against Persia gave Herodotus the chance to introduce Athens and Sparta into his narrative back in his first book. Aristagoras' quest for allies likewise lets Herodotus catch us up on the goings-on in these *poleis*. In Croesus' day, fifty-odd years before the Ionian Revolt, Sparta was a military powerhouse and already in control of most of the Peloponnese. Sparta had a dual kingship, and the kings at that time were Anaxandridas (560–520) and Ariston (550–515). By the time Aristagoras came asking for help, Anaxandridas had been succeeded by his oldest son, Cleomenes, and Ariston by his son Demaratus. Herodotus tells us that Cleomenes was rumored to be mad. He doesn't go into detail here, but later we'll learn of the horrible form this madness took. While he listened to what Aristagoras had to say, at any rate, Cleomenes' behavior was normal enough.

During his interview with Cleomenes, Aristagoras showed the Spartan king a map of the world and made a long speech asking for the Spartans' help in freeing the Ionian cities from Persian control. The Persians wouldn't stand a chance against the Spartans, Aristagoras said, and they were, besides, impossibly wealthy: the campaign would make the Spartans rich. He pointed out where the various nations that had been subsumed by Persia were located on the map—the Lydians and Phrygians and so on—and in particular he pointed out the Persian capital of Susa, where the Great King lived and kept his treasure. When Aristagoras was done with his spiel, Cleomenes answered briefly, as befitted a king of the laconic Spartans: "Milesian friend, I will postpone answering until the day after tomorrow." When the two men met again, Cleomenes asked Aristagoras how many days' journey it was from the coast of Asia Minor to Susa. Aristagoras told him the truth, that the trip took three months, and he thereby lost any hope of bringing the Spartans on board. Cleomenes' response this time was only slightly longer than before: "Milesian friend," he said, "get out of Sparta before the sun sets. No speech you make will be pretty enough if you want the Spartans to journey three months from the sea."

Cleomenes' reply showcases another Spartan characteristic: they were notoriously unwilling to travel far from the Peloponnese. Sparta was a military state whose full citizens—Spartiates—lived a life of constant training for combat: there's a reason *spartan* means "strict" and "austere" in English. (The Spartan kingship, meanwhile, was a hereditary military command, and the men who held the office were as battle-hardened as their subjects: Sparta's kings were not the sort of monarchs who sat around wearing silk stockings and eating giant turkey legs.) The Spartans lived off the backs of an enslaved population, the helots (which means "the captured ones" in Greek), who were tied to their land and regularly abused by their masters. Since the Spartiates were a minority within their own state, they lived in constant fear of helot revolt. Their need to have sufficient numbers of warriors close to home at all times to guard against this possibility was an important factor in their foreign policy decisions. Sending an army across the Aegean and on a three-month jaunt inland from there was simply out of the question.

Aristagoras, however, was unwilling to take no for an answer. He followed Cleomenes home and begged the king to listen to him, asking that Cleomenes send his daughter out of the room so that they could talk freely. The girl, whose name was Gorgo, was a precocious eight- or nine-year-old. Cleomenes told Aristagoras he could speak freely in front of her, and so the Milesian played his final card, offering Cleomenes a bribe if he would agree to join the Ionians' cause. Aristagoras started his bid at ten talents and raised his offer in increments. When he hit fifty talents, Gorgo allegedly cried out, "Father, the stranger will corrupt you if you don't walk away!" Cleomenes, pleased with what his daughter had said, did just that. The interview over, Aristagoras left Sparta and made his way to Athens.

The Expulsion of the Pisistratids from Athens (5.55–65)

After the death of Hipparchus (the son of Pisistratus, and brother of the tyrant
Hippias), who, in spite of the clear warning he had received concerning his fate
in a dream, was slain by Harmodius and Aristogiton (men both of the race of the
Gephyraeans), the oppression of the Athenians continued by the space of four
years; and they gained nothing, but were worse used than before.   (5.55)

When last we heard about Athens, back when Croesus was making his inquiries, Pisistratus was tyrant. Herodotus now picks up where he left off, providing
a capsule history of Athens from the end of Pisistratus' tyranny to the Ionian
Revolt. Pisistratus died in 528 or 527 and was succeeded by his oldest son, Hippias. In 514 Hippias' brother Hipparchus was assassinated at the Panathenaia,
an important annual festival in Athens. The assassins, Harmodius and Aristogiton, are conventionally referred to as tyrannicides even though the man they
killed was not in fact Athens' tyrant. The event was celebrated afterwards in
Athens as the first blow against tyranny: statues of Harmodius and Aristogiton
were erected, their descendants were given special privileges (Demosthenes,
Against Leptines 127), songs were sung of their exploits (Athenaeus, 15.695).
But despite the tyrannicides' celebrity, Herodotus tells us surprisingly little
about the assassination itself. He mentions only that Hipparchus had dreamt
of his death the night before the Panathenaia, and after consulting with dream
interpreters the next morning he went out to fulfill his responsibilities at the
festival anyway. Later authors, particularly Thucydides (6.53–59) and Aristotle
(*The Constitution of Athens* 18–19), fill in the blanks. The details provided vary,
but in brief, the whole thing started because Hipparchus (or another brother,
according to Aristotle) tried and failed repeatedly to seduce Harmodius, who
was Aristogiton's lover. Aristogiton was worried that Hipparchus would take
Harmodius by force, and he therefore began plotting to overthrow the tyranny.
Hipparchus, meanwhile, decided to revenge himself on Harmodius by publicly
insulting his sister: she was invited to take part in a procession (surely not the
Panathenaia, as Aristotle has it), and when she showed up, Hipparchus and his
brother sent her away, saying that she wasn't worthy of the honor. The insult
merely fueled the would-be tyrannicides' anger. They and a small cadre of co-
conspirators intended to assassinate Hippias and Hipparchus at the Panathenaia, but in the event only Hipparchus was killed. Harmodius was caught and
killed on the spot, and Aristogiton was arrested and later killed, perhaps, as

Aristotle has it, after first being interrogated and tortured. After Hipparchus' murder, Hippias became more despotic in his rule.

Herodotus, having for once failed to pass on a good story where there was one to be told, picks up the narrative again. Back in chapter one we heard about Megacles, a prominent Athenian from a distinguished and wealthy family, the Alcmaeonids, whose daughter had married Pisistratus. The tyrant, not wanting to have sons by an Alcmaeonid, had not had sex with her in the "conventional way," which brought an end to the honeymoon between their families. Later, after Pisistratus came to power for the third and final time, Megacles and the rest of the Alcmaeonids went into exile (1.64, 6.123). They and some other exiles had been trying to return to Athens by force and free the state from Pisistratid rule, but so far to no avail. They now hit on a scheme to entice the Spartans to help them out. The Alcmaeonids bribed the oracle at Delphi and got the priestess there to urge any Spartiates visiting the shrine to help the Athenians get rid of Hippias. After repeatedly receiving this same message from the oracle, the Spartans finally took action, sending an army by sea to Attica. They landed at Athens' harbor but were quickly thwarted by the Pisistratids and their Thessalian allies, and so this first Spartan expedition against Athens came to nothing.

The Spartans later sent another expedition, this time by land and with Cleomenes at its head. The Spartans quickly defeated the Thessalian cavalry, then laid siege to the Acropolis, where the Pisistratids had holed up. Herodotus explains that under normal circumstances, the Spartans' siege wouldn't have accomplished anything. Not having prepared for a lengthy campaign, they would have stayed in Athens for only a few days, and the Pisistratids, who were well supplied on the Acropolis, would have waited them out. But something unexpected happened. The children of the Pisistratids, who were secretly being conveyed out of the country for safekeeping, were captured. The Spartans now had a huge bargaining chip, and they used it to force the Pisistratids to leave Athens. Thus Hippias, after thirty-six years of rule, left Athens and retired to Sigeum on the Hellespont. And the Alcmaeonids, finally, went back home.

Cleisthenes and Isagoras (5.66–76)

The chief authority was lodged with two persons, Clisthenes, of the family
of the Alcmaeonids, who is said to have been the persuader of the Pythoness,
and Isagoras, the son of Tisander, who belonged to a noble house, but whose
pedigree I am not able to trace further.   (5.66.1)

In the wake of the Pisistratids' removal from Athens, two men vied for power:
Cleisthenes, the Alcmaeonid who was said to have bribed the oracle, and Isagoras, another aristocrat who, according to Aristotle, had been a supporter
of Hippias (*The Constitution of Athens* 20). In an attempt to increase his support in Athens, Cleisthenes took the *demos*—the mob, if you will—into his faction. ("Democracy" derives from the Greek words *demos* and *kratos*, "power.")
With the support of these average Athenians—in particular, poor Athenians—
Cleisthenes gained the upper hand, but Isagoras in turn asked his guest-friend
Cleomenes for help.

Cleomenes sent a herald to Athens demanding that the Athenians banish
Cleisthenes and the rest of the Alcmaeonids because they were polluted by
blood guilt. In fact, the Alcmaeonids *were* under a curse. Over a hundred years
earlier, in 632 (probably), a man named Cylon, an Olympic victor, had tried to
set himself up as tyrant in Athens. (Herodotus' account at 5.71 can here be supplemented with Thucydides 1.126.) The Athenians resisted the coup and laid
siege to the Acropolis, where Cylon and his party had taken refuge. Cylon and
his brother managed to escape, but those who were left behind took up position as suppliants at an altar. They were persuaded to give themselves up on the
understanding that they would not be killed, but when they surrendered, they
were killed anyway, and the man who was held responsible for the impiety was
an Alcmaeonid, Cleisthenes' great-grandfather Megacles. The Alcmaeonids
were exiled from Athens afterwards, but they were allowed back in the 590s. As
we've seen, they were exiled again after Pisistratus came to power—though that
time it wasn't because of the family curse. Now, with Cleomenes demanding
they be driven out again, the Alcmaeonids left Athens for the third time. But
that wasn't the end of the business.

Cleomenes marched on Athens with a small force and banished some seven
hundred families. He then tried to replace the current government with a narrow oligarchy comprised of Isagoras and some three hundred of his partisans,

but the Athenians didn't stand for it. When Isagoras and his supporters, Spartan and Athenian, seized the Acropolis, the rest of the Athenians laid siege to their own citadel. On the third day of the siege, Isagoras and the Spartans withdrew from Athens under a truce, but Isagoras' Athenian supporters were captured and executed. Meanwhile, Cleisthenes and the other Athenians who had been expelled at Cleomenes' bidding were recalled.

The Spartan force that had seized the Acropolis with Isagoras was a small one, insufficient to the task. Now Cleomenes, insulted at his ouster from Athens, began assembling a larger force with the idea of marching on Athens again and installing Isagoras as tyrant once and for all. The Athenians, meanwhile, were aware that they were likely to face Spartan retaliation, and they made their own preparations, sending to Persia, of all places, to ask for an alliance. Although allying with Persia was not at this point the sinister act it would become in a few years' time, it's not clear what the Athenians were hoping to accomplish by seeking an alliance. The Spartans, living right next door in the Peloponnese, could mobilize much more quickly than the Persians, even assuming they agreed to send help. So a Persian force was unlikely to be of any use in the face of imminent invasion from the Peloponnese. Still, an embassy was sent to Artaphernes in Sardis, who required that the Athenians give earth and water to the Persians in return for an alliance. Earth and water, remember, were tokens of submission in the Persian parlance. What the Persians demanded in return for their protection, in other words, was that the Athenians become vassals of the Great King.

I can almost hear you scoffing at the very idea. The Athenians, having cast off the yoke of Pisistratid tyranny and given Isagoras and his Spartan cronies the heave-ho, weren't about to hand the state over to Persia just like that. And yet, that's exactly what they did—or at least, that's what their ambassadors did. They gave the Persians earth and water, and when they returned home the Athenians were angry with them. According to Herodotus, the envoys had acted on their own authority in acceding to the Persian demands, but this is hard to believe. Perhaps instead, as some scholars have suggested, the envoys were acting under orders, but by the time they returned to Athens the situation was no longer so desperate: the Spartan invasion by that time had come to naught—see below— and the Athenians had the leisure to repent their earlier choices. We aren't told whether the Athenians, in addition to censuring their envoys, also rejected the alliance the men had brokered, but it hardly matters if they did: as far as the

Persians were concerned, the Athenians, whatever their regrets the morning after, had submitted to them.

Meanwhile, the Spartans gathered their allies and invaded Attica, but the expedition fell apart before much was accomplished. Some of Sparta's allies abandoned the campaign, and a disagreement between the two Spartan kings, Cleomenes and Demaratus, led to the latter going back home as well. The Spartan invasion that had so frightened the Athenians died with a whimper. Isagoras didn't have a future as an Athenian tyrant, but as we'll see, the Spartans weren't quite finished with trying to effect a change in Athens' leadership.

Herodotus doesn't go into much detail about what it meant for Cleisthenes to have appealed to the *demos* when he was vying against Isagoras, or what Cleisthenes accomplished later in Athens, except to mention that he reorganized the citizen body into ten new tribes from an earlier four. This may not sound like much, but it was far from insignificant. While the old tribes were hereditary, membership in the new tribes was based on geography: the state was divided into thirty units, and three of these units, from different parts of Attica, were combined into a single tribe, associating Athenians from diverse areas with one another and breaking up old allegiances. The basic unit of the state became the local village, or deme, and the organs of state—the new Council of Five Hundred that Cleisthenes introduced, the military, the archonships (public offices)—were now organized around the new tribal structure. (For readers interested in the particulars, Aristotle provides more information about the Cleisthenic reforms at *The Constitution of Athens* 20–22.) The power of the hereditary aristocracy was decreased by Cleisthenes' reforms while the authority of the *demos* increased. Cleisthenes, who is sometimes called the Father of Democracy, may not have intended as much, but his reforms left Athens a more democratic state. Further reforms later in the century would make it radically so.

We don't know what happened to Cleisthenes after he instituted his reforms. Some late sources hint that he was ostracized, that is, sent into exile for a period of ten years by vote of the citizenry. But this solution to the mystery of his fate is a little too tidy, since the institution of ostracism in Athens was another one of Cleisthenes' innovations. (Votes were cast in ostracisms on *ostraka*, bits of broken pottery, hence the name of the procedure. Here, I think, it is de rigueur to mention W. G. Forrest's quip that if Cleisthenes was in fact ostracized he was "hoist with his own potsherd.")[4] Many scholars have assumed that Cleisthenes, even if he was not ostracized, did fall out of favor because he was held responsible for the unpopular embassy to Persia. But the simplest explanation for Cleisthenes' disappearance from the historical record is perhaps the most likely, that he died soon after enacting his reforms or, at least, retired from public life.

The Further Intrigues of Hippias (5.90–96)

On the return of Hippias to Asia from Lacedaemon, he moved heaven and earth to set Artaphernes against the Athenians, and did all that lay in his power to bring Athens into subjection to himself and Darius.   (5.96.1)

Sometime after Cleomenes had failed for a second time to install Isagoras as tyrant, the Spartans decided to take action against Athens again. In general, they were feeling ill-disposed toward the Athenians. They had somehow found out about the Alcmaeonids' bribery of the oracle at Delphi, back when the Spartans were tricked into helping to expel the Pisistratids from Athens. In addition, while holed up on the Acropolis, Cleomenes had gotten his hands on some oracles, previously owned by the Pisistratids, which prophesied enmity between Sparta and Athens. And, generally speaking, the Athenians were not conducting their affairs as the Spartans would have wished. So it seemed best to try to replace the current Athenian government with one that was more congenial to Spartan interests. They sent for Hippias, who had retired to Sigeum on the Hellespont with the rest of his family, and when he arrived the Spartans tried to sell their allies on the idea of reinstalling Hippias as tyrant in Athens. The allies, however, chief among them Corinth, were opposed to the project. (The Corinthian representative at this meeting is depicted as giving a speech about the evils of tyranny in which he catalogues the abuses of the Corinthian tyrants Cypselus and Periander, some of which we've discussed already in chapter five.) Because of their allies' intransigence, the Spartans' plans for Athens were checked, and Hippias returned to Asia.

Disappointed in his hopes of being restored to Athens by the Spartans, Hippias went to Sardis and tried to stir up anti-Athenian sentiment there, hoping that Artaphernes might take up his cause. The Athenians somehow caught wind of Hippias' activities and sent a delegation themselves to Artaphernes urging him not to listen to Hippias, but he was unlikely to take their side in the matter: while they had repudiated the alliance their envoys had brokered with Persia, Hippias' appeal for Persian help showed he was perfectly comfortable with the idea of submitting Athens to Persian rule, provided he got to play the puppet tyrant. Artaphernes ordered the Athenians to take Hippias back "if they wished to be safe"—he was speaking to vassals of the Great King, remember, and could expect to be obeyed. But the Athenians bravely shrugged off the threat and, in not submitting to the demand, showed themselves to be openly at enmity with Persia.

The Ionian Revolt, Part II: Athens and the Burning of Sardis (5.97–105)

These ships were the beginning of mischief both to the Greeks and to the barbarians. (5.97.3)

It was at this point that Aristagoras came to Athens looking for an ally. The Athenians, having so recently ousted their own tyrant and more than a little peeved with Persia over the Hippias business, were more receptive than the Spartans had been to the idea of freeing the Ionians. Aristagoras made his case before the Athenian assembly, and the Athenians voted to send a fleet of twenty ships to help. "These ships," Herodotus writes, "were the beginning of evils [*arche kakon*] for the Greeks and the barbarians." If Herodotus sounds unusually dramatic here, it's probably because he is—surely consciously—echoing a passage in *The Iliad* (5.62–64) in which the ships that brought Paris to Sparta (where he would steal Helen and provoke the Trojan War) are described as "the beginning of evils" (*archekakous*) for the Trojans.

The Athenian fleet, joined by five ships from Eretria on Euboea, sailed off to Ionia and met up with the Ionian forces at Ephesus, north of Miletus on the coast of Asia Minor. The combined forces marched inland to Sardis, which lay about 150 miles to the northeast. They captured the city and burned it, although they were unable to capture the acropolis, which Artaphernes was defending. That done, the Ionians and their allies returned to Ephesus, but there they were caught and severely defeated by a Persian army that had trailed them from Sardis. The battle marked the end of Athens' brief involvement in the revolt. The Athenians sailed back home and refused Aristagoras' entreaties to help further. But in taking a hand in the burning of Sardis, they and the Eretrians had roused the anger of the Great King. Herodotus reports that when Darius heard of the burning of Sardis, he made little of the Ionians' involvement, as he was confident he would put down their rebellion. But he asked who the Athenians were—evidently having forgotten that they were, at least on papyrus, among his newest subjects and having forgotten as well whatever he may have learned about Athens from the spies he sent off to Greece with Democedes. When he got his answer, Darius shot an arrow into the sky and prayed for revenge. "Zeus," he said, "grant me the opportunity to punish the Athenians." And lest he forget about the Athenians this time, he ordered one of his servants to say to him three times whenever dinner was served, "Master, remember the Athenians." That was how one set daily repeating reminders before the advent of PDAs and smartphones.[5]

Herodotus' account suggests that the Athenians were foolish to support the Ionian Revolt, both because it called down Persian fury on their heads and because, he implies, the revolt was a doomed enterprise from the start. In describing Aristagoras' successful visit to Athens, Herodotus rather maliciously comments, "It is easier to mislead many men than one, since Aristagoras was not able to fool Cleomenes alone of the Lacedaemonians but he did fool thirty thousand of the Athenians." But the very fact that it took Darius five years to put down the Ionian Revolt, at such great cost, shows that the Ionians' cause was not inherently hopeless. And it's hard to believe that Athens and the rest of Greece weren't already in Persia's crosshairs, with or without the Athenians' intervention in Ionia. The Persians, with their campaigns in Thrace, were paving a road across the north Aegean coast to Macedon and northern Greece. And the Athenians had already come to the attention of the Persians when they gave earth and water to Artaphernes but refused to install Hippias as tyrant. It seems inevitable that the Persian juggernaut would be rolling west to swallow up the Greek states as it had Lydia and Ionia. As How and Wells write in their commentary at 5.97.2, the Athenians' mistake was not in supporting the Ionians but in deserting them.[6]

The Ionian Revolt, Part III: The Battle of Lade and the Fall of Miletus (5.108–123; 6.7–33)

The Persians, when they had vanquished the Ionians in the sea-fight, besieged Miletus both by land and sea, driving mines under the walls, and making use of every known device, until at length they took both the citadel and the town, six years from the time when the revolt first broke out under Aristagoras.   (6.18)

The Ionian Revolt continued without the Athenians, with many cities joining the cause after the fall of Sardis. Byzantium and other *poleis* around the Hellespont rebelled, as well as many cities to the south of Miletus and most of the island of Cyprus (5.103). But after these initial successes, things went downhill for the rebels. The Persians retook Cyprus, then began to reduce the rest of the Greeks, recapturing cities in the Hellespont and Caria and then moving into Ionia and Aeolia. In 494 the Persian forces descended on Miletus, where Aristagoras had hatched the revolt five years earlier. A great naval battle was fought at Lade, a small island in the Milesian harbor, 600 Persian ships, Herodotus says, ranged against the combined Ionian fleet of 353 ships. The Persians tried to undermine the rebels by having the tyrants who had been deposed send messages to their former subjects. They promised the rebels lenient treatment if they betrayed their fellow Greeks. The alternative, should the Greeks lose the battle, would be horrible to contemplate: enslavement, the castration of their sons, the seizure of their daughters. The Samians alone took the Persians up on their offer. When the fleets met, Herodotus says—though he admits he has heard conflicting reports and cannot be certain what happened—forty-nine of the Samians' sixty ships deserted the Greek lines, the commanders of eleven ships bravely ignoring their orders to withdraw. The Samians' mass defection, meanwhile, prompted other contingents to pull out. Of the Greeks who stayed to fight, the Chians fared the worst. After the Greeks lost the battle, some of the Chians made for home, but those whose ships had been disabled fled overland to Ephesus. Arriving in the middle of the night, the Chians were not recognized by their fellow Greeks. The men of Ephesus thought the Chians were there to steal their women, who were celebrating a festival (the Thesmophoria), and they came out and killed them.

After the Battle of Lade the Persians invested Miletus by land and sea. The city fell to the Persians in 494, and the Milesians suffered the expected results of their rebellion; most of their men were killed, and the women and children were taken captive. The city was burned. The Athenians took the Milesians' fate hard—hard enough, at least, that when the playwright Phrynichus staged a play entitled *The Capture of Miletus* in 493 he was fined a thousand drachmas for reminding his tearful audience of the tragedy. Future production of the play was forbidden in Athens. No fragments of it have survived.

After the fall of Miletus the Persians mopped up resistance around the Aegean, receiving the surrender of rebel cities in Caria and Ionia or reducing them by force. They castrated the most attractive boys they found in Ionia and sent the best-looking girls off to Darius. The Persians also captured the islands of Chios, Lesbos, and Tenedos and "netted" the inhabitants by way of hunting them down: we've seen this before, when Darius had Samos trawled with a net prior to handing it over to Syloson to govern. Syloson's son Aeaces, who had convinced the Samians to betray the Greek cause during the Battle of Lade, was restored as the island's tyrant. Samos, Herodotus says, was the only rebel state whose cities and temples weren't burned by the Persians—the Samians' reward for having deserted the Greeks.

Around this same time the Persians took the opportunity to expand their empire. They captured a number of cities on the European side of the Hellespont—the Thracian Chersonese—which had not previously been in Persia's possession. As we'll see in the next chapter, the Persians' actions in the area were to have consequences on the other side of the Aegean, since the tyrant who had been governing the Chersonese, an expatriate Athenian whom we've met briefly before, was forced by events to return home. Had Miltiades been permitted to live out his days by the Hellespont, he might have wound up living longer, but he probably wouldn't have made it into our history books.

The Further Adventures and Complicity of Histiaeus (5.106–107; 6.1–6, 26–30)

Darius, when he learnt what had taken place, found great fault with the men engaged in this business for not bringing Histiaeus alive into his presence, and commanded his servants to wash and dress the head with all care, and then bury it, as the head of a man who had been a great benefactor to himself and the Persians.   (6.30.2)

Aristagoras had not been present for the fall of Miletus. When the Persians began marching against Ionia, but before the Battle of Lade, Aristagoras and some of his followers fled north to Myrcinus in Thrace, the city Darius had given to Histiaeus as a reward after the Scythian expedition. According to Herodotus Aristagoras' flight was motivated purely by cowardice: having supposedly begun the revolt for selfish reasons—because he was worried about his position in Miletus after the failed expedition to Naxos—Aristagoras abandoned his allies when the going got rough. Scholars have suggested that other, less blameworthy considerations may have prompted Aristagoras' move to Thrace: that he was hoping to defeat the Persians who had remained in Europe, or that he wanted to secure revenue from the Thracian mines to bankroll the revolt. Whatever his motives, though, the move to Myrcinus didn't work out well for him. Aristagoras was killed while laying siege to a neighboring Thracian town.

It remains to discuss the fate of Aristagoras' alleged co-conspirator in the revolt, Histiaeus. When last we heard from him, Histiaeus was unhappily stuck in Darius' court at Susa, so homesick for Miletus that he sent a tattooed messenger to Aristagoras urging him to revolt. His plan, we're told, was to use the unrest as his ticket home: once Miletus had revolted, Darius would send him back to the coast to subdue it. The scheme was an unlikely one, but, at least as Herodotus tells the story, that's exactly what happened. After the Ionians and their allies burned Sardis, Darius confronted Histiaeus. He accused him of being complicit in the revolt since it was Histiaeus' deputy, Aristagoras, who had started it. But Histiaeus denied any involvement and suggested that it might not have happened had he remained in Ionia. He asked that Darius send him back home to restore order, and he promised to hand Aristagoras over to the king. Strangely, Histiaeus sweetened the pot by promising to subdue the island of Sardinia too. (Sardinia?! His throwing in a promise to capture a largish island on the other side of Italy seems incredible, but thus, allegedly, spake Histiaeus.) In denying his involvement in the revolt, Herodotus says, Histiaeus was lying, but he fooled Darius, who sent him off with the request that he return to Susa once he'd taken care of things in Miletus.

Darius' half-brother Artaphernes was not so easily taken in. When Histiaeus arrived in Sardis, Artaphernes accused him of having planned the revolt, whatever his denials. "Here's what happened, Histiaeus," he said. "You sewed the shoe, and Aristagoras put it on." Because Artaphernes had his number, Histiaeus quickly left Sardis for the coast. Again Herodotus tells us that Histiaeus had lied to Darius: he had said he would capture Sardinia, but he really meant to become the leader of the Ionian Revolt.

It's not always clear what Histiaeus was up to after he left Sardis, or whose side he was on. But in short, after trying and failing to regain the tyranny of Miletus, he wound up gathering a small army in the north Aegean and making piratical raids on the islands there. Finally a Persian army attacked Histiaeus' forces, and he was taken alive. He was captured rather than killed, in fact, because in the thick of the fighting, when he was about to be stabbed to death, he spoke in Persian, identifying himself to his assailant. Histiaeus hoped that, if he could make it out of the battle alive, Darius might forgive him any trespasses. He may have been right. Artaphernes, at least, seemed worried about just this outcome. Rather than sending Histiaeus off to Darius, where he might manage to wangle himself into a position of influence again, he had Histiaeus impaled. Then he cut off Histiaeus' head, had it embalmed, and sent it to the king in Susa. Darius, when the head arrived, was furious that Histiaeus hadn't been sent to him alive. He gave his minions a good talking-to, then ordered that Histiaeus' head be washed and properly buried, since the man had been of such great service to Persia.

Herodotus, with the wisdom of hindsight, presents the story of the Ionian Revolt as if its failure were a foregone conclusion. Aristagoras and Histiaeus are portrayed as having instigated the insurrection for selfish reasons, the one because of his failure in Naxos, the other out of a desire to return home from Susa. The truth of the matter was surely much more complicated, that both men—if indeed both had a hand in starting the revolt—were merely the most prominent actors in a larger story of growing anti-Persian, anti-tyrannical, pro-democratic sentiment in the Greek *poleis* of Asia Minor. A lot of ink has been spilled in particular over the enigmatic figure of Histiaeus. Herodotus seems to have no doubt about his complicity in the revolt: Histiaeus, according to Herodotus, sent the tattooed slave to Aristagoras urging him to revolt, and he lied to Darius when he denied having any involvement in the insurrection. But if you subtract from Herodotus' account his hostile commentary and the story of the tattooed messenger—the fantastic elements and too-convenient timing of which make one skeptical anyway—then all that's left is suspicion: Megabazus was reportedly suspicious of what Histiaeus' intentions were in Myrcinus; Darius was suspicious of Histiaeus because of his deputy Aristagoras' role in the revolt; Artaphernes was even more suspicious. All this adds up to a lot of smoke, and Histiaeus' metamorphosis into a piratical, opportunistic adventurer late in his career muddies our assessment of him. But it's not clear that Histiaeus, biding his time at the royal court in Susa, was in fact an architect of the revolt. In assuming he was, Herodotus may have been listening too uncritically to sources that were hostile to the tyrant.

With the Ionians subdued, the Persians turned their attention to further expansion in the west. Thanks to the Athenians' participation in the burning of Sardis, Darius was focused particularly on their punishment. He wasn't allowed to forget them, after all, since his reminder was delivered in triplicate every dinner time: "Master, remember the Athenians."

CHAPTER TEN

Miltiades, Madness, and Marathon

The First Persian War

WHILE THE PERSIANS WERE MOPPING things up in the Aegean after their defeat of the Ionians, the Greek tyrant of the Chersonese, Miltiades, decided it was time to pull up stakes and return to his native Athens. Miltiades, as we've seen, had a walk-on part in Herodotus' *History* during the Persians' Scythian expedition, when he advised the Ionians to abandon the bridge across the Ister. Now, as part of the build-up to his account of the battle of Marathon—during which Miltiades and his colleagues were destined to change the course of history—Herodotus provides us with Miltiades' backstory, beginning with an account of how his uncle, the elder Miltiades, won the tyranny of the Chersonese.

Miltiades in the Chersonese (6.34–41)

He now no sooner heard that the Phoenicians were attacking Tenedos than he
loaded five triremes with his goods and chattels, and set sail for Athens.

(6.41.1)

In the middle of the sixth century, the Chersonese was controlled by a Thracian tribe called the Dolonci who were faring poorly at the time in a war with a
neighboring tribe. Their kings went to Delphi to consult the oracle about the
war, and they were told that they should bring back as the "founder" of their
state whoever first offered them hospitality after they left the temple. So the
kings took off traveling down the so-called Sacred Road, which wound some
seventy-five miles to the southeast through Phocis and Boeotia until it hit Athens. It wasn't until the kings had reached Athens that anyone paid any attention
to them. Miltiades, the son of Cypselus, was on his porch when he saw them
walking by. He knew they were foreigners from their dress and the fact that
they were carrying spears—which wasn't the done thing in Athens—and he
called out to them and invited them to spend the night in his home. They took
him up on the offer, and at some point during the evening they let him know
about the oracle they'd received. Miltiades, since he wasn't crazy about how
things were being run in Athens—Pisistratus was tyrant at the time—agreed to
go with them. He gathered a group of colonists and sailed off to take possession
of his new homeland, where the Dolonci made him tyrant.

Once in power, Miltiades set about securing the area by building a wall
across the isthmus near its base, effectively turning the Chersonese—the name
literally means "land island" or peninsula—into an island. Miltiades also made
war on some of his new neighbors, including the people of Lampsacus, on the
Asian side of the Hellespont. The Lampsacenes in fact captured Miltiades during the hostilities, but they released him on the say-so of Croesus of Lydia, a
fan of Miltiades, who threatened to destroy the Lampsacenes "like a pine tree"
if they didn't comply. The threat reportedly had the Lampsacenes scratching
their heads for a while until they realized what Croesus meant: the pine tree
Croesus had in mind (the Corsican pine, or *Pinus Laricio*) is a tree which, once
cut down, doesn't put out new shoots. Croesus, that is, meant business. (What
Herodotus fails to mention is that the city of Lampsacus had earlier been
called "Pityousa," meaning "abounding in pine trees." So Croesus' arboreal
threat was a clever play on words, and one which the Lampsacenes themselves

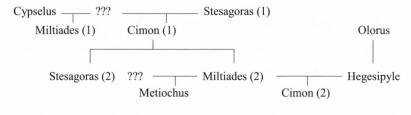

Miltiades' Family Tree

were likely to have understand at once, despite Herodotus' claim to the contrary.)

Miltiades ruled in the Chersonese for several decades. When he died, the tyranny passed to his nephew Stesagoras, the son of Miltiades' half-brother Cimon. But Stesagoras himself was soon dead—somebody hit him in the head with an axe—and the tyranny devolved upon Stesagoras' brother, the younger Miltiades. Miltiades duly sailed from Athens to the Chersonese and firmed up his position there by arresting some of the leading men of the area and marrying the daughter of the Thracian king, Olorus. (This Thracian Olorus, by the way, may have been the great-grandfather of the historian Thucydides, whose father's name was likewise Olorus.)

As we've seen, Miltiades took part in Darius' Scythian expedition in 513. Sometime after that—it's not clear from Herodotus' account precisely when or for how long—Miltiades was forced to flee the Chersonese because the Scythians were making inroads in the area. But he returned and took up his rule again in 496, when the Ionian Revolt was in full swing. Three years later, Miltiades was forced to leave the Chersonese for good. After the Ionians were defeated, the Persian fleet set about conquering islands off the coast of Asia Minor. When Miltiades heard that the Persians were at Tenedos, a tiny island only some fifteen miles from the mouth of the Hellespont, he set sail for Athens with a fleet of five ships. But before he'd even lost sight of the Chersonese, the Persians were on him. Miltiades himself escaped with four ships, but the Persians captured the fifth, which was commanded by Miltiades' son Metiochus. The Persians sent Metiochus off to Darius, thinking him a great prize, since he was the son of the man who'd argued in favor of abandoning the Ister bridge. But Darius, when Metiochus arrived, treated him well. Metiochus was given a house and a Persian wife, and the children he had with her were treated as Persians. Miltiades himself, having lost his son to Persia, made it safely to Athens, where he would soon win renown fighting against his son's adopted compatriots.

The Expedition of Mardonius (6.43–45)

But here a violent north wind sprang up, against which nothing could contend, and handled a large number of the ships with much rudeness, shattering them and driving them aground upon Athos.   (6.44.2)

In the spring of the following year Darius took his first stab at avenging himself on Athens and Eretria for their role in the burning of Sardis. He appointed his son-in-law/nephew Mardonius general and sent him off with an army and a large fleet. (Mardonius was the son of Darius' sister and Gobryas, one of the seven conspirators. Darius' daughter was married to Mardonius, and Darius himself was married to Gobryas' daughter, so Gobryas was at the same time father-in-law to both Darius and his daughter.)

Mardonius' army marched north through Ionia and west across Thrace while his fleet skirted the coast. Initially, the expedition was successful: the Persians conquered the island of Thasos and enslaved the Macedonians. (Herodotus' reference to the reduction of Macedon here is an apparent contradiction of his earlier report that the Macedonians surrendered to Persia back in 510. This is further reason to doubt Herodotus' story about Alexander I and the alleged murder of the Persian envoys by a bunch of guys in drag.) Mardonius would surely have followed up these successes with a march south through Greece, but fortune intervened to postpone the inevitable invasion. Mardonius' fleet was all but destroyed in a storm while he was attempting to sail around Athos, the easternmost of the three fingers of the Chalcidicean peninsula, which juts into the Aegean from the Thracian coast.[1] According to Herodotus, three hundred ships were lost and more than twenty thousand men killed, either drowned or battered to death on the rocks or eaten by the sharks that infest the area. The Persian army, meanwhile, was later attacked by the Brygi, a Thracian tribe. Many Persians were killed in the encounter, and Mardonius himself was

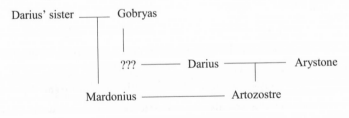

Darius' Marital Ties with Gobryas

injured. He stayed around long enough to conquer and enslave the Brygi, and then his battered fleet and army limped back to Asia, leaving Greece unmolested for the time being.

The Persian Heralds of 491 (6.48–49; 7.133–137)

When Darius some time before sent messengers for the same purpose, they were thrown at Athens into the pit of punishment, at Sparta into a well, and bidden to take therefrom earth and water for themselves, and carry it to their king.   (7.133.1)

Before he mounted yet another expedition against Greece, Darius sent heralds across the Aegean to demand earth and water from the various Greek states. Herodotus tells us that Darius sent men to both Sparta and Athens on this occasion but his messengers met with abuse in both *poleis*. The Spartans, we're told, threw the heralds into a well and told them to get their earth and water from there. The Athenians, so the story goes, threw the corpses of the heralds who visited them into a pit, the *barathron*, a natural chasm that the Athenians used for disposing of the bodies of wrongdoers.

The Athenians, as far as Herodotus was aware, escaped punishment for their treatment of the Persian heralds, but the Spartans suffered divine retribution because of their actions. There was a shrine in Sparta to Talthybius, the herald who led the captive woman Briseis from Achilles' tent in the first book of Homer's *Iliad* (1.320–323). His (purported) descendants, the Talthybiadae, served in Sparta as a hereditary class of heralds (cf. 6.60). After the Spartans' murder of the Persian heralds, the wrath of Talthybius fell on them, an otherworldly anger that manifested itself in the Spartans failing to obtain favorable omens when they performed sacrifices. Disturbed by this, the Spartans repeatedly met in assembly and finally resolved to send two scapegoats to Persia to atone for their offense. Two men volunteered for the job, Sperthias and Bulis. They traveled all the way to Susa and surrendered themselves to Xerxes—Darius was dead by this time—offering their lives as recompense for the lives of the Persian heralds (although they refused, as free men, to make obeisance to the king while they were there). Xerxes, however, refused to kill them, both because he didn't want to do to the Spartans what they'd done to the Persians and because he didn't want to absolve the Spartans of their guilt by killing their representatives in turn. So Sperthias and Bulis returned to Sparta, and the wrath of Talthybius hung over the Spartans' heads for another sixty years until they were finally punished for their offense.

In 430, during the early stages of the Peloponnesian War, the Spartans and some of their allies in the Peloponnese sent an embassy to Persia to ask the king to ally with them against Athens. (Herodotus' account of this embassy can be supplemented by Thucydides 2.67.) The Spartans contributed three men to the group, two of whom were Aneristus and Nicolas, the sons, respectively, of Sperthias and Bulis. They never made it to Persia. The Peloponnesians were captured *en route* by Thracians and handed over to Athens. The Athenians killed the envoys without giving them a hearing and threw their bodies into a pit—perhaps the *barathron*, though neither Herodotus nor Thucydides says that specifically. Herodotus sees divinity at work in the incident because of the coincidence of the parties involved, that the Spartan envoys killed by the Athenians should be the sons of the men whose deaths were meant to assuage Talthybius. But because heralding was a family business in Sparta, the coincidence is perhaps not as striking as it at first appears. It would make sense if the Spartans who volunteered to atone for the murder of the Persian heralds were themselves heralds and thus Talthybiadae. And that Aneristus and Nicolas were sent as envoys to Persia likewise suggests that they—and thus their fathers— were Talthybiadae. Since the pool of Talthybiadae available for service was a limited one, it's not very surprising that the envoys killed in 430 should be the sons of the heralds selected as scapegoats in 491. We need not, with Herodotus, see divinity at work in the incident. (The Athenians' execution of the Peloponnesian envoys, by the way, is the latest event Herodotus reports in his *History*. We know, therefore, that he must have lived until at least 430.)

Scholarly opinion differs as to whether the Persians in fact sent heralds to Athens as well as Sparta in 491, as Herodotus reports. Against Herodotus' evidence is the history of Athens' relationship with the Persian Empire. The Athenians had already given earth and water to Persia in 507 and had then repudiated their alliance. They refused to reinstall Hippias as tyrant when ordered to do so by Artaphernes, and, most dramatically, they joined the Ionians in burning Sardis in 498. Because of their perfidy, Darius had supposedly been told to "remember the Athenians" thrice daily for the previous seven years. Given all this, it seems unlikely that the Persians would approach Athens in 491 as if there were no bad blood between them. The Athenians, then, probably never threw Persia's envoys into the *barathron*. That story may have been an invention suggested by what happened to the envoys sent to Sparta.

Whatever the truth about the Persian embassy to Athens, it's clear that neither the Athenians nor the Spartans gave earth and water to Persia in 491. Many other Greeks surrendered to Persia at once, however—all of the islanders the heralds contacted and many of the mainland states as well. The expression in Greek for collaborating with the Persians was "medizing," going over to "the Mede." (The Greeks often referred to the Persians as Medians, although Persia had absorbed the Medes in the mid-sixth century.)[2] Among those who medized was the island of Aegina, a longtime commercial rival and military foe of Athens that lay in the Saronic Gulf, less than twenty miles from Piraeus, one of Athens' harbors.[3] The Athenians, understanding the Aeginetans' alliance with Persia to be a threat to themselves, called in the Spartans for help.[4] Herodotus' account of the Spartan campaign that followed introduces a lengthy discussion of Sparta's kings, Cleomenes and Demaratus.

The Deposition of Demaratus (6.50–70)

Then one of his servants came and told him the news, as he sat in council with the Ephors; whereat, remembering when it was that the woman became his wife, he counted the months upon his fingers, and having so done, cried out with an oath, "The boy cannot be mine." (5.63.2)

When the Athenians appealed to Sparta for help against Aegina, Cleomenes crossed over to the island intending to arrest the men who were most responsible for medizing. But when he attempted to do this, the Aeginetans opposed him, and in particular they objected that Cleomenes could not have been acting on the authority of the Spartan state since he was not accompanied by Sparta's other king, Demaratus. The argument, Herodotus tells us, was in fact suggested to them in a letter from Demaratus, who was back in Sparta saying nasty things behind Cleomenes' back. Apparently the Aeginetans' complaint was technically valid, too, because it prompted Cleomenes to go back to Sparta without arresting anyone. Once back home, Cleomenes set about trying to get rid of Demaratus, who'd been a thorn in his side since at least 506, when he had abandoned the campaign to install Isagoras as tyrant in Athens (5.75).

Demaratus had been king for some twenty years already, but Cleomenes sought to depose him on the grounds that he was ineligible for the monarchy. Unfortunately for Demaratus, there was reason to suspect his legitimacy. Before he became king, Demaratus' (purported) father Ariston had ruled in

Sparta. After marrying two wives in succession he was still childless, and so he sought to marry a third time. In particular, he was lusting after the beautiful wife of his best friend, Agetus. He determined to steal her from Agetus by trickery. He suggested to his friend that they make a trade: each of them could choose whatever they liked of the other's possessions. Agetus agreed, not suspecting what Ariston was up to, and they sealed the deal with oaths. Agetus made his selection first, whatever it was, and then Ariston chose his friend's wife for himself. Agetus wasn't happy about it, and presumably their friendship was never the same again, but Ariston got the girl. Less than nine months later, he also got a bouncing baby boy. He was sitting in council with other Spartan officials when a messenger came and told him he had a son. Ariston counted up the months on his fingers (*epi daktulon*), then said something he would later come to regret: "He could not be my son." The officials who were with him heard the remark but, incredibly, made nothing of it. These men, Sparta's five ephors— the name literally means "overseers"—were elected officers who were tasked with keeping an eye on the kings and were concerned in particular with the maintenance of the two royal houses. The ephors had actually sat and watched when Cleomenes' half-brother Dorieus was born to make sure everything was legitimate: there had been some question as to whether the woman was in fact pregnant (5.41). And yet here the king himself was swearing the baby his wife had just delivered wasn't his own, and they did nothing! But that, at any rate, is how the story goes. Ariston later decided the baby was in fact his, and when he died Demaratus succeeded him on the throne, apparently without anyone calling his legitimacy into question.

Cleomenes set out to change that. When he got back from Aegina he came to an understanding with a certain Leotychidas, who was a member of Demaratus' royal house and thus himself eligible for kingship. Leotychidas was the perfect guy for Cleomenes to approach because he hated Demaratus: some time back, the king—like father, like son—had stolen the girl Leotychidas was slated to marry. Demaratus had in fact actually seized the girl, abducting her and making her his wife before Leotychidas could have her, a so-called marriage by capture or abduction marriage. So Leotychidas was happy enough to plot with Cleomenes to steal his kinsman's throne. And he promised, if Cleomenes made him king, that he would go over to Aegina with Cleomenes to take care of the unfinished business there.

Leotychidas lodged a complaint saying that Demaratus was unfit to rule because he wasn't Ariston's son. There was a trial. The ephors who'd witnessed

Ariston's comment when Demaratus was born, who were probably well into their eighties at this point, were dragged in to testify. Finally, after much debate—and at the suggestion of Cleomenes—they decided to refer the matter to the oracle at Delphi. This must have been Cleomenes' plan all along. He arranged things so that the oracle would give the answer he wanted. He knew a guy with influence at Delphi, and that guy somehow got the priestess to play along. So when the Spartans consulted the oracle, the priestess told them that Demaratus was not Ariston's son, and he was removed from the kingship. Later on, when Cleomenes' shenanigans were discovered, the priestess lost her job, and the man who'd acted as intermediary was banned from Delphi.

Demaratus remained in Sparta for a time after he lost the kingship, and he was in fact elected to some office or other—Herodotus doesn't say what it was. But when he was sitting in the stands at the Festival of Naked Boys—a festival which involved choruses of, you guessed it, naked boys—Leotychidas' servants came over and made fun of him, asking how he liked holding an elected office after being king. That pushed Demaratus over the edge. The remark, he said, would be the beginning of either ten thousand evils or ten thousand blessings, but what he really meant was the former: they'd be sorry. He went home, packed his bags, and summoned his mother, and when she got there he did what he probably should have done years before: he begged her to tell him the truth about his birth. Was he in fact Ariston's son? Or the son of her former husband? Or was there some truth to the rumors he'd heard about her and their mule driver?

The truth, it turns out, was a little more complicated than he had imagined. Demaratus' mother explained that three days after she'd come to live with Ariston, a phantom that looked exactly like her new husband had had sex with her and given her garlands. When the phantom left, Ariston himself came in and asked her where she'd gotten the garlands. She said something like, "From you, silly," which led to the expected confusion, and finally they figured out that she'd had sex with the phantom of a hero whose shrine the garlands had been stolen from. She also had sex with Ariston that night, which is the night she got pregnant, so Demaratus' father was either Ariston himself or the Ariston-shaped ghost of a dead hero. Meanwhile, Demaratus was born prematurely, which is why Ariston had leapt to the conclusion that he wasn't the baby's father. But he just hadn't understood at the time that babies could be born early. He had come to acknowledge his mistake later.

Demaratus, having finally gotten the truth from his mother (such as it was), left town, saying he was going to Delphi. In fact, he meant to leave Greece. The Spartans suspected he was trying to run away, and they went after him and tried to arrest him. This may be because there was a law on the books forbidding the descendants of Heracles—that is, members of the Spartan royal houses— to live among foreigners (Plutarch, *Agis* 11). (As commentators have pointed out, though, if Demaratus was illegitimate, then he wasn't a Heraclid and so shouldn't have been covered by this law.) Demaratus gave his would-be captors the slip, however, and made his way finally to Persia, where he became an advisor to the king. We'll be hearing more from him later in Herodotus' *History*.

The Madness of Cleomenes (6.73–84)

So Cleomenes came back; but had no sooner returned than he, who had never been altogether of sound mind, was smitten with downright madness.   (6.75.1)

With Demaratus out of the picture and Leotychidas installed in his place, there was nothing to stop Cleomenes from dealing with the Aeginetans. The two kings went over to Aegina and took ten of the island's leading men as hostages, and they gave them for safekeeping to the Aeginetans' enemies, the Athenians. (The Athenians' refusal to return these hostages later was the cause of renewed hostility between Athens and Aegina [6.85–93].) Presumably the men were intended to serve as guarantors of Aegina's behavior if—when—the Persians came.

Soon after the Aegina business was settled, the truth about Cleomenes' treatment of Demaratus came out. Fearing what the Spartans would do, Cleomenes fled to Arcadia, the area north of Sparta in the middle of the Peloponnese, and tried to organize the Arcadians into an anti-Spartan league. To get him to stop, the Spartans invited Cleomenes to come back and rule again as king. He returned but, almost immediately, he went crazy—or more crazy, since Herodotus says there were signs earlier too that he was disturbed. Now, whenever he encountered one of the Spartiates, he'd hit him in the face with his stick. Finally Cleomenes' family locked him up in "the wood," a device similar to our stocks but designed to detain a prisoner by the foot or feet. Cleomenes was also kept under guard. Unfortunately, the human element in the Spartans' security system proved to be its weakness. Cleomenes asked his guard for a knife. The man at first refused him, but Cleomenes threatened him with future abuse. The guard was just a helot, so he was naturally fearful of the king's reprisals: presumably he wouldn't be locked up forever. Finally he gave his prisoner a knife, and Cleomenes put it to use:

> Cleomenes took the knife and began mutilating himself, starting from the calves. Cutting his flesh lengthwise he advanced from his calves to his thighs, and from his thighs to his hips and loins until he got to his belly; he cut this in strips as well and so died.

The Greeks offered various explanations for Cleomenes' insanity, but most agreed that he went mad because he had somehow offended the gods: he'd corrupted the priestess in the Demaratus affair (as most Greeks thought), or he'd ravaged a sacred precinct in Eleusis (the Athenians), or he'd murdered Argive prisoners and burned down a sacred grove (the Argives). The Spartans themselves offered a more natural explanation, that Cleomenes' went crazy because he'd been drinking unusually strong wine after spending time with a bunch of Scythian ambassadors. Some modern scholars, more cynical than Cleomenes' contemporaries, have suspected the story of his suicide was a cover-up. They suggest the ephors lured Cleomenes back from Arcadia to Sparta and had him murdered, a final solution to the troubles he was causing them. But the truth of what happened, unfortunately, is lost to us.

The Persian Advance: Naxos and Eretria (6.94–101)

> These were no sooner entered within the walls than they plundered and burnt all the temples that there were in the town, in revenge for the burning of their own temples at Sardis; moreover, they did according to the orders of Darius, and carried away captive all the inhabitants.   (6.101.3)

Darius, meanwhile, was keeping busy, preparing to send another expedition against Athens and Eretria. He replaced his son-in-law Mardonius—whose expedition to Greece via Thrace had been such a failure—with two new generals, Datis and Artaphernes, the latter the son of Darius' half-brother Artaphernes. These men gathered their forces in Cilicia, on the southeast coast of Asia Minor, and sailed west with a fleet of some six hundred ships. (So Herodotus reports, but the number is probably too large: generally speaking, Herodotus cannot be relied on to get the numbers right when discussing the size of Persian forces.) This time, the Persians would avoid the dangers of sailing around the Athos Peninsula in Thrace—where Mardonius' fleet had been destroyed—by cutting across the Aegean, subduing the Cycladic Islands along the way. The Persians' first piece of business was to capture Naxos: the island had not been destined for destruction back in 499, when Aristagoras of Miletus made his failed expedition, but the Naxians' reprieve was over. This time the Persians took the island and enslaved as many of its inhabitants as they could catch. The people of Delos, meanwhile, which lay to the northwest, fled north while the Persians were at Naxos. But Datis sent a herald to assure them that they could return home safely: Delos was the birthplace of the twin gods Artemis and Apollo, and as such neither it nor its inhabitants would be harmed. In sparing the Delians, the Persians may have wanted to avoid offending their Ionian sailors, or they may have shown restraint per the request of their resident Greek expert: accompanying the Persians was none other than the ousted Pisistratid Hippias, now an old man intent on regaining the tyranny of Athens before he died.

After Naxos the Persians sailed around the Aegean, taking hostages and gathering troops and generally intimidating the Greeks into surrendering without a fight. The first real show of resistance came from the people of Carystus, a city on the southern coast of Euboea, but they didn't hold out for long: the Persians laid siege and ravaged the country, and in the end the Carystians medized like all the rest. The Eretrians, with this vast Persian armada sailing against them intent on their destruction, weren't sure what to do. Some of them argued for abandoning their city and hiding out in the heights of Euboea. Others were in favor of surrendering. They begged Athens to send help, but the Athenians had problems of their own to worry about: they were next on the Persians' list. They did, however, arrange to have help sent from Chalcis, which lay very near Eretria on Euboea. About fifteen years earlier the Athenians had established four thousand colonists in the city (5.77). It was these men who now came to Eretria's defense, at least briefly. After they'd arrived, a leading Eretrian, who understood his city was likely to be betrayed from within, urged the Athenian colonists to abandon the Eretrians and save themselves. They took his advice, and left not only Eretria but Euboea itself, crossing over to mainland Greece.

When the Persians came, the Eretrians opted to stay behind their walls. They were hoping to survive a siege, but they managed to hold out for only six days. On the seventh, the city was betrayed. The Persians burst in and plundered the city and burned its temples—recompense for the Eretrians' burning of Sardis—and they enslaved the inhabitants. The Athenians, awaiting events to the south, had little time left now before their own day of judgment.

Marathon, Part I: Premonitions and Other Preliminaries (6.102–108)

So they waited for the full of the moon.   (6.106.3)

After a few days in Eretria, the Persians sailed to Attica. They landed at Marathon, in the northeast corner of the *polis*, an area that offered both a sheltered harbor and a plain suitable for cavalry action: the Persians had brought horses across the Aegean. The Persians were guided to Marathon by Hippias, whose father, Pisistratus, had likewise landed at Marathon, in 546, before his third, successful attempt to gain the tyranny of Athens (1.62). Hippias' hopes of being restored as tyrant in Athens had been nurtured by the dream he'd had the previous night. In it he was sleeping with his mother, a vision Hippias understood to mean that after reestablishing himself in Athens he would die in his native country. But his optimism on that score was short-lived. Not long after the Persians disembarked, while he was arranging them in battle order, Hippias had a coughing fit so violent that one of his teeth, which was already loose, fell out of his mouth and onto the ground. Hippias searched frantically for the tooth, but he couldn't find it, and he was finally forced to accept the implications of the loss: it was not he but his tooth that was destined to end its days embraced by Attic soil. More to the point, as he announced to those around him, the loss of his tooth meant the Persians would not be subjugating Athens after all. Hippias was right, of course, but the Persians wouldn't be taking his word for it: the battle had yet to be fought and lost.

After the Athenians learned of the fall of Eretria, they sent a runner to Sparta to relay the news and ask for help. The man—whose name was either Phidippides or, more probably, Philippides—was a *hemerodromos*, a professional long-distance runner or "day runner." Philippides made it to Sparta, some 136 miles away, the day after he left Athens, so in something less than 48 hours. (This impressive feat may sound unlikely, but it is by no means impossible: the "Spartathlon"—a race from Athens to Sparta commemorating Philippides' run—has been held annually since 1983. The current record for completion of the race is 20 hours, 25 minutes, set by Yiannis Kouros in 1984.) The Spartans' response to Philippides' message, meanwhile, must have been transmitted back to Athens somehow, but though later sources credit Philippides with running back to Athens in time to fight at Marathon, Herodotus doesn't say anything about his return trip. (That he also ran at high speed back to Athens seems impossible, but again, it's been done: Yiannis Kouros has made the run from Athens to Sparta and back in 53 hours and 43 minutes.)[5]

Herodotus likewise makes no mention of a runner being dispatched from Marathon after the battle to report the news at Athens. That story, probably more familiar to modern readers, appears only in much later sources—Plutarch (*Moralia* 347c) and Lucian (*Pro Lapsu* 3), who wrote in the first and second centuries A.D., respectively. That runner allegedly fell dead upon reaching Athens and giving his news—a sensational detail that was probably a later embellishment to the story, given that Herodotus elected not to mention it in his *History.* The shorter run from Marathon to Athens—between 22 and 26 miles depending on the route taken by the runner—was the inspiration for our modern marathon race, an event created for the first modern Olympics in 1896. (Marathon has crept into our common parlance also, less happily, by giving us the -athon suffix, which is to events impressive for their duration—walk-a-thons, Toyotathons, and so on—what -gate has become for political scandals since Watergate.)

The Spartans thus received word of the Persians' imminent arrival in Attica soon after the Athenians themselves knew of it, but though they were eager to help their neighbors, they were unable to act immediately. When Philippides arrived it was the ninth day of the first phase of the moon, and the Spartans said they would not be able to march out until the moon was full. This has usually been understood to mean that the Spartans were celebrating the Carnea, an important festival of Apollo that lasted from the 7th to the 15th of the Spartan month of Carnea (our August or September), though Herodotus doesn't spell this out. But the inability of the Spartans to march at once, if alarming for the Greeks whose lives hung in the balance, is something of a gift for the storyteller, since it heightens the tension of what happened next. The clock was now ticking: once the moon was full, the Spartans would come. If the Athenians could delay the fight long enough, they wouldn't have to face the Persians alone. Their city—their lives and the lives of their children—might yet be saved.

Unlike the Eretrians, who had opted to try their luck at withstanding a siege, the Athenians decided to march out and meet the Persians. (Herodotus doesn't mention anything about the debate within Athens that must have preceded this decision, though Aristotle, writing in the fourth century B.C. [*Rhetoric* 1411a10], refers to a decree passed at the time that called for the Athenians to provision themselves and take the field.)[6] The Athenians marched to Marathon and took up position there in a sanctuary of Heracles. They were soon joined by the full army of Plataea, a town in Boeotia—the area just north of Attica—that had allied with Athens some thirty years earlier. Scholars estimate that the Athenians had about 10,000 men in the field, the Plataean contingent adding perhaps a thousand more. Estimates for the size of the Persian army vary, but most historians would put the number of fighting men—that is, not counting support staff—at about 20,000 or 25,000.[7] The Athenians and their allies, that is, were outnumbered by at least two to one. The Greeks had the advantage, however, when it came to equipment. They carried large shields and were protected by heavy armor—helmets and greaves (shin guards) and corselets: the equipment, *hopla* in Greek, from which the heavily armed Greek infantryman, or hoplite, took his name. The Persians, however, carried wicker shields and wore felt hats. They may not have had any body armor at all: in describing a later battle between Greeks and Persians Herodotus says that the latter fought "naked," that is, without protective clothing (9.62–63). Having taken up their positions on the Marathon plain, the Greek and Persian armies, mismatched as they were in size and accessories, waited for the battle to begin.

Marathon, Part II: The Long Wait (6.109–110)

> The Athenian generals were divided in their opinions; and some advised not
> to risk a battle, because they were too few to engage such a host as that of
> the Medes, while others were for fighting at once; and among these last was
> Miltiades.   (6.109.1)

As we've seen, the Athenians had every reason to delay the onset of battle. If they waited long enough, the Spartans would get there in time to help. They also held a good defensive position on the plain, which allowed them to block the Persians' approach to Athens. Still, as Herodotus tells the story, Athens' military commanders were not unanimously in favor of delaying the fight. The army had marched out to Marathon under the command of all ten of its generals. (Ever since Cleisthenes' democratic reforms at the turn of the century, ten generals had been elected annually in Athens, one from each of the new tribes.) Another military official was also on hand, the polemarch, or war archon. The *polemarchia* was an office in transition at this point. While the polemarch had been the principal military official in Athens before Cleisthenes' reforms, the office would begin to diminish in importance a few years after the battle at

Marathon. It's not clear precisely what the balance of power between the generals and the polemarch was in 490. Herodotus' evidence for that relationship is ambiguous: the polemarch's vote in councils-of-war seems to have weighed more heavily than that of any individual general, yet the polemarch apparently never held operational command, which was instead rotated among the generals from day to day. Herodotus, however, who was writing decades after the *polemarchia* had lost its military importance, may not have properly understood the command structure at Marathon.

According to Herodotus, the generals were divided in opinion over the question of whether to fight or not. Presumably what Herodotus means is that they were arguing about whether to fight sooner rather than later, since turning tail and marching back to Athens was surely not an option: the decision to meet the Persians in the field rather than withstand a siege had already been made. Among those who wanted to fight was Miltiades, the former tyrant of the Chersonese, who had returned to Athens in 493 and was now serving as one of Athens' generals. With the generals undecided about what to do (they may have been equally divided in their opinions, but this isn't clear from the Greek), Miltiades went to the polemarch, whose name was Callimachus, and tried to talk him into voting in favor of a fight. Miltiades didn't say anything to Callimachus about waiting for the Spartans—which would have been a point in favor of further delay. The thrust of his argument was that the longer the Athenians delayed, the more likely it was that some of them would decide to medize. Athens, that is, could be betrayed from within, just as Eretria had been. The Persians, presumably, were hoping for just such an outcome: they had Hippias with them, after all, and must have assumed—or been convinced by him—that there was a pro-Pisistratid faction in Athens that would rally on his behalf.

Miltiades' argument was persuasive. Callimachus threw his weight behind the pro-fight group and the decision was finally made: the Athenians would fight. Or they would fight sooner rather than later. At any rate, it was all systems go. The impediment to their taking immediate action was removed and so . . . they waited some more. Herodotus says that each of the generals, when his time came to command the army, surrendered his authority to Miltiades. But still, Miltiades didn't make a move until his own turn had come around, some days after the decision to fight was made. Only then did the Athenians draw up in battle order and advance against the Persians.

Herodotus' account, unfortunately, doesn't make much sense. For one thing, as we mentioned above, Herodotus is not very clear about what the generals were arguing over: whether they should fight at all—an argument that would more properly have occurred back in Athens, before they marched out—or fight at once? Nor does it make sense that the generals, having finally decided not to wait for the Spartans because of the danger posed by potential medizers, should then wait for several more days because of a technicality about whose day of command it was. These issues and numerous other questions pertaining to the Marathon campaign have been endlessly debated by modern scholars, and I would urge interested readers to dive into the secondary literature if they want to gorge themselves on the minutiae. But it makes sense, I think, to assume that Herodotus' explanation for the delay at Marathon is a distortion of the real reasons behind it: the Athenians were waiting as long as possible for the arrival of the Spartans. When they finally did fight, before the Spartans arrived, it was because they were forced by circumstances to do so.

The Athenians may have decided to initiate battle themselves because some tactical advantage had presented itself. A very late source—an encyclopedia compiled in the tenth century A.D. (Suda, "Choris hippeis" = chi 444)—preserves an anecdote not found in any other source. Supposedly, the Ionians serving in Darius' army at one point signaled to the Athenians that the Persian cavalry were "apart," evidently meaning they were somehow separated from the main force, or not where they were supposed to be. Miltiades may have initiated action to take advantage of the opportunity this presented. Alternatively, the Persians may have forced the Athenians' hand by initiating battle themselves, either because they finally despaired of getting help from Athenian medizers or because they wanted to act before the Athenians received reinforcements. However begun, though, and whatever the reasons for delay, the battle was finally on.

Marathon, Part III: The Battle (6.111–120)

There fell in this battle of Marathon, on the side of the barbarians, about six thousand and four hundred men; on that of the Athenians, one hundred and ninety-two.　(6.117.1)

Greek infantry battles of this period were a collective affair. Heavily armed soldiers—hoplites—were arranged in a phalanx, usually eight ranks deep, to form a massive rectangle of men that marched in column. They were equipped with swords and iron-tipped spears, some seven feet long, and on their left forearms they carried great round shields. The hoplite's shield (*hoplon*) was about three feet in diameter and made of bronze-plated wood. Its weight has been estimated at sixteen pounds, a heavy burden to be carrying on one arm for any length of time. The *hoplon* protected its bearer's left side and protruded beyond him to protect the right side of the man next to him. The safety of the individual, that is, depended on his remaining stationed alongside his linemates. If he broke rank or turned and fled, he made himself more vulnerable while also endangering the cohesion of the phalanx. (Interestingly, there was a tendency for a phalanx to drift to the right when marching, as each man in the line would move so as to shelter his unprotected side more thoroughly with his neighbor's shield [Thucydides 5.71.1].)

The Athenians, now that the time had come to fight, drew up their lines for battle. The polemarch Callimachus was on the right wing of the phalanx. The Plataeans held the left. And the line was made as long as that which the Persians was fielding: the armies were probably each about a mile wide. Since the Greeks had fewer fighters than their enemy, their line had to be lengthened to equal that of the Persians. They achieved this by thinning out and extending the center. So while the wings of the army were eight or more ranks deep, the center was only a few ranks deep and thus the weakest part of the line. As Miltiades will probably have guessed, since he had fought alongside the Persians during his stint in the Chersonese, the Greeks' weak center would be facing the Persians' best troops. The Greeks advanced from their initial position about a mile from the Persians, and when they got closer—some 200 or 250 yards away—they did something no hoplite army had ever done before: they charged the enemy at a run. They thus minimized the time they would be vulnerable to the Persians' archers. The charge must also have shocked the pants off of the Persians, which was probably a second reason for adopting the tactic.[8]

The Athenians and Plataeans crashed into the Persian line, and the fight was on. Judging from what happened in the battle, the plan going in must have been for the Greek center to hold its position as long as possible, giving the stronger wings the time to defeat the Persians ranged against them. Once they'd done so, and the Persians were fleeing before them, the hoplites on the wings were to leave off pursuit, re-form, and attack the Persians' center from the rear. And that's what happened: the Greeks were victorious on both wings while the Persians eventually broke through the Greek center. The wings, now attacking the Persians from behind, put them to flight. The Persians fled to their ships and scrambled madly to get on board. Meanwhile, the Athenians were slaughtering as many of them as they could and trying to set fire to the ships. Great numbers of men probably died at this stage: among them were, on the Athenian side, the polemarch Callimachus and one of the generals, Stesilaus, son of Thrasylaus. A man named Cynegirus died in the fighting by the ships as well, after his hand was chopped off with an ax as he grabbed hold of the stern of a ship. He was the brother of the playwright Aeschylus, who also fought at Marathon (though Herodotus does not mention him). Aeschylus—the author of the *Oresteia* trilogy, among other works, known as the "father of tragedy"—is said to have made no mention of his prestigious literary career in his epitaph, which he composed himself. Instead, he mentions as his greatest distinction the fact of his having fought at Marathon: "Of his glorious might the grove at Marathon could tell, and the long-haired Medes—for they know!" (Athenaeus 14.627d, trans. Charles Burton Gulick)

The Athenians captured seven Persian ships, and the rest of the Persians, as many as got out of Marathon alive, sailed away. But they didn't go back to Persia right away. Instead, they sailed about seventy miles around the southern cape of Attica, hoping to beat the Athenian army back to Athens. Perhaps, as Jim Lacey sensibly suggests, they intended to burn Athens in retribution for the burning of Sardis, but if so, they were disappointed.[9] The Athenians marched the more than twenty miles back to Athens (this probably happened the day after the battle) and got there before the barbarians. With the veterans of Marathon standing ready to defend the city, the Persians would not set Athens aflame, at least not this time. After riding at anchor for a while in the Athenian harbor, the barbarians sailed back to Asia with some very bad news to tell their king.

Herodotus reports that 6400 Persians were killed at Marathon. Against that number only 192 Athenians died. These heroes of Marathon were buried on the battleground: the mound heaped over their mass grave is still visible on the Marathon plain.

After the full moon, finally, the Spartans arrived. Herodotus says they made it to Athens on the third day after they'd left Sparta. This may not be true: the Spartans had almost 140 miles to cover while carrying battle gear. But the implication is that they got there as quickly as they possibly could once it was permissible for them to leave Sparta. They'd missed the battle but were eager to see the Persians. They went to Marathon and looked at the rotting corpses. They praised the Athenians for their accomplishment. And they went back home.

The burial mound of the 192 Athenians who died at Marathon in 490 B.C. is still visible on the Marathon plain. Published on Wikimedia Commons by Dgcampos (http://commons.wikimedia.org/wiki/File:Tumulusmarathon.JPG); and released under the following licenses: GNU Free Documentation License; Creative Commons Attribution-Share Alike 3.0 Unported; Free Art License. It is free to reuse, including commercially.

The Shield Signal and the Alcmaeonidae (6.115, 121–131)

A shield was shown, no doubt; that cannot be gainsaid; but who it was that showed it I cannot any further determine.   (6.124.2)

Herodotus says that there was a rumor current in Athens alleging that when the Persians were already in their ships after the battle at Marathon, the Alcmaeonidae—the prominent, often-exiled Athenian family that had been instrumental in freeing Athens from Pisistratid rule in 510—signaled to the enemy by raising a shield. The signal was sent because of a prior arrangement between the Alcmaeonidae and the Persians, so the story went, and it's what prompted the Persians to sail to Athens.

The shield signal, if it was in fact given, must have been sent from a prearranged location that was relatively close to the shore, since it was visible to the Persians offshore and they will have known where to look for it. (Some have supposed that the shield was used to flash a signal to the Persians, but this has been adequately disputed. Herodotus is clear, for one thing, in saying that the signal was the raising of a shield, not its flashing. Because of its curvature, moreover, a shield of the period could not have been used to transmit a flash of light intense enough to be seen at a great distance.)[10] The message relayed, meanwhile, given the nature of the signal, must have been a simple one, also prearranged. The raising of a single shield apparently signified that the Persians should sail to Athens. We can only guess what message would have been conveyed by the lack of a signal (or by a different signal: two raised shields, perhaps).

Herodotus is firm in his belief that the shield signal was sent, but he seriously doubts the Alcmaeonidae were behind it, both because they were historically opposed to tyranny (the Persians wanted to reinstall Hippias as tyrant in Athens) and because they were such a distinguished family. The charge against them prompts Herodotus to launch into a handful of stories about prominent members of the dynasty.

The Alcmaeonidae allegedly owed their wealth to their founder, Alcmaeon himself, who was invited to Lydia by Croesus as a reward for services performed for Lydians visiting Delphi. Croesus made a present to Alcmaeon of all the gold he could carry out of the royal treasury on his person. Alcmaeon made the most of the opportunity by wearing excessively large boots and a big tunic he folded over to form a pocket. He loaded himself up as much as he could, including filling his mouth with gold dust, and emerged from the treasury scarcely able to walk. Croesus thought this was very funny, and he rewarded Alcmaeon by giving him twice as much as he was carrying. Unfortunately, the story can't be swallowed whole: Alcmaeon was the grandfather of an adult daughter during Croesus' reign in the mid-sixth century. (This is the daughter of Megacles, who was married to Pisistratus.) But according to Herodotus, Alcmaeon's gold grab predated her parents' marriage. Still, the anecdote may preserve a kernel of truth about the source of Alcmaeonid wealth.

In the next generation the position of the Alcmaeonidae would be advanced even further, since Alcmaeon's son Megacles married into what amounted to Greek royalty at the time, having won the hand of a tyrant's daughter. While Alcmaeon's adventure in the Lydian treasury reads like a game show challenge,

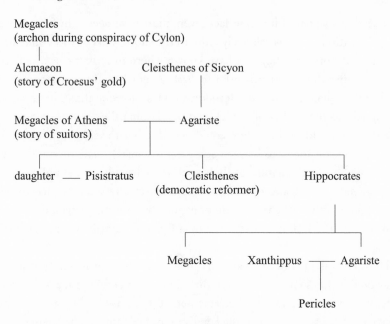

The Alcmaeonidae

Megacles won his bride in the ancient equivalent of *The Bachelorette*. Cleisthenes, the tyrant of Sicyon in the northeast Peloponnese, was looking for a husband for his daughter Agariste. With a view to finding the best man in all of Greece for her, he made a proclamation at the Olympics announcing a contest for her hand: interested suitors were to report to Sicyon within sixty days; the winner would be selected within a year after that. Cleisthenes had a race track and wrestling ground constructed for the purpose. The suitors, meanwhile, came to Sicyon from all over the Greek world: from Siris and Sybaris in the instep of Italy, from Epidamnus in modern Albania, from central Greece and throughout the Peloponnese, from Euboea and Thrace and Athens. Cleisthenes put the contestants through their paces for an entire year, observing their behavior, testing their manliness and education, talking with them one on one and watching them in larger groups. In the end he narrowed the suitors down to a short list of two, both men from Athens: Hippoclides, the son of Tisander, who was his favorite of the two, and Megacles, the son of Alcmaeon.

The day finally came when Cleisthenes would announce the winner, and the tyrant hosted a feast for all of Sicyon by way of celebration. After dinner the suitors tried to best one another in speech-making and music. Hippoclides, who may have had a bit too much to drink by this point, asked the pipe-player to play something for him, and he danced to the music. Then he had a table brought over, and he got up on top of it and danced some more. Finally Hippoclides stood on his head and danced upside down, his legs forming the steps in the air. (Herodotus doesn't say as much, but Hippoclides may have been flashing his audience at this point.) He looked, in other words, like an idiot. Cleisthenes, who was disgusted by the show, had contained himself during the first act. But the sight of Hippoclides dancing on his head was too much. "Son of Tisander," Cleisthenes spat out, "you have danced away your marriage!" And Hippoclides responded, weirdly, "Hippoclides doesn't care." The prize of marriage to Agariste fell by default to Cleisthenes' second favorite, Megacles, who had had the sense not to make an ass of himself so close to the finish line.

The story of Cleisthenes' testing of the suitors may be a fiction, but the marriage between Megacles and Agariste was historical. Their progeny would change the course of history. One son, Cleisthenes, was the man who instituted democratic reforms in Athens in the late sixth century. And their great-grandson would be one of the most famous men Athens ever produced, Pericles, the general and statesman whom Thucydides would claim effectively ruled Athens in the mid-fifth century, the first citizen in a society that was becoming a democracy in name only (2.65.10).

Miltiades' Expedition to Paros (6.132–136)

So Miltiades returned home sick, without bringing the Athenians any money, and without conquering Paros, having done no more than to besiege the town for six-and-twenty days, and ravage the remainder of the island.   (6.135.1)

Not long after the defeat of the Persians at Marathon, in late 490 or early 489, Miltiades asked the Athenians to provide him with a fleet of seventy ships and an army. According to Herodotus, Miltiades didn't tell the Athenians what he intended to do with this armada, but he promised that the expedition would make them rich. The Athenians were excited by the prospect of wealth, and Miltiades' political capital was at a high after his success at Marathon, so they agreed to his request. (That the Athenian *demos* would commit to a campaign without being informed of its objective is highly suspicious, but as I argue elsewhere, it's difficult to dismiss Herodotus' evidence for Miltiades' secrecy.)[11]

Miltiades, once he got his fleet, sailed against the island of Paros, which lay just to the west of Naxos in the middle of the Aegean. The pretext for the attack was that the Parians had medized back when the Persians were terrifying the islanders into submission. Herodotus claims, however, that Miltiades really attacked the island because of a personal grudge he held against a particular Parian. Once he'd arrived, at any rate, Miltiades issued the Parians an ultimatum: fork over a hundred talents or he would destroy them. The Parians decided to take their chances. They refused to pay Miltiades any money, and they prepared for a siege, beefing up their walls under cover of night.

Miltiades set about besieging Paros, but he was not meeting with much success, and he wasn't sure what to do next. At this point, according to Herodotus' Parian sources, a captive woman named Timo came to him. She was a priestess of Demeter and Kore, the goddesses of the underworld. She suggested that if he really wanted to conquer Paros, he should break into the Parian temple of Demeter and . . . well, and do something—Herodotus wasn't sure precisely what: probably steal a sacred object of some kind, something on which the safety of the state was thought to depend. Miltiades took her advice and went off to the temple. He climbed over the wall that enclosed it. He went toward the shrine. But when he was at the doors he started to shiver in fear, and rather than do whatever he'd gone there to do, he turned around and headed back the way he'd come. The exploit proved his undoing. When he jumped down from the wall on his way out, he injured his leg, wrenching his thigh or banging his knee, Herodotus says, though it's more likely, given what happened next, that he suffered a compound fracture. It was a serious injury, at any rate, serious enough that Miltiades aborted the siege and sailed back to Athens. His plan had been thwarted—or so the Parians' account implies—by a divine hand. When the Parians later sought to punish Timo for attempting to help the Athenians, they were told by the Delphic oracle that it was not she who'd advised Miltiades but a phantom: Miltiades' trip to Demeter's shrine, his injury, it all had the hand of a god in it. The oracle further prophesied that Miltiades was destined to end poorly.

And so he was. Miltiades' expedition to Paros had been a failure. He'd promised to make the Athenians rich, but he'd sailed away from the island after a twenty-six-day siege with nothing to show for it. Back in Athens he was brought to trial on a capital charge, accused of having deceived the Athenians. (His prosecutor was Xanthippus, the father of Pericles.) Herodotus says that Miltiades was unable to defend himself during the trial because of his wound, which had become infected. Friends spoke on his behalf as he lay in court on a stretcher, and their testimony prompted the jurors to punish Miltiades with a fine rather than execution. But while Miltiades was spared by the Athenians, he would not escape a death sentence: the wound he sustained on Paros became gangrenous and he died. Miltiades' fine was paid by his son Cimon, who would serve repeatedly as a general in Athens later in the century.

The hero of Marathon was dead, his star having fallen remarkably quickly after the Athenians chased off the Persians. The Athenians, meanwhile, had bought themselves a respite from war with Persia, but it was only a respite. Their glorious victory at Marathon was, from the Persians' point of view, merely a troubling setback, not serious enough to upset their plans of punishing Athens and expanding westward. They would be back. Athens, and the rest of Greece, could count on it.

CHAPTER ELEVEN

Feats of Engineering and Doomed Valor

The Second Persian War to the Battle of Thermopylae

W
HEN DARIUS HEARD WHAT HAD HAPPENED at Marathon, he was more intent than ever on subduing the Athenians. He sent messengers throughout the empire ordering that preparations be made for another campaign, bigger than the last: horses and transports and corn, men and ships. Everything was to be made ready for an expedition against Greece. Darius would spend the next three years preparing to march, and then, when the Greeks might have expected the Persian military machine to roll over them, events would intervene to delay the expedition yet further. That delay, as we'll see, made all the difference in the world.

The Succession of Xerxes (7.1–4)

He died in the year following the revolt of Egypt and the matters here related, after having reigned in all six-and-thirty years, leaving the revolted Egyptians and the Athenians alike unpunished.   (7.4)

While Darius was busy with his preparations for an expedition against Greece, Egypt revolted. Darius now had two big wars on his to-do list, and Herodotus implies that he was intent on leading at least one of the expeditions himself. This got his sons worried about which of them would inherit the throne in the event that dad didn't make it back alive. Two of Darius' sons were in the running for the kingship. Artobazanes was Darius' oldest son, by his former wife (the daughter of Gobryas), and he claimed the succession on the grounds of his seniority. Xerxes, however, argued that he should be king because he was the grandson of Cyrus through his mother, Atossa. Darius hadn't yet decided between the two when Demaratus arrived in Persia, on the lam from Sparta's authorities. Demaratus, remember, had recently been deposed from the Spartan kingship because of questions related to his legitimacy: his mother wasn't sure whether he was the son of the former king (her husband) or of a ghost who looked just like him. So it was ironic for Demaratus to be offering Xerxes advice on the question of succession. Nonetheless he suggested to Xerxes that in addition to playing up his connection to Cyrus, he should bring up the fact that he was born when Darius was already king, while Artobazanes was born when Darius was only a private citizen. Xerxes took Demaratus' advice, made the argument, and persuaded his father: Darius named Xerxes as his heir.

With the question of the succession resolved, Darius continued his military preparations, but he wasn't fated to subdue the Egyptians or to avenge the Persian dead of Marathon: Darius died in 486 after ruling Persia for thirty-six years. The kingship passed to Xerxes, who was the nephew and grandson, respectively, of Darius' predecessors on the throne, Cambyses and Cyrus.

The Suppression of Egypt and the Persian Council of War (7.5–11)

Artabanus, thou art my father's brother—that shall save thee from receiving the due meed of thy silly words.   (XERXES, at 7.11.1)

Xerxes wasn't keen on the idea of going ahead with the war against Greece at first, but a number of people urged him to continue with his father's plans. Mardonius, Xerxes' cousin, talked up the need to punish the Athenians, in part, Herodotus says, because he was hoping to be installed as satrap in Greece once it had been added to the Persian Empire. The Pisistratids, some of whom were in Susa, were likewise agitating for a Greek campaign. Presumably they were still hoping to regain the glory days of Pisistratid rule in Athens. And the Aleuadae, a leading family in the northern Greek state of Thessaly, sent messengers to the new king offering their support. Xerxes, finally, was sold on the idea: he would attack Greece. But first he had to deal with Egypt.

Subduing the Egyptian rebels may not have been a simple task in real life, but Herodotus dispenses with the campaign easily enough on paper. It took him nineteen sections (6.102–120)—nine pages in the translation nearest to hand as I write—to discuss the battle of Marathon and its preliminaries. Herodotus lavished forty sections on the Scythian expedition (5.83–142) and thirty-eight on Cambyses' conquest of Egypt back in the 520s (3.1–38). By contrast, Herodotus' account of Xerxes' reconquest of Egypt is astonishing for its brevity. He writes, simply: "After Xerxes was persuaded to attack Greece, in the year after Darius' death he first made an expedition against the rebels. After subduing them he made all of Egypt more harshly enslaved than it had been under Darius, and he gave the rule of the country to his brother Achaemenes, the son of Darius." Reconquest of Egypt: check. Now on to Greece.

The first thing Xerxes did was call a meeting. He summoned a counsel of Persian nobles and told them he intended to bridge the Hellespont and attack Greece via Thrace. He would burn Athens by way of reprisal for the burning of Sardis and the Persian defeat at Marathon, and he was going to subdue the rest of Greece besides. In fact, he said, he was going to conquer all of Europe. The guilty and the innocent alike would be subjected to the yoke of slavery, and in the end no one—no city or nation—would be strong enough to meet the Persians in battle. In short, at least as Herodotus tells the story, Xerxes wanted to take over the world. That was his game plan, anyway, but he didn't want to seem like the sort of megalomaniacal dictator who didn't listen to his minions, so he ended his harangue with a "What do you guys think?" and yielded the floor.

Mardonius was the first to speak, and he played the yes man to the hilt: Xerxes was the best king ever; the Athenians needed to be punished; and the Greeks, who at any rate had a stupid way of fighting, were no match for the Persians. On his own expedition through Thrace, he said, the Greeks had never even thought of fighting him. They wouldn't stand a chance against the even larger army Xerxes would be fielding. What Mardonius didn't say, of course, is that he never actually invaded Greece on that expedition back in 492. Nor did he mention that the Persians were defeated by the Greeks, those alleged cowards, at Marathon.

When Mardonius finished, the other Persians at the meeting were reluctant to say anything. One imagines them staring at the table uncomfortably or casting furtive glances at one another, silently urging somebody else to break the silence. Finally someone did, Xerxes' uncle Artabanus, the brother of Darius. As he reminded Xerxes in his speech, Artabanus had advised his brother not to fight the Scythians back in 513 (4.83), and he'd been right: the expedition had been a failure. Now Xerxes intended to take on an even more formidable enemy, the whole of Greece, when the Athenians alone had destroyed the Persian army at Marathon. There was danger too, Artabanus said, in Xerxes' plan to bridge the Hellespont: if the Greeks managed to break down the bridge, they would trap the Persian army in Europe. Again, this had almost happened during the Scythian expedition: if the Ionians hadn't maintained the bridge over the Ister, Darius' army would have been annihilated. Artabanus urged his nephew to slow down and reconsider. And, wise advisor that he was, he threw in a bit of Solonic wisdom: the gods are jealous and apt to strike down the most successful. Persia, for all its grandeur, was not immune to such vicissitudes.

Artabanus also had some harsh words for Mardonius. In order to bolster his case for war, he said, Mardonius was slandering the Greeks, saying that they were cowards and bad fighters: it wasn't true, and it wasn't nice. But if there was to be war with Greece, Mardonius should be willing to gamble on its outcome. Artabanus proposed that Mardonius lead the expedition while Xerxes remain behind in Persia and that he and Mardonius stake their own and their children's lives on the outcome of the campaign. If it was a success, Artabanus and his children would be executed; if it failed, Mardonius and his family would pay the price. But Artabanus expected Mardonius to be killed long before he could settle that debt, his body left unburied somewhere in Greece, torn apart by birds and dogs.

It had taken courage for Artabanus to raise objections to Xerxes' plans, but his efforts weren't appreciated: Xerxes was furious. He said that Artabanus was a coward and would stay home with the women while the rest of the men went off to win glory. Xerxes also allegedly framed the fight as a war of self-defense. The Athenians had started it: they'd invaded Asia and burned Sardis. If the Persians didn't go on the offensive now, Xerxes said, then the Athenians would: the coming war would determine whether the Greeks would be masters of Persia or the Persians of Greece. There could be no backing down.

This bit about Athens taking on the Persian Empire, mind you, is anachronistic nonsense. Athens at this time was a gnat in comparison with the Persian behemoth. No one at the time could seriously have thought that Athens—or indeed all of Greece combined—posed an existential threat to Persia. Not in the 480s. A hundred and fifty years later, it would be another story. Alexander the Great of Macedon would lead a Greek and Macedonian army east, soundly defeat King Darius III, and forge from the ashes of his kingdom the largest empire the world had ever seen. But it's unlikely that Xerxes could have imagined such a future as he stood before his counselors that day, laying out his own plans for world conquest.

The Dreams of Xerxes (7.12–19)

Having put on the garments which Xerxes was wont to wear and taken his seat upon the royal throne, he lay down to sleep upon the king's own bed.   (7.17.1)

But for all his apparent confidence, Xerxes was troubled by what Artabanus had said. He thought about the campaign more that night, and by the time he went to bed he'd changed his mind: there would be no Greek expedition. During the night, however, he had a dream. A man appeared to him and chastised him for changing his mind. If Xerxes altered his plans, the dream figure said, he would fare poorly, and he would not be forgiven.

Surprisingly, the vision didn't sway Xerxes from his resolve. When he woke up the next morning he summoned the same group of nobles and told them the expedition was off. He apologized for the change in plan and the nasty things he'd said to his uncle. He was a hotheaded youth, he said, who'd been listening to the wrong people, but now he would be taking Artabanus' advice.

If that had been the end of it, the history of the world might have been very different, but that night the figure appeared to Xerxes again and repeated his warning: if Xerxes didn't launch his campaign at once, he would be brought low as quickly as he had risen to power. This second appearance of the dream figure terrified Xerxes, and he jumped out of bed and sent a messenger to summon Artabanus. When his uncle arrived he told him that while he wanted to follow his advice and abandon the campaign, he was being haunted by a dream that was threatening him if he didn't go ahead with the invasion. Xerxes proposed they test the dream by seeing if it appeared to Artabanus as well. He told his uncle to put on his clothes, sit on his throne, and then sleep in his bed. If the dream came to Artabanus as well, they'd know that it was indeed sent by a god.

Artabanus had some issues with Xerxes' plan. For one thing, he wasn't keen on the idea of sitting on the royal throne. That was the sort of thing that could get you executed, and he may have worried that Xerxes was testing him to see if he'd actually do it. He also disagreed with Xerxes on the nature of dreams. He didn't believe they were sent by the gods but thought they were visions related to what one had been thinking about during the day. And even if dreams were divine, he said, why should this vision be fooled into thinking Artabanus was Xerxes just because he was wearing the royal pajamas and sleeping in the king's bed? Still, he would do what Xerxes ordered. If the dream came to him with the same message, he was inclined to believe in its divinity.

Artabanus thus put on Xerxes' clothes and sat on the throne and went to bed. And the same vision came to him. The dream figure wasn't fooled by Artabanus' getup. It recognized him as the man responsible for changing Xerxes' mind about the campaign, and it threatened him: Artabanus would not be able to alter what was fated with impunity, it said. When the dream figure looked like it was about to burn out his eyes with hot irons, Artabanus leapt out of bed, a changed man. He told Xerxes what he'd seen in the dream, and he explained his previous thinking: bad things happen when a man desires too much, he said. The pattern was there to see in the campaigns of Xerxes' predecessors: Cyrus lost his life fighting against the Massagetae; Cambyses fared poorly against the Ethiopians; Darius barely made it out of Scythia alive. Artabanus had hoped Xerxes could find happiness in inactivity. But apparently the gods had other ideas. "Some god-sent destruction, as it seems, has hold of the Greeks," he said. "I am changed and reverse my judgment." In the morning, Xerxes called another meeting: the war was on.

A third dream came to Xerxes that seemed to suggest this final decision was the correct one. In this vision, Xerxes wore a crown of olives, and shoots grew from it to overshadow all the world, though later the crown vanished from his head. The Magi interpreted the dream to mean that all of mankind would be subject to Xerxes. Their optimistic prophecy suggests they didn't give enough weight to the crown's ultimate disappearance from the royal head.

Artabanus, too, was guilty of jumping to an erroneous conclusion. The dream figure had told him only that he ought not attempt to change destiny. Artabanus assumed this meant that the Greeks were fated for destruction. It's the same mistake Croesus made back when he assumed that the mighty empire he was bound to destroy was that of the Persians.

The Canal at Athos and the Bridging of the Hellespont (7.20–36)

"Well dost thou deserve that no man should honour thee with sacrifice; for thou art of a truth a treacherous and unsavoury river." (XERXES, at 7.35.2)

Xerxes spent the next four years (484–481) putting together the largest expedition the world had ever seen. Compared to the army Xerxes collected, the force Darius led against Scythia in 513 was nothing. This would be bigger than Marathon, bigger than the Greek armada that chased Helen to Troy. Throughout the empire troops and horses and ships and grain were readied and transported and collected and stored, the myriad tasks associated with the expedition divvied up among Xerxes' subject peoples: this nation to build horse transports, that one to provide ropes of papyrus or grain. In the north Aegean, gangs of men were put to work building a bridge across the Strymon River and digging a canal—traces of it still survive—through the Athos Peninsula at its narrowest point, not quite a mile and a half across: Xerxes' fleet would cut through the peninsula rather than risk the treacherous waters that had destroyed much of Mardonius' fleet back in 492. The men digging the canal handed buckets of soil up the sides of their trenches, their overseers standing by with whips. Sometimes the walls of a trench would collapse, because they had been made too steep, and the work would have to be done all over again. The Phoenicians alone avoided this problem, as they had the foresight to make their section of the channel twice as wide at the top as it was at the bottom.

Meanwhile, Xerxes' great host was on the move. The troops mustered in Cappadocia and marched west with the king, crossing the Halys River, which had once divided Croesus' kingdom from Persia. In Celaenae, at the headwaters of the Maeander, a Lydian named Pythius, the son of Atys, entertained Xerxes and his army. He offered to contribute money toward the expedition as well, impressing Xerxes with his generosity and wealth. Indeed, Xerxes was told that after himself Pythius was the richest man in Persia. Herodotus doesn't say as much, but Pythius may in fact have been the grandson of Croesus, whose son Atys had been killed by Adrastus during that boar hunt. He would in that case have inherited his family's storied wealth. The two men talked money for a while, Pythius enumerating precisely how much he had, so much in gold and so much in silver, and he offered it all to Xerxes. He would live off his slaves and the proceeds of his estates, he said. But Xerxes was too delighted with the man to accept his offer. Instead, he made Pythius his guest-friend and rewarded the man's selfless generosity with a gift of money.

From Celaenae the army marched to Sardis, and Xerxes sent heralds off throughout Greece to demand earth and water of the various *poleis*, though not Sparta and Athens. Given what had happened to Darius' heralds when they visited those states in 491—one envoy supposedly thrown into a pit, the other into a well (see chapter ten)—Xerxes already knew what their answer to his messengers' "resistance is futile" ultimatum would be.

To the north, Xerxes was having a bridge built across the Hellespont, from the territory of Abydus, on the Asian side of the strait, to a rocky headland that jutted into the sea from the European side. It was a significant piece of land, the place where Europe would be yoked to Asia and the setting Herodotus chooses for the final scene of his *History*. Herodotus refers to that concluding image now: not much later, he says, the Athenians would haul the Persian satrap of Sestus there and crucify him. We'll consider the significance of that cruel punishment later.

Constructing a bridge that was some three quarters of a mile long and able to withstand the Hellespont's strong currents was a tremendous feat of engineering. The Persians got it wrong the first time. A storm came up and battered the completed bridge, smashing it to pieces. Xerxes was furious when he heard the news, furious with the men who'd supervised its construction and furious with the water itself. He ordered that the Hellespont be whipped three hundred times, as though it were a slave in need of correction, and that fetters be lowered into it. The water got a verbal spanking as well. Xerxes ordered the men who were whipping it to deliver a harangue as they did so: "O bitter water," they said, "your master imposes this penalty on you because you injured him, having suffered no wrong from him. King Xerxes will cross you, whether you like it or not. It's fitting that no one sacrifices to you, who are a foul and briny river." Bad river! Herodotus heard as well that Xerxes had the water branded—this would presumably involve dipping hot irons in the water—again, just as a slave might be. As for the humans who'd supervised the shoddy construction of the bridge, they were beheaded.

Two new bridges were built, under new supervisors with, it was to be hoped, better heads on their shoulders. It was a stunning achievement. Two lines of ships were positioned across the Hellespont, 674 ships in all, arranged side to side and each anchored fore and aft. Across the tops of the ships flexible roadways were constructed. Six cables per bridge were strung across the Hellespont, each almost a mile long and weighing, it's been estimated, a whopping 162,000 pounds each. The cables formed the basis of the roadway, which was built of planking covered by brushwood and soil. And barriers were built on either side so that the baggage animals and horses, when they crossed, wouldn't realize they were over water and panic. This time the supervisors kept their heads.

Eclipses and Corpses: Leaving Sardis (7.37–39)

At the moment of departure, the sun suddenly quitted his seat in the heavens, and disappeared, though there were no clouds in sight, but the sky was clear and serene.   (7.37.2)

Finally everything was ready. The bridges across the Strymon and the Hellespont were built, and the Athos Peninsula was bisected by Xerxes' canal. The Persians, after wintering at Sardis, marched out in April of 480 bound for the bridges at Abydus. Their departure, Herodotus tells us, was rendered more dramatic by the occurrence of a solar eclipse, a good omen according to the Magi, who said it signified the Greeks' upcoming abandonment of their cities. (Grene's translation, "the god was declaring to the Greeks the eclipse of their cities," is a satisfying play on words that captures the Greek nicely: the noun Herodotus uses is *ekleipsin*, which means "abandonment" as well as "eclipse.") Unfortunately the story isn't true. No solar eclipse was visible from Sardis in the spring of 480—though partial eclipses were visible in Greece and Asia Minor in October of 480 and February of 478.[1] (Herodotus mentions the latter at 9.10.3.) It may be that Herodotus or his sources have transposed one of these historical eclipses to the dramatic launch of the expedition from Sardis.

The sun's sudden disappearance was said to have terrified Xerxes' old friend Pythius, the rich Lydian who'd entertained the king back in Celaenae, but his anxiety would be easy to understand even without any unusual celestial phenomena: Pythius had five sons, and they were all going off to Greece. The old man came to Xerxes as the army was leaving Sardis, thinking that their guest-friendship and his previous generosity to the king might count for something, and he begged Xerxes for a favor. Xerxes, not anticipating what the request would be, told Pythius he need only ask for whatever he wanted. Encouraged, Pythius explained that all of his sons were serving with the army. He begged that one of them, the oldest, be released from service so that he could take care of his father and the family property.

Pythius' request may not seem unreasonable to us, but it infuriated Xerxes. Here he was, marching out with all his sons and his brothers, his friends and his servants, with everything on the line, and Pythius—Xerxes' slave, for heaven's sake—comes along and asks that one of his sons be allowed to stay home. By all rights, Pythius himself should be marching with the army, Xerxes said. And Pythius' wife as well! Readers may remember what Darius did when Oeobazus asked for a similar favor back before the Scythian expedition. Unfortunately, Xerxes had learned a thing or two from his dad: in response to Pythius' request, he ordered his men to find the Lydian's oldest son and cut him in half. The two halves of the boy's body were then placed on either side of the road so that the army could march between them. Herodotus doesn't mention it, but this horrific bit of savagery seems to have had a point to it. Passing between the two halves of a sacrificial animal was thought to purify or protect those doing it. So the execution of Pythius' son and the disposition of his corpse was like a purification ceremony taken to the next level, since the animal that was sacrificed was human. It may be that the Persian rank and file, far from being disgusted by the sight, took some comfort in marching past the halved remains of their slain comrade.

The Wisdom of Artabanus (7.40–52)

Lay thou to heart the old proverb, which says truly, "The beginning and end of a matter are not always seen at once." (ARTABANUS, at 7.51.3)

Xerxes' great army marched out of Sardis between the two halves of Pythius' son. They drove up the coast of Asia Minor, crossing the Caicus River and the

Scamander. At Troy, where the enmity between East and West had once set a city aflame, Xerxes sacrificed a thousand cattle to the Trojan version of the goddess Athena. Finally they arrived at Abydus, and Xerxes climbed a hill and sat on a marble throne that had been built for him. He surveyed his army and fleet from above: the Hellespont was filled with ships, the shore teeming with men. The spectacle moved Xerxes to tears because, as he explained to his uncle Artabanus, great as the army was, in a hundred years not one of the men before him would be alive. Sadder yet, Artabanus said, is that life, though brief, is so filled with hardship that there is no one who doesn't wish for his own death many times over before it comes.

The two men talked also about Artabanus' earlier resistance to the war, and Artabanus confessed that he was still worried. The Persian army and fleet were certainly large enough to inspire confidence, but their very size was a problem: there wouldn't be enough harbors available to shelter the fleet if a storm came up. That meant the Persians were going into the expedition more than usually at the mercy of circumstances beyond their control. Also, he said, the chances of the army running out of food increased the more land they managed to capture. These were causes for concern: the best of men should be cautious in planning, he said, contemplating such worst-case scenarios, and bold in action.

Xerxes countered Artabanus' pessimism with his own "don't worry, be happy" philosophy: overthinking things can be paralyzing; sometimes you have to do something and suffer the consequences rather than do nothing for fear of them; big risks bring big rewards. Besides, he said, they wouldn't have any trouble with the food supply. They were bringing a lot with them, for one thing, and they'd be able to supplement it by living off the land. The Greeks, after all, were not nomads but farmers—which is to say that there would be crops available for the taking. (That last bit was a reference to Darius' disastrous expedition against the nomadic Scythians, which informed Artabanus' concerns to a large extent.)

Artabanus tried a different tack. If nothing else, he said, let's at least leave the Ionians home: we can win without them, and there's a chance they'll betray us and help their fellow Greeks. It was a reasonable point, and Artabanus followed it up with a bit of wisdom that could have been delivered by Solon himself: "Consider the old saying, how well expressed it is, that the end of everything is not always clear from its beginning." It's the last line Artabanus delivers in Herodotus' *History*.

Xerxes had an answer for his uncle's final piece of advice as well. The Ionians wouldn't betray the Persians, he said, because they hadn't done so back when it counted, when they could have destroyed the bridge over the Ister and left Darius' army to the mercy of the Scythians. (Since then, of course, the Ionians had revolted from Persia, causing Darius to spend much of the 490s putting down their insurrection, but Xerxes seems to have forgotten that part.) More importantly, the Ionians had left behind their families and property, which were now essentially being held hostage for their good behavior. They wouldn't dream of betraying the Persians.

Their interview over, Xerxes dismissed Artabanus and sent him back to Persia to run things in his absence. The empire was thus left in the hands of a capable regent, but Xerxes, in shipping his Debbie Downer of an uncle back to Susa, was depriving himself of a trustworthy counselor. Meanwhile, Xerxes had now received the same advice from his own wise advisor that Croesus had heard from Solon before his fall. Always look to the end of things: no one is guaranteed a successful conclusion in life. Xerxes' peripety, like Croesus', wouldn't be long in coming.

From the Hellespont to the Borders of Greece (7.53–132)

Hereby it was shown plainly enough, that Xerxes would lead forth his host against Greece with mighty pomp and splendour, but, in order to reach again the spot from which he set out, would have to run for his life.   (7.57.1)

It was time to go. The Persians waited until sunrise the next morning and then, after performing various rites involving incense and libations and myrtle branches, they began the crossing, the baggage animals and cavalry and spearmen and infantry and chariots and Xerxes himself. Even with the Persians using the two bridges simultaneously and never taking a break, it took seven days and seven nights for the whole army to cross. They made it to the European side of the strait without incident, but for anyone with eyes to see, it was clear that trouble lay ahead. When the Persians were again on the march they saw an ominous (and unlikely) portent: a horse gave birth to a hare. The omen's meaning, Herodotus says, was perfectly obvious: the Persians would ride into Greece in magnificent style—that's the horse part—but they would be running like rabbits on the way out. Still, Xerxes ignored this clear indication of disaster to come and plowed ahead, east through the Chersonese and then west to Doriscus in Thrace. There the army met up with the fleet and the captains beached their ships so that they could be prepared for the campaign ahead (thoroughly dried out and perhaps recaulked). And there, Herodotus says, Xerxes decided to review and number his army.

We can skip the ten-odd pages that follow in which Herodotus describes the various contingents of the army—their equipment and attire and the names of their commanders. What is interesting, however, is the way Xerxes is said to have gone about counting his men: 10,000 troops were crowded together into a tight area, and a circle was drawn around them. The Persians then built a low wall along the circumference of the circle, and this walled-in enclosure was used as a measure for subsequent groupings of 10,000. The infantry alone, thus counted in myriads, allegedly amounted to 1,700,000, on top of which were 80,000 cavalry, 20,000 camel drivers and charioteers, and the crews of 1207 triremes—wooden warships named for their three banks of oars. Herodotus estimates the total number of fighting men who crossed into Europe from Asia at 2,317,610, and that's not counting the servants and male noncombatants. Still more troops were added to Xerxes' force as he marched through Greece, so that by the time the army reached central Greece, it had swelled to 5,283,220, by Herodotus' estimate. Plus there were women in untold numbers—cooks and prostitutes—as well as innumerable pack animals.

Xerxes' army was big, but it can't have been that big. In the early 1900s Hans Delbrück noted that if the army were really as enormous as Herodotus says it was, "the march column of the Persians would . . . have been 2,000 miles long, and when the head of the column was arriving before Thermopylae, the end of the column might have been just marching out of Susa, on the far side of the Tigris."[2] Modern estimates for the size of Xerxes' army and fleet vary. Readers interested in pursuing the question might start with Michael Flower's helpful summary in Appendix R of *The Landmark Herodotus*: he argues for 80,000 as an upper limit for the size of Xerxes' original land army, with a lower limit of 40,000, and he puts the number of triremes in Xerxes' fleet at 600 at most, and perhaps as few as 300.[3]

After numbering his army and taking notes on the various contingents, Xerxes sent for Demaratus, the exiled king of Sparta, who was traveling with the army. He asked Demaratus whether he thought the Greeks would actually engage them when they invaded. Xerxes himself expected the enemy to surrender without a fight once they saw the immensity of his army. They couldn't possibly stand their ground against us, he said, nor could all the Greeks and all other westerners put together, at least not unless they made a united stand. But

Demaratus said that the Spartans—for those were the people he knew best— would certainly fight the Persians no matter how outnumbered they were: they would never willingly be slaves to Persia. Xerxes thought this was nonsense, both because of the numbers involved—how, say, could one Spartan take on ten Persians at once, or twenty, or a thousand?—and because the Spartans were free men and thus not under compulsion to show such extraordinary courage.

Demaratus' stirring response—and this from a man who'd been mistreated in Sparta and welcomed in Persia—is the sort of thing that could move a battle-scarred hoplite to tears: "Fighting singly," he said, "the Spartans are no worse than other men. But fighting together they are the best of all. For while they are free men they are not free in all respects: the law is their master, which they fear much more than your men fear you. They do what it commands, and it commands always this: never to flee from battle, but to remain in position and conquer or die." Demaratus was dead serious, but Xerxes dismissed him with a laugh and carried on with his invasion.

The Persians marched west from Doriscus through Thrace, conscripting troops along the way. They were divided into three lines, Herodotus says, a third of the army marching along the coast beside the fleet and the other two divisions taking routes farther inland. The army was so vast that it drank rivers dry and bankrupted any communities that were required to play host: a citizen of Abdera, which had spent months preparing a dinner for the king and his troops, remarked afterward that they should be grateful Xerxes was accustomed to eat only once a day; if they'd had to provide a second meal as well, they would have been ruined. When the Persians reached Acanthus on the Athos Peninsula, the fleet sailed through the canal Xerxes had built, then rounded the other two prongs of the Chalcidic peninsula and sailed north to Therme. They waited there, on the border of Greece, until the land army could catch up. When the fleet and army were reunited, Xerxes lingered for some time in the area. He sailed south to scout the mouth of the Peneus River in Thessaly, and he set a third of his army to clearing a road along the slopes of Mount Olympus—home of the Olympian gods—to facilitate his army's passage through the mountains and south to the Thessalian plain.

The Formation and First Congress of the Hellenic League (7.145–169)

"As ye are resolved to yield nothing and claim everything, ye had best make haste back to Greece, and say, that the spring of her year is lost to her."

(GELON, at 7.162.1)

The Greeks hadn't been sitting on their hands this whole time. In the fall of 481, those who were "of the better way of thinking about Greece"—that is, those who weren't inclined to medize in response to the invasion—met in a congress and agreed to form a coalition of states, which modern historians call the Hellenic League, to respond to the common threat. (It was clear that the invasion was aimed at all of Greece this time rather than just Athens [7.138].) They exchanged pledges and resolved to end any ongoing wars among them— this was no time for distractions. They also swore an oath—either at this first congress or later on[4]—that any Greeks who submitted to the Persians when not under compulsion to do so would have one tenth of their property confiscated and dedicated to the god at Delphi. (This may not seem like much of a punishment, but what Herodotus probably means is that a tithe would be taken from the property of medizing states after their cities were destroyed and their populations sold into slavery. In the event, however, so many states wound up medizing that the threat could not have been enforced.) The allied states also agreed to give Sparta command of the League's military operations, both on land and at sea. Athens, which contributed the most ships to the cause, initially claimed leadership of the fleet, but yielded the command in the interest of League harmony when objections were raised by some of the member states (8.3).

The allies also took two further measures at this congress: they sent spies to Sardis, where Xerxes had collected his host, and they sent ambassadors to ask for help from Argos (in the Peloponnese), Sicily, Crete, and Corcyra. Herodotus tells us what happened on each of these missions. The spies who were sent to Asia were captured and tortured. They were about to be executed when Xerxes found out what was happening. Rather than have them killed, he ordered his men to give the spies a tour of his army. That way they could go back home with an accurate report of what the Greeks would be up against: Xerxes suspected that the spies' information would frighten many of the Greeks into surrendering before the Persians had to raise a finger.

The embassy to Argos met with no success. According to the Argives, they agreed to join the Hellenic League on two conditions, that the Spartans conclude a thirty-year peace with them and that they be given half of the command of the League. The first stipulation was up for consideration, but the Spartans weren't about to surrender half of their authority to Argos. (They did offer to give the Argive king a vote in League affairs equal to that of each of Sparta's kings, but the Argives rejected the offer.) Herodotus says that the Argives demanded a leadership role because they knew that this would be unacceptable to the Spartans, whose rejection of the proposal would then justify Argive neutrality. There was also a story that the Argives had already come to some kind of agreement with Persia by this point and even that they had invited the Persians into Greece, but Herodotus is emphatic in denying the latter accusation, even as he is noncommittal about the former.

The ambassadors who sailed to Sicily for an interview with Gelon of Syracuse had a similar experience. Gelon was not inclined to get involved, but he said that he would supply a sizable fleet and army if the Greeks gave him the command. Again, this was a deal-breaker, as was Gelon's proposed compromise, that he be given command of either the fleet or the army. Thus these ambassadors returned to Greece empty-handed as well, but for Gelon's message to the Greeks in which he likened his army—what would have been the flower of a united Greek host—to springtime, the best part of the year. "Tell Greece," he said, "that her spring has been taken from the year." Gelon later sent three ships east to await events: if the Persians were victorious, his ambassadors were to give earth and water; if the Greeks won, his men were to sail back home.

The League ambassadors who sailed to Crete were likewise sent packing after the oracle at Delphi advised the Cretans not to join the alliance. The Corcyraeans, on the other hand, promised to send help, and in the event they did launch sixty ships, but their fleet lingered around the Peloponnese and never made it far enough east to take part in a battle. The Corcyraeans later claimed that they had been prevented from joining the rest of the Greek fleet by the winds around Cape Malea, the southernmost point of the Peloponnese. The excuse is plausible, since navigating the waters around the Cape was notoriously difficult.[5] But Herodotus says the Corcyraeans were playing both sides of the fence, not committing fully to the Greek defense in case the Persians won, as seemed likely, while appearing to the Greeks as if they had tried but failed to join the cause.

The news, then, was not good. No help was promised by any of the states to which the Greeks had appealed except Corcyra, and that assistance never materialized. And the Greek spies, when they returned from Sardis (probably early in 480), would report that the Persian king was fielding an army the likes of which the Greeks had never seen before.

The Expedition to Tempe (7.172–174)

The Thessalians did not embrace the cause of the Medes until they were forced to do so; for they gave plain proof that the intrigues of the Aleuadae were not at all to their liking.   (7.172.1)

The representatives of the Hellenic League met for a second time (and the last time we know of; subsequent decisions would be made in councils-of-war) in the spring of 480. The Thessalians, learning that Xerxes was in Abydus and ready to cross into Europe, sent envoys to the congress, which was being held somewhere on the Isthmus of Corinth. By this point some Thessalians had already medized, or were at least leaning in that direction: the first of all the Greeks to go over to the Persians were the Aleuadae, Herodotus says, a powerful family in Thessaly (7.130). But the Aleuads didn't represent all Thessalians. The envoys who addressed the allied congress came on behalf of those in Thessaly who were not disposed to surrender.[6]

The Thessalians were in a difficult position. Their country, which lay just south of Macedon, would be the first one Xerxes attacked. The Thessalians wanted to resist the Persians, but they couldn't possibly do it alone. They asked the Greeks to send an army north to help them guard the pass at Tempe, between Mount Olympus and Mount Ossa, to stop the Persians before they could descend into the Thessalian plain. If the Greeks didn't send help, they said, they would be compelled to save themselves by submitting to the enemy.

The Greeks promptly sent an army of ten thousand men north, while the Persians were still at Abydus.[7] They made camp at Tempe and stayed in position for a few days, but then messengers arrived from Alexander, the king of Macedon. He advised the Greeks to abandon the pass because they would not be able to hold it against Xerxes' army, which, he said, was enormous. It's not clear whether in warning the Greeks Alexander was acting as an agent of the Persian king (he was an ally of Persia at this point) or in his own interests (hoping to get the war out of his back yard) or out of genuine concern for his southern neighbors. The Greeks, at any rate, decided to abandon Tempe, either because of Alexander's warning or, Herodotus suggests, because they'd learned of other routes into Thessaly that the Persians could take. Whatever the reason, the Greeks withdrew to the south after Alexander's intercession, abandoning the Thessalians, who had no alternative now but to medize.

The Oracle of the Wooden Wall (7.140–144)

He therefore counselled his countrymen to make ready to fight on board
their ships, since they were the wooden wall in which the god told them to
trust.   (7.143.2)

At some time during the buildup to the Persian invasion, the Athenians consulted the oracle at Delphi. Their envoys performed the customary rites beforehand and were about to put their question to the priestess when she spat out a prophecy before they could so much as speak. Her response was disheartening, to say the least: twelve lines of dactylic hexameter (the meter of epic: dum diddy dum diddy dum diddy dum diddy dum diddy dum dum), the purport of which can be summarized roughly as "Run away! The Persians are going to kill you all." (The oracle Herodotus preserves is in dactyls, but it may have been delivered in prose—or even gibberish—and versified after the fact—though presumably before the Athenians back home received it.) The envoys were crushed. It certainly wasn't the sort of news they wanted to bring back home. But at the suggestion of a Delphian, Timon, they begged for a second response from the god, saying that otherwise they would stay in Delphi until they died. The envoys' stubbornness won them another twelve lines of hexameter:

Pallas Athena cannot appease Olympian Zeus,
Although begging with many words and clever counsel.
I will say the same thing to you, making it like adamant [that is, really strong]:
For, when everything is being captured, as much as the boundary of Cecrops [a
     mythical Athenian king]
Contains and the dell of holy Cithaeron [a mountain in Boeotia],
Wide-seeing Zeus grants to the Triton-born [Athena] that a wooden wall
Alone will be untaken, which will save you and your children.
Do not await the cavalry and infantry,
The great host coming from abroad, but turn your back
And withdraw; you will meet them another day.
O divine Salamis, you will destroy the children of women
Either when Demeter [seed] is sown or when she is harvested.

The first oracle had advised the Athenians to "flee to the ends of the earth." This time the advice was the same: "turn your back and withdraw." But the second oracle wasn't quite as grim as the first because the god also gave the Athenians some cause for hope, adding that a "wooden wall" would save them. It wasn't much, but it was better. The envoys brought the oracle back to Athens, and the debate over its interpretation began.

Specifically, the Athenians debated what the god meant by the "wooden wall," which he foresaw as their only salvation. The most natural interpretation of the phrase, of course, is that it was a reference to, well, a wall constructed of wood. But as we've seen, the interpretation of oracles was a tricky business: leaping to conclusions about their meanings was a sure way to court disaster. And even if the phrase was a straightforward reference to a real wooden wall, which wall did Apollo have in mind? A lot of different interpretations were floated, but Herodotus mentions only the two main ones. Some thought the god meant the Acropolis would be saved: it had once been fenced in by a thorn hedge, which was wooden wall–ish enough to fit the bill: in the event, the Athenians did leave the Acropolis defended by a garrison, just in case this was what Apollo had in fact intended (8.51–53).

Others suggested that the wooden wall referred to Athens' navy. Less than a decade earlier the Athenians had had to borrow ships from Corinth because they didn't have enough of their own for an attack against Aegina (6.89). But times had changed. The south of Attica was rich in silver, which was mined by private contractors who shared the proceeds with the state. In 483 there was a surplus of revenue from the mines—a windfall from the discovery of rich new seams, perhaps—and the Athenians were debating what to do with the state's share of the extra money. (On the mines, see also Aristotle, *The Constitution of Athens* 22.7, 47.2.) The prevailing opinion was that it should be distributed equally among the citizenry, with each getting ten drachmas. But the Athenians were persuaded to put the money to better use: Themistocles, the son of Neocles, argued that they should instead use the surplus funds to enlarge their fleet. Herodotus tells us that Themistocles convinced them by saying the ships could be used against Aegina, but it's hard to believe that he and most everyone else in Athens wasn't also thinking about the looming Persian threat.

By the time they were debating the meaning of the wooden wall oracle, the Athenians had a fleet of two hundred ships at their disposal, the largest navy in Greece.[8] It thus made sense that the god intended them to rely on their ships—to withdraw rather than face the enemy on land, where they would

surely be overrun, and meet the Persians at sea. The problem with this interpretation, though, was that Apollo had added a frightening coda to his second
oracle: if the Athenians fought a naval battle around Salamis, a lot of "children
of women" were going to end up dead. How could that be a good thing?

This is where Themistocles made his second great contribution. He argued
that the ones who were fated to die around Salamis were the Persians, not the
Greeks. After all, Salamis is referred to by the oracle as "divine," he said. Were
it destined to be a site of devastation for the Greeks, the god would have called
it "cruel" instead. Themistocles' argument about the epithet applied to Salamis
may be a bit weak, but what's nice about his interpretation is that he thought
outside the box. Unlike Croesus—who leapt to the conclusion, upon receiving
his oracle, that he would destroy someone else's mighty empire rather than his
own—Themistocles recognized the ambiguity in the Athenians' prophecy and
looked past its most obvious meaning: those dead children of women didn't
have to be Greeks. The Athenians liked his interpretation too. They resolved to
resist the Persians at sea, together with as many Greeks as would join them.

It's worth noting here how different things might have been. Had the Persian invasion of Greece not been delayed by the Egyptian rebellion and Darius'
death earlier in the decade, the Athenians would not have had the time or the
money needed to expand their fleet before the barbarians came. There would
have been no "wooden wall" on which to hang their faith in 480. Without Athens' navy, the Persian invasion would likely have ended in the subjugation of
Greece, and western civilization itself would have developed along very different lines.

Historians disagree about when the Athenians sent envoys to Delphi.
Herodotus indicates by his placement of the story that the oracle was consulted
before the first congress of the Hellenic League in the autumn of 481. But the
defeatist tone of the god's responses and the mention of Salamis in the second
oracle have suggested to some that the god was consulted in the following year,
after Tempe had been abandoned, when the invasion of Attica was more imminent and Salamis was more likely to have been mentioned as a potential theater
of war. The timing of the consultation has some bearing on how we reconstruct
the Athenians' response to the impending invasion. But apart from the difficulty of the early reference to Salamis in the oracle, which can be explained
away—given its location, the Athenians could be expected to take refuge there,
and a battle at sea off Attica was likely enough[9]—there is no compelling reason
to abandon Herodotus' implied chronology. And doing so would require us

to assume that the Athenians waited until after the formation of the Hellenic League to consult the god about their strategy. As A. R. Hands writes, "It would be pertinent to ask what business had the Athenians to be consulting about resistance in the spring of 480, after they had already joined with Sparta in initiating the defense of Greece, which should have indicated that they had made up their minds on that question, in the previous autumn."[10]

Thermopylae and Artemisium: The Greeks' Strategy and First Blood (7.175–183)

Weighing well all that was likely to happen, and considering that in this region the barbarians could make no use of their vast numbers, nor of their cavalry, they resolved to await here the invader of Greece.   (7.177)

When the Greeks returned to the isthmus from Tempe, they debated where they should make their stand against the Persians. They decided to send an army north to central Greece to guard the pass at Thermopylae. (The name "Thermopylae," which means "hot gates," comes from the thermal springs located there and the three constrictions or "gates" that punctuate the pass.) The pass ran about three miles west to east, a narrow stretch bounded by the sea to the north and steep hills to the south, the spurs of Mount Oeta. (Herodotus mistakenly describes the pass as running north to south, with the mountains to the west and the Malian Gulf to the east.) The pass was hourglass-shaped, roughly speaking: at the western and eastern ends or "gates," the track was very narrow, only wide enough for a single wagon to pass through, and in the middle there was another constriction where the path was about fifty feet wide. The Greeks who lived in the area had once built a defensive wall across the pass at this middle gate, but it had since fallen into disrepair. (Visitors to Thermopylae nowadays won't see the topography Herodotus describes. The pass is much wider now than it was in 480 because the sea has silted up and receded several miles to the north.) The advantage of fighting in the pass was that because of the confined space, the Persians would be unable to take advantage of their superiority in numbers or use their cavalry. The problem with Thermopylae, however, as the Greeks found out when they got there, was that there was a narrow goat path, the Anopea Path, that snaked some twenty or so miles over the mountains to the south of Thermopylae and emerged behind the east gate. Thermopylae, that is, could be turned.

While a land army guarded the pass at Thermopylae, the Greek fleet would be stationed at Artemisium, a beach on the northern coast of Euboea, which was close enough to Thermopylae that the two forces would be able to communicate with one another (cf. 8.21). Though Herodotus does not make this very clear in his account, the contingents sent to Thermopylae and Artemisium would be two prongs of a single amphibious operation, each dependent on the other: the land army would attempt to prevent the Persians from overrunning southern Greece, while the fleet was there to keep the Persians from outflanking Thermopylae by sea. That was the hope, anyway. When the second congress of the Greek allies broke up, the Greek land and naval forces advanced to their various posts.

The Persians were soon on the move. Their ten fastest ships set out on a reconnaissance mission from Therme in Macedonia and sailed south toward Sciathus, a small island to the northeast of Artemisium. The Greeks, who were now in position at Artemisium, had an advance guard of three ships posted off Sciathus (perhaps, some scholars have argued, rather farther to the north of the island than Herodotus' account suggests). When they spotted the Persian squadron, the three ships fled. Two of them were captured by the Persians. An unfortunate crewman on the first ship taken, a man named Leon, became the first Greek casualty of the war. The Persians selected him because he was the best-looking of the men on board, and they thought his death would be a good omen. They hauled him to the prow of the ship and slit his throat. The third Greek ship managed to escape the Persians. It ran aground near the Tempe pass in the north of Thessaly. Its Athenian crew abandoned the ship and the crewmen made their way overland back to Athens.

News of what had happened was signaled to the rest of the fleet from Sciathus. Herodotus says that the Greeks reacted to the news by abandoning their position at Artemisium and moving the entire fleet south to Chalcis to guard the Euripus, the channel that separates the island of Euboea from mainland Greece. Chalcis was on the Euboean side of the strait, roughly at the island's midpoint, where the channel is at its narrowest, some forty yards wide. It made sense for the Greeks to post ships there to guard against all or part of the Persian fleet encircling the island and approaching Artemisium from the rear. But it would have been foolhardy to guard Chalcis while leaving Artemisium itself undefended, since that would have left the flank of the land army at Thermopylae vulnerable. Instead, the first sighting of Persian ships by the Greeks' advance guard must have signaled to the Greeks that it was time to send a part of their fleet south to Chalcis: I accept J. B. Bury's argument that the ships that were dispatched to the Euripus at this point are the fifty-three mentioned later returning to Artemisium (8.14). The rest of the Greek fleet will have stayed in position in the north.[11]

Three of the ten Persian ships that had chased off the Greeks' advance guard ran aground on an underwater reef between Sciathus and the mainland. The Persians marked the reef with a white pillar as a warning to the rest of their fleet, then returned to Therme to report that the way was clear. The full fleet now sailed from Therme, eleven days after their army had marched out. After a long day's sail they made it to Sepias, a beach on the coast of mainland Greece roughly fifty miles north of the tip of Euboea.

The First Storm (7.188–195)

But at dawn of day calm and stillness gave place to a raging sea and a violent storm, which fell upon them with a strong gale from the east—a wind which the people in those parts call Hellespontias.   (7.188.2)

The Persian fleet was too big for all the ships to line up along the beach at Sepias, so most of them rode at anchor in the harbor, a parking lot of triremes arrayed eight deep, their prows pointed seaward, the sterns of one row of ships tucked between the prows of the preceding row. They were in a dangerously exposed position. A great wind storm came up as they lay at anchor the next morning and battered the fleet for three days straight. Herodotus says that no fewer than four hundred of the Persians' ships were destroyed, driven against the rocks or wrecked along the shore—just the sort of thing Xerxes' uncle, Artabanus, had worried might happen (7.49). The Greek ships, meanwhile, which were in relatively sheltered locations—some at Artemisium, some in the Euboean Gulf—apparently suffered no damage.

The story may sound almost too good—from the Greeks' perspective—to be true, that the storm just happened to come up and take out a hefty percentage of the Persian fleet while leaving the Greek ships intact. We need not take as gospel Herodotus' report of the number of ships destroyed, but wind storms are not unusual in the area. Dry, northerly winds sweep down the Aegean during the summer every year, sometimes blowing at gale force. Gusting wind storms like Herodotus describes can last for many days at a time. These "etesian" winds—the name comes from the Greek word for "annual"—made sailing north during the summer months difficult. (Nearly a century and a half later, Philip of Macedon—according to his nemesis, Demosthenes [*First Philippic* 31]—would coordinate his attacks with the winds so that the Athenians would be unable to sail north and oppose him.)

In connection with the destruction of the Persian ships in the storm, Herodotus mentions a local man, Aminocles, who made a fortune from the stuff he found washed ashore afterwards—gold and silver cups and so on. Herodotus mentions Aminocles in order to contrast his good fortune with the tragedy that followed on its heels, something having to do with the death of his son: the son may have been murdered or was perhaps killed accidentally by his father (cf. Plutarch, *On the Malice of Herodotus* 30 = *Moralia* 864c). Herodotus' cryptic reference to the boy's death is of course compelling, but what's nice about the anecdote also is that it shrinks the epic story of the Persian invasion to a human scale by creating a simple image: a man walking along the beach after the Persians have left, picking through the wreckage dotting the shore. The war affected whole nations, of course, in big ways; it's no exaggeration to say that in 480 and 479 the future of western civilization hung in the balance. But it's easy to forget that the invasion brought changes on a smaller scale as well. It affected the lives of real people we've never heard of, in ways that might never occur to us—like Aminocles finding a fortune on the beach.

When the storm finally ended and the seas had calmed, the Persians left Sepias and sailed south along the Magnesian shore. They rounded the cape of Magnesia and anchored at Aphetae, where their ships will have been visible to the Greeks at Artemisium, about ten miles to the southwest across the strait. Fifteen of the Persians' ships were delayed for some reason, however, and they lost contact with the rest of their fleet. Sailing into the strait, they saw the Greek ships at Artemisium and blithely sailed to join them, thinking they were Persian. The Greeks saw these stragglers, realized what was going on, and sailed out to capture them. They interrogated their prisoners—Herodotus names several of the captives and provides some backstory for each—and after finding out what they wanted to know about Xerxes' army, they sent the Persians off in chains to the Isthmus of Corinth.

Thermopylae, Part I: Preliminaries (7.196–209)

> He had now come to Thermopylae, accompanied by the three hundred men
> which the law assigned him, whom he had himself chosen from among the
> citizens, and who were all of them fathers with sons living.   (7.205.2)

Xerxes' land army, meanwhile, which had set out from Macedon before the
fleet, wound its way south through Greece. When the Persians finally arrived
at the Malian Gulf, they set up camp west of Thermopylae, while the Greeks
encamped within the pass itself. The Greek army was about seven thousand
strong and included contingents from Boeotia, Phocis, and Locris in central
Greece and from across the Peloponnese, including three hundred Spartiates.
Each city's forces had their own commander, but the commander of the entire army was the Spartan king Leonidas, whose importance to the story is un-
derscored by Herodotus' introduction of him, a rolling litany of patronymics
that traces Leonidas' ancestry back twenty generations to his mythical forbear
Heracles:

> There were other generals for these contingents, each city having its own, but the
> one who was especially admired and who was the leader of the entire army was the
> Lacedaemonian Leonidas—the son of Anaxandridas, son of Leon, son of Eurycra-
> tides, son of Anaxandrus, son of Eurycrates, son of Polydorus, son of Alcamenes,
> son of Teleclus, son of Archelaus, son of Hegesilaus, son of Doryssus, son of Le-
> botes, son of Erchestratus, son of Agis, son of Eurysthenes, son of Aristodemus,
> son of Aristomachus, son of Cleodaeus, son of Hyllus, son of Heracles—who had
> gained the kingship in Sparta unexpectedly.

Leonidas' kingship was unexpected because he was only the third-oldest son
of Anaxandridas (5.39–41). But his older brother Dorieus had been killed in
Sicily (5.42–48), and his half-brother Cleomenes, the previous king, had died
without having sons. Leonidas was next in line for the throne, and his position
was bolstered by his marriage to Cleomenes' daughter Gorgo, the girl who, as a
precocious eight-year-old, had urged her father not to allow himself to be corrupted by Aristagoras of Miletus.

The three hundred Spartans who served under Leonidas at Thermopylae
had been selected for the campaign from among those Spartiates who had living sons. At first read it may sound as if the kids back home were serving al-

most as guarantors of their fathers' good behavior: these Spartans, who were probably all in their thirties or older, had more to fight for by virtue of their parenthood. But fighting and dying proudly in battle is what the Spartans did as a matter of course. The warrior ethos was instilled in them with their mothers' milk. (Those same mothers, as the famous story goes, would later hand their sons their shields and send them off to war with the admonishment "With it or on it." That is, either come back with your shield or with it serving as your bier. The third alternative—throwing it away so as to flee the enemy unencumbered—was not an option [Plutarch *Moralia* 241F].) The Spartans, then, didn't need the incentive of children to urge them on to heroics. Instead, the criterion that they have sons may have served a different purpose: it meant that they had replacements lined up. Their families wouldn't become extinct if they died. The survival of Sparta, after all, depended on the continued existence of a sufficiently large pool of elite citizen warriors. (Sparta's decline, roughly a hundred years after the battle at Thermopylae, was due to her loss of four hundred Spartiates—a quarter or more of her fully enfranchised citizens at the time— at the Battle of Leuctra [Aristotle, *Politics* 1270a33–34; Xenophon, *Hellenica* 6.4.15].)[12] This is not to say the Spartans went into Thermopylae assuming it was a suicide mission—as some historians have argued—but this also wasn't the sort of fight to which they were accustomed. The Greeks were engaged in an existential battle against an enemy that had already defeated and absorbed numerous civilizations. The stakes here were higher than ever.

Alternatively, it's been suggested that the fatherhood criterion for the Spartiates sent to Thermopylae had some connection we don't understand to the fact that the Spartans were celebrating the Carnean festival at the time. As we saw in chapter ten, the Spartans' celebration of the Carnea was probably what prevented them from marching out in time to help the Athenians at Marathon. This time they sent an advance force north under the leadership of one of their kings—which will have signaled to the rest of the Greeks that they were seriously invested in the campaign—and Herodotus says that they intended to send out additional troops after the Carnea. J. F. Lazenby has suggested that in assembling the advance force, the younger men may have been "passed over as being particularly bound by the taboos surrounding the Karneian festival, and that the 300 were selected by the king, perhaps by lot, from those over thirty."[13] As it happened, the Thermopylae campaign coincided with the celebration of the Olympic festival as well as the Carnea, so that other states likewise sent only a part of their forces, with the promise to send more when the games were over. No one imagined, Herodotus says, that the campaign would be decided as quickly as it was.

But hold! Another explanation that has been offered for the fatherhood criterion is that it was fabricated, a later addition to the story that Herodotus picked up from his sources. In other words, the interpretation of the information Herodotus provides is, once again, far from straightforward. As I suggested in my introduction, pretty much everything in Herodotus' *History* has been the subject of scholarly debate, perhaps nothing more so than his account of the expeditions to Thermopylae and Artemisium. Readers can assume that nearly every detail Herodotus provides about the expedition has been doubted and dissected in print: the fatherhood criterion, the degree of damage caused by the first storm, the mooring method employed by the Persians at Sepias, the size and location of the beach at which they anchored, the location of the rocks against which they were wrecked, the location of the Greek advance guard that first spotted the Persians, the fact that the crew that ran aground at Tempe returned to Athens rather than Artemisium, the reason that the fifteen Persian ships captured by the Greeks were delayed, the reason the Greeks withdrew from Artemisium, how many of them withdrew, whether the Greek land army was really expecting reinforcements or if that was propaganda fed to the allies, and so on. And bigger questions are asked as well, of course. What were the Greeks attempting to accomplish at Artemisium and Thermopylae? Did they intend to beat back the Persians or merely delay them until Xerxes ran out of supplies? Or until Attica could be evacuated? Was Thermopylae a suicide mission from the outset? Did it turn into one? Was the land army that was mustered sufficient for its purpose, whatever that purpose was? Was the naval arm of the expedition its more important component, or the infantry? Scholars have vastly different views on these questions: see the bibliography to this chapter for a small taste of what's out there. But people should be aware that if they read a popular history of the Persian Wars, including these chapters, they are necessarily being fed the author's particular version of it. And with that caveat offered, back to the story.

When the Greeks at Thermopylae finally caught sight of the enemy, they panicked. The Peloponnesians were terrified and wanted to retreat to the isthmus, an idea that was of course vehemently opposed by the contingents from central Greece, whose countries would in that case be abandoned to the Persians. Leonidas kept his head and opted to stick with the original plan, but he also sent out messengers to various cities, unnamed by Herodotus, asking for help.

Leonidas and his seven thousand soldiers, then, could expect reinforcements—from back home and perhaps from these recently contacted cities. They were vastly outnumbered, but their position within the pass minimized the Persians' advantage in size. If their inevitable losses could be made good with fresh troops, they might be able to hold the pass indefinitely, or at least until Xerxes' supplies ran out and he was forced to retreat. They rebuilt the wall across the middle gate of the pass, took up position behind it, and waited.

From his position west of Thermopylae, meanwhile, Xerxes sent out a mounted spy to see how many Greeks were guarding the pass and what they were up to. The spy was more than a little surprised by what he saw. Most of the Greeks were behind the wall, so he couldn't observe them. But there were a number of Spartans out in front of it, and Xerxes' man got an eyeful. Some of the Spartans were exercising (*gumnazomenous*), which isn't strange under the circumstances, but one's mental image has to be adjusted for the fact that they probably were doing it stark naked. (Our *gymnastics* and, of course, *gym* come from the Greek word *gumnos*, meaning "naked"—something your average gym-taking fourth-grader would probably be happy to know.) More surprising, the rest of the Spartans, those who weren't engaged in the ancient equivalent of naked sit-ups,[14] were instead sitting around combing their hair. This was probably as jarring an image for Xerxes' spy as, say, a marine checking his lipstick before battle would be to us. But he duly took note of their numbers and went off to report to the king.

Xerxes was shocked by what he heard, and he called in his resident Greek expert, Demaratus, to explain the Spartans' behavior. Demaratus told Xerxes that the Spartans were getting ready to risk their lives: combing their hair was what they did before battle. And he tacked on another paean to the Spartans' martial spirit. These were the bravest men the Greeks were going to throw at them. If Xerxes beat the Spartans, there was no nation on earth that could stand against him.

Thermopylae, Part II: The Battle (7.210–225)

Now, as the king was in a great strait, and knew not how he should deal with the emergency, Ephialtes, the son of Eurydemus, a man of Malis, came to him and was admitted to a conference.   (7.213.1)

Despite what Demaratus had said, Xerxes thought that the Greeks would run away, and according to Herodotus he gave them a chance to do just that.[15] He took no action for several days, but on the fifth day, with the Greeks showing no sign of being scared off, he ordered an assault, sending his Medians and Cissians against the Greeks. It wasn't the walk in the park Xerxes had expected. The Persian contingents suffered very high casualties, wave after wave of men falling before the Greeks' spears. The Medes and Cissians were eventually replaced on the front lines by the so-called Immortals. These were Xerxes' best troops, an elite corps whose name, Herodotus says, came from the fact that the unit was always kept at a strength of ten thousand men (7.83). But they didn't fare any better than the others had. The fighting in the pass was close, and the Greeks benefited from their superior armor and weaponry: the Persians had shorter spears, for example, so they could be spitted by the Greeks before they got close enough to use their own weapons. The Spartans were also able to implement a feigned retreat on multiple occasions, a move that required a great deal of discipline and skill. They would turn their backs as if to flee, and when the Persians had broken ranks to pursue them, the Spartans would wheel around and slaughter them. The Greeks, too, were serving in relays, the various contingents fighting and resting by turns so that none of them was overwhelmed by fatigue. Finally, after scarcely denting the Greek resistance, the Persians withdrew for the day. Herodotus pithily remarks that it was clear to everyone at this point that though there were many men (*anthropoi*, that is, humans) among the Persian troops, there were few *men* (*andres*, men as opposed to women.)

The second day of fighting went much like the first, and by the end of it Xerxes didn't know what he was going to do. The answer came in the form of a Greek traitor, Ephialtes, the son of Eurydemus, a local who wasn't averse to selling out his fellow Greeks if it meant he'd get a reward from the Persian king.[16] Ephialtes told Xerxes about the Anopea, the circuitous path south of Thermopylae by which the Greeks could be outflanked. (One sometimes sees mentioned in this context the fact that the word *ephialtes* means "nightmare" in modern Greek. But this is just a coincidence: "Ephialtes" or "Epiales" was the name of a nightmare-causing demon in antiquity. The name is apparently related etymologically to the Greek verb *ephallomai*, meaning "spring upon," and has nothing to do with Ephialtes the traitor. [Alcaeus, *Etymologicum Genuinum* Fragment 406].) Xerxes acted on Ephialtes' information at once. He ordered his Immortals—perhaps all ten thousand of them, or what was left of them, though Herodotus doesn't specify—to take the Anopea and surprise the Greeks from their rear. They set off, with Ephialtes serving as guide, in the evening of that second day of battle, "around the time the lamps were lit," as Herodotus puts it.

After the Greeks had arrived at Thermopylae, they'd found out about the Anopea Path. It was a troubling problem, but not troubling enough that it necessitated retreat. Leonidas dispatched a thousand Phocians to guard the path. The Phocians, whose own country lay not far to the south, had volunteered for the job. They'd been on guard duty already for some days when, at the break of dawn on what would be the third day of fighting down in the pass, the Immortals crested the summit of the Anopea, where the Phocians were stationed. The Phocians weren't prepared. They apparently hadn't posted sentries, and so were alerted to the enemy's presence only by the sound of the leaves crunching under their feet. They jumped to arm themselves, but the Persians were on them almost at once. The Immortals drew up for battle and dislodged a volley of arrows at the Phocians, who withdrew to the top of a hill. In describing the Phocians' actions, Herodotus seems to be repeating what they must have said in self-defense after the fact. As one scholar has put it, it's a "ludicrously lame" apology.[17] The Phocians withdrew, Herodotus says, because they assumed that they were the object of the Persians' attack. The logic seems to be that they were retreating to a more defensible position, and the Persians were expected to follow them up the mountain and have it out. But the Persians didn't care about the Phocians, and they were in a hurry. They left them on the mountain and rushed down the path to where the real action was, in the Thermopylae pass. (The Phocians seem at the very least to have been incompetent, but perhaps Herodotus' defense hides an uglier truth, that they retreated not in order to fight on more favorable ground but to save themselves, the Greeks in the pass be damned.)

Back at Thermopylae, word came from the Greeks' scouts, who ran down from the peaks at daybreak, that the Immortals were on their way. The Greeks had to decide what they were going to do very quickly, before the Persians descended from the Anopea. There were three main options:[18]

1.   The entire Greek army could remain in position and attempt to fight the Persians on two fronts. But in that case their supplies would be limited, and they would eventually be compelled to retreat anyway (if they weren't all killed).

2. The entire Greek army could retreat at once. But this would be dangerous, particularly during daylight, because the Persians would harass them from the rear.

Herodotus says the Greeks' opinions were divided between these two positions. But Leonidas opted for a third possibility:

3. Some of the Greeks could retreat while a picked force remained behind as a rearguard, delaying the Persians until the others were safely away.

According to Herodotus, Leonidas opted to stay because retreat would have been dishonorable for the Spartans, because he wanted to hoard the glory that would be won for his own country, and because of an oracle the Spartans had received at the beginning of the war. Either Sparta would be destroyed, the priestess had allegedly said (again, in dactylic hexameter), or a Spartan king would be: Leonidas would be that king. But whatever his expectations of glory (and of course Herodotus wouldn't have been privy to Leonidas' thoughts), and whatever his opinion of the oracle (which most historians think was actually a later invention, composed after the war was over), Leonidas surely made the best tactical decision.

The Spartans would be among those staying behind, of course—along with the helots they had with them—but they couldn't hold off the Persians by themselves. In the end they were joined by the Theban and Thespian contingents, from Boeotia in central Greece, who had contributed 400 and 700 troops, respectively. Herodotus claims Leonidas forced the Thebans to stay—and that he had pretty much forced them to serve at Thermopylae in the first place (7.205)—but for logistical reasons alone this seems unlikely: how do you make 400 armed men stay somewhere if they don't want to? It seems clear that Herodotus is repeating anti-Theban propaganda in his account (cf. Plutarch, *Moralia* 866). There was arguably good reason to hate the Thebans for their later behavior—as we'll soon see—but what they did afterwards, under duress, does not imply that they were unwilling participants in the campaign from the get-go or that Leonidas had to force them to stay and fight after the Greeks' position had been compromised.

Herodotus implies that the 2000-odd Greeks who remained at Thermopylae that morning had now knowingly signed onto a suicide mission. And according to Plutarch, Leonidas made no secret of the hopelessness of their situation. He reportedly urged his men to eat a good breakfast before the fighting started because, as will be familiar to anyone who's seen Gerard Butler scream the line in the movie *300*, "Tonight we dine in hell!" (or in Hades, as the Greeks would say; Plutarch, *Moralia* 225C).[19] Certainly the Greeks couldn't hope to defeat the Persians, not a couple thousand of them against Xerxes' myriads. But it's not impossible that they expected to survive, to hold the pass for as long as was necessary to cover the retreat of their compatriots and then slip away themselves to a defensive position farther south. Unfortunately, that's not what happened.

Xerxes advanced later that morning. By prior arrangement with Ephialtes he attacked at the time when people back home would be doing their shopping, perhaps at nine or ten in the morning. The two prongs of the Persian army were apparently attempting to coordinate their movements—not an easy thing to do in the absence of modern communications technology—either so they'd rush the Greeks from the front and rear simultaneously or perhaps so the Greeks would already be engaged at the pass when the Immortals came up behind them. The latter, at any rate, is what happened. Xerxes attacked and the fight was on, neither side holding back. The Greeks, who had remained in the narrows of the pass, guarding their wall, on the two previous days of fighting, now made forays into the wider part. They fought in a frenzy, Herodotus says, without regard for their lives which, at any rate, they viewed as forfeit. Many of them were reduced to fighting with their swords, as most of their spears had been broken. The entire Persian army, meanwhile, was sent against the Greeks, not just individual contingents as in the previous days. They were whipped on from behind so that they would continue to press forward, and in the violent push some of them were trampled and some drowned in the sea that flanked the pass to the north. It was in this stage of the fighting, Herodotus says, that Leonidas was killed.

When the Immortals showed up, the fight changed. The Greeks withdrew to a hill behind their wall. Most of them, at least: the Thebans opted to save themselves at this point. They threw up their hands and surrendered, saying (but who could have heard them and reported this to Herodotus' sources?) that they had been compelled to fight and were really on the Persians' side. Some of the Thebans were killed by the Persians in the confusion. The rest were taken prisoner and later branded as slaves (7.233). As for the Spartans and Thespians, they made their last stand on the hill, fighting now with whatever weapons they had left—their daggers, their bare hands, their teeth. They were surrounded by the enemy and killed to a man, taken down, finally, by a hail of missiles.

Thermopylae, Part III: Epilogue (7.228–238; 8.24–25)

No sooner had these words been uttered, than it became difficult to get a boat, so great was the number of those who desired to see the sight.   (8.25.1)

After the battle, Xerxes and Demaratus had another sit-down. Xerxes asked Demaratus what strategy he thought the Persians should adopt, and Demaratus gave him some good advice. He recommended distracting the Spartans from the defense of Greece by establishing a base on the island of Cythera, which lay just south of the Peloponnese, and harassing the coast from it. The Spartans would inevitably return to defend their homeland, thus dividing the Greek forces, and Xerxes would be able to conquer the Greeks separately. Otherwise, he said, Xerxes could expect to fight tougher battles than Thermopylae in the days to come, specifically at the Isthmus of Corinth. But Xerxes' brother Achaemenes, who was also present, advised against Demaratus' strategy. The army and navy needed to work in conjunction with one another, he argued, and if Xerxes sent part of the fleet south to the Peloponnese, the Persians would lose their numerical advantage over the Greeks as far as ships went. Xerxes wound up taking his brother's advice: the Persian fleet would not be split up. And then he went out to take a walk among the corpses. There was work to be done.

After the battle at Marathon, you may remember, when the Spartans had finally arrived, they went out to view the Persian corpses. We now see that the Persians likewise enjoyed a good gander at dead people. But first the stage had to be set. Xerxes, so Herodotus tells us, had the 4000 Greeks who died at Thermopylae piled in a heap—with the notable exception of Leonidas, or at least his head, which Xerxes, in a fit of pique, ordered to be cut off and impaled on a post. Xerxes then ordered that 19,000 of the 20,000 Persian dead be buried in a mass grave. The grave was then covered with brush so that the earth wouldn't appear to have been disturbed. The other 1000 Persian dead were left sprawled where they lay. The point was to make it appear as if the battle at Thermopylae hadn't been won at such a high cost. Soon afterwards Xerxes sent a herald to the fleet to invite anyone who was interested to come and take a look at the corpses, and the party was on: so many Persians wanted to go to Thermopylae that you could scarcely find a boat to take you there, Herodotus says. The Persians spent the day looking at the battlefield, then sailed back to their posts the next morning. It was a good time, but the Persians hadn't been fooled by Xerxes' trickery:

it was clear to them that more than a thousand of their brothers in arms had died in the pass.

The Greeks were eventually buried on the battlefield, although forty years later, according to the Greek geographer Pausanias, Leonidas' bones (or what were thought to be his bones) were dug up and brought home to Sparta (3.14.1). On the hill where the Spartans and Thespians made their last stand, the Greeks erected a statue of a lion, a tribute to Leonidas (whose name means "lion's son") (7.225). The statue is no longer extant, but in its place now there is a marble slab inscribed with the two-line epitaph the poet Simonides (probably) wrote as a tribute to the fallen Spartiates (all of the dead of Thermopylae having merited a separate, less moving epitaph):

> Go tell the Spartans, stranger passing by,
> that here obedient to their laws we lie.[20]

The Greek forces at Thermopylae had a man in position ready with an oared boat to bring news to the fleet at Artemisium if something were to happen to the army. This man, an Athenian by the name of Abronichus, sailed off with the news after Thermopylae fell. His arrival would trigger the fleet's immediate evacuation of Artemisium. But before we get to that, it's necessary to backtrack and see what had been happening on the naval front since the Persians anchored at Aphetae, just across the strait from the Greek fleet.

CHAPTER TWELVE

Trial by Trireme

The Battles at Artemisium and Salamis

CHAPTER TIMELINE

480 (Aug.)	Battles at Artemisium
480 (Sept.)	Battle of Salamis

T HE GREEKS HAD 271 TRIREMES AT ARTEMISIUM—the bulk of them, 127, supplied by Athens—with a further 53 Athenian ships stationed to the south, guarding the strait between Euboea and the mainland. The Greek fleet had apparently not suffered any major damage from the storm that had battered the Persians. Herodotus says that some four hundred of the Persians' ships had been wrecked against the coast. His numbers may be off, but we can believe that the Persians suffered significant damage. Still, in the eyes of the Greeks at Artemisium, the Persian losses were disappointingly small.

Panic at Artemisium (8.4–5)

He likewise made his own gain on the occasion; for he kept the rest of the money, and no one knew of it.   (8.5.3)

When the Persians pulled into Aphetae after the storm, the Greeks, eyeing the still vast Persian fleet from their position on the other side of the strait, were reportedly terrified. They were so frightened, in fact, that they wanted to abandon their position at Artemisium and hightail it south. According to Herodotus, this wasn't merely the sentiment of the average crewman; Eurybiades himself, the Spartan commander of the fleet, was ready to leave. The Greeks of Euboea were aware that the fleet was on the brink of pulling out, and they begged Eurybiades to stay long enough for them to evacuate: if the Greeks left Artemisium, they would be abandoning Euboea to the Persians. But Eurybiades wasn't swayed, and so the Euboeans tried a different tack. They got in touch with Athens' general at Artemisium, Themistocles, and bribed him: thirty talents bought his assurance that the Greeks would stay put. (Themistocles was the guy who had talked the Athenians into building a fleet from surplus funds a few years earlier and who argued in favor of the naval interpretation of the "wooden wall" oracle.) Themistocles, so the story goes, spent eight of the thirty talents buying his colleagues' cooperation: five talents went to Eurybiades and three to Adeimantus, a Corinthian leader. Themistocles kept the rest.

It's a good story. Themistocles, that wily trickster, manages to save the day while pocketing a fortune. Unfortunately, the tale is highly suspicious for a number of reasons. The Greeks' strategy depended on the coordinated defense of Thermopylae and Artemisium. If the leaders of the fleet decided unilaterally to abandon their position, they would in effect be signing the death warrant of the seven thousand Greeks who were guarding the pass at Thermopylae. Without the Greek fleet there to stop them, the Persians would outflank Thermopylae by sea and land an army behind Leonidas' back. Apart from that, as How and Wells point out in their commentary, it's unlikely that the Euboeans would have given Themistocles a thirty-talent bribe when Eurybiades, had they broached the subject, could have been bought for five.[1] And in the event the Euboeans didn't take the opportunity they had purchased at such cost to evacuate the island (8.19–20). J. B. Bury points out that Themistocles' role in the story is nearly identical to the one he would later play at Salamis.[2] I would add that the story is suspiciously parallel to what we are told happened early on at Thermopylae. When the Greeks first caught sight of the enemy on land, Herodotus says, they panicked and wanted to abandon their position. The local Greeks, whose territory would be surrendered to Persia if the army pulled out, were against leaving, and the idea of withdrawal was eventually rejected by the Spartan commander on the scene (7.207). There may have been grumbling when the Greeks saw the Persian fleet was still formidable after the storm, but I can't believe that retreat from Artemisium was seriously considered at this point.

The Second Storm and the Fighting at Artemisium (8.6–23)

By this plan they thought to enclose the Greeks on every side; for the ships detached would block up the only way by which they could retreat, while the others would press upon them in front.   (8.7.1)

After their arrival at Aphetae, the Persians sent two hundred of their ships off to circumnavigate Euboea. The ships sailed around the far side of the island of Sciathus in order to keep their movements secret from the Greeks at Artemisium (whose view would be obstructed by the island), then headed south. The idea was to block the Greeks' escape route, trapping them in the narrow waters between Euboea and the mainland. The Persians intended to wait until their ships were in position in the south before they attacked the Greeks at Artemisium.

Meanwhile, a professional diver who was serving in the Persian fleet deserted to the Greeks. The story was that the diver, Scyllias of Scione, swam underwater all the way from Aphetae to Artemisium, about ten miles. But Herodotus suggests—far more plausibly (though swimming the strait freestyle, say, would not have been impossible)—that he came instead by boat. Scyllias arrived with information about how the Persians had fared in the storm, and he also told them about the ships the Persians had sent around Euboea. In light of Scyllias' news, the Greeks decided to sail out after midnight to meet the Persians' two hundred ships. Presumably this means that the Greeks intended to send a part of their fleet south down the Euripus while maintaining their position on Euboea's northern coast: sending the whole fleet would have implied abandoning Artemisium and leaving the troops at Thermopylae unprotected, which, as we've suggested above, was unacceptable. If we are right that the Greeks already had a fleet of fifty-three ships guarding the Euripus, the decision they took now will have been to send reinforcements south to join them.

But whatever their plans for later that night, the Greeks had work to do before it got dark. Late in the afternoon they took advantage of the fact that the Persian fleet was now divided by attacking. This was the first of what would be three days of fighting in the strait, and according to Herodotus it was the same three days during which the land forces fought at Thermopylae. Thus while the Greeks under Leonidas were cutting down wave after wave of poorly equipped Persians—the Medians and Cissians and the Immortals, on that first day—the Greek fleet was fighting it out at sea. The Greeks sailed out, probably with only a portion of their fleet, and allowed themselves to be surrounded. On a signal, the Greeks formed their ships into a circle, sterns together, prows out. When a second signal was given, the circle exploded outwards, the Greek ships ramming whatever enemy vessel was close at hand. The Persians had begun the battle contemptuous of the Greeks. But by the time night fell, they had reason to reconsider. That first day the Greeks captured thirty Persian ships. The Persians, apparently, captured none.

We've mentioned triremes before—the Greeks had so many, so many were destroyed in the storm—without going into much detail about them. Triremes were the state-of-the-art warships of the day. The vessels were made of wood and could travel under sail, but they bristled with 170 oars arranged in three banks on either side, 30 in the top row, 29 in the middle, 26 on the bottom. The ships were about 130 feet long—a bit more than the length of three school buses—and 18 feet wide, more than twice that with their oars fully extended. They were long and thin and relatively fragile but built for speed and maneuverability: for short bursts they could reach a top speed of nine or ten nautical miles per hour. The ship carried about two hundred men: 170 rowers who sat on fixed wooden benches in the cramped, airless hold, blind, most of them, to what was happening in the battle; ten marines, a handful of archers, the captain, a piper, a rowing master, various deck hands. The ships were equipped with a wooden ram coated in bronze that extended from the prow at waterline. The principal tactic of the era was ramming, that is, smashing into an enemy ship at top speed with a view to opening a hole in its hull. Fights at sea could also sometimes approximate land battles, the marines on board engaging in hand-to-hand fighting with their counterparts on an enemy vessel after their ships had drawn together. Some historians believe that a trireme might also be made to disable an enemy ship by shearing off its oars by sailing alongside it with one's own oars drawn in.[3] The fitter and more experienced the crew, the better its chance of surviving a battle: 170 men rowing and backing water in unison, straining at the oars, straining to hear the orders being relayed from the rowing master; the rowing master in turn obeying the ship's helmsman, who piloted the ship as it was chased and gave chase in choppy waters, seeking to outmaneuver the enemy while protecting his own vessel's flanks. The movements of scores or hundreds of ships were coordinated in a deadly water ballet, the fate of the crews' families and cities hanging in the balance: this was hellish work that required considerable skill and fortitude. The Athenians' navy was relatively new, most of the ships having been constructed only in the previous few years. And the Greek states had never fought alongside one another before in such numbers. But their prowess was in evidence on that first day of fighting at Artemisium, when they burst from their defensive circular formation to take thirty Persian ships. The Persians would learn at some cost that the Greek fleet, if inferior in size to their own, would not easily be subdued.

The Greeks, having had the better of the day's fighting at sea, never got around to sending reinforcements south. Presumably they were prevented from doing so by the storm that came up that night—not a windstorm like the one that had wrecked so many Persian ships a few days earlier but a violent thunderstorm with a hard rain. During the storm the wreckage from the day's battle drifted toward Aphetae, where the Persian fleet was moored. The storm waves slapped corpses and other debris against the prows of the Persian ships and tangled them in their oar blades. It was worse for the two hundred ships that were sailing around Euboea. They were caught in the open sea and driven against rocks. The fleet was destroyed (some scholars have suggested that any survivors were dispatched by the fifty-three ships the Greeks had at Chalcis), another boon granted to the Greeks by the gods.

In the afternoon of the next day the fifty-three ships that had been guarding the Euripus arrived in Artemisium: since the Persians' circumnavigating fleet had been destroyed, their presence at Chalcis was no longer necessary. At roughly the same time—the ships from Chalcis may in fact have brought the news—the Greeks at Artemisium learned what had happened to the Persian fleet in the storm. Bolstered by the news and by the addition of the fifty-three ships to their ranks, the Greeks attacked the Persians again later in the afternoon. They put to sea against a squadron of ships from Cilicia and destroyed them.

On the third day, for the first time, the Persian fleet took the offensive, and the fighting was hard. The Greeks emerged as victors at the end of the day, but their losses, while less than what the Persians suffered, were significant. Herodotus says that roughly half of the Athenian ships, nearly a hundred, were disabled. (This is hard to credit, though, since the Athenians had 180 ships in the water not much later at Salamis [8.44]: perhaps the damage to many of them was easily repaired.) Because of their losses, the Greeks were supposedly ready to retreat again. This is the third time that Herodotus claims that the Greeks either intended to leave or actually left Artemisium. The first was after the Persians captured two of the three Greek ships that had been stationed as an advance guard around Sciathus (7.183). (The entire fleet withdrew to Chalcis on that occasion, according to Herodotus, but it makes more sense to assume, as we have, that the Greeks instead sent a squadron south to guard the Euripus.) Again, the Greeks allegedly panicked and wanted to flee when they first saw the Persian fleet at Aphetae (8.4). Their flight was allegedly stayed only by the Euboeans' bribery of Themistocles. We've argued before that the Greek fleet would not have unilaterally abandoned its position because the allies' strategy depended on a coordinated defense of the Thermopylae-Artemisium line. The same is true now: it's unlikely that the Greeks were contemplating a withdrawal from Artemisium because of their losses after the third day of battle. The decision to withdraw would instead be made a few hours later, after—but only after—Abronichus arrived in his oared boat with the news: Thermopylae had fallen (cf. Plutarch, *On the Malice of Herodotus* 34 = *Moralia* 867B–C).

Remaining in Artemisium, once Thermopylae was lost, was out of the question. The Persian land army would be heading south, and the Greeks would have to be ready to meet it. Once they got the news, then, they began preparing to evacuate, which they would do under cover of night, hoping to slip away without the Persians seeing them from Aphetae. The Greeks slaughtered as many of the Euboeans' sheep as they could get their hands on—better for the Greeks to eat them than the Persians, when they landed—and roasted them in fires lit along the beach. The fires would also serve to deceive the enemy into thinking that the Greeks were still encamped at Artemisium. They sailed away during the night, the various contingents peeling off in the order in which they were posted, the Athenians leaving last of all. The Persians had no idea that the Greeks had evacuated until a messenger came with the news before sunrise. They could hardly believe it, but spies confirmed the story: the Greeks were gone. The Persians sailed over to Artemisium themselves that morning and quickly set to overrunning northern Euboea. That's what they were up to when, as we've seen, a messenger arrived with Xerxes' invitation to view the dead of Thermopylae.

Before the Greek withdrawal from Artemisium, Themistocles had messages inscribed on rocks around the area where the crews of the enemy fleet were sure to see them—near fresh water springs, for example. (Given the length of Themistocles' message, this sounds like a time-consuming operation. Perhaps his notes—which unfortunately have not survived—were painted rather than inscribed.) The inscriptions were addressed to the Ionian Greeks who were serving in Xerxes' fleet. They urged the Ionians, as fellow Greeks, to desert the Persians or, if that was impossible, to remain neutral or at least prove cowardly

Themistocles, the architect of Athen's navy and hero of Salamis. The bust is a second-century A.D. Roman copy of a Greek original. Werner Forman / Art Resource, NY

in the fighting. Herodotus imagines that in leaving the notes Themistocles hoped for one of two results: either he would in fact influence the Ionians' behavior, or he would make Xerxes distrust them enough to keep them out of the fighting. Either result would benefit the Greeks. Themistocles' strategy here is fascinating as an early example of psychological warfare, the ancient equivalent of dropping pamphlets behind enemy lines to encourage desertion. Themistocles, as he'll prove again shortly, was a clever fellow.

A bust of Themistocles was discovered at Ostia, the port city of Rome, in 1939. It's a Roman copy, probably made in the second century A.D., of a Greek original. The original, which no longer survives, may have been sculpted during Themistocles' lifetime. The statue is inscribed with Themistocles' name and is in good shape but for its nose having broken off. At least a couple of historians have spilled their excitement over the bust in print. Barry Strauss, in his very readable book *The Battle of Salamis*, writes, "The bust conveys irresistible force, as if of a powerful and intelligent man who needed only his will to wrest an enemy into submission."[4] But this is nothing compared to Peter Green's swoon over the statue in *The Greco-Persian Wars*:

> That big round head, simple planes recalling the early cubic conception, poised squarely above a thick, muscular, boxer's neck; the firm yet sensuous mouth, showing a faint ironic smile beneath those drooping moustaches; wiry crisp hair lying close against the skull—all tell an identical story. What we have here is the portrait of a born leader: as Gisela Richter wrote, "a farseeing, fearless, but headstrong man, a saviour in times of stress, but perhaps difficult in times of peace." There is, surely, nothing conventional or stylised about that broad forehead and bulldog jaw; they have an ineluctably Churchillian quality.[5]

I wouldn't read quite so much into the man's physiognomy myself. I see a guy with a beefy neck and thick hair, a close beard, his eyes a bit too close together, more on the ugly side of the continuum than not. But I fear I may lack imagination when it comes to interpreting the visual arts.

The Greeks Gather at Salamis (8.31–63)

"With thee it rests, O Eurybiades! to save Greece, if thou wilt only hearken unto me, and give the enemy battle here, rather than yield to the advice of those among us who would have the fleet withdrawn to the Isthmus."

(THEMISTOCLES, at 8.60.A)

After leaving Thermopylae, the Persians marched south through Phocis, burning and ravaging and raping their way down the Cephisus River. The Phocians refused to medize and fled before the horde, but some of them were caught, and some of the women, Herodotus says, died from the sheer number of the men assaulting them. The greater part of the army then marched through Boeotia toward Athens, the Boeotians (though not the trusty Plataeans and Thespians) medizing at every turn. A smaller force marched toward Delphi with a view to plundering the shrine there, Herodotus says, but they were prevented from doing so by a combination of manpower and miracles. Most dramatically, great chunks of rock allegedly broke off from the cliffs that tower over the shrine and crushed many of the barbarians, coming to rest by the sanctuary of Athena Pronaia, part of the temple complex. Great chunks of rock certainly did fall from the cliffs at some point: Herodotus saw them, and two big boulders are there to see among the ruins of the temple today. But the timing of their crash to earth may not have been as fortuitous as Herodotus suggests. The story of the Persians' attack on the shrine has been doubted: they may have been thwarted by more mundane means, or they may never have intended to take Delphi at all, due to its unique importance in the ancient world. (The Persians had given Delos a pass, remember, on their way across the Aegean in 490.) But for whatever reason, Delphi was spared. Athens wouldn't be so fortunate.

After the Greeks pulled out of Artemisium, they sailed south down the Euripus. They dropped the Plataeans off en route, near Chalcis, so that they could evacuate their city, and the rest of them proceeded to Salamis. Herodotus says that they stopped at Salamis at the request of the Athenians, who needed to begin evacuating Attica: upon their arrival, they issued a proclamation urging the Athenians to save their families and households as best they could. But evacuating Athens was a big job—probably at least a hundred thousand people had to be moved[6]—and the Athenians didn't have a lot of time. Despite what Herodotus says, the evacuation had surely begun long before. The proclamation issued after Artemisium was probably a last call, urging anyone who hadn't already left to do so at once. The evacuees were shipped to Salamis and Aegina as well as Troezen, on the east coast of the Peloponnese. Attica was left all but deserted: there were a few stragglers left behind for whatever reason who were subsequently taken prisoner by the Persians (9.99.2), and a garrison remained in place on the Acropolis. Herodotus says it was manned by just a handful of temple stewards and some indigents, people who maintained that the "wooden wall" destined to save Athens was not its fleet but the city's citadel. But if so, they were uncommonly virile temple stewards and indigents, who were able to withstand a Persian siege, once the Persians got there, "for a long time," and who rolled boulders down on their attackers. In the end, they would all be butchered.

The Greek fleet that returned from Artemisium was joined in the harbors of Salamis by more allied ships. These sailed over from Troezen, where they had mustered from across the Greek world—from the Peloponnese and the mainland, from the Cycladic Islands, and one lone ship had come all the way from Croton on the southern coast of Italy (the hometown of Darius' old doctor Democedes). The Greeks now had 368 triremes in their fleet as well as a handful of penteconters (fifty-oared boats).[7] The little island of Salamis, only some thirty-six square miles in area, was now bursting with boats, its population swelled by the evacuees that had shipped over from Athens and by the nearly seventy-five thousand men who were manning the allied fleet (8.42–48).

The Greek commanders who were gathered at Salamis met to discuss what their next line of defense should be. Attica was as good as lost. Indeed, while the Greeks were arguing over what they should do, word came that the Persians had arrived in Athens and had defeated the small cadre defending the citadel: the Acropolis had been put to flames. The only good news was that because the Athenians had left Attica virtually deserted, Xerxes had had to vent his wrath on property, for the most part, rather than on people. The Greeks, who could probably see and even smell the smoke rising from the Acropolis some ten miles to the east, were themselves enflamed by the news that Athens was taken. But where would they fight? The Peloponnesians were already building a wall across the Isthmus of Corinth, which was less than five miles wide at its narrowest point. They'd begun building it as soon as they'd heard about the fate of Thermopylae—thousands of men working nonstop under the command of Cleombrotus, Leonidas' brother, carrying in stones and bricks and wood and crates of sand for the purpose (8.71).[8] Most of the Greeks thought that it made sense for the fleet to likewise defend the Peloponnese. That way they'd have a friendly shore at their back and the land army near at hand. If, on the other hand, they fought around Salamis and were defeated, they'd be trapped on the island without any hope of help coming to them through a Persian blockade. They resolved, therefore, to stake the fate of Greece on a fight at the isthmus. Then the conference broke up, and the Greeks returned to their ships to pass the night. It would be an even less restful one than they probably expected.

When Themistocles went back to his ship, he told a political ally of his, Mnesiphilus, that the Greeks had decided to fight at the isthmus. Mnesiphilus urged him at all costs to get Eurybiades to change his mind. He argued that once the Greeks left Salamis, they would scatter to their own cities, and Greece would be lost: they should instead fight at Salamis. Themistocles agreed and went to talk to Eurybiades. He repeated what Mnesiphilus had said—without giving the man credit, Herodotus says—and he added some arguments of his own. He convinced Eurybiades—a "dull, well-meaning nonentity," Peter Green calls the poor guy[9]—to summon a second conference of the allied commanders that very night. Once they were gathered, Themistocles repeated the arguments he'd made to Eurybiades (though he didn't insult the Greeks by mentioning Mnesiphilus' concern that they would all scatter to their own cities):

1. It was to the Greeks' advantage to fight in a confined space rather than in the open sea because their ships were heavier than the Persians' (and

thus slower; this may have been due to their design or because they had not been dried out as recently and were waterlogged) and because their fleet was smaller. (Just as it was to the advantage of the Greeks under Leonidas to fight in the narrow pass at Thermopylae, because it neutralized the Persians' advantage in numbers, so fighting in the straits of Salamis would benefit the Greeks' smaller fleet.)

2. By retreating to the isthmus, the Greeks would be yielding the city of Megara to the barbarians as well as the islands of Salamis and Aegina— where many of the Athenians had sent their families for safekeeping. (Evacuating them a second time to the Peloponnese would probably be impossible at this point. So allowing the Persians to gain possession of the islands was unthinkable.)

3. If the Greeks retreated to the isthmus, they would be bringing the war that much closer to the Peloponnese. (Herodotus doesn't say as much, but a defeat off of the Peloponnese would necessarily spell the end of Greece: there would be no fall-back position.) But by fighting at Salamis, the Greeks would be defending the Peloponnese just as much as if they were at the isthmus, without leading the enemy farther south.

4. Themistocles also mentioned the "wooden wall" oracle, which, he said, had prophesied a Greek win at Salamis. (But bringing up the oracle was dangerous ground, since the optimistic interpretation of its reference to Salamis as the place where a lot of "children of women" were destined to die was hardly uncontroversial.)

One can poke holes in some of Themistocles' arguments,[10] but on the whole he makes a strong case for fighting at Salamis. Still, he was reportedly given trouble by the Corinthian Adeimantus—the man he was said to have bribed, along with Eurybiades, to stay put at Artemisium. Adeimantus berated Themistocles as a "cityless man" and said that he should only be allowed to voice an opinion if he had a *polis* behind him. It was a low blow, given those plumes of smoke still rising from the Acropolis: Themistocles was "cityless" only because he'd just lost his *polis* to the Persians. But Themistocles had two hundred ships at his back, and that was city enough. He added a further argument to his litany of reasons that the Greeks should stay where they were:

5. If the Greeks refused to fight at Salamis, the Athenians would pull out of the war effort and emigrate to Italy.

Without the Athenians, who were contributing more than half of the fleet's ships, the Greeks had no chance of winning. And so Eurybiades and the other Greeks caved. The great sea battle against the Persians would be fought at Salamis.

Some scholars have seen an anti-Themistoclean bias at work in Herodotus' story of the Salamis debate. The game plan for which Themistocles would later be lauded—fighting in the straits of Salamis rather than withdrawing to the isthmus—is here portrayed as an idea stolen from Mnesiphilus. But the arguments Themistocles is said to have made for fighting at Salamis were compelling, while Mnesiphilus' contribution—that the allies would scatter if the fleet withdrew to the isthmus—makes no sense. Why should the fleet's retreat necessarily lead to its dissolution? The Mnesiphilus story may or may not have been the product of a tradition hostile to Themistocles, but even if we accept it as historical, Themistocles still emerges from Herodotus' pages as the true architect of the battle at Salamis.

Themistocles wasn't claiming that a fight in the straits of Salamis would necessarily result in a Greek victory—nor that fighting at the isthmus implied their defeat. He was arguing from probabilities: if things went as he expected (8.60.β), he says, the Greeks would win at Salamis. War is a game in which one has to play the odds. There was one potential problem with the Greeks' choice of battleground, however: they couldn't force the barbarians to fight there. If the Persians elected to bypass the Greek fleet and sail to the Peloponnese, the Greeks' hard-fought decision to fight in the straits would be purely academic.

The Persian Conference at Phalerum (8.66–69)

"Spare thy ships, and do not risk a battle; for these people are as much superior to thy people in seamanship, as men to women."   (Artemisia, at 8.68.α.1)

The Persian fleet, having delayed in the north of Euboea, arrived in Attica nine days after the final battle at Artemisium. (Herodotus' account suggests that Xerxes' army, or at least a part of it, was already there by the time the fleet showed up.) The Persians moored their ships in Phalerum Bay, the natural harbor of Athens, a semicircle of beach southwest of the city. The Persians had more ships now than they'd had right after Artemisium, since the Greeks who medized after the battles in central Greece had now joined them. But none of the Persians' new allies were great sea powers, so they won't have been able to contribute very many ships. Herodotus is surely wrong when he says that the Persian fleet was now as big as it had been when it first pulled into Sepias, before the two storms and fighting at sea had taken out, according to his account, more than six hundred of their triremes. But the Persian fleet still outnumbered the Greeks', even after their losses, perhaps by about two to one.

Now that the Persians were in Attica, there was work to be done: the Acropolis was besieged and set on fire, Athenian stragglers were rounded up in the countryside, and the sailors were probably busy making repairs to their triremes. But after some delay Xerxes went down to Phalerum in person and canvassed the commanders of his fleet. We are not to imagine that the king conducted the interviews himself: he sat on a throne, and the generals and officers of the fleet took their places around him while Xerxes' cousin Mardonius asked for their opinions. The question was, should the Persians fight a sea battle or not? Surrounded by yes men as Xerxes was, it's hardly surprising that the answers Mardonius brought back to the king were all resounding affirmatives—with one exception. The commander of the ships serving in Xerxes' fleet from Halicarnassus and a handful of nearby islands was neither a yes man nor, in fact, a man at all: Artemisia, the queen of Halicarnassus, had ruled on her own after her husband's death and had elected to serve with the fleet in person. Unlike everyone else who served under Xerxes, Artemisia, by virtue of her sex, had not been obliged to fight (7.99). Presumably she could have appointed a general to serve in her stead. Insofar as her participation in the campaign was voluntary, she had more in common with the Greeks she was fighting against than she did with her allies.[11] Artemisia also turned out to be the only one of Xerxes' minions who was confident enough to speak truth to power. While Xerxes' other commanders said what they thought the king wanted to hear, Artemisia played the wise advisor and argued against a naval battle. The Greeks were better at sea than the Persians, she said, better—and here she played with her androgynous role in Xerxes' military—by as much as men are superior to women. Xerxes therefore shouldn't risk a naval engagement. Instead, she suggested that he send his land army down the isthmus, toward the Peloponnese, and wait: eventually the Greeks would scatter, both because their supplies on Salamis would run out and because the Peloponnesians among them would want to go and protect their homeland. Besides, having sacked Athens, Xerxes had gotten what he had come for.

The others commanders, hearing Artemisia's response to Mardonius, assumed that she was in trouble. One didn't mouth off in front of the king like that without paying a price. But Xerxes was in fact pleased with her advice and praised her, even if he didn't listen to her. He decided to go with the majority opinion—with his own opinion—and fight it out at sea. Sure, the Persians hadn't fared as well against the Greeks before as they might have, but Xerxes figured there was a big difference between Artemisium and Salamis: he hadn't been watching at Artemisium. Xerxes assumed that his men would try harder if they knew their king was keeping an eye on them, and he was probably right: the Greeks, after all, were fighting for the survival of their families and their communities; the Persians were fighting because the king had told them to. They needed to be incentivized.

It's interesting that the question Xerxes posed to his commanders was whether they should fight at sea at all—not where they should fight. If the Persians had bypassed Salamis and sailed to the isthmus, where the wall was being built (close to the juncture of the isthmus and the Peloponnese), it would have forced the Greeks to follow them and fight in the open sea, which would have been to the Persians' advantage. But in that case the Persians would have had to operate off of a hostile coastline (assuming the Persian land army had not yet broken through and conquered territory within the Peloponnese, which was unlikely to happen quickly). With the Greeks holding the shore, the Persians would not be able to beach their ships or procure food by land or, should it come to that, swim to salvation—those of them who *could* swim. Fighting in the straits of Salamis, with conquered territory at their back, was preferable to the alternative. And if they could manage to defeat the Greek fleet, then victory on land was a done deal, since they'd be able to land troops behind enemy lines whenever they wished.

Themistocles' Ruse (8.70–82)

"The Athenian commander has sent me to you privily, without the knowledge of the other Greeks." (SICINNUS, at 8.75.2)

After the Persians decided to fight at sea—but probably not immediately after, as Herodotus' account suggests—they sailed out and drew up for battle off of Salamis, outside of the strait, hoping to entice the Greeks to come out and fight. The Greeks didn't bite, and the Persians soon withdrew, since it was already late in the day. That same evening, the Persian army started its march toward the Peloponnese. Meanwhile, things were falling apart in the Greek camp, at least from Themistocles' perspective. The Peloponnesians among them weren't happy with the decision the generals had made to stay at Salamis. And the news that the Persian army was en route to the Peloponnese—the sound of tens of thousands of men on the march, probably carrying across the water—can't have helped their mood. They wanted to go back home and defend the isthmus. The sailors' whispered criticisms eventually erupted into public complaints and culminated finally in a meeting, where the whole question of where to fight was debated anew. This time around, Themistocles' viewpoint wasn't winning. He decided to help it along.

Themistocles, the story goes, slipped out of the meeting and got hold of one of his servants, Sicinnus, a Greek (probably) who was what we might today call a "manny": he looked after Themistocles' kids. Themistocles sent Sicinnus off to Phalerum in a small boat with a message he was to deliver to the Persians:

> The general of the Athenians sent me without the knowledge of the other Greeks (for it so happens that he favors the king and he would prefer that your side prevail rather than that of the Greeks). I am to say that the Greeks are very afraid and are planning to flee. It is now in your power to accomplish the most glorious of all actions, unless you let them run away. For they are arguing with one another and they will not oppose you: you will see them fighting at sea against themselves, those who favor you against those who do not.

Herodotus doesn't say much about Sicinnus' adventure—which (of course) some scholars have doubted ever happened—but it was surely tailor-made for the movies: the mild-mannered manny sneaking off under cover of darkness, a treasonous message burned in his memory; ink-black waves slapping against the small boat's hull; the cry of a Persian sentry when Sicinnus' craft heaves into view; the tense moments in the enemy's camp while the barbarians decide whether to believe him or kill him. In the end, they believed him, and after all, much of what he said was true: the Greeks were arguing amongst themselves; the Peloponnesians did want to run off. And the report that one of the Greek generals and some of the sailors were ready to turn traitor, well, that was exactly what Xerxes wanted to hear, and that rendered it credible enough. Battles in antiquity were often decided by the actions of traitors. Some historians have been skeptical of the story because the Persians let Sicinnus go rather than keep him hostage to events. But perhaps he made it clear that he'd need to report back to Themistocles, to let Xerxes' man on the inside know that his plans for betraying the Greeks during the battle were a go. For his service this night, Themistocles would later help Sicinnus become a citizen of Thespia in Boeotia, after the war, when the Thespians were seeking to rebuild their population. And a rich citizen at that. But first Sicinnus and his wily patron would have to survive another year of war.

The Persians got busy at once. They had intended to fight at Salamis to begin with. But Sicinnus' message had the effect of moving up the timetable: if a pro-Persian contingent within the fleet was ready to turn on the other Greeks, Xerxes would want to engage the enemy as soon as possible, before the Peloponnesians had a chance to withdraw to the isthmus. Salamis was looking like it could be a decisive win for Xerxes, a chance to crush the Greek fleet once and for all with the aid of a fifth column. The Persians put to sea in the middle of the night and sailed—as quietly as possible—into the strait between Salamis and Attica, where the Greek fleet was stationed.

Salamis lies not quite a mile off the west coast of Attica in the Saronic Gulf. The island is shaped like a horseshoe or a backwards C, its mouth open to the west. At about the island's midpoint a long, thin peninsula, the Cynosura (the name means "dog's tail"), juts from its eastern shore toward Attica. Between the eastern tip of Cynosura and the mainland, just to the south of the peninsula, the rocky little island of Psyttaleia breaks up the strait into two passages. The Greek fleet was moored to the north and west of Cynosura. Precisely what the Persians' movements were during the night is a question that has exercised scholars. But it seems that part of their fleet sailed north along the Attic coast, past Cynosura, past where the Greeks were stationed across the channel, and took up position off of Mount Aegaleus, which bulges into the strait from Attica opposite the northern part of Salamis. In the end they were in position to block the Greek fleet from fleeing northward, up into the Bay of Eleusis and counterclockwise around the island. In the south, another part of the Persian fleet was probably strung out along the Attic shore east of Psyttaleia, positioned to challenge any ships that tried to sail out of the strait. More Persian ships may have been massed to the southeast, outside of the straits. The Persians also stationed men on Psyttaleia itself. During the battle survivors and wrecks could be expected to wash ashore there. The Persians on the island would be able to save their allies and kill any Greeks that struggled to shore.

While the Persians were moving their ships into position across the channel, the Greeks were still arguing, oblivious, as Herodotus' account has it, to what their enemy was up to. The Persians were moving as quietly as they could through the strait. Still, the passage of hundreds of ships less than a mile away would inevitably make some noise and, as Barry Strauss points out,[12] the Persians might even have been smellable across the channel, the sweaty bodies of tens of thousands of overworked Persian oarsmen generating a not inconsiderable stench. But if they had an inkling that something was up, the Greeks wouldn't have known in the dark just what was happening. That revelation awaited the arrival of the Athenian Aristides, the son of Lysimachus, who sailed over to Salamis from Aegina in the middle of the night. Aristides was an old political rival of Themistocles. He had been ostracized a few years earlier, but the Athenians recalled their exiles prior to the Persian invasion, all hands being needed on deck, as it were (cf. Aristotle, *The Constitution of Athens* 22). Aristides, Herodotus says, was the justest man in all of Athens, and that was certainly his reputation in antiquity, so much so that he's commonly referred to as "Aristides the Just." While sailing in, Aristides had seen the Persian fleet taking up position in the strait. (He'd had to elude their ships in the dark, perhaps by hugging the shore of Salamis.) When he came to the Greeks' meeting, he pulled Themistocles aside—whatever their former enmity, they were now working together—and told him the Greeks were now effectively surrounded: they wouldn't be getting out of the strait without a battle.

Themistocles was pleased. By sending Sicinnus off to the Persian camp, he had hoped to prompt the enemy to act before the Peloponnesians could scatter. Themistocles hadn't made any tactical suggestions to the Persians—specific instructions might have seemed suspicious—but he couldn't have hoped for a better outcome. The Greeks would be compelled to fight at Salamis, and they would be fighting in conditions that favored their slower, smaller fleet. And if there weren't any surprises, they would, by Themistocles' calculation, be victorious. Themistocles told Aristides that he was responsible for what the Persians were doing: he had had to force the Greeks to fight at Salamis against their will. He asked Aristides to report the news about the Persians' movements to the Greeks, because, he said, if he told them they wouldn't believe it.

As it happened, the Greeks didn't believe Aristides, either, but later that night his information was confirmed. A ship that had been serving under Xerxes, from the island of Tenos in the Cyclades, deserted to the Greeks. Its commander filled the Greeks in on everything the Persians were doing. So now everybody knew: the next day—September 28, probably, but at any rate a day in late September—would be one for the history books.

"Woe, in Triple Banks of Oars":[13] The Battle of Salamis (8.83–96)

Yet the Persians fought more bravely here than at Euboea, and indeed surpassed themselves; each did his utmost through fear of Xerxes, for each thought that the king's eye was upon himself.   (8.86)

The Greeks, convinced by the Tenians that they were indeed surrounded, got ready to fight. In the morning, before dawn, Themistocles and the other generals gave their inspirational pre-battle harangues to the troops, and then the Greeks boarded their triremes and launched their ships. As they were doing so, the Persians attacked. Far from being on the verge of fleeing or of turning traitorously against their allies, as the Persians had been led to expect, the Greeks, relatively well rested after a night on shore, were ready to fight. The Persians, by contrast, while superior as far as numbers went, were probably already exhausted. They'd been at their oars all night. They hadn't slept. They may have been hungry. And they would soon find that their superiority in numbers counted against them in the narrow waters east of Salamis.

Herodotus doesn't give us a big-picture view of what happened in the battle. His account consists primarily of anecdotes, stories he picked up from his sources about this or that incident in the melee. And really, that was all anyone in the thick of the fighting could possibly have been aware of, their slice of a battle that involved a thousand or more ships fighting in roughly a square mile of sea. The only person who got a bird's-eye view of the proceedings was Xerxes—and whatever attendants were with him—who was seated on a throne on Mount Aegaleus watching the battle as if it were a football game. He had a clerk nearby who kept track of the Persian captains whose actions Xerxes would want to recognize afterwards: ramming an enemy vessel while the king was watching had its rewards. Artemisia, in fact, managed to rise even higher in Xerxes' estimation by conspicuous ramming—though Xerxes missed an important detail while watching that particular episode. Artemisia's trireme was being pursued by a Greek ship at one point during the battle, and in order to escape it—or perhaps it was just an accident—she rammed a Persian vessel, not only one of her allies, but in fact one of the ships under her command (7.99). The captain of the Greek ship that had been chasing her, assuming that her trireme was now fighting on the Greeks' side, left off pursuit. (Had he known it was Artemisia he'd been after, he would never have let her go. The Athenians had put a price on her head, ten thousand drachmas for anyone who captured her alive: they were scandalized that a woman had dared to wage war against them.) Xerxes was watching when Artemisia rammed the ship and naturally assumed she had taken out a Greek trireme, not one of his own. Nor would he be disabused of this idea later, since no one on the ship Artemisia had rammed survived to tell the tale. Xerxes, delighting in her manly valor from his perch on the mountain, reportedly observed, "My men have become women and my women men!"

Among the anecdotes Herodotus includes in his account is a story about the Corinthian Adeimantus. Adeimantus allegedly hoisted sail and fled in panic at the start of the battle, followed by the rest of his countrymen. Before they got to the Bay of Eleusis, however, they encountered a mysterious little boat—sent by the gods, it seemed to them—whose crew told Adeimantus that while he was running away, the rest of the Greeks were back in the front lines winning the battle. Adeimantus was persuaded to turn around, but by the time the Corinthians got back, the battle was over. This story, Herodotus tells us, was reported only by the Athenians: the Corinthians denied the accusation that they had run away, and the rest of Greece bore witness to their having performed well at Salamis. Nor is there any other evidence that corroborates the charge, which appears to be nothing but a baseless piece of slander that Herodotus' Athenian sources were spreading around. Adeimantus, in fact, is maligned throughout Herodotus' pages: he was bribed to stay and fight at Artemisium; he rebuked Themistocles as a "cityless" man at that second conference of the Greek allies. The reason for the Athenians' animosity toward Adeimantus may lie in events that occurred half a century later. Adeimantus' son Aristeus was a Corinthian commander during the early stages of the Peloponnesian War. He caused the Athenians a good deal of trouble in the north Aegean before he was executed by them: he was one of the envoys who was thrown into a pit along with the sons of Sperthias and Bulis in 430 (7.137; Thucydides 1.60, 1.65, 2.67: see chapter ten). The venom directed at Adeimantus by Herodotus' sources, that is, may in part have been prompted by the deeds of his son.

The Persians fought better under the king's eye at Salamis than they had at Artemisium, but it wasn't good enough. In the close-quarter fighting in the straits, the Greek triremes rammed ship after ship, crippling some, sinking others. Some of the Persian triremes managed to escape back to Phalerum, but many ran afoul of their own boats while trying to flee, the ships toward the rear of the action pressing forward to join the fray. Others were dispatched by the Aeginetans, who lay in wait, ready to pounce on any Persian vessels trying to flee to the south, past Psyttaleia. Herodotus doesn't provide figures for the losses on either side, but according to the historian Diodorus (11.19.3), who wrote some four hundred years later, the Persians lost at least two hundred ships in the battle. Diodorus' figure may be exaggerated, but whatever the number was, it was enough to put the fear of Zeus into Xerxes. The Persian sailors who went down with their ships, meanwhile, tended to stay down: most of them weren't able to swim.

Among the Greeks who fought at Salamis that day was the playwright Aeschylus, whose brother, as we've seen, had fought and died at Marathon a decade earlier, bleeding out after his hand was chopped off. In 472, eight years after the Greek victory at Salamis, Aeschylus' play *The Persians* was performed in Athens to an audience that must have been filled with veterans of the battle. The play—the only extant Greek tragedy that has a historical rather than a mythological subject—is set in the Persian capital of Susa. It depicts the moment when news of the Persians' devastating defeat arrives in the capital via a herald. The herald provides poetic descriptions of the course of the battle that can be used to supplement what we get from Herodotus:

> First the floods of Persians held the line,
> But when the narrows choked them, and rescue hopeless,
> Smitten by prows, their bronze jaws gaping,
> Shattered entire was our fleet of oars.
> (lines 412–415, trans. Seth Benardete)

Neither Herodotus nor Aeschylus, then, gives us anything like a clinical account of the battle. We do get a few specifics. The Athenians held the Greeks' left wing, for example, opposite the Phoenicians, and the Spartans were on the right across from the Ionians. Some of the Ionians—but not many—followed the instructions Themistocles had had chiseled in the rocks around Artemisium and proved themselves willful cowards in the fighting. But primarily what we have is impressionistic—anecdotes and poetry—from which we get a feel for the fighting. And the estimated numbers of the dead on either side likewise tell a story. There would have been some forty thousand men on the two hundred ships the Persians reportedly lost. Most of them drowned, but some were dispatched by the Greeks in the water or while clambering ashore. "Like tuna or some catch of fish," Aeschylus writes, "with fragments of oar and bits of wreckage the Greeks went on beating them, slicing them up" (lines 424–426). The strait and, eventually, the beaches ringing it were littered with their corpses. Nor were the Persians posted on Psyttaleia safe. Aristides—Themistocles' one-time rival—rounded up some men, went over to the island, and slaughtered those holding it. Against these Persian losses, the Greeks lost forty ships (Diodorus 11.19.3): eight hundred men, then, but the Greeks could swim, and many of these probably made it to shore safely. The battle, that is, was a huge victory for the Greek side, its importance probably not apparent even to the Greeks that evening, as they towed in the hulls of the damaged triremes and saw to their dead and wounded and wondered what the Persian fleet—still large enough to cause trouble even with these recent losses—was going to do next. But Salamis changed everything.

The Withdrawal of the Persian Fleet (8.97–102, 107)

"Depart home, if thou art so minded, and take with thee the bulk of thy army; but first let me choose out 300,000 troops, and let it be my task to bring Greece beneath thy sway." (MARDONIUS, at 8.100.5)

Back when Xerxes sacked Athens, he'd sent news of the triumph to Susa, where his uncle Artabanus was serving as regent (8.54). That first message had prompted celebrations in the capital, but now Xerxes had bad news to share. He sent word of the defeat at Salamis by mounted courier, which gives Herodotus a chance to marvel at the efficiency and speed of the communication network the Persians had in place: the message was carried in relays, one man and horse per day, with replacements posted at intervals along the route—a Persian pony express, in other words. Its carriers, famously, were available to ride at all times and in all weather, prevented from finishing their routes by neither snow nor rain nor heat nor night. . . . If that sounds familiar, it's because Herodotus' description of the Persian express at 8.98.1 has served as an unofficial motto of the United States Post Office for the last century. A translation of the line was inscribed on the facade of the main post office building in New York City (at 8th Avenue and 33rd Street), which opened in 1914: "Neither snow nor rain nor heat nor gloom of night stays these couriers from the swift completion of their appointed rounds." At any rate, when the mail came to Susa this time, perhaps as little as a week after Xerxes sent the message, his subjects fell to lamenting and rending their garments. They also blamed Mardonius for having talked Xerxes into going to Greece in the first place (7.5). In all likelihood, they wouldn't be the only ones pointing the finger of blame at Mardonius.

Herodotus alleges that Xerxes wanted to withdraw from Greece at once after Salamis: he was terrified that the Greeks would destroy the bridges over the Hellespont and trap him and his men in Europe. However bad the defeat at Salamis had been, though, the war was by no means over. Xerxes' fleet was still larger than what the Greeks could put in the water, and the Greeks themselves fully expected to have to fight at sea again (8.96.1, 8.108.1). The retreat of the Persian fleet from Greece, that is, was not an inevitable result of the battle at Salamis. Still, that's what wound up happening.

The idea to send the fleet back to Asia allegedly came from Mardonius. He was worried about what the Persian defeat at Salamis might mean for his future: it didn't look good. He figured he could save his skin by subduing Greece on his own. Alternatively, he'd die in battle, but that would be preferable to enduring whatever punishment Xerxes might inflict on him. He suggested two possible plans of action to Xerxes: either the Persians should stay in Greece in full force and attack the Peloponnese, or Xerxes should return to Asia with the fleet and the bulk of the army and leave Mardonius behind with a force of three hundred thousand troops. Mardonius, in that case, would deal with things in Greece and hand the country over to Xerxes properly enslaved. Before deciding which plan to adopt, Xerxes consulted Artemisia. She, after all, had offered him the best advice before, when she'd urged him not to risk a naval battle at Salamis. Artemisia threw her weight behind Mardonius' second option. If Mardonius succeeded in enslaving Greece, she explained, Xerxes would get the credit for his servant's victory, but if Mardonius failed, it was no big deal: Xerxes and his house would be safe, and the Greeks would live to lose the war another day, having gained little by defeating Xerxes' minion.

Xerxes was delighted with Artemisia's advice, and he gave Mardonius the go-ahead to select the troops that would be staying behind. Later that night, per Xerxes' instructions, the Persian fleet slipped away from Phalerum, hurrying back to the Hellespont and the safer waters bordering Asia.

The Kids, the Queen, and the Castrated (8.103–106)

The Hermotimus of whom I spoke above was, as I said, a Pedasian; and he, of all men whom we know, took the most cruel vengeance on the person who had done him an injury.   (8.105.1)

Before Xerxes left Athens, however, he asked Artemisia to do him a favor. He had a bunch of his kids on campaign with him, bastards who were presumably too young to serve in the military and needed looking after, and he asked Artemisia to take them back with her by boat to Ephesus: he'd be making the trip back home overland. Ephesus, on the coast of Asia Minor, is where the Royal Road to Susa started. The kids would presumably be traveling from there by land back to the capital. Now, it's true that Xerxes was unusually fond of Artemisia, and she was a woman, after all, but what we know of her—that possibly intentional ramming of her own ally during the battle at Salamis, to say nothing of the whole Amazon warrior princess persona—doesn't scream "mother figure" to me, even if she did have a son of her own (7.99). Still, even if Artemisia wasn't exactly nanny material, Xerxes trusted her. He also sent along his most trusted eunuch, Hermotimus, to serve as the party's bodyguard, the manly woman paired with the womanly man.

Hermotimus may literally have lacked cojones, but figuratively speaking he had them to spare. Herodotus distinguishes him as someone who, after having been wronged, exacted the greatest vengeance of anyone known. I would argue that Astyages out-vengeanced him back when he made Harpagus eat his own son, but Hermotimus probably comes in second. Although not having testicles had proved to be a good career move for him—Hermotimus was a trusted member of the royal court—he harbored some resentment over what had been done to him. Hermotimus was originally from Pedasa, which was right near Halicarnassus on the coast of Asia Minor. He'd been captured by enemies as a boy and sold into slavery. The guy who bought him, Panionius of Chios, castrated him and put him back up for sale. That's how Panionius made his living, by buying attractive boys, increasing their value through castration, and then marking them up for resale.

When Xerxes was in Sardis mustering his troops for the invasion of Greece, Hermotimus happened to go down to the coast opposite Chios, and he ran into Panionius. Hermotimus, like Astyages before him, pretended to be happy with what Panionius had done to him: castration had given him a brilliant career, and Hermotimus wanted to reward his castrator in turn. He would set him up nicely somewhere, he said; Panionius should bring the wife and kids. Panionius accepted the offer, and then, when he and his family were settled, Hermotimus showed his true colors. He gave Panionius a talking to, for one thing, saying that Panionius had made him "a nothing rather than a man." And then he made Panionius chop off his four sons' testicles. And then he had the boys chop off dad's. Vengeance extracted.

Hermotimus, presumably, wouldn't hesitate to use any means necessary to protect Xerxes' bastard boys on the trip home, so Xerxes had chosen well. As for Artemisia, this is the last we hear of her in the *History*. It's an odd sendoff for the warrior queen, being dispatched by Xerxes to play nanny for the duration of an Aegean cruise. One wonders if Herodotus meant anything by it.[14]

Secrets, Sieges, and Scandal: Themistocles and the Athenian Fleet after Salamis (8.108–112, 121–125)

Accordingly, they came in to his views; whereupon he lost no time in sending messengers, on board a light bark, to the King, choosing for this purpose men whom he could trust to keep his instructions secret, even although they should be put to every kind of torture.   (8.110.2)

When the Greeks woke up the morning after the Persian fleet had withdrawn, they assumed the enemy was still in position at Phalerum: after all, the Persian land forces were still nearby. They were shocked when they found out the fleet was gone. The Greeks jumped in their ships—some of them, at least, with some surely left behind to watch Salamis—and sailed off in pursuit. They may have been looking for a fight, hoping to pick off vulnerable stragglers, or perhaps they just wanted to make sure the Persians had indeed left the area. But after sailing as far as Andros, the large island to the southeast of Euboea, they hadn't spotted a single ship, and they paused there to debate their options. Themistocles was in favor of sailing straight to the Hellespont and destroying Xerxes' bridges, thereby trapping the Persian land army in Europe. But Eurybiades, the Spartan commander-in-chief, argued that it was better for the Greeks if the Persians were allowed to leave. If they were trapped, they might, in their desperation, do a lot of damage, and the cities of Greece could fall to them one by one. In the future, he said, they would take the war to Asia rather than fight in their own homeland. We might add that it would have been unwise for the

Greek fleet, or a large portion of it, to sail to the Hellespont when Xerxes was still back in Attica ready to wreak havoc with his army. Now was not the time to divide the allied forces. Eurybiades' view prevailed, and Themistocles was left to explain the decision to the Athenians, who were reportedly as eager as he was to sail to the Hellespont. Themistocles repeated Eurybiades' arguments, making a convincing show of being in agreement with them, and he bade the Athenians to start rebuilding their lives, repairing their property, planting their crops. In the spring, he said, they could go east and renew the fight.[15]

But according to Herodotus, Themistocles had another trick up his sleeve. Since he hadn't gotten his way in the debate, he decided to use the Greeks' decision not to sail to the Hellespont to his advantage. He sent Sicinnus off on yet another secret mission, this time bearing a message he delivered to Xerxes personally. Sicinnus allegedly told the king that Themistocles had convinced the Greeks not to go to the Hellespont and destroy the bridges: Xerxes could withdraw from Greece at his leisure without fear that his passage across the Hellespont would be in jeopardy.

On the face of it, the story is hard to believe. Could Xerxes really be expected to believe a second secret message from Themistocles after the first had led to disaster at Salamis? Well, maybe. Themistocles, after all, hadn't chosen the time and place of the battle; that was Xerxes' doing. And if the Greeks had neither fled nor turned traitor during the fighting, as Themistocles had suggested they would, that had been out of his hands: the discord in the Greek camp that he'd told Xerxes about had been real enough. But what makes Herodotus' story more likely than not to be true, however unlikely it may seem, is that Thucydides apparently believed it. In his *History of the Peloponnesian War* he quotes a letter that Themistocles sent years later to Xerxes' son Artaxerxes. In the letter Themistocles mentions the services he had rendered to Artaxerxes' father during his invasion of Greece: "He wrote about the announcement of the retreat from Salamis and that of the bridges, which he falsely took credit for, that they were not broken up on account of him" (1.137.4). Thucydides was no slouch, and he was not averse to refuting Herodotus when he thought it appropriate, so his belief that Themistocles really did send two secret messages to Xerxes carries considerable weight.

But what was the point of the second message? The motivation Herodotus attributes to Themistocles is pretty nasty. It was also clearly written with knowledge of what lay in Themistocles' future—more on which in a bit.

Herodotus says Themistocles sent the message in order to store up some credit with Xerxes in case the Athenians ever turned on him and he needed a refuge. It's hard to believe, though, that the architect of Salamis, who was being lauded throughout Greece at the time, was really prescient enough to imagine that sort of a future for himself. But if the message was indeed sent and its content was as Herodotus describes, it's not clear what other purpose it could have had.[16]

After deciding not to sail to the Hellespont, the Greeks demanded that the people of Andros, who had medized, pay money to the Greek allies. When the Andrians refused—citing as their reason the dictates of their gods, Penury and Helplessness—the Greeks laid siege to the island. The siege was ultimately unsuccessful, however, and the Greeks went on to devastate Carystus, in southern Euboea, which had likewise medized (6.99, 8.66, 8.121). Herodotus' account of the allies' actions against medizers in late 480 is blatantly anti-Themistoclean. Herodotus says that Themistocles, operating without the knowledge of his colleagues, was sending threatening messages around the Aegean demanding that the islands pay him money and threatening them with reprisal from the fleet. He was motivated purely by greed, according to Herodotus, and the money was intended for his private coffers. But it's ridiculous to think the fleet was being used for Themistocles' personal benefit. Clearly the allied Greeks were working together, extracting war indemnities from cities that had sided with the Persians, and backing up their demands with military action.

Themistocles, at this point, was at the pinnacle of his career. People were saying he was the cleverest guy in Greece, and he was almost everybody's second choice (after themselves) to win the prize for valor after the battle (which would be something like voting him the MVP of Salamis). The Spartans gave him the ancient equivalent of a ticker-tape parade: they gave him gifts and provided him with a military escort on his way out of town. But not everybody was thrilled with the attention Themistocles was getting. When he got back to Athens, Timodemus of the deme Aphidna, whose only claim to fame was that he was Themistocles' enemy, and who was mad with jealousy, criticized Themistocles for taking credit for what had been a communal action: Themistocles had gotten those gifts from the Spartans because of Athens, he said, not on his own account. "Here's the truth of it," Themistocles shot back. "If I were from Belbina"—a tiny speck of island southwest of Attica, in other words Nowheresville—"I would not have been honored by the Spartans; but neither would you, Sir, although you are an Athenian."

End scene. Exit Themistocles. This is the last we hear from him in Herodotus' *History*.[17] Herodotus' presentation of Themistocles may be negative at times, but he certainly gave the guy a great exit line.[18]

Herodotus leaves Themistocles on top, but as I've hinted above, his later career wasn't all sunshine and bunnies. In the early 470s he was instrumental in getting Athens and its harbors refortified, but he was ostracized in 472. While he was in exile, the Spartans sent an embassy to Athens accusing him of collaboration with Persia. They had allegedly found evidence implicating Themistocles while looking into a treasonous plot involving their own general, Pausanias. (Stay tuned for that story.) The Athenians sent men to arrest Themistocles, who at the time was living in Argos in the Peloponnese, but he got wind of what was happening and fled. Thucydides' account of Themistocles' life on the run reads like something from a Jason Bourne novel. From Argos he went to the island of Corcyra, his would-be captors close on his heels. Then he was in Molossia in northwest Greece begging the Molossian king for help. From there he went to Macedon, where he booked passage on a merchant ship bound for Ionia. A storm blew the ship uncomfortably close to the Athenian fleet, which was laying siege to Naxos at the time, but after bribing and threatening the captain of the merchant ship Themistocles made it safely to Ephesus. He traveled inland and wrote that letter to Artaxerxes that we already mentioned, offering his services to the king. He learned Persian. And he lived out the rest of his days in the city of Magnesia in Asia Minor, which Artaxerxes gave him to govern. Themistocles died in 459, probably from natural causes, though there were rumors he'd committed suicide. His bones were secretly brought back to Athens by his relatives and buried in Attic soil (Thucydides 1.135–138).

Xerxes' Retreat (8.113–120, 126–130)

Plague too and dysentery attacked the troops while still upon their march, and greatly thinned their ranks.   (8.115.3)

After the retreat of the fleet from Phalerum, the Persian army also withdrew, its march toward the Peloponnese having been aborted after Salamis. The entire army went north to Thessaly, where Mardonius had decided to spend the winter. When the Persians got there, Mardonius selected the troops that would be staying behind with him in Greece, then Xerxes set off for home with the rest of the army. They were escorted to the Hellespont by sixty thousand of Mardonius' chosen troops, who were under the command of Artabazus. Herodotus or his sources may have exaggerated the difficulties that Xerxes' army faced en route, but as he tells the story, at least, things were pretty bad. There was very little food available, and the Persians had to resort to eating grass and leaves and tree bark. Many died from illness along the way. Others had to be left behind to recuperate in the cities they passed through. Still, they made it to the Hellespont in forty-five days, roughly half the time it had taken the Persians to get from the Hellespont to Athens going in the other direction (8.51). (There is an alternate story that Xerxes traveled by ship from Thrace to Asia while the rest of the army went on foot, but Herodotus emphatically dismisses it.)

When Xerxes got to the Hellespont, the bridges turned out to be unusable. They had been damaged in a storm and were no longer securely fastened. After all Xerxes' earlier concern about the Greeks sailing across the Aegean and breaking down the bridges, here they were, already out of commission. It's a bit anticlimactic. More anticlimactic yet, it doesn't seem to have mattered very much. The Persian fleet was on hand to ferry the army across the strait to Abydus. There, having gone hungry for forty-five days, the Persians ate like pigs and made themselves sick. More of them died. The rest returned with Xerxes to Sardis.

The sixty thousand troops that had escorted Xerxes to the Hellespont—or what was left of them—took their time returning to Thessaly. Along the way they laid siege to cities that had revolted from Persian rule. They captured Olynthus in Chalcidice easily enough and slit the throats of its inhabitants. But their siege of Potidaea, on the westernmost prong of the Chalcidic peninsula, was less successful. Many of the Persians died when they tried to cross the peninsula during an ebbtide: when the flood tide came in, lots of them drowned because they couldn't swim, and many of those who could swim were killed by the Potidaeans, who came after them in boats. But eventually, probably in February or March of 479, the army limped back to Thessaly, having lost perhaps a third of their original number (9.66). As for the Persian fleet, it passed the winter at Cyme, on the coast of Asia Minor. In the spring the ships would sail to Samos to keep an eye on the Ionian Greeks, lest they get it in their heads to revolt again.

With Mardonius' troops all tucked in their beds for the winter up in Thessaly, the allied Greeks had a bit of breathing room. The Athenians moved back to Attica. The Peloponnesians kept working on the Isthmian wall. And everybody waited for the spring, when Mardonius' men would stir and shake their spears and march south again. The Persian army that remained in Greece was still a formidable war machine, but with Xerxes' fleet removed from the equation, the subjection of Greece would not be easy: it would be more difficult to supply the army, and the Persians would no longer be able to outflank the Greeks by sea. In depriving the Persians of their naval arm, the Greek victory at Salamis had gone a long way toward leveling the playing field. The allied fleet had done its job admirably: but the fate of Greece would be decided in the coming year by sword and spear.

CHAPTER THIRTEEN

Concluding Scenes

The Battles of Plataea and Mycale and the Siege of Sestus

CHAPTER TIMELINE

479 (June)	Second Persian occupation of Attica
479 (Aug.)	Battles of Plataea and Mycale

W HILE HE WAS WINTERING IN THESSALY, Mardonius sent a man out—Mys, a Greek from Caria in Asia Minor—to consult various oracles. Mys visited shrines throughout central Greece (though not the oracle at Delphi), among them the sanctuary of Ptoan Apollo in Boeotia. The prophet there spat out a response in a language the Thebans on hand couldn't identify but that Mys understood: the god was speaking Carian. Mys grabbed a tablet from the Thebans, wrote down the prophecy, and carried it back to Mardonius. Herodotus doesn't know what Mys had been sent to ask the god about, but his guess is that the oracle suggested that Mardonius try to make Athens his ally (8.133–136). That, at any rate, is what Mardonius endeavored to do next.

The Stones of Salamis (8.137–9.5)

"So long as the sun keeps his present course, we will never join alliance with Xerxes." (THE ATHENIANS, at 8.143.2)

As soon as he read the response Mys brought back from Boeotia, Mardonius sent Alexander of Macedon to Athens as his messenger. When last we heard from the Macedonian king, he had sent messengers to Tempe in northern Greece to urge the Greeks to abandon their position. Now Alexander passed along a message Mardonius had received from Xerxes outlining his proposal for a Persian-Athenian alliance. The Persians wanted to lure the Athenians away from the Greek cause: if Athens' fleet were on their side, the Persians would quickly gain mastery of the sea, and Greece would be all but won. Accordingly, the terms they offered were very generous:

1. The Athenians would be forgiven for all past offenses.
2. They would be given their land back.
3. They would also be given any other territory they wanted.
4. They would be autonomous.
5. Xerxes would rebuild the Athenian shrines he had destroyed.

The price, of course, would be Athens' betrayal of the rest of Greece. Alexander, after delivering the message, urged the Athenians to accept the offer: they couldn't hope to hold out against Xerxes forever, he said, and Athens was sure to be destroyed in the course of the war.

The Spartans had heard that Alexander was in Athens with a message from Mardonius, and they'd sent envoys of their own. (The Athenians had delayed Alexander, in fact, to give the Spartans a chance to get there.) After Alexander spoke, the Spartans said their piece, urging the Athenians to stay the course. For one thing, they said, the whole business had been the Athenians' fault: they'd brought the war with Persia to Greece. Moreover, it would be intolerable if the other Greeks wound up being enslaved because of the Athenians, who had always enjoyed a reputation as liberators. They understood that the Athenians were suffering, since they'd already lost two harvests (this reference is a little unclear, but apparently what is meant is the harvest of 480 and the one that would come in 479), and they offered to take care of all of Athens' noncombatants for as long as the war lasted. But by no means, they said, should the Athenians be swayed by Alexander or trust the barbarians, who were lying to them.

The Athenians answered Alexander first: "As long as the sun travels in its current course," they said, "we will never come to terms with Xerxes. Trusting in the gods and the heroes as our allies, we will fight him in defense of ourselves." Their response doesn't quite have the power of Churchill's "we shall fight on the beaches" speech, but it's a stirring response in the face of the Persian threat. Appended to the speech was a veiled threat directed at Alexander: don't come to us with this sort of advice again, they said, "We wouldn't want anything bad to happen to you."

The Athenians next addressed the Spartans. There wasn't enough gold in the world, they said, to make Athens betray the Greeks, with whom the Athenians shared a common heritage. As long as a single Athenian survived, they would not come to terms with Xerxes. They declined the Spartans' generous offer to maintain Athens' noncombatants but asked that the Spartans send an army as quickly as possible so that they could meet the enemy in Boeotia: Mardonius would surely be moving south as soon as he heard the response Alexander was bringing back.

The Athenians were right. Mardonius did march south as soon as Alexander returned, though as it turns out, it was already late spring by the time he got on the road. He'd been hoping to score a diplomatic coup by turning the Athenians and had been waiting out the result of his overtures, but now that his diplomatic efforts had come to nothing, it was time to move. He had a terrible yearning, Herodotus says, to take Athens for a second time. While he was marching through Boeotia, the Thebans suggested that he stop there and try to divide the Greeks by liberally bribing Greece's leading men, but Mardonius wouldn't be swayed from his plans. (In fact it's quite possible, as we'll see, that he had already tried his hand at bribery by this time.)

When Mardonius got to Athens, in June of 479, the Athenians weren't home. They'd evacuated for a second time, and most of them, again, were at Salamis with the fleet. Mardonius, figuring the Athenians might reconsider now that he was in Attica, decided to give diplomacy another shot. He sent a man over to Salamis to make the same offer Alexander had made—territory and autonomy and amnesty and so on in return for their switching sides. Once again, the Athenians didn't even want to consider the offer. Or more specifically, the members of Athens' Council of Five Hundred, which had the responsibility of meeting with envoys from foreign states, didn't want to consider it. Except for one guy. One of the councilors—Herodotus calls him Lycidas, though other sources give his name as Cyrsilus—said that Mardonius' offer should be put to the assembly for consideration. Herodotus suggests that Lycidas may have been on Mardonius' payroll, and it is certainly possible that he had been bribed, but what he suggested was not procedurally out of line. The council, at its discretion, could introduce foreign envoys to the assembly, or not. But in the context of the times, Lycidas' suggestion seemed downright treasonous. Consider the Athenians' situation. They had had to evacuate their homes for the second time, and for the second time a foreign army was occupying Attica. Their temples had been burnt. Many of them were separated from their families. Athenians had died in Attica and in the battles at Salamis and Artemisium, while Athens' allies had perished in greater numbers on land, the Spartans and Thespians under Leonidas killed to a man at Thermopylae. Now they were facing a second season of war, and Mardonius was wiggling his carrot under their noses again. All the Athenians had to do to save themselves was to take part in the enslavement of their fellow Greeks, alongside whom their friends and neighbors had died while trying to preserve Greek liberty. The Athenians had already said no to Alexander. Now here was Lycidas, in the face of all the devastation the Persians had brought to Greece, suggesting they consider Mardonius' offer after all. The Athenians were in no mood for his brand of cowardice. What followed is one of the more shocking episodes in Athenian history.

The Athenian councilors surrounded Lycidas and stoned him to death, an extraordinary instance of mob violence in Athens.[1] It was an ugly scene, and things would get uglier yet. When word of what Lycidas had said and what the councilors had done spread, a sort of mob mentality seized hold of the Athenian women who had evacuated to Salamis. A bunch of them got together on their own initiative and marched on Lycidas' house, the women recruiting others as they went along, and they stoned to death the dead man's wife and children.

Mardonius' messenger, doubtless to his great relief, was sent away unharmed. The Athenians' answer to the terms Mardonius had proposed was an emphatic no.

The Road to Plataea (9.6–19)

When the envoys had spoken, the Ephors declared to them with an oath: "Our troops must be at Oresteum by this time, on their march against the strangers."

(9.11.2)

There was some delay on the Greek side in getting their army together, and some indication that cracks were beginning to appear in the Greek alliance. Before they'd evacuated to Salamis for the second time, the Athenians had waited in Attica for as long as they could, Herodotus says, expecting the Spartans to send an army north so that they could meet the enemy in Boeotia. When no Peloponnesian army materialized on the Attic border, the Athenians evacuated and sent messengers to Sparta. The messengers reproached the Spartans for letting Mardonius invade Attica a second time, and they told the Spartans about Mardonius' second offer of an alliance. The Athenians said they would never "willingly" agree to Mardonius' terms, but they warned the Spartans that if they didn't send help, the Athenians might have to save themselves by other means. Still, the Spartans delayed further. They were celebrating yet another festival—the Hyacinthia this time—and they were putting the final touches on the Isthmian wall.[2] The Spartans told the Athenian messengers they'd have their answer the next day, but one day turned into two, then three, and finally ten days had passed. By the eleventh day the Athenians had had enough. They went to the Spartan ephors (elected officers) and said that because the Spartans had betrayed them, the Athenians would have to ally with Persia. And at that point the ephors delivered their punchline: as far as they knew, they said, the Spartan army was already in Orestheum (northwest of Sparta), en route to Boeotia. The Athenians were dumbfounded—doubtless the ephors enjoyed their confusion—and they set off back home, accompanied by five thousand hoplites—not Spartiates but *perioikoi*, literally "dwellers around," free inhabitants of Spartan territory who were, however, not full Spartan citizens.

The Spartans had secretly dispatched an army during the previous night: 5000 Spartiates and, if Herodotus is to be believed, 35,000 helots under the command of Pausanias, who was serving as regent during the minority of his cousin Pleistarchus, the son of Leonidas. (Pausanias was the son of Leonidas' brother Cleombrotus, who had supervised the construction of the Isthmian wall but had since died [8.71].) Herodotus says the Spartans decided to send the army out after a man from Tegea, north of Sparta, reminded them that the Peloponnese was vulnerable to attack by sea, which meant that they needed the Athenians. But this can't be the whole story. It's impossible to believe that anyone in Sparta had forgotten for a moment that the Spartan defenses at the Isthmian wall could be outflanked by sea. It's not clear what was going on during the Spartans' lengthy delay, nor why they played their trick on the Athenian messengers. But at least the Spartans were now on the move. They marched up the isthmus and were joined by other Peloponnesians and by the Athenians themselves, who crossed over from Salamis. The Greeks mustered at Eleusis, on the coast of Attica near its juncture with the isthmus, and advanced from there into Boeotia.

Argos, northeast of Sparta in the Peloponnese, had refused to join the Greeks back in the fall of 481 when the allies sent envoys around to various cities requesting help. Now, Herodotus says, the Argives had promised Mardonius that they would prevent the Spartans from leaving the Peloponnese. But when they found out that the Spartans were already heading north, they sent a runner to Mardonius to warn him that the Spartans were coming and that the Argives would not be able to stop them. When Mardonius heard the news, he burned Athens—he'd been holding off until now, thinking that the Athenians might yet change their minds. He destroyed whatever had been left standing in Athens after the first invasion, and then he withdrew. He wanted to meet the enemy in Boeotia because it was more suited to cavalry action than Attica and because he'd be closer to Thebes, which was squarely on the Persian side. He sent a part of his army, perhaps only the cavalry, down as far as Megara on the isthmus: as it turned out, this was the farthest the Persians would ever penetrate into Greece. According to Herodotus, Mardonius hoped to catch and destroy an advance force of Spartans he'd heard had arrived in Megara, but in the event his men just ravaged the territory and withdrew. With the rest of his army Mardonius marched into Boeotia. The Persians built a fortress on the northern side of the Asopus River, which ran roughly east-west across much of Boeotia and served as the border between Theban and Plataean territory (cf. 6.108). And there they waited for the Greeks.

Plataea, Part I: Baggage Trains and Mysterious Strangers (9.20–49)

"Now, however, they have determined to let the victims pass unheeded, and, as soon as day dawns, to engage in battle."   (ALEXANDER, at 9.45.2)

In contrast to Herodotus' spare accounts of Marathon, Artemisium, and Salamis, his discussion of the battle at Plataea and its preliminaries feels bloated and unfocused: it's all troop strength and battle formations, the positioning and repositioning of armies, endless delays. For our purposes his narrative can be abbreviated significantly.

After the Greeks had mustered at Eleusis, they marched into Boeotia and took up position in the foothills of Cithaeron, the range that separates Attica from Boeotia. Mardonius, when the Greeks didn't move further into the Boeotian plain, sent his cavalry against them and inflicted some damage, particularly on the Megarians, who were in the most vulnerable position. But the Greeks made out better overall in the fighting than the Persians, who eventually withdrew after losing a large number of men, including their cavalry commander, Masistius. Masistius' death prompted dramatic expressions of grief back in the Persian camp, but it was a big coup for the Greeks. They put his body on a wagon and drove it up and down the ranks so that the soldiers could see it, another instance of the ancients enjoying a good look at an enemy corpse.

After this first skirmish the Greeks moved down from the foothills into the plain, primarily, Herodotus says, because they would have better access to water. They encamped around Plataea, south of the Asopus. Herodotus describes their battle order and strength at some length: the 10,000 Spartan hoplites (both Spartiates and *perioikoi*) held the right wing and Athens' 8000 hoplites held the left (after a dispute with the Tegeans over who should have the honor; the Tegeans wound up being posted right next to the Spartans). In all, the Greeks fielded 38,700 hoplites and had 69,500 lightly armed troops besides. Scholars have doubted that there really were 35,000 helots serving in the army, so this last figure may be too large. In addition, there were 1800 Thespians on the Greek side, but they had no body armor. (Seven hundred Thespians had died at Thermopylae with Leonidas. Their city had been destroyed afterwards, when Xerxes marched through Boeotia on his way to Athens. But the Thespians themselves had fled to the Peloponnese [8.50].) According to Herodotus, whose numbers are probably exaggerated, the Persian army was more than three times as large: Mardonius reportedly had 300,000 barbarian infantry as well as some unknown number of Greeks fighting on his side—Herodotus guesses about 50,000. When the army was lined up for battle, the Persians were arrayed opposite the Spartans, and the Macedonians and Thessalians were opposite the Athenians.

Once the armies were in place, the Persians to the north of the Asopus, the Greeks to the south, the long wait began. Both sides performed sacrifices prior to initiating action, hoping to obtain favorable signs from the gods. This would have involved sacrificing an animal and examining its innards, perhaps putting an organ or two on the fire to see how they and the fire behaved. Despite their religious differences, both the Persians and the Greeks were in fact performing the same sorts of rituals at Plataea: the Persians had hired a Greek seer for the purpose, Hegesistratus of Elis, in the Peloponnese. (As Macan points out in his commentary at 9.37, this shows how far the invasion of Greece was from being a religious crusade against the Greeks.)[3] Herodotus tells an interesting story about Hegesistratus. Years earlier he'd lived through one of those nightmarish what-if questions people sometimes ask themselves: what if you were chained up and somebody was going to kill you and the only way you could escape was if you sawed off your foot? Well, Hegesistratus sawed off his foot. He escaped from his captors—the Spartans, as it happens, who were going to execute him for some unspecified offenses—somehow managed not to die from an infection, got himself a wooden foot, and was now on the other side of the Asopus trying to get the sacrifices to bode well for a Persian offensive. But the gods had the same message for both the Persians and the Greeks: they would be okay if they fought in self-defense, but not if they crossed the Asopus and began the fight. And so they waited.

Eight days went by during which more Greeks were continually streaming in over the mountain to join the allied army. Finally Mardonius sent some cavalry up to block the passes through Cithaeron. They managed to intercept a train of five hundred baggage animals that was bringing in provisions for the Greeks. The Persians killed the men who were tending the animals and many of the animals as well, Herodotus says, though the latter detail seems unlikely: it would have been foolish for the Persians to engage in the frenzy of wasteful slaughter Herodotus describes when they had an army to feed. But whatever in fact happened to the beasts, the Persians had scored a big coup in depriving their enemy of the captured supplies, which they now drove back to the Persian camp. Mardonius was also routinely sending his cavalry out to harass the Greeks, but apart from these skirmishes there was no action of consequence. Neither the Persians nor the Greeks were prepared to start the fight by crossing the river. And so two more days passed.

On the eleventh day of the wait at Plataea, Mardonius had a chat with Artabazus—the guy who had escorted Xerxes to the Hellespont with sixty thousand troops and ravaged his way back through Thrace to Thessaly. Artabazus suggested that the Persians withdraw to Thebes, where they had plenty of supplies stored up, and that Mardonius try to bribe the Greeks rather than risking everything on a pitched battle. (This was the same advice the Thebans had given Mardonius previously.) But Mardonius would have none of it. Despite his delay at Plataea, he is consistently portrayed by Herodotus as being eager to fight. He was so eager for battle, in fact, that he now decided he would initiate hostilities the next day without waiting for Hegesistratus' sacrifices to turn out favorably.

In the middle of that night, a lone horseman rode up to the Athenian guards and asked to speak with their commanders. The generals were summoned, and the mystery rider told them that Mardonius, despite the trouble he was having with his sacrifices, had decided to attack the next morning. But if he didn't, for some reason, the stranger bade the Greeks to maintain their positions anyway, because the Persians were running low on supplies. He ended his speech by announcing his identity—"I am Alexander of Macedon," he said—and then he rode off into the night.

The story has been doubted. For one thing, the Persians probably weren't running out of supplies. They had plenty waiting for them at Thebes, and they had just commandeered the Greeks' wagon train. Further, one wonders how

Alexander got past the sentries guarding the Persian camp and why he wasn't recognized by the Greek generals, who had probably met him back when he brought Mardonius' offer of alliance to Athens (8.136). Beyond that, it has seemed too implausible to some that the Macedonian king was riding around in the middle of the night bearing messages: "The whole idea of kings of Macedonia riding about the Plataian landscape in the darkness is ludicrous," J. F. Lazenby writes, "and notions that he was engaged in some kind of deception plan on Mardonios' behalf worse. The episode smacks of later attempts to exonerate the king of Macedonia from charges that he had collaborated."[4] Certainly we should at least be suspicious of the story as it stands.

Alexander's information, at any rate, allegedly prompted some last-minute adjustments in the Greek lineup. Pausanias suggested that the Athenians switch places with the Spartans since they'd fought against the Persians before, at Marathon, while the Spartans never had. (More accurately, the only Spartans who had ever fought the Persians were lying dead up in Thermopylae.) So the two contingents switched positions, but when Mardonius saw what they were doing, he started to switch his left and right wings as well. And when the Greeks saw what the Persians were doing, they switched back to their original arrangement. Or so Herodotus tells us. It may be that he's trying to make sense of some information he didn't fully grasp and that this comical exchange of positions on both sides of the river was what he came up with. In the end, both armies were left in their original places, and nobody crossed the Asopus, so Alexander's secret message, if it really was delivered, had come to nothing. During that day the Persian cavalry continued harrying the Greeks, as they had before. But this time, finally, they did something that changed the status quo: they stopped up the spring from which the Greeks had been getting their water.[5]

Plataea, Part II: The Battle (9.50–89)

Sometimes singly, sometimes in bodies of ten, now fewer and now more in number, they dashed forward upon the Spartan ranks, and so perished.   (9.62.3)

Having their water supply cut off was an enormous problem for the Greeks: it meant that they would no longer be able to hold their current position. In addition, they weren't able to get supplies from beyond Cithaeron anymore because of the Persian cavalry, and the cavalry, too, was constantly harassing their troops. The Greeks decided to withdraw to a new position—their third since entering Boeotia—where they would have ample water and the Persian cavalry would pose less of a problem. Herodotus calls this proposed new position "the island." Modern scholars have not been able to establish its exact location, but it was somewhere "in front of the city of the Plataeans." Herodotus describes it as a strip of land, about a third of a mile wide, that was surrounded by two branches of the river Oëroë, which divided upstream from it and then joined up again later.

The plan was for half of the army to withdraw to the island in the middle of the night while the other half went to Cithaeron to liberate a baggage train the Persians had blocked. But in the event, the withdrawal was botched. As Herodotus tells the story, the center part of the army—everybody but the Spartans, Athenians, and Tegeans—fled in panic and wound up at the temple of Hera outside of Plataea. More likely, these Greeks had not intended to disobey orders but had instead lost their way in the confusion of withdrawing in the dark in unfamiliar territory. As for the Spartans (and the Tegeans, who were with them), they were ready to withdraw according to the agreed-upon plan but were reportedly delayed because one of their regimental commanders, Amompharetus, refused to retreat. Hours of pleading with him to obey orders allegedly followed, which seems extremely unlikely. It may be that his unit "delayed" because it was tasked with covering the retreat of the rest of the army. But whether Amompharetus was in fact insubordinate or there was some other reason for his unit being behind the rest, the Spartans were late in getting under way. The Athenians, in turn, weren't sure what to do. Pausanias basically told them to follow the Spartans' lead.

The result of all this movement in the middle of the night was that the Greek army was divided into three divisions at daybreak. The Greeks who should have formed the army's center were drawn up in front of the temple of Hera, while the Spartans and Athenians, the right and left wings respectively, were separated from one another but endeavoring to close the gap while retreating. Mardonius woke up to the pleasant surprise that the Greeks had deserted their earlier positions—from cowardice, he assumed—and he immediately attacked, thinking he could catch them in the disorder of retreat and win an enormous victory. The Persians charged across the Asopus and made straight for the Spartan contingent. (They were unable to see the Athenians at this point.) Pausanias sent a mounted messenger to the Athenians to let them know the Spartans were under attack, but the Athenians weren't able to help: they had been attacked themselves by the Greeks who were serving under Mardonius. So the two wings of the Greek army fought in isolation from one another. The Greek center, meanwhile, for the moment had no part in the fighting.

With the various contingents of the Greek army unable to offer one another assistance, the battle could have been a debacle. In fact, it marked the end of the Persian War in Europe. The fighting between the Spartans and Persians was fierce and close, too close for the Persians to use their bows. They fought bravely, but they were no match for the better trained and better armed Spartans. The Persians threw themselves against the Spartan phalanx in wave after wave, small groups of men rushing against the Spartans' nearly impenetrable wall of shields, and they were destroyed. After Mardonius and those around him were killed, the rest of the Persians fled in disorder to their fortification north of the Asopus.

Meanwhile, most of the Greeks who were fighting against the Athenians fought badly on purpose, perhaps melting away from the scene to flee to their homes in central Greece when they saw the way things were heading. The Thebans alone fought intensely, but after the Athenians killed three hundred of their best troops, they fled as well, back to Thebes.

At this point the Greeks who were at the temple of Hera finally saw some action. They heard that there had been a battle and that Pausanias had won, and they started marching to join the Spartans. They were met then by the Boeotian contingent of Xerxes' cavalry, which was attempting to cover the retreat of their allies. The cavalry attacked this body of Greeks and pursued them all the way to Cithaeron, killing some six hundred of them.

The Greeks pursued the Persians who had fled to their fortification and after some struggle breached the walls and poured in. The Persians were trapped, and the Greeks butchered them in enormous numbers. Herodotus says that no more than 3000 of them survived. That means that, according to Herodotus' numbers, 257,000 barbarians were killed at Plataea, doubtless an exaggeration, but at any rate far more Persians died that day than allied Greeks. In addition to the 600 men from the Greek center who were cut down by the Boeotian cavalry, 91 Spartans, 16 Tegeans, and 52 Athenians died at Plataea.

The Persians had fled from the battle in three divisions, the Thebans back to Thebes, the Persians who had been fighting against the Spartans to their fortification beyond the Asopus, and a third group north to Phocis. Herodotus says that Artabazus, when he saw the Persians fleeing before the Spartans, took the forty thousand men under his command and fled north, racing to make it to the Hellespont as soon as possible. He lied through his teeth along the way, telling the Phocians and Thessalians, when he got there, that his was an advance army that would soon be followed by the rest of the Persians. He figured that if he told them the truth—that the Persians had been routed and he was fleeing for his life—the medizing Greeks would butcher him and the rest of his army. He pushed on north, then east through Thrace, where some of his men were hacked to death by the Thracians. Others died along the way from hunger or exhaustion. Eventually Artabazus and his men made it to the Hellespont, which they crossed by boat. Artabazus' army was the last substantial body of Persian troops to leave Greece. The Greek mainland had been liberated from Persian control.

There was the usual stuff to take care of after the battle. The Greeks assigned prizes for valor. They buried their dead. They collected booty from the barbarians' tents and stripped their corpses. They dedicated tenths of the spoils to various gods—among them, of course, the god at Delphi—and they divided the rest, including the Persians' pack animals and concubines. There was one concubine, however, who emerged from the ordeal a free woman: she came to Pausanias after the battle and explained that she was originally from the island of Cos and had been captured by the Persians. As it turned out, her father, Hegetoridas, was Pausanias' guest-friend. Pausanias entrusted the woman to the Spartan ephors for safekeeping and she was eventually sent to Aegina, "where she herself wanted to go." A man from Aegina, meanwhile, Lampon, son of Pytheas, came to Pausanias after the battle and suggested that he cut off Mardonius' head and impale it on a stake in return for what Xerxes had done to Leonidas after Thermopylae. But Pausanias was appalled at the suggestion: such barbarism was unworthy of Greeks. So Mardonius' body remained intact, though it's not clear what happened to it otherwise: it was stolen after the battle and buried, Herodotus says, but he wasn't able to determine who had done it. The rest of the barbarian dead were apparently left to rot where they lay. (This was standard procedure in the case of enemy corpses that hadn't been collected by their compatriots after a battle.)

Ten days after the battle, when the business of war was finished at Plataea, the Greeks marched on Thebes and demanded that the Thebans surrender the ringleaders of the pro-Persian contingent there, including their leaders Timagenidas and Attaginus. When the guilty weren't immediately handed over, the Greeks laid siege to the city and ravaged the surrounding countryside. After nineteen days of this, the Thebans agreed to surrender the men. Attaginus escaped, but his children were caught and brought to Pausanias. He released them, however, as they were not implicated in their father's offenses. The other Thebans who were handed over to Pausanias assumed (strangely, perhaps) that there would be a hearing and that they'd be able to bribe their way out of a guilty verdict, but there was no trial: Pausanias brought them to Corinth, and they were executed.

Pausanias comes off well in Herodotus' account of Plataea: his treatment of Mardonius' corpse, the children of Attaginus, and the lady from Cos speak highly of him, to say nothing of the fact that he won the war. But Herodotus alludes elsewhere in his *History* to the trouble Pausanias would get into just a year later (5.32, 8.3). Herodotus doesn't go into detail, but Thucydides provides the story at 1.128–134. Pausanias was suspected of collaborating with the Persians while leading the allied Greek forces in operations around the Hellespont in 478. He was recalled to Sparta, tried, and acquitted. Later he went out again to the same area, though not in an official capacity, and he allegedly intrigued with the Persians again. Generally speaking, too, he behaved badly, putting on airs and dressing like a Persian, surrounding himself with a court as if he were an Oriental monarch. The Spartans again required that he return to Sparta. He was imprisoned but subsequently released because there was insufficient proof of his guilt. Later, more damning evidence came to light. He was on the verge of being arrested—as the story goes, he saw the ephors coming after him in the street and started running—but he escaped and took refuge at a temple (specifically, the temple of the Goddess of the Brazen House). It wasn't much of a refuge. The Spartan authorities boarded up the place and waited for him to starve. When he was near death, they brought him outside so that they wouldn't be guilty of killing him in the temple—that's the sort of thing the gods frowned upon—and he died as soon as he was carried out. Pausanias thus joins Miltiades and Themistocles in the club of successful Greek generals whose glorious victories over the Persians were followed up by ignominy.

The Battle of Mycale (9.90–106)

Ionia, therefore, on this day revolted a second time from the Persians.   (9.104)

In a coincidence that will seem to us cynical moderns too good to be true—but Herodotus insists on the synchronism—the Greeks won a second victory on the same day as the battle at Plataea. In the spring of 479 the allied Greek fleet—110 ships, at any rate—had met at Aegina and sailed from there to Delos

(8.131–132). The fleet was under the command of the Spartan king Leotychidas, who had succeeded Demaratus on the throne. Athens' general on the scene was Xanthippus, the man who had prosecuted Miltiades after his failed expedition to Paros a decade earlier. While the fleet was at Delos, three messengers came to the Greeks from Samos. The men—Lampon, Athenagoras, and Hegesistratus—had been sent by the Samians, or some faction within Samos, without the knowledge of the island's pro-Persian tyrant. Hegesistratus, speaking for his colleagues, urged the Greeks to sail to Ionia. If the Ionians saw the Greek fleet nearby, he said, they would immediately desert the Persians, and the Persian fleet was in no condition to withstand an attack. When Hegesistratus had finished, Leotychidas asked him his name and was much encouraged by the answer, since Hegesistratus means "leader of the army." The Greeks agreed to do as the Samians suggested, and after the Samians had sworn an oath of alliance, the fleet was off, Hegesistratus sailing back with the Greeks because of the portent of his name.

The Greeks sailed east to Asia Minor and anchored off of Samos, ready to fight the Persians at sea. But the Persians were unwilling to risk a naval battle. Their Phoenician ships had been sent away—it's not clear why or when—but the rest of the Persian fleet sailed toward the mainland so that they could be close to their army, which was encamped at Mycale, the peninsula opposite Samos. The Persians beached their ships, built a stockade around them, and settled in for a siege.

Initially the Greeks weren't sure what to do in response to the Persians' flight, but they followed them to Mycale, finally, and when they saw the situation—the Persian ships drawn up on land inside the stockade and the army deployed along the shore—Leotychidas took a trick from Themistocles' playbook. He sailed along the beach and had a herald call out to the Ionians, saying they should think about their freedom and pass along to one another the watchword "Hebe." (This would be used in the thick of fighting, or during retreat, to recognize friendly forces.) Again, as at Artemisium, the purpose of this was either to get the Ionians to join the Greeks or to make the Persians mistrust them. The plan worked perfectly. When the Persians saw that the Greeks were ready to fight, they disarmed the Samians. They didn't trust them, both because of the message Leotychidas had delivered and because the Samians had previously released some Athenian prisoners of war and sent them back home—those unfortunates who had been stranded in Attica and were captured when Xerxes invaded. The Persians also ordered the Milesians in their army to guard the passes to the peaks of Mycale, a job that would keep them away from the battlefield and thus out of trouble—or so they thought.

After delivering their message to the Ionians, the Greeks landed and lined up for battle, Herodotus says, but he's clearly leaving out an important step: they can't have disembarked with the Persian army looking on, as they'd surely have been slaughtered in the process, cut down while they were out of formation and unprepared. The Greeks must instead have sailed off a ways before landing, then returned on foot. Herodotus describes their advance: the Athenians, on the left wing, were walking along the flat ground near the shore, while the Spartans, on the right, had to cross rougher terrain. As a result, the Athenians wound up coming to blows with the Persians before the Spartans arrived. Thus the Greeks' subsequent victory was largely due to the Athenians. They drove the Persians back until they fled behind their stockade. And when the Greeks took the walls, most of the barbarians fled, though the Persians stayed on. The Spartans were present for this last act. The Ionian Greeks, meanwhile, deserted the Persians in the melee and joined in attacking them.

Up in the mountains the Milesians did their share as well. As the barbarians fled along the passes toward the heights of Mycale, the Milesians misled them, sending them back against their enemies, and finally they killed them themselves. Ionia, once again, was in revolt from Persia.

As their last act at Mycale, the Greeks burned the Persians' ships and stockade and then sailed off to Samos, where they debated what to do next. The idea that was considered and dismissed was a radical one: the Spartans were in favor of abandoning Ionia to the barbarians, moving its Greek population back to the mainland and settling them in territory confiscated from the medizing Greek states back home. The thinking was that Ionia, because of its location, could never properly be defended from the Persians. Better to reestablish a firm, defensible division between east and west. But the Athenians would not stand for the evacuation of Asia, so the idea was rejected. The Chians and Lesbians and other islanders who had fought with the Greeks were formally brought into the alliance. And the Greeks sailed off to the Hellespont to break down Xerxes' bridges, which they believed to be still intact, yoking together the continents of Europe and Asia in violation of the natural order of things.

Royal Love Affairs (9.107–113)

Amestris waited, accordingly, for this day, and then made request of Xerxes, that
he would please to give her, as her present, the wife of Masistes.   (9.110.2)

Some of the Persians who were present at the battle managed to escape by
fleeing to the heights of Mycale, and from there they made their way to Sardis.
Among these fortunate few was Xerxes' brother Masistes. As it happens, a lot
had been going on back in the capital during his absence.

While Xerxes was biding his time back home, waiting to see what was going
to happen in Greece, he wound up falling in love with Masistes' wife, who was
also in Sardis at the time. Xerxes made repeated overtures to her, but he didn't
get anywhere. Herodotus says that Xerxes did not use violence to have his way
with her because she was his brother's wife, the implication being that in the
usual scheme of things violence would have been the natural next step. (Forcing
women is one of the things tyrants typically do, after all, as Herodotus says elsewhere [3.80.5].) Instead, Xerxes resorted to a roundabout scheme he thought
might win her over. He arranged for his son Darius to marry the daughter of
this woman and Masistes. (Masistes' wife, the object of Xerxes' lust, is never
named in the story.) One may doubt whether the plan was likely to work from
the get-go: arranging for the cousins to get married doesn't seem like a surefire
way to get to sleep with your son's new mother-in-law. But the thinking must
have been that Masistes' wife would be so grateful for this additional connection between her family and the royal power that she'd do whatever Xerxes
wanted. In the event, however, Xerxes' plan backfired rather badly. After the
wedding Xerxes went to Susa, and his niece/daughter-in-law came to live in
the palace with her husband's family. Suddenly Masistes' wife didn't look so hot
anymore. Xerxes switched his affections to his son's new wife, Araynte, who,
it turned out, wasn't quite as virtuous as her mother. Uncle Xerxes apparently
didn't have any problem getting her into bed.

Meanwhile, Xerxes' wife Amestris had woven her husband a beautiful cloak.
Xerxes loved it, and he paraded around with it in front of Araynte. He was
happy with the cloak and happy with her, and in his delight he promised to
give her anything she asked for. Unfortunately, she asked for the cloak. That
wouldn't do. Amestris, if she saw Araynte with it, would figure out what the two
of them were up to. The thought filled him with dread. He offered to give her
anything but the cloak—gold, cities, an army to command—but she wouldn't

change her mind. He was forced finally to hand it over, since he'd sworn to give her whatever she wanted. But there would be hell to pay with Amestris.

When she saw her daughter-in-law with the cloak, however, Amestris got the wrong idea: somehow she thought that Araynte was blameless but that her mother was involved—Masistes' wife, who had in fact done nothing wrong at all. Amestris may have thought, as Macan suggests in his commentary at 9.110, that Xerxes was visiting Araynte by way of meeting up with her mother and that the cloak had been given to Araynte in this context.[6] Whatever the case, Amestris had it in for her sister-in-law. She waited for Xerxes' birthday, when the king would distribute gifts to the Persians, and when the day came she asked him for her present: she wanted Masistes' wife. Xerxes wasn't happy about it. His sister-in-law had done nothing wrong, and he had an inkling of what Amestris had in mind. But he felt helpless about the business, since the law required that he give whatever was asked of him at his birthday party—though one suspects that Xerxes, being Xerxes, could have declined the request if he'd put his mind to it. He handed over Masistes' wife and told Amestris to do what she wanted.

Hoping to forestall trouble with Masistes, Xerxes summoned his brother and told him that he should no longer live with his current wife. Instead, Masistes could marry one of Xerxes' daughters. Xerxes didn't give a reason—the king doesn't have to explain himself—other than to say that that was what he wanted. Normally, one did what the king wanted, but Masistes actually liked his wife, and he had children by her. He didn't want to throw her aside. He thanked Xerxes for the offer of his daughter, but he refused to do as his brother wished. Enraged, Xerxes told Masistes that now he would have no one: he couldn't have Xerxes' daughter and he couldn't have his own wife anymore either. Masistes stormed out with a "You haven't seen the last of me!" and ran off home, worried that something very bad might have happened. Of course, he was right. Amestris had ordered Masistes' wife to be mutilated: her breasts and nose and ears and lips were cut off and thrown to the dogs and her tongue was cut out and she was sent home.

Masistes found her like that after he left Xerxes. At once he set off with his sons to the province he governed, Bactria, intent on fomenting a rebellion against the king. But he was intercepted en route by Xerxes' men, and he and his sons and his supporters were all killed. "That," Herodotus concludes, "is the story of Xerxes' passion and of Masistes' death."

On the face of it, this tale of domestic intrigue seems an odd insertion so close to the end of Herodotus' *History*. But in fact, as commentators have pointed out, its similarities with the story of Gyges and Candaules, with which Herodotus begins his account, make it a fitting concluding piece. Herodotus' *History* is thus framed by two stories of a king whose erotic love for a family member leads to his transgression of conventional behavior. Candaules falls in love with his own wife and offers his spearman Gyges a look at her while she's naked, while Xerxes has an affair with his son's wife. In both cases someone is presented with a difficult choice. Gyges is compelled by Candaules' wife—who is blameless and who, like Masistes' wife, is never named—either to kill himself or to kill the king. Xerxes is forced to hand over his sister-in-law or transgress Persian gift-giving customs—evidently a tough decision for Xerxes, if not quite as dramatic a choice as Gyges faced. Both men, against their will, consequently sacrifice someone important to them. Gyges' regicide leads to a dynastic change in Lydia. The surrender of Masistes' wife leads to an aborted uprising and the extermination of Masistes' line.

The parallels between the two are imperfect, and the roles of the various actors are switched around in the two stories, but in both cases the behavior of the king showcases the transgressions that were typical of tyrants: this is the sort of thing that happened in Oriental monarchies. The punishment inflicted by Amestris on her sister-in-law was likewise barbaric: excessive, unduly cruel, the sort of thing that would have disgusted the Spartan general Pausanias, just as he was appalled by the suggestion that he behead the corpse of Mardonius after Plataea (9.79). This is not to say that Greeks were incapable of barbarism. The extralegal stoning of Lycidas and his family on Salamis is proof—and Herodotus has more evidence on hand, as we'll soon see—that under the right conditions, even Greeks could descend to barbarity (9.5). But among the Greeks such behavior was aberrant, while monarchies bred outrageous behavior by their very nature (3.80).

The Siege of Sestus and the Conclusion of Herodotus' *History* (9.114–122)

> So they led Artaÿctes to the tongue of land where the bridges of Xerxes had been fixed—or, according to others, to the knoll above the town of Madytus; and, having nailed him to a board, they left him hanging thereupon.   (9.120.4)

After their victory at Mycale, the Greeks had sailed to the Hellespont to break down Xerxes' bridges. They had long since been damaged in a storm, of course,

so that job was done. The war was over. And as far as the Spartans were concerned, it was time to go home: they dusted off their hands and sailed back to
Greece. But the Athenians decided to stay behind and lay siege to Sestus, the
strongest city in the area, which lay on the European side of the Hellespont and
was still in Persian hands.

Sestus was under the control of Xerxes' satrap Artayctes, whom Herodotus reviles for his sacrilegious behavior. Back when the Persians were advanc-
ing toward Greece, Artayctes had persuaded Xerxes to give him a gift of some
property in the Chersonese, in Elaeus, almost at the very tip of the peninsula.
In asking for the gift, Artayctes had said to the king that the "house" he wanted
belonged to a Greek who had made an expedition against the king's land and
had justly been killed in the process—a very vague description of the property.
"Give me this man's house," Artayctes said, "so that everyone may learn not to
attack your land." Xerxes was easily persuaded: the business was of little consequence to him. But what Artayctes failed to mention was that the house he
wanted was in fact the shrine of a local hero, Protesilaus. Xerxes had no idea
of the religious significance of the property he'd given to Artayctes, nor that it
contained treasure—gold and silver drinking cups and other dedicatory offer-
ings.

Once Protesilaus' shrine was declared his by royal fiat, Artayctes took all
the treasure in it back with him to Sestus. As for the precinct itself, Artayctes made a profit by farming the land—this was not so unusual, but it was apparently inappropriate in this instance. Worse, whenever he went back to visit
the place, he'd have sex with women in the innermost part (the adyton) of the
shrine (though, as Deborah Boedeker writes, "it might be objected that the
adyton (9.116.3) of a Greek temple is not a place well suited to trysting").[7] For
Herodotus, who found the idea of sexual intercourse in temples particularly
distasteful (2.64), the man was a veritable monster.

Artayctes was in Sestus when the Athenians laid siege to the city. Herodotus
also mentions by name another Persian who was in town at the time, Oeobazus.
Though he doesn't say as much, this may be the same Oeobazus whose three
sons were killed by Darius during the buildup to the first Persian invasion of
Greece, when their father made the mistake of asking the king if one of them
could be released from military service (4.84).

The siege of Sestus continued into the fall, the Athenian generals remaining
in place despite some grumbling in the ranks. Inside Sestus, meanwhile, things
were getting bad, the starving residents reduced to eating boiled leather. When

the boiled leather ran out, the Persians in the town, including Artayctes and Oeobazus, ran off in the middle of the night, climbing down a wall at the rear of the city, where the Athenians had fewer men posted. In the morning the people of Sestus let the Athenians know what had happened, and they opened their gates.

Oeobazus and his followers fled to Thrace, where they were set upon by the savage Thracians. The Thracians killed all of the Persians, but they gave Oeobazus special treatment, sacrificing him to a local god. Herodotus doesn't give us any details about what the ritual would have entailed, but it can't have been pretty. Meanwhile, Artayctes and his party, who had started later, never made it out of the Chersonese. The Athenians caught up to them near Aegospotami (where, about seventy-five years later, the Spartans would defeat the Athenians in the final battle of the Peloponnesian War). Some of the Persians were killed and others captured. Artayctes and his son, among others, were brought back to Sestus in chains.

While Artayctes was awaiting his fate, one of the men who was guarding him had a strange thing happen to him. While he was frying up some fish, some fish that were on the hot coals suddenly started jumping around as if they were still alive. Everyone gathered around to see what was going on, and Artayctes, when he saw what was happening, called out to the man who was cooking: the portent, he said, was a message to him from Protesilaus, whose shrine he had despoiled. Protesilaus was indicating that, even though he was dead, he still had the power to punish the man who had wronged him. Artayctes thus proposed the following punishment for himself: he'd pay a hundred talents for the property he'd stolen from the shrine, and he'd give the Athenians two hundred talents in return for his and his son's release.

It was a lot of money. The Athenians could have paid the crews of their fleet for a month or more with the two hundred talents Artayctes was offering. But the people of Elaeus, enraged by Artayctes' sacrilege, wanted blood, and Xanthippus, Athens' general on the scene, felt the same. Rather than allow Artayctes to buy his freedom, then, the Athenians brought him to the headland where Xerxes' bridges had yoked the Hellespont (although some said that the Athenians took him to a different place, not far from this spot). They fastened him to a board—probably with an iron collar around his neck, wrists, and feet—and they hung him up to die. They also stoned his son to death while he watched. And then the Athenians went home:

Having done these things, they sailed off to Greece, bringing other spoils with them and in particular the gear of the bridges, in order to dedicate it at their shrines. Nothing further happened during this year.

Herodotus might have ended his *History* there, but he tacked on a final section. Artayctes, he says, was the grandson of a man named Artembares,[8] who had once suggested to Cyrus the Great that the Persians, now that they were masters of all Asia, should move from their rocky land to some better place. Do what you want, Cyrus answered, but be prepared in that case to be ruled rather than to rule others: "Soft countries breed soft men. For it is not possible for the same land to bear both wonderful fruit and men who are good at war." So the Persians took Cyrus' advice, and they opted to rule, dwelling in a wretched land, rather than to sow the plains and be slaves to others.

Within a few generations, however, the Persians had forgotten Cyrus' wise advice. Far from battle-hardened, Persia's leaders now went on campaign bedecked in gold jewelry, while their servants prepared extravagant meals for them in their richly furnished tents. After the Greek victory at Plataea, the Spartan general Pausanias, for a laugh, had Mardonius' servants prepare the same sort of meal for him that they would have served their master, and Pausanias' servants prepared his usual fare. The contrast between the two spreads was exquisite, and Pausanias mocked the dead Persian leader for his stupidity, that having a banquet such as his servants had laid out he had come to take away the Greeks' meager fare (9.82). Herodotus' final reference to Cyrus and the early days of Persian dominance thus recalls the downward trajectory of the empire, which had met with reversal at the hands of men who, like the Persians of Cyrus' day, were hardened by their upbringing on difficult soil.

The Cyrus anecdote is linked to the final scene of Herodotus' *History* by the familial relationship between Artembares and Artayctes, whose horrific—even barbaric—execution at the hands of the Greeks doubtless strikes most readers as overkill. Artayctes' sacrilege, gauche though it may have been, hardly seems to warrant execution, let alone the double punishment of his son's stoning. But whatever the motives behind the historical act, Herodotus, with his climactic placement of the story, invites readers to reflect on the underlying significance of the penalty. What Herodotus doesn't specifically mention in his story—though his readers, who were suckled on Homer, will have known it— is that the hero, Protesilaus, against whom Artayctes had offended, was peculiarly important in the history of East-West relations. Protesilaus, a Thessalian prince, was the first Greek to be killed in the Trojan War (*Iliad* 2.701–702). Thus the execution of Artayctes, the last Persian killed in the war as described by Herodotus, appears as retribution for the death of Protesilaus and for all of Persia's subsequent transgressions against the Greeks. Moreover, Artayctes is killed, according to Herodotus, at the same place where Xerxes yoked the continents with his bridges, the greatest symbol of his violation of natural boundaries and of his intention to enslave all of Greece.

Some scholars have seen in Herodotus' conclusion also a veiled warning to the Athens of Herodotus' day. After the Persian War, the alliance of Greek states that had put aside their differences to combat the common threat against Greece morphed into the Delian League. This association of states, headed by Athens, was founded in 478 to continue the war against Persia. But over the course of the fifth century, the League evolved into an Athenian empire. While effectively dealing with the Persian menace, Athens came to use the league for its own purposes and superintended the alliance with a heavy hand. Athens—radical democracy at home, but tyrant abroad—had become the world's first imperial democracy by the time Herodotus was in his prime. As the Aegean's reigning superpower, Athens might, like other empires before it, be destined for a fall. Or so Herodotus may be suggesting. We can't know whether Herodotus intended any such admonition in fact, but it's there to see if one looks for it, which is a tribute to the author's multivalent conclusion.

The victory of the Hellenic League over the Persians in 480 and 479, an incomparable triumph for the small, squabbling states of Greece, did not, of course, spell the end of the Persian Empire. Xerxes lived to lick his wounds for another fourteen years before he was assassinated by the commander of his bodyguard and succeeded by his son Artaxerxes. The Persian Empire would survive for almost 150 more years. In 334 B.C. Alexander the Great—great-great-great-grandson of the Alexander who allegedly rode in the night to warn the Greeks before Plataea—would lead an army of Macedonians and Greeks against the Persian Empire and forge a vaster empire yet from its ashes. If one looks to the end of things, as Solon advised Croesus back in the day, then Persia would fall, and Athens too would be subsumed into Alexander's empire, and then Rome's. All empires and all men ultimately perish, but some lucky few end their days well, before the vicissitudes of fate have chanced to bring them misery.

Appendix
Xerxes' Heralds and the Medizing of the Greek States (7.131–132)

131. Xerxes spent many days around Pieria [an area in southern Macedon], for a third of his army was clearing the Macedonian mountain [Olympus] so that the entire army could go through by that route to Perraibia [a mountainous region in northern Thessaly]. The heralds who had been sent to Greece to demand earth had arrived, some empty-handed, some bearing earth and water.

132. The Greeks who gave earth and water were the Thessalians, Dolopians, Enienes, Perrhaebians, Locrians, Magnetes, Melians, the Achaeans of Phthiotis, the Thebans, and the rest of the Boeotians except the Thespians and Plataeans. Against these the Greeks who were undertaking the war against the barbarian swore an oath. The oath was this: they vowed, when their affairs were going well, to tithe to the god at Delphi those Greeks who surrendered themselves to Persia while not under compulsion. Such was the oath of the Greeks.

1. When did the states listed at 7.132 medize?
The most natural interpretation of 7.131–132 is that the states named medized when they were visited by the heralds Xerxes had dispatched from Sardis. Those messengers left Sardis in the fall of 481, made their way west, interacted with the Greeks, and reported back to Xerxes, having received earth and water from some but not all the states they'd visited. A quick read of Herodotus 7.131 suggests that they reported back to Xerxes while he and the Persian army were in Pieria, which is to say in the summer of 480. N. G. L. Hammond has shown, however, that 7.131 has been misunderstood: Herodotus doesn't specify when the heralds returned to Xerxes, except to say that they made their report some time before he reached Pieria.[1] At any rate, the heralds met with Xerxes no later than the summer of 480.

If the states listed in 7.132 gave earth and water when Xerxes' heralds visited them, then their medizing would necessarily predate Xerxes' invasion of Greece. But this is problematic. The list of states includes the Locrians and Thebans, both of whom sent contingents to fight at Thermopylae in the fall of 480, which means that they were not allied with Persia at that time. They must have medized under compulsion after the Greek retreat from Thermopylae and Artemisium.

Hammond suggests that the Greeks listed in 7.132 gave earth and water to Xerxes' heralds in the fall of 481 but then recanted after the Greeks took their oath against medizing states.[2] This solution would explain why the Locrians and Thebans were fighting at Thermopylae (and how the Thebans can be made to say at 7.233 that they were among the first to give earth and water to the king). We would have to believe in that case, however, that Herodotus fails to mention that the states he names in 7.132 later recanted (and after recanting, medized again when compelled to do so). P. A. Brunt offers a better solution.[3] He suggests that "Herodotus' list is of all Greek states that ever medized." In other words, the states named did not necessarily medize when they were first approached by Xerxes' heralds (though Thessaly, or contingents within Thessaly, may have). This understanding is not precluded by Herodotus' wording, and it removes the difficulties in timing described above. (The reference to early Theban medizing at 7.233 may be the product of Herodotus' anti-Theban sources.) It seems to me the neatest solution to the problem.

2. When did the Greeks swear their oath against medizers?

A related question has to do with the oath the allies swore against the Greek states that medized willingly. The wording of 7.132 suggests that the Greeks swore to punish the states that are mentioned in the passage, that is, that the states were in fact named in the oath. If that's true, however, the oath would have to have been taken after they had all medized, thus after Thermopylae. But the states in central Greece that medized after Thermopylae could certainly claim to have done so only under compulsion.

Alternatively, the Greeks may have sworn a general oath against medizing states early on, perhaps at their first congress in the fall of 481, before any states had actually medized. This would mean (as we also suggested above) that Herodotus has, a little misleadingly, preceded his reference to the oath with a list of all the states he knew subsequently medized, willingly or no. This recreation of events makes more sense: as Brunt argues, an oath sworn in advance of medizing had the potential to frighten any Greeks who were thinking of surrendering into staying the course.[4] Further, it was unrealistic to talk of tithing the medizing states after Thermopylae, when so many of them had given earth and water and when the allies could scarcely hope to survive the invasion.

Notes

CHAPTER ONE: How to Destroy a Mighty Empire

1. The story of Candaules and Gyges figures prominently in the 1996 film *The English Patient*.

2. Kirby Flower Smith, "The Tale of Gyges and the King of Lydia," *American Journal of Philology* 23 (1902): 278.

3. *P. Oxy.* 2382, ll. 1–5. The translation is by Roger Travis, "The Spectation of Gyges in P. Oxy 2382 and Herodotus Book 1," *Classical Antiquity* 19.2 (2000): 330.

4. In 1994 Diane Duyser of Florida made a grilled cheese sandwich she thought bore the image of the Virgin Mary. Rather than eating it, she stored it in a plastic box for a decade, during which time—surely a miracle!—it never became moldy. More miraculous yet, Duyser sold the sandwich on eBay.com in 2004 for thousands of dollars. " 'Virgin Mary' Toast Fetches $28,000," accessed August 23, 2011, http://news.bbc.co.uk/2/hi/4034787.stm.

5. I have preserved Rawlinson's capitalization of God, though the capital is misleading given that the ancient Greeks were polytheistic.

6. Christopher Pelling has suggested that Solon was being intentionally indirect during his conversation with Croesus: he was, after all, speaking to a tyrant, which tends to make one more circumspect. Pelling, "Educating Croesus: Talking and Learning in Herodotus' Lydian *Logos*," *Classical Antiquity* 25 (2006): 152.

7. Julia Kindt notes that Croesus is here reversing the procedure normally followed when consulting the oracle: in this case Croesus already knows the answer to the question he's posing, and the god is challenged to puzzle out the obscure thing Croesus is doing. Croesus' subversion of the norms in this instance may be read as presumptuousness, a willingness to transgress the recognized bounds between the human and divine spheres. Kindt, "Delphic Oracle Stories and the Beginning of Historiography: Herodotus' Croesus *Logos*." *Classical Philology* 101 (2006): 37–39.

8. In fact, the timing is confused. Although the dates of Pisistratus' tyrannies aren't certain, Croesus' appeal to Athens appears not to overlap with Pisistratus' third and final period of power. But the embassy to Athens was probably an invention inserted to parallel the embassy sent to Sparta.

9. Pelling notes the similarity between this passage and *Iliad* 24.480–484, the scene in which Priam, the Trojan king, shows up at the tent of his enemy, Achilles, hoping to get the body of his son returned to him: Achilles and his minions gaze upon the old man in awe. In both the Homeric and the Herodotean passages, the enemies sense a shared human vulnerability. Pelling, "Educating Croesus," 160.

CHAPTER TWO: Cannibals and Conquests

1. According to other sources Astyages and Cyrus were not related. Thus Herodotus' account of Cyrus' early career is very likely pure fiction, myths that had grown up around the Great King over a century.

2. David Asheri et al., *A Commentary on Herodotus Books I–IV* (Oxford and New York: Oxford University Press, 2007), 160.

3. On Persian modesty, see Xenophon, *Cyropaedia*, 8.1.27–33.

4. The historicity of the encounter between Cyrus and the Greeks is of course questionable. We also don't know for sure whether the story of the piping fisherman is Greek or Near Eastern in origin, or whether it in fact goes back to Aesop or was attributed to him in subsequent centuries.

5. The mule oracle allegedly predated Persia's conquest of Media, but it was almost certainly composed after the fact.

6. George G. Cameron, "Cyrus the 'Father,' and Babylonia," *Acta Iranica* 1 (1974): 45–48.

7. Pelling, "Educating Croesus," 171.

CHAPTER THREE: Horny Goats and Medicinal Urine

1. The implication of the remark, that Greek men only urinated while standing, is belied by a passage in Hesiod's *Works and Days*—a mix of mythology and practical advice written in verse around 700 B.C.: "Do not stand upright facing the sun when you make water, but remember to do this when he has set and towards his rising. And do not make water as you go, whether on the road or off the road, and do not uncover yourself: the nights belong to the blessed gods. A scrupulous man who has a wise heart sits down or goes to the wall of an enclosed court" (ll. 727–732, trans. H. G. Evelyn-White). An internet search of likely terms, meanwhile, suggests that urinating while upright likewise has its devotees among women in the modern world.

2. Pierre-Henri Larcher and William Desborough, *Larcher's Notes on Herodotus* (London: Whitaker and Co., 1844), 336.

3. Tracy R. Twyman, *Solomon's Treasure: The Magic and Mystery of America's Money* (Portland, OR: Dragon Key Press, 2005), 207.

4. Alan B. Lloyd, *Herodotus: Book II* (Leiden, the Netherlands: Brill Academic Publishers, 1975), 2:357, 360.

5. Lloyd, *Herodotus*, 365. Anyone who has found Herodotus' discussion of embalmment and necrophilia interesting will enjoy Mary Roach's *Stiff: The Curious Lives of Human Cadavers*, a delightful, sometimes gruesome account of the afterlives of modern corpses.

6. *Ancient Greek Ideas on Speech, Language, and Civilization* (Oxford, U.K.: Oxford University Press, 2003), 93.

7. George Gordon Coulton, *From St. Francis to Dante: Translations from the Chronicle of the Franciscan Salimbene (1221–1288) with Notes and Illustrations from Other Medieval Sources* (London: David Nutt, 1907), 242.

8. Larcher and Desborough, *Larcher's Notes*, 433.

9. Belief in the therapeutic effects of urine survives in the modern era. It is commonly supposed, for example, that urine is an effective cure for conjunctivitis. Similarly, in an

interview with David Letterman in 1994, Madonna touted the benefits of urinating in the shower as a cure for athlete's foot. But the alleged health benefits of urine aren't limited to its external application. Morarji Desai, the prime minister of India from 1977 to 1979, famously announced in a *60 Minutes* interview with Dan Rather that he regularly drank his own urine (initially as a cure for hemorrhoids). A quick Google search for "urophagia" will show that Mr. Desai is far from alone in the practice. (I owe this reference to Desai to my husband, for whose familiarity with urine therapy I am, I suppose, grateful.)

   10. Asheri et al., *Commentary on Herodotus*, 327.

CHAPTER FOUR: Madness and Mummies

   1. "War and the Rape-Motif, or Why Did Cambyses Invade Egypt?" *Proceedings of the American Philosophical Society* 116 (1972): 410.
   2. W. W. How and Joseph Wells, *A Commentary on Herodotus in Two Volumes* (1912, reprint, Oxford and New York: Oxford University Press, 1991), 256.
   3. Asheri et al., *Commentary on Herodotus*, 410.
   4. *Knights*, 83–84. See also Plutarch, *Themistocles* 31 and Diodorus 11.58.3.
   5. Amélie Kuhrt, *The Persian Empire: A Corpus of Sources of the Achaemenid Period* (New York: Routledge, 2007), 130.
   6. *Egypt Today*, January 2004, quoted in "NUNTII: Cambyses' Lost Army," www.atrium-media.com/rogueclassicism/2004/01/02.html (last modified April 4, 2005). Herodotus' story has also inspired at least one recent piece of fiction, Paul Sussman's 2002 novel *The Lost Army of Cambyses*.
   7. The date of the death of the bull buried in 524 is unknown, but given the rules of Apis bull succession, it must have died before May of 525, when its successor was born. Leo Depuydt, "Murder in Memphis: The Story of Cambyses's Mortal Wounding of the Apis Bull (ca. 523 B.C.E.)," *Journal of Near Eastern Studies* 54 (1995): 121.
   8. As quoted at Plato, *Gorgias* 484b, Pindar's phrase is a justification for the rule of the stronger.

CHAPTER FIVE: Meanwhile, Elsewhere in the Mediterranean

   1. J. E. van der Veen argues that what mattered most to Polycrates, and what he should have surrendered to avoid destruction, was his power. "The Lord of the Ring: Narrative Technique in Herodotus' Story on Polycrates' Ring," *Mnemosyne* 46 (1993): 442.
   2. Stewart Flory, "Laughter, Tears, and Wisdom in Herodotus," *American Journal of Philology* 99 (1978): 411.
   3. Herodotus repeatedly mentions Arion's gear in the story. For bibliography on his choice of emphasis, see Vivienne Gray, "Herodotus' Literacy and Historical Method: Arion's Story (1.23–24)," *American Journal of Philology* 122 (2001): 14n15.
   4. Gray, "Herodotus' Literary and Historical Method," 14.

CHAPTER SIX: Earless Imposters and Randy Mounts

1. *The Athenian Democracy in the Age of Demosthenes* (Oxford, U.K.: Blackwell, 1991), 14.

2. "Swift's Gulliver could not outdo this whopper. . . ." L. P. Coonen, "Herodotus on Biology," *Scientific Monthly* 76 (1953): 66.

3. R. W. Hutchinson, "The Flying Snakes of Arabia," *Classical Quarterly* 8 (1958): 101.

4. John Kerrigan, *Revenge Tragedy: Aeschylus to Armageddon* (Oxford, U.K.: Clarendon Press, 1996), 37.

5. Alan Griffiths points to a disturbing modern parallel to Antigone's favoring of an irreplaceable family member over a replaceable one, the choice made by a "lady Texan dog-fancier," as reported in an article that appeared in the *Dallas Times Herald* (September 24, 1983): "Denying permission for her Rotweiler dog, Byron—who killed her four-week-old daughter—to be destroyed, Mrs. Rognaldsen of Dallas said: 'I can always have another baby, but I can't replace Byron.'" "Democedes of Croton. A Greek Doctor at the Court of Darius," in *Achaemenid History II. The Greek Sources*, ed. H. Sancisi-Weerdenburg and A. Kuhrt (Leiden, 1987), 38n2.

6. Herodotus places the Babylonian revolt after the Persians' capture of Samos, but it may have preceded it. Pinning down the chronology is a difficult and ugly business but, fortunately, one that we needn't be very concerned about here.

7. "Mule's Foal Fools Genetics," July 26, 2007, www.denverpost.com/search/ci _6464853.

CHAPTER SEVEN: The Trouble with Nomads

1. "Bosporus," by the way, means pretty much what "Oxford" does in English: a ford where cows can cross a body of water. The Bosporus, however, was allegedly so named after it was crossed by one particular cow, Io, who was one of Zeus' lovers. Zeus reportedly turned Io into a cow *post coitum* to hide her from his jealous wife Hera. But Hera recognized the bovine Io for the hussy she was and sent a gadfly to plague her. Io wandered around in misery for a while as a result, crossing the strait from Asia to Europe during her travels. The Ionian Sea was likewise named after her. Aeschylus, *Prometheus Bound* 729–734.

2. See, for example, Reinhard Hoeppli, *Parasites and Parasitic Infections in Early Medicine and Science* (Singapore: University of Malaya Press, 1959).

CHAPTER EIGHT: Stuttering Kings and Lousy Deaths

1. "Worms and the Death of Kings: A Cautionary Note on Disease and History," *Classical Antiquity* 1 (1982): 2. I was delighted to discover while working on Pheretime that there is a genus of earthworm named Pheretima. It was named by J. G. H. Kinberg in 1866. I haven't found confirmation of my suspicion that the genus takes its name from Herodotus' worm-eaten Pheretime, but that Kinberg also used the name "Nitocris" when describing certain earthworms suggests that he was indeed using Herodotus' *History* as a source of nomenclature.

CHAPTER NINE: Tattooed Slaves and Ousted Tyrants

1. During the Ionian Revolt, at the suggestion of Aristagoras of Miletus, many of the Paeonians would escape from Persia and return to Thrace (5.98).

2. For other examples of ancient Greeks wearing women's clothes, see my "Ancient Greeks in Drag," *Military History Quarterly* 14.4 (Summer 2002): 82–88.

3. Reginald Walter Macan, *Herodotus. The Fourth, Fifth, and Sixth Books* (London: Macmillan and Co., 1895), 1:178.

4. *The Emergence of Greek Democracy* (New York and Toronto: McGraw-Hill, 1966), 203.

5. Darius, of course, had a lot more on his mind than the Greeks. As George Cawkwell writes, "It must have been very far from the truth that the King had them constantly in mind. Herodotus' pretty story (5.105.2) of Darius appointing a servant to remind him of the Athenians each day before dinner was perhaps truer than Herodotus knew. The King had more important matters to think about." Cawkwell, *The Greek Wars: The Failure of Persia* (Oxford, U.K.: Oxford University Press, 2005), 1.

6. How and Wells, *Commentary*, 57.

CHAPTER TEN: Miltiades, Madness, and Marathon

1. Nowadays Athos is a self-governed monastic state, home to twenty Eastern Orthodox monasteries. Entrance to Athos is restricted to males, and only adult male members of the Eastern Orthodox Church are allowed to live there.

2. Ironically, in referring to the Greeks as "Greeks," we are doing pretty much the same thing—calling all of a people after one of its constituent groups. The Romans called the Greeks *Graeci* because they were familiar with one Boeotian tribe, the *Graikoi*, that emigrated to Italy in the eighth century B.C.

3. Later in the century, the Athenian statesman Pericles would famously refer to Aegina as "the eyesore of the Piraeus" (Plutarch, *Pericles* 8.7). That, at least, is the standard translation, though the word Pericles used actually meant "pus." It's a more disgusting and more forceful image: Aegina, like the discharge of an eye suffering from conjunctivitis, had to be scraped from its socket, so to speak.

4. It has been suggested that Aegina at this time was already a member of the league of states that Sparta headed, the Peloponnesian League. The island's surrender to Persia would in that case have been incompatible with her obligations to Sparta and the rest of the League—thus calling on Sparta for help made sense. But the question of Aegina's relationship to Sparta at the time, like so much else in Herodotus, has been much debated.

5. "Yiannis Kouros World Records," www.yianniskouros.com/records.html (last modified June 29, 2009).

6. The decree is attributed to Miltiades, but as I argue elsewhere, he is unlikely to have been the proposer. Hamel, *Athenian Generals: Military Authority in the Classical Period* (Leiden, the Netherlands: E. J. Brill, 1998), 164–166.

7. See, for example, N. G. L. Hammond, "The Campaign and the Battle of Marathon," *Journal of Hellenic Studies* 88 (1968): 34; and J. F. Lazenby, *The Defence of Greece 490–479 BC* (Warminster, U.K.: Aris and Phillips, 1993), 46.

8. And the Persians actually wore pants they could be shocked out of, unlike the Greeks, who found trousers barbaric and unmanly (5.49.4).

9. *The First Clash: The Miraculous Greek Victory at Marathon—and Its Impact on Western Civilization* (New York: Bantam Books, 2011), 187.

10. Trevor A. Hodge, "Reflections on the Shield at Marathon," *The Annual of the British School at Athens* 96 (2001): 243–246.

11. Hamel, *Athenian Generals*, 168–171.

CHAPTER ELEVEN: Feats of Engineering and Doomed Valor

1. See NASA's Catalog of Solar Eclipses in the 5th century B.C., catalog numbers 03645 and 03649: http://eclipse.gsfc.nasa.gov/SEcat5/SE-0499--0400.html (last modified July 21, 2010).

2. Hans Delbrück, *Warfare in Antiquity*, trans. Walter J. Renfroe Jr. (1920; repr. Lincoln, NE, and London: University of Nebraska Press, 1990), 35.

3. *The Landmark Herodotus*, edited by Robert B. Strassler (New York: Pantheon Books, 2007).

4. For the timing of this oath, see the appendix.

5. I discuss this in Hamel, *Athenian Generals*, 135n45.

6. Herodotus includes the Thessalians in a list of Greek states that gave earth and water to Persia (7.132), but it's not clear when those states medized. For more information, see the appendix.

7. At first blush it seems odd that the Greeks should want to move into position so early, before the Persians had even crossed the Hellespont. But as Noel Robertson points out, the Persians had already established a base at Athos. Their next move might be to send an advance force to Olympus. "The Thessalian Expedition of 480 B.C.," *Journal of Hellenic Studies* 96 (1976): 110.

8. Herodotus says at 7.144 that the Athenians built two hundred ships with the money, but the ships they built were added to an existing fleet. The grand total was two hundred ships (8.61).

9. "It required little ingenuity for the priests at Delphi in September 481 to foretell Persia's capture of Attica and a killing of persons on Salamis, the nearest haven for troops and refugees, and to wrap it up in ambiguous words." N. G. L. Hammond, "The Narrative of Herodotus VII and the Decree of Themistocles at Troezen," *Journal of Hellenic Studies* 102 (1982): 80n24.

10. "On Strategy and Oracles, 480/79," *Journal of Hellenic Studies* 85 (1965): 59–60.

11. "The Campaign of Artemisium and Thermopylae," *The Annual of the British School at Athens* 2 (1895/1896): 88–94. Bury also makes the interesting point that the Greeks' "position at Artemisium resembled, in fact, the position at Thermopylae, in so far as both positions were weakened by the necessity of defending a collateral, though less easy and direct, passage" (88).

12. In 480 Sparta had about eight thousand citizens (7.234), but the population decreased sharply in the fifth century due in part to a devastating earthquake in c. 465. See Thomas J. Figueira, "Population Patterns in Late Archaic and Classical Sparta," *Transactions and Proceedings of the American Philological Association* 116 (1986): 165–213.

13. *The Defence of Greece 490–479 BC* (Warminster, U.K.: Aris and Phillips, 1993), 136.

14. I've stolen this delightful phrase from Peter Birkenhead's memoir *Gonville* (New York: Free Press, 2010), 122.

15. More likely, Xerxes delayed at Thermopylae because he was waiting for his fleet to move into position.

16. In the end Ephialtes' perfidy went unrewarded. The Persians lost, and Ephialtes went into exile. A price was put on his head. He was eventually killed by a man named Athenades, not very far from Thermopylae, although for an unrelated reason that Herodotus doesn't go into (7.213).

17. J. A. R. Munro, "Some Observations on the Persian Wars (Continued)," *Journal of Hellenic Studies* 22 (1902): 314.

18. These are summed up nicely in R. Hope Simpson, "Leonidas' Decision," *Phoenix* 26 (1972): 6–7.

19. Plutarch credits Leonidas with another memorable saying at Thermopylae. When Xerxes suggested that the Greeks buy their lives by handing over their weapons, Leonidas allegedly said simply "*Molon labe*," that is, "Come and get them" (Plutarch, *Moralia* 225C). The expression has been adopted by supporters of the Second Amendment for its "from my cold, dead hands" message.

20. This translation appears in Steven Pressfield's 1998 novel *The Gates of Fire*. In his acknowledgments Pressfield credits the translation to Dr. Ippokratis Kantzios of the Richard Stockton College of New Jersey. It is an updated version of a translation by William Lisle Bowles (1762–1850): "Go tell the Spartans, thou who passest by, / That here, obedient to their laws, we lie."

CHAPTER TWELVE: Trial by Trireme

1. *Commentary on Herodotus*, 237.

2. "Campaign of Artemisium and Thermopylae," 87.

3. But for doubts, see Lazenby, *Defence of Greece*, 193.

4. *The Battle of Salamis: The Naval Encounter That Saved Greece—and Western Civilization* (New York: Simon and Schuster, 2004), 12.

5. *Greco-Persian Wars*, 24.

6. This may be a conservative estimate. The Athenians had thirty-six thousand men manning 180 ships at Salamis. Their wives and children and parents and slaves would have to be moved to safety.

7. Herodotus says they had 378, but that doesn't tally with his city-by-city numeration of the ships: according to his individual numbers, there were 366 triremes, plus two ships that deserted from the Persians (8.82).

8. Herodotus says the Athenians were disappointed, upon sailing south from Artemisium, to find that the Peloponnesians were not defending Boeotia, as they had expected (8.40). But because of its geography, it's unlikely that Boeotia was ever seriously considered as the next defensible position in Greece. See How and Wells, *Commentary on Herodotus*, Appendix XX.2.

9. *The Greco-Persian Wars* (Berkeley and Los Angeles: University of California Press, 1996), 171.

10. See Lazenby, *Defence of Greece*, 160–162, for some hole-poking.

11. The point is made by Rosaria Vignolo Munson, "Artemisia in Herodotus," *Classical Antiquity* 7 (1988): 95.

12. *Battle of Salamis*, 137.

13. Aeschylus, *The Persians*, l. 1074, trans. Seth G. Benardete in *Aeschylus II: The Sup-*

pliant Maidens; The Persians; Seven against Thebes; Prometheus Bound, 2nd ed. (Chicago: University of Chicago Press, 1991), 86.

14. Macan seems to be suggesting as much in his note at 8.103: "The commission was no doubt a mark of royal favour, and recorded as such; yet is there no 'malice' in Hdt.'s notice of this *exit* of Artemisia?" *Herodotus. The Seventh, Eighth, and Ninth Books* (London: Macmillan and Co., 1908), 1.2:519.

15. Themistocles seems to be implying with this talk of rebuilding that the Persians had left Attica already, but Herodotus elsewhere implies that they had not. For a discussion of the problem, see Lazenby, *Defence of Greece*, 202–203. As he suggests, it's probably unreasonable to expect precision in a speech Herodotus invented decades after the fact. Herodotus, after all, will have known—whereas Themistocles did not at the time—that the Persian land army would soon be retreating from Attica.

16. Lazenby, *Defence of Greece*, 201, suggests that the purpose was to leave the door open in the future for Athens to come to favorable terms with Persia. The favor, that is, would be repayable to *Athens* if it proved necessary, not to Themistocles. But I'm not convinced.

17. Well, his name comes up once again, at 9.98, but only as a passing reference to the messages he had left behind for the Ionians at Artemisium. Themistocles the character is gone for good.

18. Themistocles probably did say this to Timodemus: it's the kind of witty comeback that would have been remembered. But Herodotus chose to end his account of Themistocles' career with it.

CHAPTER THIRTEEN: Concluding Scenes

1. The execution of Lycidas and his family is the first of only two known instances in which Athenians were communally stoned. The other incident occurred in 409 (Xenophon, *Hellenica* 1.2.13).

2. Macan, *Herodotus*, 1.2:603, writes in his commentary on 9.7, "This wall at the Isthmos has been a most unconscionable time a-building. . . ."

3. *Herodotus*, 1.2:672.

4. *Defence of Greece*, 231.

5. The Persian cavalry will have prevented the Greeks from getting water from the Asopus.

6. *Herodotus*, 1.2:815.

7. "Protesilaos and the End of Herodotus' *Histories*," *Classical Antiquity* 7 (1988): 40.

8. It's possible that this Artembares was the father of the boy whom Cyrus whipped during a game, the act that led to the revelation of Cyrus' true identity (see chapter two).

Appendix

1. "The Narrative of Herodotus VII and the Decree of Themistocles at Troezen," *Journal of Hellenic Studies* 102 (1982): 76–79.

2. "The Narrative of Herodotus," 81.

3. "The Hellenic League against Persia," in *Studies in Greek History and Thought* (Oxford, U.K.: Clarendon Press, 1993), 81.

4. "The Hellenic League," 48–50.

Translations

Below is a list of English translations of Herodotus that are readily available in book-stores or online. The sample text provided for each is from the beginning of Herodotus' story of Candaules and Gyges (1.8.1).

The History of Herodotus. Translated by George Rawlinson. 1858–1860.
  Available online at The Internet Classics Archive.

> "Now it happened that this Candaules was in love with his own wife; and not only so, but thought her the fairest woman in the whole world. This fancy had strange consequences. There was in his body-guard a man whom he specially favoured, Gyges, the son of Dascylus. All affairs of greatest moment were entrusted by Candaules to this person, and to him he was wont to extol the surpassing beauty of his wife."

The Histories (Everyman's Library). Translated by George Rawlinson. J. M. Dent and Sons, 1992. With an introduction by H. Bowden.
Histories. Translated by George Rawlinson. Wordsworth Editions Limited, 1996. With an introduction by Tom Griffith.

> Both the Wordsworth and Everyman editions reprint the 1910 Everyman edition of Rawlinson with few changes other than the modernization of spelling and orthography and the replacement of Roman names for deities (which Rawlinson had used) with their Greek equivalents (which Herodotus, of course, had used).

The Histories of Herodotus. Translated by George Campbell Macaulay. 1890.
  Available online at Project Gutenberg.

> "This Candaules then of whom I speak had become passionately in love with his own wife; and having become so, he deemed that his wife was fairer by far than all other women; and thus deeming, to Gyges the son of Daskylos (for he of all his spearmen was the most pleasing to him), to this Gyges, I say, he used to impart as well the more weighty of his affairs as also the beauty of his wife, praising it above measure."

The Histories. Translated by George Campbell Macaulay. Barnes and Noble Books, 2004. Revised, with introduction and notes by Donald Lateiner.

> "This Candaules then of whom I speak fell passionately in love with his own wife; and so, he deemed that his wife was fairer by far than all other women. To Gyges the son of Daskylos (for he of all his spearmen most pleased him), he used to entrust the more weighty of his affairs and also he praised to excess the beauty of his wife."

The Persian Wars. Translated by A. D. Godley. Loeb Classical Library, 1920. Published in four volumes, translation with facing Greek text. Also available online at The Perseus Digital Library.

"This Candaules, then, fell in love with his own wife, so much so that he believed her to be by far the most beautiful woman in the world; and believing this, he praised her beauty beyond measure to Gyges son of Dascylus, who was his favorite among his bodyguard; for it was to Gyges that he entrusted all his most important secrets."

The History. Translated by David Grene. University of Chicago Press, 1987. With notes and introduction by David Grene. (Grene died in 2002. His memoir, *Of Farming and Classics*, was published posthumously in 2006.)

"This Candaules fell in love with his own wife; and because he was so in love, he thought he had in her far the most beautiful of women. So he thought. Now, he had a bodyguard named Gyges, the son of Dascylus, who was his chief favorite among them. Candaules used to confide all his most serious concerns to this Gyges, and of course he was forever overpraising the beauty of his wife's body to him."

Herodotus: The Histories. Translated by Walter Blanco. W. W. Norton & Company, 1992. Contains selections from Herodotus only—not the complete text. Edited by Walter Blanco and Jennifer Tolbert Roberts, with selections from other Greek authors and early modern and twentieth-century criticism.

"Now, this Candaules actually fell in love with his own wife, and, being in love, he thought that she was the most beautiful of all women. Candaules had a favorite bodyguard, Gyges the son of Dascylus, whom he talked to about his most important affairs, and—since Candaules had this opinion of his wife—he kept carrying on to Gyges about his wife's good looks."

The Histories. Translated by Robin Waterfield. Oxford University Press, 1998. With notes and introduction by Carolyn Dewald.

"Now, this Candaules became enamoured of his own wife and therefore thought she was the most beautiful woman in the world. One of the members of his personal guard, Gyges the son of Dascylus, was an especial favourite of his, and Candaules used to discuss his most important concerns with him; in particular, he used to keep praising his wife's appearance, because he thought she was so beautiful."

The Landmark Herodotus. Translated by Andrea L. Purvis. Pantheon Books, 2007. Edited by Robert L. Strassler, with an introduction by Rosalind Thomas. With maps, annotations, appendices, and encyclopedic index.

"Now this Kandaules fell in love with his own wife and, being in love, thought he had the most beautiful of all women. Therefore, he used to tell his favorite among his bodyguards, Gyges son of Daskylos, not only about serious matters but [especially] about the beauty of his wife, and with extravagant praise."

Bibliography

The bibliography on Herodotus is enormous, wide-ranging, and hydra-headed: one can hope only to make a dent in the secondary literature relevant to one's specific interests. Below are the titles I consulted while working on this book. I have prefixed with an asterisk those I found particularly useful or interesting. Following the chapter-by-chapter bibliography is a list of commentaries on the Greek text of Herodotus and lists of other books, stories, films, and audio recordings of interest.

General

Bowen, A. J. *Plutarch: The Malice of Herodotus*. Warminster, U.K.: Aris and Phillips, 1992.

Briant, Pierre. *From Cyrus to Alexander: A History of the Persian Empire*. Translated by Peter T. Daniels. Winona Lake, IN: Eisenbrauns, 2002.

Brosius, Maria. *Women in Ancient Persia, 559–331 BC*. Oxford: Oxford University Press, 1998.

Cawkwell, George. *The Greek Wars: The Failure of Persia*. Oxford: Oxford University Press, 2005.

*Christ, Mathew R. "Herodotean Kings and Historical Inquiry." *Classical Antiquity* 13 (1994): 167–202.

Dewald, Carolyn, and John Marincola, eds. *The Cambridge Companion to Herodotus*. Cambridge: Cambridge University Press, 2006.

Evans, J. A. S. "Father of History or Father of Lies: The Reputation of Herodotus." *Classical Journal* 64 (1968): 11–17.

Fairbanks, Arthur. "Herodotus and the Oracle at Delphi." *Classical Journal* 1 (1906): 37–48.

Gould, John. *Herodotus*. New York: St. Martin's Press, 1989.

Green, Peter. *The Greco-Persian Wars*. Berkeley and Los Angeles: University of California Press, 1996. (Revised edition of *Xerxes at Salamis*, Praeger, 1970.)

Holland, Tom. *Persian Fire: The First World Empire and the Battle for the West*. New York: Anchor Books, 2005.

Kuhrt, Amélie. *The Persian Empire: A Corpus of Sources of the Achaemenid Period*. New York: Routledge, 2007.

Lateiner, Donald. *The Historical Method of Herodotus*. Toronto, Buffalo, and London: University of Toronto Press, 1989.

Lattimore, Richmond. "The Wise Adviser in Herodotus." *Classical Philology* 34 (1939): 24–35.

Loomis, William T. *Wages, Welfare Costs, and Inflation in Classical Athens*. Ann Arbor: University of Michigan Press, 1998.

Parke, H. W. "A Note on the Delphic Priesthood." *Classical Quarterly* 34 (1940): 85–89.
Pearson, Lionel. "Credulity and Scepticism in Herodotus." *Transactions and Proceedings of the American Philological Association* 72 (1941): 335–355.
*Romm, James. *Herodotus*. New Haven and London: Yale University Press, 1998.
Rose, H. J. "Some Herodotean Rationalisms." *Classical Quarterly* 34 (1940): 78–84.

CHAPTER ONE: How to Destroy a Mighty Empire

Anderson, Graham. *Fairytale in the Ancient World*. New York and London: Routledge, 2000.
Arieti, James. *Discourses on the First Books of Herodotus*. Lanham, MD: Littlefield Adams Books, 1995.
Barker, Elton. "Paging the Oracle: Interpretation, Identity and Performance in Herodotus' History." *Greece and Rome* 53 (2006): 1–28.
*Cairns, Douglas L. " 'Off with Her ΑΙΔΩΣ': Herodotus 1.8.3–4." *Classical Quarterly* 46 (1996): 78–83.
Chiasson, Charles C. "Herodotus' Use of Attic Tragedy in the Lydian *Logos*." *Classical Antiquity* 22 (2003): 5–36.
*Cohen, Ivan M. "Herodotus and the Story of Gyges: Traditional Motifs in Historical Narrative." *Fabula* 45 (2004): 55–68.
Crane, Gregory. "The Prosperity of Tyrants: Bacchylides, Herodotus, and the Contest for Legitimacy." *Arethusa* 29.1 (1996): 57–85.
*Danzig, Gabriel. "Rhetoric and the Ring: Herodotus and Plato on the Story of Gyges as a Politically Expedient Tale." *Greece and Rome* 55 (2008): 169–192.
Evans, J. A. S. "Herodotus and the Gyges Drama." *Athenaeum* 33 (1955): 333–336.
———. "What Happened to Croesus?" *Classical Journal* 74 (1978): 34–40.
Greenewalt, Crawford H. "When a Mighty Empire Was Destroyed: The Common Man at the Fall of Sardis ca. 546 B.C." *Proceedings of the American Philosophical Society* 136 (1992): 247–271.
Jones, H. Stuart. "Bacchylides and the Fate of Croesus." *Classical Review* 12 (1898): 84–85.
*Kindt, Julia. "Delphic Oracle Stories and the Beginning of Historiography: Herodotus' Croesus *Logos*." *Classical Philology* 101 (2006): 34–51.
Law, Helen H. "Croesus: From Herodotus to Boccaccio." *Classical Journal* 43 (1948): 456–462.
Levin, Donald Norman. "Croesus as an Ideal Tragic Hero." *Classical Bulletin* 36 (1960): 33–34.
McCartney, Eugene S. "Gaps in Magical Circles and Other Enclosures." *Classical Journal* 39 (1944): 408–412.
Miller, Molly. "The Herodotean Croesus." *Klio* 41 (1963): 58–94.
Parke, H. W. "The Days for Consulting the Delphic Oracle." *Classical Quarterly* 37 (1943): 19–22.
Pease, Arthur Stanley. "The Son of Croesus." *Classical Philology* 15.2 (1920): 201–202.
*Pelling, Christopher. "Educating Croesus: Talking and Learning in Herodotus' Lydian *Logos*." *Classical Antiquity* 25 (2006): 141–177.
*Sebeok, Thomas A., and Erika Brady. "The Two Sons of Croesus: A Myth about Communication in Herodotus." *Journal of the Folklore Institute* 15 (1978): 5–22.

Shapiro, Susan O. "Herodotus and Solon." *Classical Antiquity* 15.2 (1996): 348–364.

*———. "Learning through Suffering: Human Wisdom in Herodotus." *Classical Journal* 89 (1994): 349–355.

Smith, Kirby Flower. "The Tale of Gyges and the King of Lydia." *American Journal of Philology* 23 (1902): 261–282, 361–387.

*Stahl, Hans-Peter. "Learning through Suffering? Croesus' Conversations in the History of Herodotus." *Yale Classical Studies* 24 (1975): 1–36.

Summers, G. D. "Medes, Lydians, the 'Battle of the Eclipse' and the Historicity of Herodotus." Available at www.kerkenes.metu.edu.tr/kerk1/12propub/wwwpaper/ecl bygds/index.html, last modified March 2, 2011.

Travis, Roger. "The Spectation of Gyges in P. Oxy 2382 and Herodotus Book 1." *Classical Antiquity* 19.2 (2000): 330–359.

White, M. E. "Herodotus' Starting Point." *Phoenix* 23 (1969): 39–48.

Worthen, Thomas. "Herodotos's Report on Thales' Eclipse." *Electronic Antiquity* 3.7 (1997). Available at http://scholar.lib.vt.edu/ejournals/ElAnt/V3N7/worthen.html.

CHAPTER TWO: Cannibals and Conquests

*Avery, Harry C. "Herodotus' Picture of Cyrus." *American Journal of Philology* 93 (1972): 529–546.

Brown, Truesdell S. "Aristodicus of Cyme and the Branchidae." *American Journal of Philology* 99 (1978): 64–78.

Cameron, George G. "Cyrus the 'Father,' and Babylonia." *Acta Iranica* 1 (1974): 45–48.

Hengel, Martin. *Crucifixion in the Ancient World and the Folly of the Message of the Cross.* Philadelphia: Fortress Press, 1977.

Hirsch, Steven W. "Cyrus' Parable of the Fish: Sea Power in the Early Relations of Greece and Persia." *Classical Journal* 81 (1986): 222–229.

McCartney, Eugene S. "Engineering Superstitions Comparable to That Recorded by Herodotus I. 174." *Classical Philology* 35 (1940): 416–420.

McNeal, Richard A. "The Brides of Babylon: Herodotus 1.196." *Historia* 37 (1988): 54–71.

*Pelling, Christopher. "The Urine and the Vine: Astyages' Dreams at Herodotus 1.107–8." *Classical Quarterly* 46 (1996): 68–77.

CHAPTER THREE: Horny Goats and Medicinal Urine

Austin, Norman. *Helen of Troy and her Shameless Phantom.* Ithaca, NY: Cornell University Press, 1994.

Coulton, George Gordon. *From St. Francis to Dante: Translations from the Chronicle of the Franciscan Salimbene (1221–1288) with Notes and Illustrations from Other Medieval Sources.* London: David Nutt, 1907.

Dawson, Jim. *Who Cut the Cheese? A Cultural History of the Fart.* Berkeley, CA: Ten Speed Press, 1999.

Doniger, Wendy. *Splitting the Difference: Gender and Myth in Ancient Greece and India.* Chicago: University of Chicago Press, 1999.

Gera, Deborah Levine. *Ancient Greek Ideas on Speech, Language, and Civilization.* Oxford: Oxford University Press, 2003.

————. *Warrior Women: The Anonymous* Tractatus de Mulieribus. Leiden, the Netherlands: Brill Academic Publishers, 1997.

Grabbe, Lester L. "Of Mice and Dead Men: Herodotus 2.141 and Sennacherib's Invasion in 701 BCE." In *"Like a Bird in a Cage": The Invasion of Sennacherib in 701 BCE,* edited by Lester L. Grabbe, 119–140. London and New York: Sheffield Academic Press, 2003.

Groten, F. J., Jr. "Herodotus' Use of Variant Versions." *Phoenix* 17 (1963): 79–87.

John, Uncle. *Uncle John's Absolutely Absorbing Bathroom Reader.* Philadelphia: Running Press, 2002.

Lloyd, Alan B. "Herodotus' Account of Pharaonic History." *Historia* 37 (1988): 22–53.

Newberry, Percy E. "Queen Nitocris of the Sixth Dynasty." *Journal of Egyptian Archaeology* 29 (1943): 51–54.

Ryholt, Kim. *The Carlsberg Papyri, Volume 6: The Petese Stories II.* Copenhagen: Museum Tusculanum Press, 2006.

Sider, David. "The Blinding of Stesichorus." *Hermes* 117 (1989): 423–431.

Sułek, Antoni. "The Experiment of Psammetichus: Fact, Fiction, and Model to Follow." *Journal of the History of Ideas* 50.4 (1989): 645–651.

Thompson, Norma. *Herodotus and the Origins of the Political Community: Arion's Leap.* New Haven and London: Yale University Press, 1996.

Twyman, Tracy R. *Solomon's Treasure: The Magic and Mystery of America's Money.* Portland, OR: Dragon Key Press, 2005.

CHAPTER FOUR: Madness and Mummies

Atkinson, K. M. T. "The Legitimacy of Cambyses and Darius as Kings of Egypt." *Journal of the American Oriental Society* 76 (1956): 167–177.

Brown, Truesdell S. "Herodotus' Portrait of Cambyses." *Historia* 31 (1982): 387–403.

*Depuydt, Leo. "Murder in Memphis: The Story of Cambyses's Mortal Wounding of the Apis Bull (ca. 523 B.C.E.)." *Journal of Near Eastern Studies* 54 (1995): 119–126.

Dillery, John. "Cambyses and the Egyptian Chaosbeschreibung Tradition." *Classical Quarterly* 55 (2005): 387–406.

Flory, Stewart. "Laughter, Tears, and Wisdom in Herodotus." *American Journal of Philology* 99 (1978): 145–153.

Frost, Frank J. *Plutarch's Themistocles.* Princeton: Princeton University Press, 1980.

Gardner, Percy. "A Themistoclean Myth." *Classical Review* 12 (1898): 21–23.

Gemsege, Paul. "Dissertation on a Poison of the Ancients Called Bull's Blood." In *A Selection of Curious Articles from the Gentleman's Magazine,* vol. 2, edited by John Walker, 414–417. London: Longman, Hurst, Rees, Orme, and Brown, 1811.

Lang, Mabel L. "War and the Rape-Motif, or Why Did Cambyses Invade Egypt?" *Proceedings of the American Philosophical Society* 116 (1972): 410–414.

Lloyd, A. B. "Herodotus on Cambyses. Some Thoughts on Recent Work." *Achaemenid History* 3 (1988): 55–66.

Magner, Lois N. *A History of Medicine.* 2nd ed. Boca Raton, FL: Taylor and Francis Group, 2005.

Marr, John. "The Death of Themistocles." *Greece and Rome* 42 (1995): 159–167.

Munson, Rosaria Vignolo. "The Madness of Cambyses (Herodotus 3.16–38)." *Arethusa* 24 (1991): 43–65.

Prioreschi, Plinio. *A History of Medicine*. Omaha, NE: Horatius Press, 1996.

Stolper, Matthew W. "Flogging and Plucking." *Topoi*. Supplement 1: *Recherches récentes sur l'Empire achéménide* (1997): 347–350.

West, Stephanie. "Croesus' Second Reprieve and Other Tales of the Persian Court." *Classical Quarterly* 53 (2003): 416–437.

———. "Sophocles' *Antigone* and Herodotus Book 3." In *Sophocles Revisited: Essays Presented to Sir Hugh Lloyd-Jones*, edited by Jasper Griffin, 109–136. Oxford: Oxford University Press, 1999.

Yamauchi, E. "Cambyses in Egypt," in *"Go to the Land I Will Show You": Studies in Honor of Dwight W. Young*, edited by J. E. Coleson and V. H. Matthews, 371–392. Winona Lake, IN: Eisenbrauns, 1996.

York, George K., and David A. Steinberg. "The Sacred Disease of Cambyses II." *Archives of Neurology* 58 (2001): 1702–1704.

CHAPTER FIVE: Meanwhile, Elsewhere in the Mediterranean

Bowra, C. M. "Arion and the Dolphin." *Museum Helveticum* 20 (1963): 121–134.

*Flory, Stewart. "Arion's Leap: Brave Gestures in Herodotus." *American Journal of Philology* 99 (1978): 411–421.

Gray, Vivienne J. "Herodotus and Images of Tyranny: The Tyrants of Corinth." *American Journal of Philology* 117 (1996): 361–389.

*———. "Herodotus' Literary and Historical Method: Arion's Story (1.23–24)." *American Journal of Philology* 122 (2001): 11–28.

Hall, Jonathan M. *A History of the Archaic Greek World, ca. 1200–479 BCE*. Oxford, U.K.: Wiley-Blackwell, 2007.

Higham, T. F. "Nature Note: Dolphin-Riders. Ancient Stories Vindicated." *Greece and Rome* 7 (1960): 82–86.

Hooker, J. T. "Arion and the Dolphin." *Greece and Rome* 36 (1989): 141–146.

Immerwahr, Henry R. "The Samian Stories of Herodotus." *Classical Journal* 52 (1957): 312–322.

Konstan, David. "The Stories in Herodotus' *Histories*: Book 1." *Helios* 10 (1983): 1–22.

Malkin, Irad. *Myth and Territory in the Spartan Mediterranean*. Cambridge: Cambridge University Press, 2003.

Mitchell, B. M. "Herodotus and Samos." *Journal of Hellenic Studies* 95 (1975): 75–91.

Munson, Rosaria Vignolo. "The Celebratory Purpose of Herodotus: The Story of Arion in *Histories* 1.23–24." *Ramus* 15 (1986): 93–104.

*van der Veen, J. E. "The Lord of the Ring: Narrative Technique in Herodotus' Story on Polycrates' Ring." *Mnemosyne* 46 (1993): 433–457.

Vaughn, Pamela. "The Identification and Retrieval of Hoplite Battle-Dead." In *Hoplites: The Classical Greek Battle Experience*, edited by Victor Hanson, 38–62. London and New York: Routledge, 1991.

CHAPTER SIX: Earless Imposters and Randy Mounts

Adkins, Lesley. *Empires of the Plain: Henry Rawlinson and the Lost Languages of Babylon*. London: HarperCollins, 2003.

Coonen, L. P. "Herodotus on Biology." *Scientific Monthly* 76 (1953): 63–70.

Druce, George C. "An Account of the Μυρμηκολέων or Ant-Lion." *Antiquaries Journal* 3.4 (1923): 347–364.

Griffiths, Alan. "Democedes of Croton. A Greek Doctor at the Court of Darius." In *Achaemenid History II. The Greek Sources*, edited by H. Sancisi-Weerdenburg and A. Kuhrt, 37–51. Leiden, the Netherlands: Brill Academic Publishers, 1987.

Hardy, Clara Shaw. "Nomos and Replaceability in the Story of Intaphernes and His Wife." *Transactions and Proceedings of the American Philological Association* 126 (1996): 101–109.

Hollmann, Alexander. "The Manipulation of Signs in Herodotos' *Histories*." *Transactions and Proceedings of the American Philological Association* 135 (2005): 279–327.

Hutchinson, R. W. "The Flying Snakes of Arabia." *Classical Quarterly* 8 (1958): 100–101.

Kerrigan, John. *Revenge Tragedy: Aeschylus to Armageddon*. Oxford: Clarendon Press, 1996.

Lang, Mabel L. "Prexaspes and Usurper Smerdis." *Journal of Near Eastern Studies* 51 (1992): 201–207.

Lofholm, Nancy. "Mule's Foal Fools Genetics." *Denver Post*, July 26, 2007. Available at www.denverpost.com/haley/ci_6464853.html, last modified March 22, 2010.

McCartney, Eugene S. "The Gold-Digging Ants." *Classical Journal* 49.5 (1954): 234.

Murnaghan, Sheila. "Antigone 904–920 and the Institution of Marriage." *American Journal of Philology* 107 (1986): 192–207.

Neuberg, Matt. "How Like a Woman: Antigone's 'Inconsistency.'" *Classical Quarterly* 40 (1990): 54–76.

Ostwald, Martin. *Oligarchia: The Development of a Constitutional Form in Ancient Greece*. Stuttgart: Franz Steiner Verlag, 2000.

Peissel, Michel. *The Ants' Gold: The Discovery of the Greek El Dorado in the Himalayas*. London: Harvill Press, 1984.

Regenos, G. W. "A Note on Herodotus III, 102." *Classical Journal* 34.7 (1939): 425–426.

*Roisman, Joseph. "Maiandrios of Samos." *Historia* 34 (1985): 257–277.

Rosivach, Vincent J. "On Creon, Antigone, and Not Burying the Dead." *Rheinisches Museum für Philologie* 126 (1983): 193–211.

Sandison, A. T. "The First Recorded Case of Inflammatory Mastitis: Queen Atossa of Persia and the Physician Democedes." *Medical History* 3 (1959): 317–322.

Simons, Marlise. "Himalayas Offer Clue to Legend of Gold-Digging 'Ants.'" *New York Times*, November 25, 1996. Available at www.nytimes.com/1996/11/25/world/himalayas-offer-clue-to-legend-of-gold-digging-ants.html.

Strid, Ove. "Voiceless Victims, Memorable Deaths in Herodotus." *Classical Quarterly* 56 (2006): 393–403.

*van der Veen, J. E. "A Minute's Mirth . . . Syloson and His Cloak in Herodotus." *Mnemosyne* 48 (1995): 129–145.

West, Stephanie. "Sophocles' Antigone and Herodotus Book Three." In *Sophocles Revisited. Essays Presented to Sir Hugh Lloyd-Jones*, edited by Jasper Griffin, 109–136. Oxford: Oxford University Press, 1999.

Zaccagnini, Carlo. "Patterns of Mobility among Ancient Near Eastern Craftsmen." *Journal of Near Eastern Studies* 42 (1983): 245–264.

CHAPTER SEVEN: The Trouble with Nomads

Chiasson, Charles C. "An Ominous Word in Herodotus." *Hermes* 111 (1983): 115–118.

Gardiner-Garden, John R. "Dareios' Scythian Expedition and its Aftermath." *Klio* 69 (1987): 326–350.

Graubard, Mark. "Food Habits of Primitive Man." *Scientific Monthly* 55 (1942): 453–460.

Hoeppli, Reinhard. *Parasites and Parasitic Infections in Early Medicine and Science.* Singapore: University of Malaya Press, 1959.

Lateiner, Donald. "A Note on the Perils of Prosperity in Herodotus." *Rheinisches Museum für Philologie* 125 (1982): 97–101.

Overstreet, Robin M. "Flavor Buds and Other Delights." *Journal of Parasitology* 89 (2003): 1093–1107.

Purves, Alex. "The Plot Unravels: Darius's Numbered Days in Scythia (Herodotus 4.98)." *Helios* 33 (2006): 1–26.

Trigger, Bruce G. "The Social Significance of the Diadems in the Royal Tombs at Ballana." *Journal of Near Eastern Studies* (1969): 255–261.

Van Dijk, Jacobus. "Retainer Sacrifice in Egypt and in Nubia." In *The Strange World of Human Sacrifice,* edited by Jan N. Bremmer, 135–156. Leuven, Belgium: Peeters Publishers, 2007.

*West, Stephanie. "The Scythian Ultimatum (Herodotus iv 131, 132)." *Journal of Hellenic Studies* 108 (1988): 207–211.

CHAPTER EIGHT: Stuttering Kings and Lousy Deaths

Africa, Thomas. "Worms and the Death of Kings: A Cautionary Note on Disease and History." *Classical Antiquity* 1 (1982): 1–17.

Benham, Sir William. "Studies in Earthworms XLII: The Occurrence of the Genus Pheretima in New Zealand." *Transactions and Proceedings of the Royal Society of New Zealand* 76 (1947): 423–428.

Bondeson, J. "Phthiriasis: The Riddle of the Lousy Disease." *Journal of the Royal Society of Medicine* 91 (1998): 328–334.

Brown, Truesdell S. "Aeneas Tacticus, Herodotus, and the Ionian Revolt." *Historia* 30 (1981): 385–393.

Graham, A. J. "The Authenticity of the ΟΡΚΙΟΝ ΤΩΝ ΟΙΚΙΣΤΗΡΩΝ of Cyrene." In *Collected Papers on Greek Colonization,* edited by A. J. Graham, 83–112. Leiden, the Netherlands: Brill Academic Publishers, 2001.

Malkin, Irad. *Religion and Colonization in Ancient Greece.* Leiden, the Netherlands: Brill Academic Publishers, 1987.

Mitchell, B. M. "Cyrene and Persia." *Journal of Hellenic Studies* 86 (1966): 99–113.

Parker, Holt. "Vergil's Mysterious Siler: A Possible Identification from a Lousy Clue." *Classical Quarterly* 56 (2006): 623–629.

Watson, Patricia A. *Ancient Stepmothers: Myth, Misogyny and Reality.* Leiden, the Netherlands: Brill Academic Publishers, 1995.

CHAPTER NINE: Tattooed Slaves and Ousted Tyrants

Badian, Ernst. "Greeks and Macedonians." In *Macedonia and Greece in Late Classical and Early Hellenistic Times. Studies in the History of Art* 10, edited by Beryl Barr-Sharrar and Eugene N. Borza, 33–51. Washington, DC: National Gallery of Art, 1982.

Berthold, Richard M. "The Athenian Embassies to Sardis and Cleomenes' Invasion of Attica." *Historia* 51 (2002): 259–267.

Blamire, A. "Herodotus and Histiaeus." *Classical Quarterly* 9 (1959): 142–154.

Borza, Eugene. "Athenians, Macedonians, and the Origins of the Macedonian Royal House." *Studies in Attic Epigraphy, History and Topography Presented to Eugene Vanderpool. Hesperia,* Suppl. 19 (1982): 7–13.

———. *In the Shadow of Olympus: The Emergence of Macedon.* Princeton: Princeton University Press, 1990.

*Chapman, G. A. H. "Herodotus and Histiaeus' Role in the Ionian Revolt." *Historia* 21 (1971): 546–568.

Cromey, Robert D. "Kleisthenes' Fate." *Historia* 28 (1979): 129–147.

Evans, J. A. S. "Herodotus and the Ionian Revolt." *Historia* 25 (1976): 31–37.

———. "Histiaeus and Aristagoras: Notes on the Ionian Revolt." *American Journal of Philology* 84 (1963): 113–128.

Forrest, W. G. "Motivation in Herodotos: The Case of the Ionian Revolt." *International History Review* 1 (1979): 311–322.

Georges, Pericles B. "Persian Ionia under Darius: The Revolt Reconsidered." *Historia* 49 (2000): 1–39.

Grundy, George Beardoe. *The Great Persian War and its Preliminaries.* London: John Murray, 1901.

Hamel, Debra. "Ancient Greeks in Drag." *Military History Quarterly* 14 (2002): 82–88.

*Hansen, Mogens Herman. *The Athenian Democracy in the Age of Demosthenes.* Oxford, U.K.: Blackwell, 1991.

Holladay, James. "Medism in Athens 508–480 B.C." *Greece and Rome* 25 (1978): 174–191.

Keaveney, Arthur. "A 'Forgotten Cause' of the Ionian Revolt." *Classical Quarterly* 38 (1988): 76–81.

Lang, Mabel. "Herodotus and the Ionian Revolt." *Zeitschrift für Alte Geschichte* 17 (1968): 24–36.

*Manville, P. B. "Aristagoras and Histiaeus: The Leadership Struggle in the Ionian Revolt." *Classical Quarterly* 27 (1977): 80–91.

Murray, Oswyn. "The Ionian Revolt." In *Persia, Greece, and the Western Mediterranean c. 525 to 479 B.C.,* edited by John Boardman, N. G. L. Hammond, D. M. Lewis, and M. Ostwald, 461–490. Cambridge: Cambridge University Press, 1988.

Roos, P. "Alexander I in Olympia." *Eranos* (1985): 162–168.

Sealey, Raphael. *A History of the Greek City States, ca. 700–338 B.C.* Berkeley and Los Angeles: University of California Press, 1976.

*Solmsen, Lieselotte. "Speeches in Herodotus' Account of the Ionic Revolt." *American Journal of Philology* 64 (1943): 194–207.

Sourvinou-Inwood, Christiane. "Greek Perceptions of Ethnicity and the Ethnicity of the Macedonians." In *Identità e Prassi Storica nel Mediterraneo Greco,* edited by L. M. Castelnuovo, 173–203. Milan, 2002.

Waters, K. H. "Herodotus and the Ionian Revolt." *Historia* 19 (1970): 504–508.
West, Stephanie. "Herodotus' Portrait of Hecataeus." *Journal of Hellenic Studies* 111 (1991): 144–160.

CHAPTER TEN: Miltiades, Madness, and Marathon

Allen, Danielle S. *The World of Prometheus.* Princeton: Princeton University Press, 2000.
Bederman, David J. *International Law in Antiquity.* Cambridge: Cambridge University Press, 2001.
Billows, Richard A. *Marathon: The Battle That Changed Western Civilization.* New York: Overlook Press, 2010.
Cartledge, Paul. "Spartan Wives: Liberation or License?" In *Sparta,* edited by Michael Whitby, 131–160. London and New York: Routledge, 2001.
*Christensen, Dirk Lund, Thomas Heine Nielsen, and Adam Schwartz. "Herodotos and *Hemerodromoi*: Pheidippides' Run from Athens to Sparta in 490 BC from Historical and Physiological Perspectives." *Hermes* 137.2 (2009): 148–169.
Daly, Lloyd W. "Miltiades, Aratus, and Compound Fractures." *American Journal of Philology* 101 (1980): 59–60.
*Doenges, Norman A. "The Campaign and Battle of Marathon." *Historia* 47 (1998): 1–17.
*Donlan, Walter, and James Thompson. "The Charge at Marathon: Herodotus 6.112." *Classical Journal* 71 (1976): 339–343.
*Evans, J. A. S. "Herodotus and the Battle of Marathon." *Historia* 42 (1993): 279–307.
Figueira, Thomas J. "Aeginetan Membership in the Peloponnesian League." *Classical Philology* 76 (1981): 1–24.
Frost, Frank J. "The Dubious Origins of the Marathon." *American Journal of Ancient History* 4 (1979): 159–163.
*Gomme, A. W. "Herodotos and Marathon." *Phoenix* 6 (1952): 77–83.
Hamel, Debra. *Athenian Generals: Military Authority in the Classical Period.* Leiden, the Netherlands: Brill Academic Publishers, 1998.
Hammond, N. G. L. "The Campaign and the Battle of Marathon." *Journal of Hellenic Studies* 88 (1968): 13–57.
*Hanson, Victor Davis. *The Western Way of War.* New York: Knopf, 1989.
*———, ed. *Hoplites: The Classical Greek Battle Experience.* London and New York: Routledge, 1991.
*Hodge, A. Trevor. "Reflections on the Shield at Marathon." *The Annual of the British School at Athens* 96 (2001): 237–259.
Hunter, Virginia. "The Prison of Athens: A Comparative Perspective." *Phoenix* 51 (1997): 296–326.
Krentz, Peter. *The Battle of Marathon.* New Haven and London: Yale University Press, 2010.
Lacey, Jim. *The First Clash: The Miraculous Greek Victory at Marathon—and Its Impact on Western Civilization.* New York: Bantam Books, 2011.
*Lazenby, J. F. *The Defence of Greece 490–479 BC.* Warminster, U.K.: Aris and Phillips, 1993.
Lazenby, J. F., and David Whitehead. "The Myth of the Hoplite's *Hoplon*." *Classical Quarterly* 46 (1996): 27–33.

Leahy, D. M. "Aegina and the Peloponnesian League." *Classical Philology* 49 (1954): 232–243.

Matthews, Victor J. "The *Hemerodromoi*: Ultra Long-Distance Running in Antiquity." *Classical World* 68 (1974): 161–169.

Mikalson, Jon D. *Herodotus and Religion in the Persian Wars*. Chapel Hill: University of North Carolina Press, 2003.

Parke, D. W. "The Deposing of Spartan Kings." *Classical Quarterly* 39 (1945): 106–112.

Podlecki, A. J. "Athens and Aegina." *Historia* 25 (1976): 396–413.

Sealey, Raphael. "The Pit and the Well: The Persian Heralds of 491 B.C." *Classical Journal* 72 (1976): 13–20.

Shrimpton, Gordon. "The Persian Cavalry at Marathon." *Phoenix* 34 (1980): 20–37.

Stadter, Philip A. *A Commentary on Plutarch's Pericles*. Chapel Hill: University of North Carolina Press, 1989.

Stern, Jacob. "Scapegoat Narratives in Herodotus." *Hermes* 119 (1991): 304–311.

Wade-Gery, H. T. "Miltiades." *Journal of Hellenic Studies* 71 (1951): 212–221.

Wallace, W. P. "Kleomenes, Marathon, the Helots, and Arkadia." *Journal of Hellenic Studies* 74 (1954): 32–35.

CHAPTER ELEVEN: Feats of Engineering and Doomed Valor

*Bowen, Anthony. "The Place That Beached a Thousand Ships." *Classical Quarterly* 48 (1998): 345–364.

Bradford, Ernle. *Thermopylae: The Battle for the West*. Cambridge, MA: Da Capo Press, 1980.

Brunt, P. A. "The Hellenic League against Persia." In *Studies in Greek History and Thought*, 47–83. Oxford, U.K.: Clarendon Press, 1993. (Updated version of "The Hellenic League against Persia," *Historia* 2 [1953]: 135–163.)

*Bury, J. B. "The Campaign of Artemisium and Thermopylae." *The Annual of the British School at Athens* 2 (1895/1896): 83–104.

Cartledge, Paul. *Thermopylae: The Battle That Changed the World*. Woodstock and New York: Overlook Press, 2006.

Connor, W. R. "Pausanias 3.14.1: A Sidelight on Spartan History, c. 440 B.C.?" *Transactions and Proceedings of the American Philological Association* 109 (1979): 21–27.

Delbrück, Hans. *Warfare in Antiquity*. German edition 1920. Translated by Walter J. Renfroe Jr. Lincoln and London: University of Nebraska Press, 1990.

Evans, J. A. S. "The Dream of Xerxes and the 'NOMOI' of the Persians." *Classical Journal* 57 (1961): 109–111.

*———. "Notes on Thermopylae and Artemisium." *Historia* 18 (1969): 389–406.

———. "The Oracle of the 'Wooden Wall.'" *Classical Journal* 78 (1982): 24–29.

Figueira, Thomas J. "Population Patterns in Late Archaic and Classical Sparta." *Transactions and Proceedings of the American Philological Association* 116 (1986): 165–213.

Flower, Michael A. "Simonides, Ephorus, and Herodotus on the Battle of Thermopylae." *Classical Quarterly* 48 (1998): 365–379.

Grant, John R. "Leonidas' Last Stand." *Phoenix* 15 (1961): 14–27.

Hammond, N. G. L. "The Construction of Xerxes' Bridge over the Hellespont." *Journal of Hellenic Studies* 116 (1996): 88–107.

————. "The Narrative of Herodotus VII and the Decree of Themistocles at Troezen." *Journal of Hellenic Studies* 102 (1982): 75–93.

————. "Sparta at Thermopylae." *Historia* 45 (1996): 1–20.

Hands, A. R. "On Strategy and Oracles, 480/79." *Journal of Hellenic Studies* 85 (1965): 56–61.

Hignett, C. *Xerxes' Invasion of Greece*. Oxford, U.K.: Clarendon Press, 1963.

Holladay, A. J. "The Forethought of Themistocles." *Journal of Hellenic Studies* 107 (1987): 182–187.

Isserlin, B. S. J. "The Canal of Xerxes: Facts and Problems." *The Annual of the British School at Athens* 86 (1991): 83–91.

Isserlin, B. S. J., et al. "The Canal of Xerxes: Summary of Investigations 1991–2001." *The Annual of the British School at Athens* 98 (2003): 369–385.

Jones, C. P. "Tattooing and Branding in Greco-Roman Antiquity." *Journal of Roman Studies* 77 (1987): 139–155.

Lewis, Sian. "Who is Pythius the Lydian?" *Histos* 2 (1998). Available at http://research.ncl.ac.uk/histos/Histos_BackIssues1998.html, last modified June 11, 2011.

Mosshammer, Alden A. "Thales' Eclipse." *Transactions and Proceedings of the American Philological Association* 111 (1974): 145–155.

Munro, J. A. R. "Some Observations on the Persian Wars (Continued)." *Journal of Hellenic Studies* 22 (1902): 294–332.

Robertson, Noel. "The Thessalian Expedition of 480 B.C." *Journal of Hellenic Studies* 96 (1976): 100–120.

*————. "The True Meaning of the 'Wooden Wall.' " *Classical Philology* 82 (1987): 1–20.

*Simpson, R. Hope. "Leonidas' Decision." *Phoenix* 26 (1972): 1–11.

Stewart, Charles. "Erotic Dreams and Nightmares from Antiquity to the Present." *Journal of the Royal Anthropological Institute* 8 (2002): 279–309.

Tuplin, Christopher J. "Xerxes' March from Doriscus to Therme." *Historia* 52 (2003): 385–409.

Wallace, Paul W. "The Anopaia Path at Thermopylai." *American Journal of Archaeology* 84 (1980): 15–23.

Worthen, Thomas. "Herodotos's Report on Thales' Eclipse." *Electronic Antiquity* 3.7 (1997). Available at http://scholar.lib.vt.edu/ejournals/ElAnt/V3N7/worthen.html.

CHAPTER TWELVE: Trial by Trireme

Aeschylus. "The Persians." Translated by Seth G. Benardete, in *Aeschylus II:* The Suppliant Maidens *and* The Persians, Seven against Thebes, *and* Prometheus Bound, edited by David Grene and Richmond Lattimore. 2nd ed. Chicago and London: University of Chicago Press, 1991.

Ferrill, Arthur. "Herodotus and the Strategy and Tactics of the Invasion of Xerxes." *American Historical Review* 72 (1966): 102–115.

Frost, Frank J. "Scyllias: Diving in Antiquity." *Greece and Rome* 15 (1968): 180–185.

————. "Themistocles and Mnesiphilus." *Historia* 20 (1971): 20–25.

Grant, John R. Review of *Xerxes' Invasion of Greece*, by C. Hignett. *Phoenix* 17 (1963): 301–306.

Grundy, G. B. "Artemisium." *Journal of Hellenic Studies* 17 (1897): 212–229.

Hale, John R. *Lords of the Sea: The Epic Story of the Athenian Navy and the Birth of Democracy.* New York: Viking, 2009.

Hall, Edith. *The Theatrical Cast of Athens: Interactions between Ancient Greek Drama and Society.* Oxford: Oxford University Press, 2006.

*Hanson, Victor Davis. *Carnage and Culture: Landmark Battles in the Rise of Western Power.* New York: Anchor Books, 2001.

Lattimore, Richmond. "The Second Storm at Artemisium." *Classical Review* 53 (1939): 57–58.

Lazenby, J. F. "Aischylos and Salamis." *Hermes* 116 (1988): 168–185.

———. "The Strategy of the Greeks in the Opening Campaign of the Persian War." *Hermes* 92 (1964): 264–284.

Morrison, John S., and John F. Coates. *The Athenian Trireme: The History and Reconstruction of an Ancient Greek Warship.* 2nd edition. Cambridge: Cambridge University Press, 2000.

Munson, Rosaria Vignolo. "Artemisia in Herodotus." *Classical Antiquity* 7 (1988): 91–106.

Sealey, Raphael. "Again the Siege of the Acropolis, 480 B.C." *California Studies in Classical Antiquity* 5 (1972): 183–194.

Sidebotham, Steven. "Herodotus on Artemisium." *Classical World* 75 (1982): 177–186.

*Strauss, Barry. *The Battle of Salamis: The Naval Encounter That Saved Greece—and Western Civilization.* New York: Simon and Schuster, 2004.

Wallace, M. B. "Herodotos and Euboia." *Phoenix* 28 (1974): 22–44.

Westlake, H. D. "Aristeus, the Son of Adeimantus." *Classical Quarterly* 41 (1947): 25–30.

CHAPTER THIRTEEN: Concluding Scenes

Boedeker, Deborah. "Protesilaos and the End of Herodotus' *Histories.*" *Classical Antiquity* 7 (1988): 30–48.

Braun, Thomas. "ΞΡΗΣΤΟΥΣ ΠΟΙΕΙΝ." *Classical Quarterly* 44 (1994): 40–45.

*Desmond, William. "Punishments and the Conclusion of Herodotus' *Histories.*" *Greek, Roman, and Byzantine Studies* 44 (2004): 19–40.

Dewald, C. "Wanton Kings, Pickled Heroes, and Gnomic Founding Fathers: Strategies of Meaning at the End of Herodotus' *Histories.*" In *Classical Closure: Reading the End in Greek and Latin Literature,* edited by Deborah H. Roberts, Francis Dunn, and Don Fowler, 62–82. Princeton: Princeton University Press, 1997.

Gammie, John G. "Herodotus on Kings and Tyrants: Objective Historiography or Conventional Portraiture?" *Journal of Near Eastern Studies* 45 (1986): 171–195.

Gilula, Dwora. 2003. "Who Was Actually Buried in the First of Three Spartan Graves (Hdt. 9.85.1)? Textual and Historical Problems." In *Herodotus and His World: Essays From a Conference in Memory of George Forrest,* edited by Peter Derow and Robert Parker, 73–87. Oxford: Oxford University Press.

*Herington, John. "The Closure of Herodotus' *Histories.*" *Illinois Classical Studies* 16 (1991): 149–160.

Hunt, Peter. "Helots at the Battle of Plataea." *Historia* 46 (1997): 129–144.

Jameson, Michael H. "Sacrifice before Battle." In *Hoplites: The Classical Greek Battle Experience,* edited by Victor Davis Hanson, 197–227. London and New York: Routledge, 1991.

Larson, Stephanie. "Kandaules' Wife, Masistes' Wife: Herodotus' Narrative Strategy in Suppressing Names of Women (Hdt. 1.8–12 and 9.108–13)." *Classical Journal* 101 (2006): 225–244.

Moles, John. "Herodotus Warns the Athenians." *Papers of the Leeds International Latin Seminar* 9 (1996): 259–284.

Rosivach, Vincent J. "Execution by Stoning in Athens." *Classical Antiquity* 6 (1987): 232–248.

Verrall, A. W. "The Death of Cyrsilus, Alias Lycides. A Problem in Authorities." *Classical Review* 23 (1909): 36–40.

Woodhouse, W. J. "The Greeks at Plataiai." *Journal of Hellenic Studies* 18 (1898): 33–59.

Commentaries on the Greek Text

Asheri, David, et al. *A Commentary on Herodotus Books I–IV*. Translated by Barbara Graziosi. Oxford and New York: Oxford University Press, 2007.

Barbour, Amy L. *Selections from Herodotus*. Norman and London: University of Oklahoma Press, 1977.

Bowie, A. M. *Herodotus: Histories Book VIII*. Cambridge and New York: Cambridge University Press, 2007.

Flower, Michael A., and John Marincola. *Herodotus Histories Book IX*. Cambridge and New York: Cambridge University Press, 2002.

How, W. W., and Joseph Wells. *A Commentary on Herodotus in Two Volumes*. 1912. Reprint, Oxford and New York: Oxford University Press, 1991.

Larcher, Pierre-Henri, and William Desborough. *Larcher's Notes on Herodotus*. London: Whitaker and Co., 1844.

Lloyd, Alan B. *Herodotus: Book II*. 3 vols. Leiden, the Netherlands: Brill Academic Publishers, 1975–1998.

Macan, Reginald Walter. *Herodotus. The Fourth, Fifth, and Sixth Books*. 2 vols. London: Macmillan and Co., 1895.

———. *Herodotus. The Seventh, Eighth, and Ninth Books*. 3 vols. London: Macmillan and Co., 1908.

McQueen, E. I. *Herodotus: Book VI*. London: Duckworth Publishers, 2001.

Newmyer, Stephen T. *Herodotus Book III*. Bryn Mawr, PA: Bryn Mawr Commentaries, 1986.

Powell, J. Enoch. *Herodotus, Book VIII*. 1939. Reprint, London: Duckworth Publishers, 2003.

Scott, Lionel. *Historical Commentary on Herodotus Book 6*. Leiden, the Netherlands: Brill Academic Publishers, 2005.

Sheets, George A. *Herodotus Book I*. Bryn Mawr, PA: Bryn Mawr Commentaries, 1993.

Sleeman, J. H. *Herodotus: Book I*. 1909. Reprint, London: Duckworth Publishers, 2007.

Steadman, Geoffrey. *Herodotus' Histories Book 1: Greek Text with Facing Vocabulary and Commentary*. Createspace.com, 2009.

Waddell, W. G. *Herodotus: Book II*. 1939. Reprint, London: Duckworth Publishers, 1998.

Woods, Henry George. *Herodotus: Book I*. 1871. Reprint, Bibliobazaar, 2008.

Other Books and Stories of Interest

Bierman, John. *The Secret Life of Laszlo Almasy: The Real English Patient.* London: Penguin Books, 2005.

Grene, David. *Of Farming and Classics: A Memoir.* Chicago and London: University of Chicago Press, 2006.

Huler, Scott. *No-Man's Land: One Man's Odyssey Through* The Odyssey. New York: Crown Publishers, 2008.

Kapuściński, Ryszard. *Travels with Herodotus.* New York: Vintage Books, 2007.

Marozzi, Justin. *The Way of Herodotus: Travels with the Man Who Invented History.* Philadelphia: Da Capo Press, 2008.

Pressfield, Steven. *Gates of Fire.* New York: Doubleday, 1998.

Sussman, Paul. *The Lost Army of Cambyses.* London: Bantam Press, 2002.

Williams, Tennessee. "The Vengeance of Nitocris." In *First Fiction: An Anthology of the First Published Stories by Famous Writers,* edited by Kathy Kiernan and Michael M. Moore, 437–449. New York: Little, Brown, 1994. (First published in *Weird Tales,* 1928.)

Films and Documentaries of Interest

300. Directed by Zack Snyder. Warner Bros., 2007.

The 300 Spartans. Directed by Rudoph Maté. Twentieth Century Fox, 1962.

The English Patient. Directed by Anthony Minghella. Miramax, 1996.

The Giant of Marathon. Directed by Jacques Tourneur. Galatea Film, 1960. (It's probably best to watch the 2007 release of this one, if you must watch it at all: *The Film Crew: The Giant of Marathon,* with commentary by former *Mystery Science Theater 3000* stars Mike Nelson, Bill Corbett, and Kevin Murphy.)

"Marathon." *Decisive Battles of the Ancient World.* The History Channel, 2006.

"Thermopylae." *Decisive Battles of the Ancient World.* The History Channel, 2006.

Audio Recordings

Cartledge, Paul, et al. "Marathon2500." Series of nine lectures. Available at www.marathon2500.org.

Vandiver, Elizabeth. "Herodotus, The Father of History." Series of twenty-four lectures. The Teaching Company, Course No. 2353.

Index of Literary Texts Cited

Passages cited appear in boldface.

General Index

Page numbers in boldface refer to tables and illustrations.